Anti-Americanism in Latin America and the Caribbean

Explorations in Culture and International History
General Editor: Jessica C.E. Gienow-Hecht

Volume 1
Culture and International History
Edited by Jessica C.E. Gienow-Hecht and Frank Schumacher

Volume 2
Remaking France
Brian Angus McKenzie

Volume 3
Anti-Americanism in Latin America and the Caribbean
Edited by Alan McPherson

ANTI-AMERICANISM IN LATIN AMERICA AND THE CARIBBEAN

Edited by
Alan McPherson

Berghahn Books
New York • Oxford

First published in 2006 by
Berghahn Books
www.berghahnbooks.com

©2006, 2008 Alan McPherson
Paperback edition reprinted in 2008

Library of Congress Cataloging-in-Publication Data

Anti-Americanism in Latin America and the Caribbean / edited by Alan McPherson.
    p. cm. – (Explorations in culture and international history ; v. 3)
  Includes bibliographical references and index.
  ISBN 1-84545-141-4 (hdbk. : alk. paper) – ISBN 1-84545-142-2 (pbk. : alk. paper)
   1. Anti-Americanism–Latin America. 2. Latin America–Relations–United States. 3. United States–Relations–Latin America. I. McPherson, Alan L. II. Series

  F1418.A635 2006
  303.48'23073–dc22

                      2006040745

British Library Cataloguing in Publication Data

A catalogue record for this book is available from the British Library

Printed in the United States on acid-free paper

ISBN 1-84545-141-4 hardback
ISBN 1-84545-142-2 paperback

Contents

Part II: Comparative and Transnational Approaches

Part III: Explaining the Absence of Anti-Americanism

LIST OF ABBREVIATIONS

AACC	Anglo-American Caribbean Commission
ACI	Andean Counterdrug Initiative
AD	Acción Democrática, Venezuela
AFL	American Federation of Labor, United States
AGNM	Archivo General de la Nación, Mexico
AID	Agency for International Development, United States
AMRE	Archivo del Ministerio de Relaciones Exteriores, Lima
AMREC	Archivo del Ministerio de Relaciones Exteriores y Culto, Buenos Aires
APRA	Alianza Popular Revolucionaria Americana, Peru
AREM	Archivo de la Secretaría de Relaciones Exteriores de México, Mexico City
ATLAS	Agrupación de Trabajadores Latinoamericanos Sindicalistas
AUC	Autodefensas Unidas de Colombia
AULH	Archive of Union and Labor History, Wayne State University, Detroit, Michigan
CADA	Compañía Anónima Distribuidora de Alimentos, Venezuela
CCMC	Corporación de Comercio Mayorista, Venezuela
CEPAL	Comisión Económica para América Latina
CERMLC	Centro de Estudios de la Revolución Mexicana Lázaro Cárdenas, Jiquilpan, Michoacán, Mexico
CGSB	La Coordinadora Guerrillera Simón Bolívar, Colombia
CGT	Confederación General de Trabajadores, Argentina
CIA	Central Intelligence Agency, United States
CIO	Congress of Industrial Organizations, United States

COPEI	Comité de Organización Política Electoral Independiente, Venezuela
CTM	Confederación de Trabajadores Mexicanos
CTV	Condederación de Trabajadores Venezolanos
CVF	Corporación Venezolana de Fomento
CWTP	Charles W. Taussig Papers
DDRS	Declassified Documents Reference System
DEA	Drug Enforcement Administration, United States
EEUU	Estados Unidos
ELN	Ejército de Liberación Nacional, Colombia
EWMC	Eric Williams Memorial Collection, University of the West Indies, St. Augustine, Trinidad
FALN	Fuerzas Armadas de Liberación Nacional, Venezuela
FARC	Fuerzas Armadas de la Revolución Colombiana
FDRL	Franklin D. Roosevelt Library, Hyde Park, New York
FMLN	Frente Farabundo Martí de Liberación Nacional, El Salvador
FRUS	U.S. Department of State, *Foreign Relations of the United States*
FSR	Fundación Simon Rodriguez, Buenos Aires
FTAA	Free Trade Area of the Americas
GAO	General Accounting Office, United States
HSTL	Harry S Truman Presidential Library
IBEC	International Basic Economy Corporation
IMF	International Monetary Fund
IMFA	International Monetary Fund Archives, Washington, D.C.
ISI	Import substitution industrialization
JPL	Jamaica Progressive League
LBJL	Lyndon Baines Johnson Library, Austin, Texas
LOC	Library of Congress, Washington, D.C.
MIR	Movimiento Izquierdo Revolucionario, Venezuela
MNR	Movimiento Nacionalista Revolucionario, Bolivia
MRIC	Memoranda Regarding Individual Countries, National Archives, College Park, Maryland
MUDD	Mudd Library, Princeton University, New Jersey
NA	National Archives, College Park, Maryland

NAACP	National Association for the Advancement of Colored People, United States
NAACPP	NAACP Papers, Library of Congress
NAFTA	North American Free Trade Agreement
NAR	Nelson A. Rockefeller
NLJ	National Library of Jamaica, Kingston
NSAEBB	National Security Archive Electronic Briefing Book
NSC	National Security Council, United States
NSF	National Security File
OAS	Organization of American States
OPEC	Organization of Petroleum Exporting Countries
PCV	Partido Comunista de Venezuela
PDVSA	Petroléo de Venezuela
PNP	People's National Party, Jamaica
PRC	Partido Revolucionario Cubano
PRO	Public Record Office, Kew Garden, United Kingdom
PT	Partido dos Trabalhadores, Brazil
RAC	Rockefeller Archive Center, Tarrytown, New York
RASS	Records of the Assistant Secretaries of State for Inter-American Affairs, Subject File, Argentina Folder, Record Group 59, National Archives, College Park, Maryland
RG	Record Group
RG 4	Records of the U.S. Food Administration, National Archives, College Park, Maryland
RG 59	Records of the U.S. Department of State, National Archives, College Park, Maryland
RG 84	Records of the Foreign Service Posts, National Archives, College Park, Maryland
RG 273	Records of the National Security Council, National Archives, College Park, Maryland
RG 306	Records of the United States Information Agency, National Archives, College Park, Maryland
SCCF	Schomburg Center Clipping File
SELA	Sistema Económico Latinoamericano
SRE	Secretaría de Relaciones Exteriores, Mexico
STPRM	Sindicato de Trabajadores Petroleros de la República Mexicana

UD	Unión Democrática, Argentina
UP	Unión Patriótica, Colombia
URD	Unión Republicana Democrática, Venezuela
USIA	United States Information Agency
VBEC	Venezuela Basic Economy Corporation
WHCF	White House Central Files, Lyndon B. Johnson Library, Austin, Texas
WINC	West Indies National Council
WSF	World Social Forum
WTO	World Trade Organization

Illustrations

TABLES

INTRODUCTION

Antiyanquismo: Nascent Scholarship, Ancient Sentiments

Alan McPherson

Only deeper and broader probing can uncover the many rich motivations, articulations, contexts, and buried representations of resistance. It is with this insight in mind that the contributors to this volume inquired into the career of anti-Americanism in Latin America and the Caribbean throughout the long history of the region's relations with the United States. Analyzing this career, they agreed, must include re-imagining the sources, forms of expression, visions, and implications for policy of anti-US resistance.

The authors agreed not to be bound by any specific definition of anti-Americanism. Yet they operated from the assumption that anti-Americanism should be treated as an ideology in the cultural sense of the word, a protean set of images, ideas, and practices that both explain why the world is how it is and set forth a justification for future action.[1] This definition of ideology assumes that anti-Americanism contains some negative stereotypes and simplifications, much as all ideologies do, especially those with the prefix "anti-." But it also advances that, as a complex system of thought, anti-Americanism cannot be dismissed as a mere political tool used by elites to manipulate the masses. It was, and is, meaningful to those who have embraced it, often ordinary people who rallied to integrate their shared values into resistance movements built at great sacrifice across national, class, racial, and other divides.

In this view, all criticisms of the United States developed out of *some* cultural process. To chart these expressions of hostility, crossbreeding the "new cultural history" with international perspectives was necessary.[2] As Jessica Gienow-Hecht and Frank Schumacher explained in the inaugural volume of this series, such a method sought "to decenter diplomatic history while at the same time integrating the cultural approach into the study of foreign relations."[3] Their repertoire for "culture" was already vast, ranging from dreams and ideas to cultural theory, perceptions, the creation of memory, lifestyles, emotions, art, scholarship, and symbolism.

This volume certainly draws on these now-accepted sources of cultural history—from the comedy of Mexico's Cantinflas to the cartoons of irreverent magazines in almost every country, to the classic novels and pamphlets that envisioned Latin America's racial, religious, and "spiritual" rejection of US norms. Yet it expands even further the material allowed in cultural interactions with international history because of the deeply ingrained meanings and emotions that Latin Americans attached to such concrete manifestations of US "hard" power as the landing of Marines or the mismanagement of US banana plantations. Cultures of resistance, especially resistance to imperialism, tend to be bound to the visceral need to halt injustice. For that reason, their motivations tend to be material rather than abstract, and their representations straightforward rather than subtle. In this volume, therefore, more traditional cultural evidence—novels, paintings, cartoons, and the like—stands shoulder to shoulder with debates over national identity, with diplomatic rhetoric, with theological disputations, and with visions of economic development. Moreover, because anti-Americanism has tended to include appeals to mass participation, the "culture" of anti-US resistance also includes manifestations of mobilization such as parades, rallies, and even riots. Finally, this volume's contributors avoided an approach so jargon-filled that it would fall into the trap about which scholar Florencia Mallon warned students of the subaltern: a discourse so esoteric that it excludes those it is meant to help.[4]

The contributors shared a final assumption: that anti-Americanism below the Rio Grande had much to teach the rest of the world. Among these teachings, a first lesson relates to the cumulative impact of time on anti-Americanism. As Mary Louise Pratt wrote, "the United States and Latin America have been entwined and entangled in a way that other places have not," and they have been so for centuries.[5] In that time, a generational sedimentation of grievances shaped historical memories and national mythologies. Latin America's resentments fed one another over time and grew in complexity and intensity. As a result, while US diplomats often ridiculed "latent anti-Americanism" for harping over past injustices, Latin Americans were not convinced that any injustices were merely in the past or that they were irrelevant even if they had passed. This phenomenon has most recently erupted in the Middle East, where anti-US resentments united cross-sections of generations and boosted nationalism.

A second lesson from Latin America regards the unique attraction to anti-Americanism in poor countries. While Britain and France may have expressed an equally old anti-Americanism, Latin America's was much less abstract or theoretical because of the reality of US economic domination there. "Latin America, not Europe, was the area most exposed to American power," scholars Barry Rubin and Judith Colp Rubin reminded us.[6] Being "under the boot" of US power was often quite literal, given the hundreds of landings by US forces, and so Latin America more than the rest of the world has experienced US domination through violence and capital, both forms that affected the poor far more than the well-to-do. Now that, in the early twenty-first century, many other poor regions of the world perceive their poverty to be tied to the wealth of the United States, Washington should expect economic grievances to undergird much of contemporary anti-Americanism.

A final lesson from Latin America relates to the type of resistance that tends to emerge from powerlessness. The individual countries of Latin America began and remained relatively impotent vis-à-vis the United States. They learned, therefore, to resist with the "weapons of the weak"—not conventional warfare or political arm-twisting, but either passive resistance such as boycotts and civil disobedience or more desperate tactics such as guerrilla struggles and spontaneous rioting.[7] In all these ways, today's leaders and non-state actors around the world may see parallels to their own situations in Latin American history.

To locate the reader better within this trajectory, this introduction provides intellectual and historical contexts to the chapters that follow it. It first traces scholarship on anti-Americanism in Latin America and the Caribbean since the 1920s, making the case that a generation of more disinterested and historically-minded scholars of anti-Americanism may be finally emerging. It then outlines major periods in the history of anti-Americanism from 1783 until 2005, laying the groundwork for the case studies of each chapter, which it then briefly summarizes.

The Scholarship: A Historiography of Anti-Americanism in Latin America and the Caribbean

Scholarship on US power in Latin America and the Caribbean is certainly plentiful, but literature on the resistance to that power has been restrained by political polarization and a lack of sources—and imagination. However, since the 1990s, and especially since September 11, 2001, new analytic sophistication and political balance in this literature have demonstrated the potential that that traumatic day has held to re-open minds to the past as well as the future of anti-Americanism.

Perhaps the earliest wave of US writings on Latin America's hostility towards the United States focused on "Yankeephobia" in the 1920s.[8] Like most commentators on US-Latin American affairs during this decade,[9] most of its participants were not historians or other scholars but government bureaucrats or students who had recently traveled to Latin America, where they personally experienced animosity. They tried to make sense of past criticisms, but their explanations were fraught with clunky analysis and the need to justify US domination of the Caribbean and Central America at the time.

As the word "Yankeephobia" itself suggested, these observers tended to discard out-of-hand all criticism of the United States as an irrational fear of the progress that US military occupation or investment were forcing on a foolishly reluctant Latin America. Mistrusting US power was, to them, an engrained pathology that must be exposed to be healed. It was to be pitied, even, growing as it allegedly did out of Latin America's failed culture—its violent Spanish heritage, priest-ridden Catholicism, abiding social inequalities, and European-dependent antimodernism. The trope of anti-Americanism-as-pathology was so consensual among 1920s observers that the construction itself suggested fear—US fear of allowing any uncovering of its wrongdoing or hypocrisy abroad. The pathology consensus sometimes even denied that Latin Americans were responsible for their own political culture. One author characterized anti-Americanism in Latin America as a "campaign" by Germans who scattered there after World War I. In a typical appraisal of the time, he was flattered because anti-Americanism was therefore a reaction to the spread of democracy, "an inevitable step in the evolution of mankind."[10]

This 1920s wave also suffered from methodological problems, mostly because sources were almost exclusively the "great texts" of anti-Americanism. Many 1920s authors were students of Latin American literature who valued the pithy phrases of well-heeled authors, the defiant speeches by great statesmen, and the angry verses against US agribusiness. They failed, however, to seek anti-Americanism in unpublished popular sources. One author who wished for more popular evidence of anti-US sentiment expressed frustration that it simply could not to be found among simple folk in Brazil. "Being largely passive and uneducated, the Brazilian common people afford us but vague inlets toward their ideas. We can thus only approach their minds by personal experience, by the testimony of Brazilian scholars, who have studied their native countrymen, or by actual incidents in which North Americans have been brought into direct contact with the sentiments and actions of the populace."[11] Even with a less disdainful researcher, the obstacles to obtaining popular evidence of anti-Americanism were serious, since none of these early chroniclers uncovered a single poll of Latin American public opinion, neither on images of the United States nor on any other topic. This first collective effort toward understanding the phenomenon, therefore, suffered from a defensive US nationalism and from the elite view that only other elites could be valid historical voices. The flawed perspective of 1920s Yankeephobia scholarship foreshadowed future failures.

A second wave of scholarship on anti-Americanism in Latin America and the Caribbean washed over the Anglo-American world from the late 1950s until the mid-1960s. While this wave benefited from more evidence than the first, it also spread more assumptions—albeit more evenly across both ends of the ideological spectrum. Moved into action by attacks on Vice President Richard Nixon in South America in 1958 and by the Cuban Revolution, a broader variety of scholars now tried to explain the anti-Americanism of Fidel Castro's generation. Institutions that funded scholarship on US-Latin American relations had multiplied since the 1920s, and so had the reading public. As a result, sociologists, economists, and political scientists now blended their insights with those of travelers, journalists, educators, and Cold Warriors.[12]

Most still worked with limited evidence. Despite the fact that the United States Information Agency conducted pathbreaking polls in Latin America starting in the 1950s, few seemed aware of them. Moreover, although this generation had more direct interactions with ordinary Latin Americans, few conducted systematic surveys or creative analyses of popular sentiment rejecting US power. They focused their energies instead on extrapolating the ideas and actions from small groups of communists and guerrillas to the majority of Latin Americans. And they continued to rely heavily on the writings of intellectuals.[13]

One result was—again—a fear that Latin sentiment was running amok. The Cold War catapulted this fear into the highest reaches of Washington, where policymakers from the Oval Office to Congress to the Pentagon associated nearly any criticism of the United States, no matter how mild, with communist propaganda. Reflecting this paranoia, scholars couched their conclusions, again, in pathological metaphors. One called anti-Americanism a "disease" and spoke of "Yankeephobe contagion" measured on a "Yankeephobe fever chart."[14] Allen Dulles, director of the Central Intelligence Agency (CIA), called the spread of Cuba's revolutionary rhetoric "Castro-itis."[15] As they had in the 1920s, pathology metaphors reinforced the belief that Latin Americans were unable to forge their own arguments. They had to be "infected"—this time not by Germany, but by Moscow and Beijing.

In the 1970s and early 1980s, mainstream interest in anti-Americanism remained low and could hardly be considered a "wave." Latin Americans, who had long since realized the deep roots on *antiyanquismo,* now contributed historical scholarship. Yet they often merely reprinted the "great texts" of anti-Americanism without much comment or analysis.[16] In the United States and Europe, the anti-Vietnam War protests produced a backlash of sorts against criticism of US foreign policies everywhere—the first wave of what could be called "anti-anti-Americanism." This focus on anti-Americanism became the refuge of scholars obsessed with branding critics abroad—and the counterculture at home—as unpatriotic, xenophobic, or opposed to democracy.[17]

Slowly, some more analytic and empirical treatments of anti-Americanism emerged, cresting slowly into a third wave by the late 1980s and 1990s. This wave seemed motivated by a combination of the declining Western paranoia that the developing world would turn to communism and the demonizing of the United States by Islamist movements in the wake of the Iranian Revolution. Political scientists stood at the forefront of devising definitions, taxonomies, and case studies—on Latin America and elsewhere. While Alvin Rubinstein and Donald Smith's *Anti-Americanism in the Third World* presented itself as a potential model for comparative global studies, it also suffered from the abiding tendency to defend the United States from its critics rather than understand the critics on their own terms.[18] Nevertheless, progress was evident. Some scholars inquired into deeper strains of anti-Americanism that lay behind the official propaganda of communist states in the twentieth century.[19] Most attention focused on the reasons why otherwise friendly nations such as France,[20] Germany,[21] Canada,[22] and South Korea[23] had developed such antipathy to the United States during the Cold War. Much of this excellent work remained obscure, however, for lack of an audience.

Precociously belonging to this third wave, Carlos Rangel's *The Latin Americans* appeared in 1977 and became the first book, in Latin America or elsewhere, to offer a sweeping interpretation of Latin America's image of the United States. It was a smash in France and in Rangel's home country, Venezuela. The book relied on sometimes thin psychological meta-narratives, but Rangel usefully underscored what few dared declare in public: that Latin America's images of the United States were deeply ambivalent.[24] Almost simultaneously, others added context to that perspective. Carlos Rama in Spanish, and then John Reid, and F. Toscano and James Hiester in English, all joined their otherwise unremarkable "great text" anthologies with observations of the material and cultural conditions that produced historical shifts in anti-Americanism in the hemisphere—the sharing of books, the increase in commerce, the development of universities.[25] By the 1990s, Latin American anti-Americanism more fully entered the purview of historians. One group of Mexican scholars provided one of the best social histories of the phenomenon, *Estados Unidos desde América Latina,* which paid serious attention to social psychology, institutional context, and how anti-Americanism varied from one social group to another and one country to another.[26] And the topic continued to attract a broad audience in Latin America. In 2000, a group of Latin American scholars updated Rangel's critique of reactive anti-Americanism in the hemisphere in their popular *Guide to the Perfect Latin American Idiot.*[27]

A fourth and defining wave of scholarship swelled quickly when the world stood agape at the destruction wrought on September 11, 2001 upon the US sense of invulnerability. That day opened up scholarship on *antiyanquismo* by allowing hemispheric scholars to participate in a worldwide conversation on anti-Americanism with the broader public and by building a stronger bridge between scholars regardless of their politics. To be sure, some perils lingered in this scholarship. Just as anticommunism had distorted the understanding of anti-Americanism in the 1960s, the fear of terrorism now threatened to derail informed scholarship in the 2000s. The nationalistic cant swirling around the media and the simplistic reassurance from the Oval Office that foreigners hated the United States "because we are free" demonstrated the need for disinterested scholarly attention.

The longing for balanced histories of anti-Americanism would not easily be satisfied. Two edited volumes published in 2004 illustrated the continuing political polarization of what could increasingly be called anti-Americanism studies. The first, Paul Hollander's *Understanding Anti-Americanism,* stood firmly to the right of this polarization. Hollander, a Hungarian expatriate, pioneered much of the scholarship on anti-Americanism in the 1980s and 1990s. He often exposed the institutional background and facile scapegoating of anti-Americanism, especially among the left-leaning US intelligentsia. But he too often slapped the term "anti-American" onto anyone inside or outside the United States who criticized its policy or society with any consistency.[28] In *Understanding Anti-Americanism,* his rhetorical technique was in evidence throughout: to string together seemingly intemperate quotations out of context and thus whip up the unwitting reader's outrage at critics of the United States. While Hollander himself was careful to state that anti-Americanism could be either rational or irrational, he and his contributors tended to illustrate only the latter.[29] Several chapters exclusively charted "irrational" anti-Americanism and paid only lip service to the "rational" variety. Typical of this false balance was Roger Kimball's assertion that "there may be—in fact there assuredly are—many things to criticize about the United States. But anti-Americanism has almost nothing to do with *criticism.* It is more a pathology than a position, operating not by evidence but emotion."[30] Kimball and others were indeed keen on perpetuating the image of anti-Americanism as a disease. Michael Radu, another contributor to *Understanding Anti-Americanism,* called Mexican intellectuals' anti-Americanism "Pavlovian" and Argentine versions "fashionable." The end result was not, in fact, an "understanding" of anti-Americanism but rather the reinforcement of the shopworn nationalistic assumption that "they hate us" because of who we *are:* free, modern, democratic, wealthy, and so on. At its worst, this argument made a mockery of the term "anti-American" when its users abused it to bully dissidents into silence the way Joseph McCarthy did with the term "un-American."[31]

Andrew Ross and Kristin Ross's *Anti-Americanism,* meanwhile, gathered several think pieces from New York University scholars who emphasized—with more sophistication than did Hollander—the view from the left that there has been no "hate" for what the United States *is.* Instead, anti-Americanism has been well-deserved resentment for what the United States *does:* denies freedom to the oppressed, chooses war over peace, exploits the world's poor, and so on. The Rosses' discussion of Latin American anti-Americanism emphasized that the region epitomized the most "organic" and "purest" resistance given the record of US domination.[32] Much as authors on the left had done before, contributors to *Anti-Americanism* focused so much on US misdeeds that they barely analyzed the criticisms of those deeds. *Anti-Americanism* also inverted the rhetoric of Hollander by briefly admitting that some criticisms of the United States may be emotional or prejudicial, then promptly ignoring them. The Rosses allowed, for instance, that "caricature is intrinsic to the standpoint known as anti-Americanism," but then returned to listing what the United States had done to deserve the caricature.[33] Siding too easily with the critics, *Anti-Americanism* often ended up joining anti-US discourse rather than engaging it.

Despite the lingering politicization, the events of September 11th allowed more moderate and diverse scholars to delve into the complexities of anti-Americanism. More rigorous, comprehensive, and detached scholarship now existed alongside the usual fire and brimstone. Some of the best scholarship on anti-Americanism to emerge after September 11, 2001 was more balanced between US and foreign sources,[34] based on quantitative data,[35] attuned to personal narratives,[36] realistic about political opportunism,[37] attentive to generational shifts,[38] and sensitive to anti-Americanism's cultural and social meanings.[39] While some intellectual sins of the past remained—the generalizations, dismissals, polarizations, and the distortion of evidence—a new opening had been breached for a public seemingly awakened to the importance of foreign opinion to US international relations. Jean-François Revel's work on French anti-Americanism, translated and abridged, even became a hit in the United States in 2003.[40] No longer did one need to be a zealot for US influence in the world nor a sworn enemy of it to be interested in anti-Americanism. Since the extreme versions of anti-Americanism now concerned everyone in the United States—and, arguably, the world—the public seemed willing to explore not only the extreme but the less harmful forms of hostility, and to inquire about the roots and branches of both.

The Phenomenon: A Brief History of Hostility, 1783–2005

Keeping the distortions of past scholarship in mind, the task of painting the broad strokes of anti-US hostility in Latin America and the Caribbean should involve great care in giving equal attention to shifts in the following three elements: US actions that prompted resistance; elite and popular groups who led anti-US arguments; and movements and policies championed by those groups. Causes, sentiment, and strategy: these three pillars help to define six periods in the history of anti-Americanism in Latin America and the Caribbean—1783 to 1830, 1831 to 1897, 1898 to 1933, 1934 to 1958, 1959 to 1990, and 1991 to 2005. The metaphor of a tree of anti-Americanism aptly expresses the narrative arc during these periods. Roots and nutrients were buried deep at the outset of the late eighteenth century, when anti-Americanism remained a shrub. But it took nurturing, the right climactic conditions, and the capricious winds of history to plunge the roots deeper, thicken the trunk, and grow the branches. Throughout it all, the causes of anti-Americanism increasingly became concrete abuses of US power, its sentiment grew to integrate the cultural and political, and its strategy became increasingly effective at countering US power.

1783–1830: Independence and Disappointment

During this first period, Creole leaders of the republics newly freed from the moribund Spanish empire saw their hopes of a New World alliance with the United States dashed. This disappointment was perhaps the greatest driver of anti-Americanism in the decades following the victory of the thirteen North American colonies over England. It was rooted in the fact that US help to Latin America against Spain remained paltry and tied to US self-interest.

The US founding fathers, to be sure, were glad to see others rebelling against European monarchies. They also had long traded with Latin America—often smuggling around Spanish monopolies—and, during the revolutions against Spain, they continued to build ships for Latin America and to sell wheat, flour, and slaves there. Yet the founders remained suspicious of the self-governing ability of those who had remained for so long under the rule of an empire that was brutal yet neglectful, Thomistic yet unruly, devoutly Catholic yet unable to proselytize natives. They judged the Creoles who emerged from that rule as lazy, fractured, and superstitious. As a result, US leaders only offered cooperation or protection if it corresponded to their own interests. President James Monroe's "doctrine" of 1823, for instance, clearly meant to open Latin America to more US shipping as much as it warned Europeans not to re-colonize it.

Latin American views of the United States during these years, good or bad, were largely confined to the Creole elite. They were the ones who traveled to the United States, traded with it, or read its news and novels. Within these small groups, hope of a hemispheric rebirth had taken root. Creoles admired the success and moderation of the American Revolution and foresaw the making of a continent-wide "America" united against an outdated Europe.[41] As the Lima daily *El Satélite del Peruano* exuded in 1812, "the whole vast extension of both Americas is what we conceive of as our fatherland. . . . All of us who inhabit the New World are brothers . . . worthy of constituting a nation."[42] Creoles also shared the goals of the US founding fathers: ending monarchy and solidifying republicanism, spreading citizenship to white men of property, and gaining wealth through freer commerce. Finally, Latin Americans sought a military alliance with the prosperous neighbors to the north. For this reason, the majority may have welcomed the Monroe Doctrine even though they may not have expected much to follow from it. Venezuela's Francisco de Miranda typified Latin America's early optimism. Traveling from South Carolina to New England in 1783–84, he was perhaps the first Creole to visit the new union, and the only independence leader to also participate in the American and French Revolutions. In his travelogue, Miranda expressed admiration for the prosperity, strong health, and constitutional politics of the United States.[43]

Events, however, soon brought these broadly defined "American" hopes crashing down. In 1806, Miranda organized raids against the Spanish, but US Secretary of State James Madison failed to support them. Four years later, when the Caracas elite declared its independence, again the US government refused to second it. One Venezuelan diplomat expressed the bitter lesson learned: "Every day I am more persuaded that it is necessary for each country to rely on its own resources; foreign aid always depends upon the rewards that are expected."[44] Naked expansionism, racism, and cut-throat trade practices were giving US citizens a bad reputation. As far back as 1787, in fact, Mexicans may have taken to referring negatively to US citizens as *gringos*.[45] In 1819, Antonio José de Irisarri, Chilean minister to London, resented "the contempt with which . . . the United States have viewed us; they send their merchant ships to our ports as they would send them to an uninhabited coast, threatening it with their warships as they would the blacks of Senegal."[46]

In one of the earliest characterizations of the United States as a "colossus," a Cuban economist in 1811 summarized the interlaced fears of the elite that lay behind anti-Americanism. "We see rising up . . . in the northern portion of this world a colossus which has been constructed by all castes and languages and which threatens to swallow up, if not all our America, at least the northern portion. . . . This precious isle [Cuba] is exposed to the terrible risks of proximity to the Negro King Enrique Cristobal and to the United States."[47] Unwittingly perhaps, the Cuban expressed the three fundamentals that made up anti-Americanism in this first period: fear of US expansion; fear of diversity; and fear of uprisings by the masses of poor, dark-skinned peoples in Latin America and the Caribbean who might take seriously the exhortations of the founding fathers and undertake a radical social revolution.

From this turn of events, some Creoles took the lesson to harden their hearts while others closed their political systems to the Yankee. Among his peers, Venezuela's Simón Bolívar, bitter at the scant support he received from Washington, stood out for his suspicion that the Monroe Doctrine was a harbinger of US expansionism. In

1825, Bolívar advocated a military alliance with London rather than with Washington, and in 1826, he kept US diplomats at arm's length during that year's inter-American conference. "The North Americans . . . are foreigners to us," Bolívar warned. He feared that, for "selfish" reasons, US citizens would be his "greatest opponents."[48] In 1829, not only had Bolívar lost all faith in any union in either his continent or between it and the north, but he warned of the unusual peril that grew out of US hypocrisy. "The United States appears destined by Providence to plague our America with misery in the name of Liberty."[49]

1831–1897: Filibustering and Fury

Concern that the hunger for land of the former British colonies would be satisfied only at the expense of Latin America characterized this second period. Early evidence of US rapaciousness came out of Texas. There, white settlers' demand for statehood led to the Mexican War, at the end of which the US government took as its spoils almost all Mexican lands north of the Rio Grande. Simultaneously, fueled as much by greed and racism as by nationalism, proslavery advocates pursued expansion southward. In 1854, after one US envoy thought he had been insulted by locals in Nicaragua, he ordered the destruction of their small village of San Juan del Norte. More common than this brutal shelling by gunboats were the filibustering expeditions of the antebellum period. The boldest of these was William Walker's war against Nicaragua, which installed him as president from 1855 to 1857. The US building of a railroad on the Isthmus of Panama from 1850 to 1855 was another milestone in blending anti-expansionist feeling with anti-Americanism.

In response to this expansion, the idea spread in cities and small towns of Latin America that US ambitions for the hemisphere went beyond self-interested relations between equals and toward outright piracy and domination. More than ever, animalistic metaphors seemed to apply to the Yankee. In 1856, Chile's Francisco Bilbao used simultaneous images of eagles and snakes to illustrate rapacity. The United States "extends its talons . . . against the south," he wrote. "Already we see fragments of America falling into the jaws of the Saxon boa . . . as it unfolds its tortuous coils. Yesterday it was Texas then it was northern Mexico and the Pacific that meets a new master."[50] Walker's efforts to turn Nicaragua into a Southern colony for slavery, though they met a fatal end in 1860, left a particularly bad taste with Latin Americans. Few had expected such bare-bones racist aggression from the north; this fully contradicted the democratic ethos of a perennial Latin American favorite, Walt Whitman. It was mostly in response to

Walker's adventures that Latin American leaders called a special congress in Lima in 1856.

Resistance now expanded from the Creole elite to two separate groups. The first consisted of the second-generation leaders, well bred, often in Europe. This group broadened its anti-Americanism by disdaining US materialism while predicting a political confrontation with the North Americans. Before the Civil War, elite anti-Americanism aimed criticisms at US society because of the widespread dislike of Southern slavery and the filibustering it encouraged. After the war, that argument largely disappeared, even if a disapproval of Jim Crow racism remained. Taking center stage was revulsion against the US love of the dollar. Material pursuits seemed to many Latin Americans to have become the sole measure of success in the "Colossus of the North" and the root of its insatiable expansion.[51]

A second, newer group joining the chorus of disapproval consisted of the occupants of land—the small farmers and cattle ranchers—who, faced with US expansion, developed a more violent, ground-level resistance. The Mexican War and the laying of the railroad in Panama sparked some of the most violent backlashes by ordinary Latin Americans. Much of the fighting against US invaders in Mexico City in 1847 and 1848, for instance, did not come from the elite or even Mexican regulars, but from urban poor and peasants who organized guerrilla warfare.[52] And as the number of US merchants and Marines who landed in Latin American ports increased, so did the commonness of scuffles, rumbles, and bar fights. Latin American and US men fought over money, women, and real or perceived slights. In 1891, one of these incidents sparked a major international scandal when two US sailors from the vessel *Baltimore* were killed during a saloon brawl in the Chilean port of Valparaíso.

Such incidents of anti-Americanism "from below" still remained largely isolated from each other and, except for particularly public episodes such as the *Baltimore* affair, ignored by Latin American leaders and by Washington. Perhaps because of this persistent lack of cross-class collaboration, no government declared itself openly hostile to what the United States did or was, so anti-Americanism did not yet shape policies in any comprehensive way. As a result, Cuban patriot José Martí's 1890 declaration that "the time has come for Spanish America to declare her second independence" sounded hollow to many.[53] Still, hostility had now spread beyond the elite, beyond the ports, and beyond one or two particularly aggrieved countries. By 1893, one Brazilian could plausibly claim, "There is no Latin American nation that has not suffered in its relations with the United States."[54]

1898–1933: Bad Neighborliness and Backlash

During this third period, the relatively easy defeat of Spain in 1898 and the hegemony the United States exercised over Cuba and small neighboring republics in the decades that followed sparked perhaps the most virulent hostility in the history of US-Latin American relations. In 1901, the United States set the pattern for twentieth-century informal control by coercing Cuba into passing the Platt Amendment, which codified US control of the island's revenue, treaties, and politics. Then, in 1903, Washington encouraged a nationalist revolution in the department of Panama against Colombia and in return demanded the right to build and operate there a waterway between the oceans.

The Panama Canal opened in 1914, coinciding with the outburst of hostilities in Europe. Both of these events set in motion further developments. For the next twenty years, US governments occupied Cuba, Panama, Mexico, Nicaragua, Haiti, the Dominican Republic, and other republics at one time or the other. Preceding or following the Marines were great capitalists such as Minor Keith, who converted Guatemala into a massive plantation for the United Fruit Company by bribing local autocrats, building monopolistic infrastructures, and forcing small banana growers out of the market. Direct US investment in Latin America grew from $50 million in 1896 to $1.3 billion in 1924.[55]

In reaction, Latin Americans lost much of the admiration for the United States that remained. While some agreed that temporary US interventions might bring some stability and even prosperity to the circum-Caribbean, long-term occupation was just too much of a humiliation to accept. Washington showed little respect for national sovereignty or international practices, and occupiers were often brutal and racist. Colombian novelist José Vargas Vila summarized how many Latin Americans now contrasted US expansion unfavorably with the European variation:

> [US presidents Woodrow] Wilson and [Theodore] Roosevelt have torn the glorious flag; they flaunt the insolent rage over the affliction of the Latin race of America, which they dream of exterminating, in the savage ferocity of their barbarous souls! English imperialism makes for civilization. Proof of this may be seen in great and prosperous India, in Egypt, in Australia and in Canada, rich and almost free. American filibusterism makes for brutality. Proofs of this are soon in the Filipinos, hunted like wild beasts; in the disappearing Hawaiians, in the despoiled natives of Panama and in the Porto Ricans, compelled by oppression to emigrate.... Wherever the Englishman goes, a village is born; wherever the Yankee goes, a race dies.

Vargas Vila had an explanation for this behavior that embraced the racial determinism of the time. US citizens were, he wrote, "A lustful race, hostile and contemptuous; a countless people false and cruel, insolent and depreciatory toward us, with monstrous ideas of their superiority and an unbridled desire for conquest! . . . Such are the men of the North, descendents of the Norsemen, pirates of the Baltic who in crudely built boats crossed black water, under misty skies, to pillage peoples."[56]

The educated elite coalesced around one book in particular: *Ariel,* by Uruguayan author José Enrique Rodo. The turgid but influential tome argued that US citizens were blindly materialistic and individualistic, whereas Latin Americans were more attuned to "spiritual" matters and the finer things in life. *Ariel* influenced modern (and modernist) writers from Nicaragua's Rubén Darío to Manuel Ugarte of Argentina, José Vasconcelos of Mexico, and José Carlos Mariátegui of Peru.[57] Arielism became quickly institutionalized into scholarly journals, newspapers, poetry, literature, and theater. Given the Social Darwinism and racial theories popular at the time, some Latin Americans such as the poet José Santos Chocano imagined cultural differences to foreshadow a full-blown racial clash between "Anglo-Saxons" and "Latins."[58]

Far more balanced and informed than *Ariel,* but stemming from the same tradition of European-influenced elite anti-Americanism, was Manuel Ugarte's *The Destiny of a Continent,* published in 1923. The Argentine writer left for Paris right after college around the time of the War of 1898. He then visited the United States and Mexico in 1900–01, apparently knowing "nothing of imperialism" at the time. His time in Texas and Mexico, especially, was educational. In Mexico, he was shocked that "among the people . . . and especially among the younger men, there was a feeling of keen resentment and marked hostility against the *gringo.* In hotels, cafés, and theatres could be noticed an obvious antagonism which was arising as great collective sentiments do arise, without logic or reflection from confused memories and instinctive perceptions." He added, "The more humble the rank in society, the more clearly did this sentiment appear."[59] Ugarte ended by drawing broad conclusions about US character. "With the exception of the group of intellectuals," he said, "the mentality of the country, from the point of view of general ideas, smacks of the rough-and-ready morality of the cow-boy, violent and vain of his muscles, who civilized the Far West by exterminating simultaneously the virgin forest and the aboriginal races in the same high-handed act of pride and domination." Disillusioned, Ugarte returned to France, and there, for the next few decades, produced pamphlets, articles, and speeches against US expansion.

Destiny added specific warnings against US expansion in Latin America to *Ariel's* general indictment of materialism. Ugarte presciently argued that US power was not at all crude but in fact more sophisticated than the European kind because it insinuated itself into the society and culture of the countries under its control. What made matters worse, said Ugarte, was that US imperialists refused to annex nonwhite nations, thus leaving them to their own devices once the US military had built bases, US administrators had taken over customs, and US corporations had bought up land. Finally, as many other Latin Americans had done and would do, Ugarte denied harboring any prejudice against the United States. "In spite of the reputation of a Yankee-hater which has been ascribed to me—a legend as false as many others—I have never been an enemy of this great nation. . . . If I have spoken of resistance it was with a view to the exigencies of the future—and this apart from all animosity, and on the firm ground of patriotism." Staking out what historians of foreign relations would call a realist position, Ugarte called for all "Latin" peoples—whether from the Americas, France, Italy, or Spain—to collaborate against the United States rather than hate it. "The United States have done and will continue to do what all the strong peoples in history have done, and nothing can be more futile than the arguments used against this policy in Latin America. To invoke ethics in international affairs is almost always a confession of defeat."[60]

In this third period, anti-US movements took shape with more coalition building and military know-how than ever before, but they still remained unable to seize national governments. In the countrysides of Haiti, the Dominican Republic, and Nicaragua, peasant guerrilla armies consisting of a blend of bandits and nationalists went to war against US occupiers. Thousands of *cacos*, *gavilleros*, and *sandinistas,* respectively, put up struggles that lasted years. All failed to bring down US-supported governments, and only the Sandinistas could be said to have prompted the departure of US troops. In the cities, meanwhile, US diplomats now faced political organizations wholly devoted to sending the Yankees back home. Journalists, lawyers, intellectuals, playwrights, writers, and sometimes even burgeoning working-class groups united. Their techniques ranged from diplomacy to international media campaigns, to boycotts of US goods, to the writing of plays and novels.[61] Poor and middling Latin Americans increasingly rejected the "spiritual" focus of Arielist politics and imagined broader social bases on which to build Latin American and Caribbean movements.

One of these bases was Hispanism, or pan-Hispanism. While both *Ariel* and *Destiny* spoke to the continuing influence of French culture upon Latin American elites,[62] a broader social group that included intellectuals, large landowners, and church leaders formulated an anti-US sentiment around a revival of their shared heritage with Spain.[63] Hispanism claimed to unite Latin Americans under the banners of the Spanish language, Catholicism, traditional gender roles, and subordination of racial minorities to a nation-state conveniently managed by Spanish Americans. In this context, adherence to Hispanic rituals and celebrations often equaled the rejection of Anglo-Saxon ways. For instance, after US administrators increased their control of the Dominican Republic in 1907 and again in 1916, the Dominican elite feared the leveling of social differences and creeping consumerism. In response, it adopted Spanish as its official language and invested great energy into parades for its Catholic patron saint.[64]

University students provided another of the new social bases for anti-Americanism. In 1918, Argentine students rose up against administrators to demand greater academic freedom and secularization, and their ultimate ideals were also directed against US imperialism. When the Argentine revolt spread to Peru in 1919 and then to other universities, it influenced the birth in 1924 of the American Popular Revolutionary Alliance (APRA). APRA was the first truly international anti-US party in the hemisphere.[65]

Still a third base of identity for anti-US movements was indigenism. Indigenism countered US power by stressing the mixed-race distinctiveness of Latin America. Poet Rubén Darío, for instance, saw in Latin America's indigenous population the moral purity of the continent that stood in opposition to the racially segregated United States.[66] Indigenism grew out of the need to find a unifying cultural identity that celebrated rather than ignored racial mixing in the Americas and that allowed a greater blending of social classes than did Arielism. Psychologically, the impact was similar to Arielism in that it allowed Latin Americans to ignore material inferiority and emphasize moral and cultural superiority to the United States.[67]

Indigenism also offered plans for action. For the Motilón Indians of Venezuela, indigenism in the 1920s justified shooting poison darts at US oil company workers. For Central Americans who looked down on black West Indians toiling on US plantations or on the locks of the Panama Canal, indigenism united descendants of both Europeans and Native Americans against the supposed corruption from these dark-skinned toilers of imperialism. For José Vasconcelos, author of *The Cosmic Race* (1925), indigenism provided the inspiration for his design of an educational system for Mexico that had at its core a "national" university celebrating the mixed-race achievements of Mexicans while largely ignoring the class and gender differences that still very much divided them.[68] For APRA's founder, Víctor Haya de la Torre, the concept of "Indoamérica" linked all Latin Americans and distinguished them from both Europe and the United States.[69] Finally, for Augusto Sandino in Nicaragua, indigenism influenced a millennial vision of violent liberation struggle against white invading Marines.[70]

1934–1958: Good Neighborliness and Nationalism

This fourth period, along with the first, was perhaps the freest from anti-Americanism. There are three good reasons behind this. First, the US government explicitly retreated from the practice of direct military intervention in the hemisphere and gave that new policy the winning name of the "Good Neighbor." Second, as historian Donald Dozer argued, Latin Americans witnessed the Great Depression of 1929 wreaking havoc on the United States and felt considerably less anger—or envy—because of it.[71] Third, the struggle against totalitarianism during World War II reminded the entire hemisphere of its substantial common ideals and interests. As Venezuela's Carlos Rangel recalled, the confluence of Franklin D. Roosevelt's policies toward the hemisphere and the advent of war "assuaged our anti-North Americanism for some twenty years."[72]

In the post-World War II period, however, relations between the United States and Latin America turned awry. Many felt that the United States had taken advantage of Latin America's raw materials during World War II and that Washington was not prepared to treat its southern neighbors as equals now that the Cold War was heating up.[73] The United States was "detestable in Latin American eyes," ventured a Mexican statesman in 1945. It "resorts to brute force or proceeds with less skillful methods and . . . it does not show the fruits of intelligence, of perseverance and of wisdom."[74] Nationalism flowed out of a combination of nation-building during US occupations, urban labor struggles, and World War II's strengthening of central governments. It also stemmed from a postwar respect for the sovereignty of the smallest republics, represented by the founding of the United Nations in 1945. Latin American nationalists now saw an opportunity to heighten their stature vis-à-vis the United States.

Argentina's view of the United States particularly declined at the end of the war because it remained close to the Axis powers and was ostracized from postwar diplomacy. Starting in 1946, Juan Perón most clearly made the United States Argentina's opposite as he decried both communism and "Yankee imperialism." As Perón softened his stance in the later 1940s, other Latin American leaders—some democrats, some autocrats—increasingly wore the mantle of national pride in their arguments against either US abuse or neglect.[75]

Unfortunately for them, the Cold War's intensification in the late 1940s and early 1950s all but eliminated the possibility for serious democratic reform. Very few national governments in the 1950s were openly anti-US in their rhetoric or policies, lest they be conflated with communists. Historian Kyle Longley, for instance, explained the un-usual success of Costa Rica during these years owing to the ability of its leader, José Figueres, to "walk the fine line between national-ism and anti-Americanism."[76]

In case the danger of overstepping that line was unclear, the CIA's 1954 overthrow of Guatemalan reformer Jacobo Arbenz brought home the point. Instead of promoting democracy, pro-US dictatorships such as the one that soon replaced Arbenz made a comeback and squelched much of the movement for independence from US power. When anti-US events did arise—for instance, when mobs attacked Vice President Richard Nixon during his South American tour in 1958—they were just that, mobs, largely disconnected from any or-ganized politics of anti-Americanism.

Perhaps in the absence of organized anti-Americanism, one flourishing expression of anti-US sentiment in the postwar period was the novel. Latin Americans, especially from the middle and lower-middle social groups, were increasingly literate, and many had di-rectly witnessed or even suffered the indignities of working for US agricultural corporations or mines during the early century. The mid-century period therefore witnesses a flurry of novels that used the literary technique of social realism to convey the harsh conditions of US labor and racial attitudes in, say, Costa Rica or Guatemala, to the general reader in faraway Argentina or Chile.[77] There is no telling how much the impression left by these novels influenced the next wave of anti-Americanism, one of the most momentous in the his-tory of US-Latin American relations.

1959–1990: Superpowerdom and Socialism

The Cuban Revolution blasted the political stakes of anti-Americanism into the stratosphere. Within a year or so of Cuban rebels overthrow-ing a US-supported dictatorship, their most charismatic leader, Fidel Castro, tore Cuba away from its dependence on the United States and aligned it with the Soviet Union. Castro also encouraged anti-US rev-olutions in surrounding countries. The Spanish-speaking Caribbean had become the focus of anti-Americanism in the world.[78]

In the 1960s, Washington reacted with a dual strategy to discour-age what it labeled "anti-American" socialism. In one hand it dangled an economic carrot—the encouragement of reform and development through aid programs such as the Alliance for Progress. In the other hand it wielded a military stick—intensified training of hemispheric soldiers and police, direct landing such as the failed invasion of Cuba at the Bay of Pigs in 1961 and the successful intervention in the Dominican Republic in 1965, and covert campaigns against liberal or Marxist reformers in British Guiana, Guatemala, Brazil, Bolivia, and Chile, among others. As the 1960s ended, Washington largely pocketed its carrot and took out an ever bigger stick. In the 1970s, it supported authoritarian military regimes in Chile and Argentina, and in the 1980s it launched low-intensity wars through proxy militaries in Nicaragua, El Salvador, Guatemala, and elsewhere.

During these decades of US superpower behavior, the core resistance to US interests in the region resided in socialist visions of the "Yankee" as the ultimate capitalist-imperialist Other. Barry Rubin and Judith Colp Rubin argued that Castro's prediction of socialist revolution in 1962 was "the enshrinement of a new theory of anti-Americanism."[79] Likewise, Mexico's former president, Lázaro Cárdenas, declared in 1961 the coming of a "new stage in the liberation of Latin America."[80] Socialism was not new in 1959 Latin America: Peru's José Carlos Mariátegui had founded the region's first socialist party in the 1920s. Sandino rejected capitalism in the 1920s and 1930s. Anarcho-Syndicalism, Marxist-Leninism, Communist parties, and other manifestations of socialism also existed long before World War II. And once the Cold War began in the late 1940s and 1950s, eminent Latin Americans such as poet Pablo Neruda turned to socialism as a tool for criticizing US imperialism.[81] Yet in the 1960s and 1970s, socialism took over nation-states and thus held out the possibility of unfurling integrated anti-US policies. In the 1980s, for instance, the Nicaraguan Sandinistas' policies of collectivizing the economy, waging war on US-backed contras, and aligning with Havana and Moscow fully followed the logic of their anthem, which declared the United States "the enemy of humanity."

Such heated rhetoric proved more apocalyptic than was public opinion at the time. Insofar as the polls available from the Cold War era convey popular sentiment, alignment with the Soviet Union was not a well-received option in Latin America. But when "socialism" was defined more moderately as the redistribution of goods and protection from US capital, it proved enormously appealing. If they defined it in this latter way, US observers were not altogether wrong to equate socialism with anti-Americanism. Socialism neatly organized several rationales for opposing US influence into one largely hermetic system of thought. The economic rationale for anti-Americanism was the most obvious: socialism rejected global capitalism as relegating Latin America and the Caribbean to the status of "dependencies" condemned to extracting (through back-breaking methods) raw materials and providing cheap sweatshop labor on the "periphery" of the world economy.[82] State-directed alternatives could break this dynamic, socialists pledged. As one scholar noted, socialism also bolstered nationalism by ridding it of the "irrational" chauvinism that hampered cooperation across borders.[83] Socialism even strengthened the cultural pillar of anti-individualism built first by Arielism and then indigenism. It did so by promising the destruction of racial, gender, and class inequalities once the capitalist system that had created them in the first place crumbled. This cultural component to socialism was often a uniquely negative attack on social inequalities, and especially racism, within the United States. According to Ana María Dopico, "the critique of racism in the United States has been perhaps the most important critical stream of anti-Americanism that came out of the [Cuban] revolution of 1959."[84] Socialism, finally, provided an explanation for US "cultural imperialism" in that US media, being dominated by the corporate ethos, distorted humanist values and brainwashed Latin Americans.[85] In all these ways, socialism made sense of anti-Americanism. It swept away the ambiguities and ambivalences of past hostilities and channeled unfocused anger and frustrations into specific explanations for why things were.

It changed the structures of resistance, too. Socialism helped spread import substitution industrialization (ISI), the raising of tariffs and other trade barriers to favor native industry. It also reshaped university—and sometimes even high school—curricula, making "sociology" courses almost exclusively based on Marxism in theory and endless denunciations of US imperialism in practice. Socialism, finally, influenced warfare as guerrilla groups led by the revolutionary Ernesto "Che" Guevara and others drew inspiration from the "foco" theory, which argued that a small group of hard-core devotees could imitate the Russian Bolsheviks and "create the conditions" for revolution even in the midst of politically passive, agricultural societies.[86]

For Washington, guerrillas were rarely a threat. The more dangerous regimes were perceived to be those of Salvador Allende in Chile (1970–1973) and of the Sandinistas in Nicaragua (1979–1990). These triumphs of socialism were largely independent from the Soviets, yet they won elections. They showed, in other words, that socialist regimes in Latin America and the Caribbean could erect anti-US policies by using the core political process of the United States—elections. The contradiction threw Washington into confusion, and the

CIA, the Pentagon, and the State Department lashed back until socialist regimes ended from exhaustion around 1990.

1991–2005: Neo-liberalism and Populism

During this sixth period, the Western Hemisphere drew inspiration
from a sudden historical turn as the Cold War ended, democratic
regimes displaced autocrats, and Washington lost interest in inter-
vening in Latin American affairs. Yet by the turn of the twenty-first
century, anti-Americanism returned as a major part of foreign and
domestic policy.

In 1990, the term "Washington consensus" came to qualify the new
orthodoxy in favor of free-market policies, also called neoliberalism.
Many in the United States and Latin America blamed ISI-type protec-
tionism for the continuing stagnation of Latin American economies.
They acted through newly emboldened bureaucracies such as the
World Trade Organization, the International Monetary Fund, and the
US Office of the Special Trade Representative to open up markets to
global competition the way Asian countries had. The North American
Free Trade Agreement (NAFTA) between Mexico, the United States,
and Canada, which went into effect in 1994, epitomized this process.
So did the spread of *maquiladoras* along the Mexican border with
the United States and in "free zones" in the Caribbean Basin. Washington's integration of the hemisphere did not stop with trade. The
Drug Enforcement Agency increasingly attacked narcotraffickers with
multinational coalitions. The State Department, meanwhile, encouraged the spread of democracy, and even designed the 1994 military
intervention in Haiti to restore President Jean-Bertrand Aristide to
office. And finally, cheaper airfares and telephone connections, cable
television, and the Internet pried open the hemisphere even further
for US culture. Throughout the 1990s, polls indicated a high regard
for the United States in Latin America.[87]

Following the September 11th attacks, however, the numbers
changed significantly. In December 2001, 58 percent of "influential"
Latin Americans agreed that US policies had caused the attacks, and
71 percent said it was "good for [the] US to feel vulnerable."[88] As one
Brazilian student explained, "I'm not against the American people,
but the United States got what it deserved."[89] Adopting the same tone,
human rights activist Hebe Pastor de Bonafini notoriously celebrated
the fact that "now [North Americans live] the same fear that they produced in us, with persecution, disappearances and torture."[90]

When the administration of George W. Bush turned the sub-rosa
struggle against terrorism into overt wars in Afghanistan and especially Iraq, anti-Americanism swelled. Seventy-nine percent of Brazil-

ians opposed a retaliatory attack even against the Taliban regime in Afghanistan.[91] Polls conducted in eight Latin American countries in 1999/2000 and 2002 showed a significant drop in the "US image" in all countries but one.[92] And perhaps the most comprehensive poll indicated a strong downward trend in "very good opinions" and "good opinions" of the United States. After they reached a combined peak of 73 percent in 2001, they sank in 2002 to 71, dropping further in 2003 to 60 percent. By that time, only 23 percent agreed with "how the US [was] managing world conflicts," and a mere 15 percent agreed "with the US actions in Irak [sic]."[93]

Polls became far bleaker for the United States before and after the invasion of Iraq in 2003. One poll of Brazilians taken in May and June 2003 asked, "In general how would you say you feel towards America?" Forty-three percent said "fairly unfavorable," and another 23 percent answered "very unfavorable." Only 24 percent felt either "very" or "fairly favorable." Brazilians disagreed with most US foreign policies, called US citizens "arrogant" and "antagonistic," and three out of every four had no desire to move to the United States.[94] After similar results were found in January 2005, the Pew Global Attitudes project concluded that "anti-Americanism is deeper and broader now than at any time in modern history."[95]

Reflecting this mass discontent, the most potent form of resistance in Latin America was of a populist flavor. Populism was difficult to describe. Its economics were more on the left than on the right since they included the protection of native industries and redistributive policies, but they respected basic tenets of the free market. More to the point, populism fought back against social inequalities. At the dawn of the twenty-first century, Latin America was the most unequal society on the globe, and many blamed that state of affairs on US neoliberalism.

In response, no longer were indigenous and women's groups satisfied with never-realized socialist promises of proletarian rule or with vague Arielist claims to "spiritual" contentment. Those long left out wanted in. They wanted to make decisions at the highest levels. Many perceived that the United States behaved with typical hypocrisy when it called for full democracy in Latin America without offering policies that could empower the poor. At times, too, given the strong indigenous participation in populist policies, anti-US visions seethed with racial resentments. As a Bolivian leader nicknamed "the condor" declared, "Whites are here as renters on our land, and we need to put a giant fence around them, a reservation, a safe place for white people to be." He was at war "against gringo neoliberalism and racism, and [wished] to change our government to an Indian one."[96]

Bolivian and Ecuadorian indigenous groups organized so effectively that, by 2005, they stood on the verge of doing just that. At the very least, said Bolivian indigenous leader Evo Morales, the Free Trade Area of the Americas (FTAA), an extension of NAFTA, was sure to go down in flames. He described the FTAA as "a neocolonization project. . . . If it is approved it would be a policy of economic genocide." He foresaw that "for the first time in Latin America the Empire could be defeated."[97]

By the early twenty-first century, populist ideas put in power national leaders who directly threatened neoliberalism. Hugo Chávez in Venezuela (first elected in 1998), Ricardo Lagos in Chile (2000), Luiz Inácio Lula da Silva in Brazil (2002), Lucio Gutiérrez in Ecuador (2002), Néstor Kirchner in Argentina (2003), and Tabaré Vasquez in Uruguay (2004) all promised to roll back policies championed by either the United States or the International Monetary Fund. In addition to domestic anti-US policies, they also developed international organizations free from US oversight such as Mercosur, the South American free trade accord. There was even talk of military and petroleum alliances that would exclude Washington. The most radical of these populist leaders was Chávez, who disagreed with almost every foreign policy of Washington, publicly partnered with Castro's Cuba, and threatened to cut off his significant oil flow to the United States. Unlike other leaders, he showed little restraint in public. He roused the participants at the World Social Forum in Porto Alegre, Brazil, in early 2005 by reviving some apparently discarded language: "Imperialism is not invincible," he said. "Capitalism must be transcended."[98] By 2005, three quarters of South America's 350 million people were now in the hands of populists. As historian Greg Grandin wrote in 2004, "Latin American-US relations appear to be on the cusp of a new period of antagonism."[99]

The Contributions: Chapter Summaries

This volume gathers research-based, never-before-published essays on anti-Americanism in Latin America and the Caribbean. These scholars of inter-American relations—eight historians, one political scientist—are all from or based in the United States, Canada, or the United Kingdom. Together they represent an effort by Anglo-American scholars to apply multinational perspectives to the newly prominent topic of anti-US hostility.[100] Each of their contributions combines a broad view of culture with a special effort to view anti-Americanism from the perspectives of both critics of the United States and US observers reacting to those criticisms. Each contributor also set out to link the present to the past.

The chapters that follow are a testament to the potential for anti-Americanism to act as a complex yet unifying concept within narratives of resistance. That narrative rejects the definition of *antiyanquismo* as the emotional, irrational, scheming disease that US patriots have been eager to deride since they coined the term "Yankeephobia" in the early twentieth century. It equally refuses to see anti-Americanism as the keen-eyed, righteous, spontaneous heroism that many in the hemisphere, north and south, wished it were. The contributions to this volume begin the work of providing case studies of attempts, scheming and heroic, to resist US power, real and perceived.

Most contributors focused on country-specific campaigns of opposition to US influences. This choice speaks not only to the power of nationalism within anti-Americanism but to the importance of central national governments as conveyors of political and cultural resistance to US power. The national politics of anti-Americanism—the theme of Part I—shaped attitudes, but the institutions of the state such as embassies, ministries of foreign relations, party newspapers, and state-run unions may have been even more powerful in stirring up a good anti-US fight than were international organizations such as the Comintern or the Organization of American States.

Chapter 1, by John Britton, emphasizes that the Mexican contribution to anti-Americanism lay in uncovering US intervention in the most subtle of places. Britton focuses on outspoken Mexican leaders who shifted their anti-US targets from the direct military intervention of 1914 to 1916 to the diplomatic intimidation and economic penetration than followed. While José M. Puig Casauranc denounced the international banking system, Jesús Silva Herzog targeted oil companies. Mass rallies demonstrated how this broadened suspicion of intervention resonated with the Mexican public. Redirecting criticism at "softer" instruments of empire might have been most likely to work in Mexico, whose long history of subjection to US intervention conditioned it to expect the worst from the *gringos*.

Glenn Dorn relates a more outwardly ambitious Argentine anti-Americanism in Chapter 2. In Argentina, Juan Perón fancied himself the new regional leader in South America in the post-World War II era. Needing to displace both US and Soviet influences to do so, Perón defined his foreign policy as encouraging state-directed social and economic development that were opposed to both communism and capitalism. Perhaps an important lesson in national narratives of anti-Americanism lies in Dorn's conclusion that Perón was far less successful in challenging US power outside his borders than Mexicans had been in cutting it short within theirs.

Darlene Rivas's Chapter 3 serves as a useful reminder that the anti-Americanism of Hugo Chávez in the 2000s operated within the confines of a dilemma deeply embedded in Venezuela's political culture. Throughout the twentieth century, Venezuelans saw their major resource, petroleum, as a godsend and a curse. Oil allowed one of the highest standards of living in Latin America, yet it also created dependency on foreign investment, exports, and goods. In confronting this dilemma, many put pressure on their main foreign partner, the United States, a pressure that at times gave way to violent outbursts in the 1950s and 1960s.

Jeffrey Taffet's study of Chile in the 1960s offers a story of a friendship gone wrong that serves as an object lesson for all US allies. In this case, US aid was the problem as well as the cure. The moderate president Eduardo Frei benefited from an infusion of dollars when he won the 1964 elections in spite of the rising popularity of his socialist counterparts, and he expressed gratitude. Yet afterwards, the administration of Lyndon Johnson demonstrated traditional US hegemonic assumptions by making unreasonable demands on Frei. Chapter 4 surveys Chilean cartoons and violent demonstrations to show how too much economic micromanaging by Washington might backfire.

Chapter 5 by Kirk Bowman rounds out Part I with a study of anti-Americanism in Brazil. Bowman's provocative thesis is that the election of Lula in 2002 culminated a process by which the social and political elite in Brazil and the United States suddenly ran out of common interests after the Cold War. Based on more than 120 interviews conducted in 2003 and 2004 and on surveys of polls and media images, Bowman's contribution suggests that Brazil's new boldness may carry abiding drawbacks for the United States.

While these national narratives argue that national political leaders were key in forging anti-US strategy out of sentiment, they also have international implications. One of these implications is that campaigns of resistance spilled over into neighboring states, for instance when Perón tried to compete with the Truman administration in South America or when Lula placed his own "heavyweight" country against the US "colossus" in South America. Part II of this volume explores transnational and comparative connections.

In Chapter 6, Jason Parker's contribution leaves Latin America proper to observe the ambivalence and strategies of West Indians during World War II. There, political leaders sharing an African heritage identified the United States as unique in two ways: one, it was not

Britain, and so could act as a lever against British colonialism; two, there were African Americans in the United States who joined West Indies in forming a diaspora in the Americas that might cooperate on the basis of race rather than nationality. Whatever anti-Americanism existed in the West Indies—and it did exist—was therefore tempered by the need to counterbalance hegemonic powers.

My own Chapter 7 compares anti-Americanism in Cuba and Panama, two equally dependent, small, Spanish-speaking countries that were traditionally of great value to the United States. Applying the concept of political culture to anti-Americanism, it identifies major differences between the two countries that existed before US control during the twentieth century and that continued to exist at the turn of the twenty-first century. In Cuba, nationalist radicalism sought the rejection of foreign influence not only out of pride but to achieve greater social justice. In Panama, meanwhile, leaders long accepted the role of foreigners in bolstering the nation's identity as a hub of commerce. Both nations rejected or welcomed US influence based on these fundamental principles.

David Ryan's Chapter 8 concludes Part II by surveying the transnational buildup of the anti-US tenets of liberation theology in the 1970s and 1980s. Ryan argues that liberation theologians did not feed upon prejudices as suggested by the "ism" of anti-Americanism, but rather came to terms with the evidence that US-led global capitalism exacerbated poverty in Central America. Focusing on El Salvador, he recalls how these theologians became the "voice of the voiceless" in arguing for the inhumanity of the local and international economy and the immorality of the national security state, its ideology, and its impact on human rights.

The sole contribution in Part III contrasts with the rest of the volume in that it argues for a minimal presence of anti-Americanism—in one country at least. In Chapter 9, William O. Walker III questions whether anti-Americanism had much of a role in the context of illegal narcotics gradually devouring public life in Colombia from 1984 to 2004. Walker's study of "quiet" anti-Americanism argues that Colombian policymakers mostly resented how the drug war, as fought by Washington, weakened the nation-state, thus not only endangering counterinsurgency efforts but the very existence of Colombia. The victory of a hard-line candidate such as Álvaro Uribe in 2002 sprang more from the desire for a strong central government than from any pro- or anti-Americanism.

As these chapters demonstrate and as this introduction has argued, the writing of the history of anti-Americanism in Latin America and the Caribbean is very much a work in progress. Like anti-Americanism itself, it is a tree of sorts, whose branches have more growing to do. The contributors to this volume endeavored to explore in greater detail a few limbs of the story briefly outlined in this introduction. What inspired them were the rich traditions of Latin American and Caribbean history, the growing method of combining US and multinational archival sources, and the concern with using cultural insights and cultural sources that the inaugural volume of this series showed could be central in understanding the meanings, articulations, and implications of power in international history.

Notes

1. This definition is similar to M. Hunt's in *Ideology and US Foreign Policy* (New Haven, 1987), 12. Hunt discussed his definition and updated the bibliography behind it in his "Ideology," in *Explaining the History of American Foreign Relations,* 2nd ed., ed. M. J. Hogan and T. G. Paterson (Cambridge, 2004), 221–40.
2. L. Hunt, ed., *The New Cultural History* (Berkeley, 1989), esp. chapters 2 and 5.
3. J. Gienow-Hecht and F. Schumacher, *Culture and International History* (New York, 2003), 3.
4. F. Mallon, "The Promise and Dilemma of Subaltern Studies: Perspectives from Latin American History," *American Historical Review* 99, 5 (December 1994): 1491–515.
5. M. L. Pratt, "Back Yard with Views," in *Anti-Americanism,* ed. A. Ross and K. Ross (New York, 2004), 32. A critic of anti-Americanism, P. Hollander agreed that "Latin American anti-Americanism has the deepest historical roots as it represents a response to past—and in some measure continued—American domination and influence in the region," in his *Anti-Americanism: Critiques at Home and Abroad* (New York, 1992), 355.
6. B. Rubin and J. C. Rubin, *Hating America: A History* (New York: 2004), 101.
7. J. C. Scott, *Weapons of the Weak: Everyday Forms of Peasant Resistance* (New Haven: 1985).
8. J. F. Rippy, "Literary Yankeephobia in Hispanic America," *Journal of International Relations* 12 (1922): Part I, 350–71; Part II, 524–33. See also W. E. Dunn, "The Postwar Attitude of Hispanic America toward the United States," *Hispanic American Historical Review* 3 (1920): 177–83; J. F. Rippy, "Pan-Hispanic Propaganda in Hispanic America," *Political Science Quarterly* 37 (September 1922); H. B. Alexander, "Present Day Attitude of South America toward the United States" (Master's thesis, Stanford, 1923); J. R. Acevedo, "Anti-Americanism in Latin America, or, Why the Ill-Feeling toward the United States" (Master's Thesis, Boston, 1927); M. W. Williams, "Latin Fears and Yankee Favors," *The American Mercury* 13 (1928): 320–25.
9. See M. T. Berger, *Under Northern Eyes: Latin American Studies and US Hegemony in the Americas 1898–1990* (Bloomington, 1995), chapter 1.
10. E. Perry, "Anti-American Propaganda in Hispanic America," *The Hispanic American Historical Review* 3 (1930): 17.
11. Alexander, "Present Day Attitude," 17.
12. For institutional background, see Berger, *Under Northern Eyes,* chapter 2. An early study, which bridged the first two waves, was M. P. Chapman, "Yankeephobia, an Analysis of Anti-United States Bias of Certain Spanish South American Intel-

lectuals, 1898–1928" (Ph.D. diss., Stanford, 1950). She noted "the absence of any thorough research into the historical beginnings of Yankeephobia," 4. See also a special issue of the *Annals of the American Academy of Political and Social Science* 295 (September 1954); W. W. Sinclair, "Los Estados Unidos de José Martí" (Master's thesis, Universidad Nacional Autónoma de Mexico, 1959); P. A. Villoldo, *Latin American Resentment* (New York, 1959); D. H. Radler, *El Gringo: The Yankee Image in Latin America* (Philadelphia, 1962); W. Wolfe, "Images of the United States in the Hispanic American Press: A Content Analysis of News and Opinions of this Country Appearing in Daily Papers from Nineteen Latin American Republics" (Ph.D. diss., Indiana, 1963); J. C. Merrill, *Gringo: The Americans As Seen by Mexican Journalists* (Gainesville, 1963); A. Scarangello, *American Education Through Foreign Eyes* (Delaware, 1964); W. Pfaff, "Yankees vs. Latins," *Commonweal,* 28 May 1965, 310; "The Anatomy of Anti-Americanism," *Senior Scholastic,* 11 February 1966; R. West, "Why Latin Americans Say, 'Go Home, Yanqui,'" *The New York Times Magazine,* 29 May 1966; a special issue of *The Annals of the American Academy of Political and Social Science* 366 (July 1966); F. Turner, "Anti-Americanism in Mexico, 1910–1913," *Hispanic American Historical Review* 47 (1967): 502–18; T. Morgan, *Among the Anti-Americans* (New York, 1967); J. Johnson, "The United States and the Latin American Left Wings," *The Yale Review* 56 (March 1967).

13. J. de Onís, *The United States as Seen by Spanish American Writers* (New York, 1952); J. De Galíndez, "Anti-American Sentiment in Latin America," *Journal of International Affairs* 9 (1955): 24–32; W. Stokes, "Cultural Anti-Americanism in Latin America," in *Issues and Conflicts: Studies in Twentieth Century American Diplomacy,* ed. G. Anderson (Lawrence, 1959).

14. Chapman, "Yankeephobia," 30, 138.

15. Dulles cited in NSC meeting, 17 November 1960, *Foreign Relations of the United States 1958–1960* (Washington, 1991), 5: 453.

16. C. Rama, *La imagen de los Estados Unidos en la América Latina: de Simón Bolívar a Allende* (Mexico City, 1975); J. G. Gómez et al., *La lucha antimperialista en Cuba* (Havana, 1976); M. Aguirre and A. Montes, ed., *De Bolívar al Frente Sandinista: antología del pensamiento anti-imperialista latinoamericano* (Madrid, 1979); Instituto de Estudio del Sandinismo, *Pensamiento antimperialista en Nicaragua: antología* (Managua, 1982); and O. Cabrera, ed., *El antimperialismo en la historia de Cuba* (Havana, 1985).

17. S. Haseler, *The Varieties of Anti-Americanism, Reflex and Response* (Washington, 1985) and *Anti-Americanism: Steps on a Dangerous Path* (London, 1986); and O. Handlin, *The Distortion of America,* rev. ed. (New Brunswick, 1995).

18. A. Rubinstein and D. Smith, ed., *Anti-Americanism in the Third World: Implications for US Foreign Policy* (New York, 1985). For similar comparative work see *The Annals of the American Academy of Political and Social Science* 497 (May 1988); R. Kroes and M. van Rossem, ed., *Anti-Americanism in Europe* (Amsterdam, 1986); and L. Krenston, *Anti-Americanism in the Middle East: Sudden War and the Problem of Oil* (Seoul, 1993).

19. N. Andrusiak, "Soviet Anti-Americanism," *Ukranian Quarterly* 26 (autumn-winter 1970): 270–76; J. G. Lutz, "The Chinese Student Movement of 1945–1949," *Journal of Asian Studies* 31 (Nov. 1971): 89–110; D. Shambaugh, *Beautiful Imperialist: China Perceives America, 1972–1990* (Princeton, 1991); Z. Yang, "United States Marines in Qingdao: Military-Civilian Interaction, Nationalism, and China's Civil War, 1945–1949" (Ph.D. diss., Maryland, 1998); E. Shiraev and V. Zubok, *Anti-Americanism in Russia: From Stalin to Putin* (New York, 2000); G. Wang, *In Search of Justice: The 1905–1906 Chinese Anti-American Boycott* (Cambridge, 2001); and H. Zhang, *America Perceived: The Making of Chinese Images of the United States, 1945–1953* (Westport, 2002).

20. D. Strauss, *Menace in the West: The Rise of French Anti-Americanism in Modern Times* (Westport, 1978); L. W. Hindsley, "In Search of an Ally: French Attitudes toward America, 1919–1929" (Ph.D. diss., Michigan State, 1980); G. Suffert, *Les nouveaux cow-boys: essai sur l'anti-américanisme primaire* (Paris, 1984); F. Costigliola, *Awkward Dominion: American Political, Economic, and Cultural Relations with Europe, 1919–1933* (Ithaca, 1984); S. D. Armus, "Primacy of the Spiritual: French Resistance to America and the Formation of French Identity" (Ph.D. diss., Stony Brook, 1998); R. Kuisel, *Seducing the French: The Dilemma of Americanization* (Berkeley, 1993); H. Laurendeau-Johnson, "French News Magazines on America 1974–1984: Influences of Political Ideology on Media Content" (Ph.D. diss., New York, 1994); and J.-F. Revel, *L'obsession anti-américaine: Son fonctionnement, ses causes, ses inconséquences* (Paris, 2000).

21. K. Sontheimer, "How Real is German Anti-Americanism? An Assessment," in *America and the Germans: An Assessment of a Three-Hundred-Year History,* vol. 2, ed. F. Trommler and J. McVeigh (Philadelphia, 1985), 117–23; D. Diner, *America in the Eyes of the Germans: An Essay on Anti-Americanism,* trans. A. Brown (Princeton, 1996); M. Klees, "The 'German Question' in the Political Culture of West Germany in the 1980s: Influence on German-American Relations between Anti-Americanism and the Recognition of the German-Polish Border" (Ph.D. diss., Fletcher School, 1998).

22. J. K. Morchain, "Anti-Americanism in Canada 1871–1891" (Ph.D. diss., Rochester, 1967); W. M. Baker, "The Anti-American Ingredient in Canadian History," *Dalhousie Review* 53 (1973): 57–77; and J. A. Granatstein, *Yankee Go Home? Canadians and Anti-Americanism* (Toronto, 1996). For a perspective from Quebec, see M. Roy, *Pour en finir avec l'antiaméricanisme* (Montreal, 1993).

23. D. Hoffman, "Culture, Self, and 'URI': Anti-Americanism in Contemporary South Korea," *Journal of Northeast Asian Studies* 12 (summer 1993): 3–20; J.-B. Lee, "Cultural Representation of Anti-Americanism: The Negative Images of the United States in South Korean Literature and Arts, 1945–1994" (Ph.D. diss., Hawaii, 1994); G.-W. Shin, "Marxism, Anti-Americanism, and Democracy in South Korea: An Examination of Nationalist Intellectual Discourse," *Positions: East Asia Cultures Critique* 3 (fall 1995): 509–13, and "South Korean Anti-Americanism: A Comparative Perspective," *Asian Survey* 36 (August 1996): 787–803.

24. C. Rangel, *The Latin Americans: Their Love-Hate Relationship with the United States,* rev. ed. (New Brunswick, [1977] 1987); R. Parsons, "Carlos Rangel's *Del buen salvaje al buen revolucionario:* A Maverick View of U.S. Imperialism," *Inter-American Review of Bibliography* 38: 3 (1988): 354–62.

25. Rama, *La imagen;* Reid, *Spanish American Images of the United States, 1790–1960* (Gainesville, 1977); and Toscano and Hiester, *Anti-Yankee Feelings in Latin America: An Anthology of Latin American Writings from Colonial to Modern Times in Their Historical Perspective* (Washington, 1982). W. L. de Arteaga, "The Historiography of Anti-Americanism in Latin America" (Master's thesis, University of Florida, 1970).

26. V. Arriaga Weiss and A. R. Suárez Argüello, ed., *Estados Unidos desde América Latina: sociedad, política y cultura* (Mexico City, 1995).

27. P. Apuleyo Mendoza et al., *Guide to the Perfect Latin American Idiot* (Lanham, 2000).

28. P. Hollander, *Anti-Americanism: Critiques at Home and Abroad* (New York, 1992) and *Anti-Americanism: Irrational & Rational* (New Brunswick, 1995).

29. P. Hollander, "Introduction: The New Virulence and Popularity," in *Understanding Anti-Americanism: Its Origins and Impact at Home and Abroad,* ed. P. Hollander (Chicago, 2004), 7–9.

30. R. Kimball, "Anti-Americanism Then and Now," in *Understanding Anti-Americanism,* 240.

31. M. Radu, "A Matter of Identity: The Anti-Americanism of Latin American Intellectuals," in *Understanding Anti-Americanism*, ed. Hollander, 146. Some conservative yet better informed studies are M. Falcoff, *A Culture of Its Own: Taking Latin America Seriously* (New Brunswick, 1998), 2; and L. Harrison, *The Pan-American Dream: Do Latin America's Cultural Values Discourage True Partnership with the United States and Canada?* (New York, 1997) and *Underdevelopment Is a State of Mind* (Lanham, 2000).

32. A. Ross and K. Ross, "Introduction," in *Anti-Americanism*, ed. Ross and Ross, 2, 3.

33. Ross and Ross, "Introduction," 1.

34. A. McPherson, *Yankee No! Anti-Americanism in US-Latin American Relations* (Cambridge, 2003); I. Buruma and A. Margalit, *Occidentalism: The West in the Eyes of Its Enemies* (New York, 2004); and T. Judt and D. Lacorne, ed., *With Us or Against Us: Studies in Global Anti-Americanism* (New York, 2005). See also the articles on anti-Americanism in *The Brown Journal of World Affairs* 10, 2 (winter/ spring 2004).

35. W. D. Connor, "Anti-Americanism in Post-Communist Russia," in *Understanding Anti-Americanism*, ed. Hollander, 214–35; S. Telhami, *The Stakes: America and the Middle East: The Consequences of Power and the Choice for Peace* (Boulder, 2002); and E. Larson et al., *Ambivalent Allies? A Study of South Korean Attitudes toward the US* (Santa Monica, 2004).

36. "What We Think of America," *Granta* 77 (spring 2002).

37. R. Crockatt, *America Embattled: September 11, Anti-Americanism, and the Global Order* (New York, 2003); P. H. Gries, *China's New Nationalism: Pride, Politics, and Diplomacy* (Berkeley, 2004).

38. Rubin and Rubin, *Hating America*. See also the September 2002 issue of the *Journal of American History* 89, published as J. Meyerowitz, *History and September 11* (Philadelphia, 2003).

39. G. McKay, ed., *Yankee Go Home (& Take Me With U): Americanization and Popular Culture* (Sheffield, 1997); Z. Sardar and M. W. Davies, *Why Do People Hate America?* (New York, 2002); J. L. Esposito, *Unholy War: Terror in the Name of Islam* (New York, 2002); P. Roger, *L'ennemi américain: généalogie de l'antiaméricanisme français* (Paris, 2002), published in English as *The American Enemy: The History of French Anti-Americanism* (Chicago, 2005); R. A. Berman, *Anti-Americanism in Europe: A Cultural Problem* (Stanford, 2004); and A. Stephan, *Anti-Americanism: The German Encounter with American Culture after 1945* (New York, 2004).

40. J.-F. Revel, *Anti-Americanism* (San Francisco, 2003).

41. G. Grandin, "The Narcissism of Violent Differences," in *Anti-Americanism*, ed. Ross and Ross, 19.

42. Cited in L. Monguió, "Nationalism and Social Discontent as Reflected in Spanish-American Literature," *The Annals of the American Academy of Political and Social Science* 334 (March 1961): 65.

43. Rangel, *The Latin Americans*, 25.

44. T. de Orea in J. Ewell, *Venezuela and the United States* (Athens, 1996), 20.

45. J. C. Merrill, *Gringo: The Americans as Seen by Mexican Journalists* (Gainesville, 1963), vii. There is some disagreement on the first use of the word. The *Oxford English Dictionary* 2nd ed. (online, 1989) and others have found it rather in 1849 after the Mexican War. There is more agreement on its etymology. The epithet most likely derived from "griego," which in nineteenth-century Spanish meant gibberish, as in "all Greek to me." Linguists also agree that, while South Americans still attach the word to most white foreigners, Mexicans reserve it for white US citizens. For various interpretations, see A. A. Roback, *A Dictionary of*

International Slurs (Cambridge, 1979); H. Rawson, *Wicked Words* (New York, 1989); and D. Carbonell Basset, *McGraw-Hill diccionario del argot* (New York, 2001).

46. Cited in P. K. Liss, *Atlantic Empires: The Network of Trade and Revolution, 1713–1826* (Baltimore, 1983), 238.
47. Cited in J. F. Rippy's introduction to M. Ugarte, *The Destiny of a Continent* (New York, [1923] 1970), viii.
48. Bolívar in Ewell, *Venezuela,* 31–32; Rangel, *The Latin Americans,* 72.
49. Translation by the author. Cited in Rama, *La imagen,* 53.
50. Bilboa in *America in Danger,* cited in Rubin and Rubin, *Hating America,* 104.
51. Examples of late nineteenth-century literature are Cuban J. M. Céspedes's *La Doctrina de Monroe* (Havana, 1893), and Brazilian E. Prado's *A Iluçao Americana* (Paris, 1895).
52. P. Foos, *A Short, Offhand, Killing Affair: Soldiers and Social Conflict during the Mexican-American War* (Chapel Hill, 2002), esp. chapter 6.
53. Translated by author. Martí cited in Rama, *La imagen,* 85.
54. E. Prado cited in Rubin and Rubin, *Hating America,* 105.
55. T. F. O'Brien, *The Revolutionary Mission: American Enterprise in Latin America, 1900–1945* (Cambridge, 1996), 208–10.
56. Both citations from Perry, "Anti-American Propaganda," 27, 31. Vargas Vila wrote *Ante los bárbaros* (Barcelona, 1917). Similar to him was R. B. Fombona of Venezuela, author of *Letras y letrados de Hispano-América* (Paris, 1908) and *La lámpara de Aladino* (Madrid, 1915).
57. D. M. Dozer, *Are We Good Neighbors? Three Decades of Inter-American Relations, 1930–1960* (Gainesville, 1959), 8.
58. Rubin and Rubin, *Hating America,* 105.
59. Ugarte, *Destiny,* 19, 20. He added that, while Argentines used the term "gringo" against *all* foreigners, Mexicans had reserved it uniquely for US citizens.
60. Ugarte, *Destiny,* xx, 12, 125.
61. On this resistance, the literature is massive. On the Dominican Republic, Haiti, and Nicaragua, one could begin with T. Castro García, *Intervención yanqui 1916–1924* (Santo Domingo, 1978); C. V. de León, *Casos y cosas de ayer* (Santo Domingo, 1972); J. U. Franco, *Nuestros grades patriotas y la intervención norteamericana del año 1916* (Santiago de los Caballeros, 1984); M. F. González, *Línea noroeste: testimonio del patriotismo olvidado* (San Pedro de Macorís, 1985); F. S. Ducoudray, *Los "Gavilleros" del Este: Una epopeya calumniada* (Santo Domingo, 1976); F. Blancpain, *Haïti et les Etats-Unis 1915–1934: Histoire d'une occupation* (Paris, 1999); G. Condé, *La ville des Cayes* (Port-au-Prince, 2002); R. Gaillard, *Les blancs débarquent,* 5 vol. (Port-au-Prince, 1981–1983); N. J. Conrady, "Le Roman haïtien d'expression française et l'occupation américaine de 1915–1934: Trois décennies d'histoire vues par quatre romanciers haïtiens engagés (Stéphane Alexis, Annie Desroy, Léon Laleau, Mme Virgile Valcin)" (Ph.D. diss., Middlebury, 1995); N. Macaulay, *The Sandino Affair* (Chicago, 1967); A. Bolaños Geyer, *Sandino* (Masaya, 2002); D. C. Hodges, *Sandino's Communism: Spiritual Politics for the Twenty-First Century* (Austin, 1992); Instituto de Estudio del Sandinismo, *Augusto C. Sandino, Padre de la Revolución Popular Sandinista y Antimperialista* (Managua, 1985); and M. A. Navarro-Génie, *Augusto "César" Sandino: Messiah of Light and Truth* (Syracuse, 2002).
62. Apart from Ugarte, R. Darío, Peru's C. Vallejo, and Mariátegui also all lived in Paris. Guatemala's M. A. Asturias was his country's ambassador there.
63. Rippy, "Pan-Hispanic Propaganda."
64. L. H. Derby, "The Magic of Modernity: Dictatorship and Civic Culture in the Dominican Republic, 1916–1962" (Ph.D. diss., Chicago, 1998), 23, 77–78.
65. V. R. Haya de la Torre, *¿A donde va Indoamérica?,* 2d ed. (Santiago, 1935).

66. Rangel, *The Latin Americans,* 88.
67. Many US observers of indigenism have been harsh in their analysis. For instance, J. Means called it "a return to the forces of a fabled past, an evasion of present realities by the substitution of gilded fiction for bitter fact." Means, "Anti-Americanism in the Neighborhood," *The North American Review* 8 (summer 1971): 10.
68. J. Vasconcelos, *The Cosmic Race/La raza cósmica,* trans. D. Jaén (Baltimore, [1925] 1997). See also Rangel, *The Latin Americans,* 91.
69. Haya de la Torre, *¿A donde va Indoamérica?,* esp. 23, 153.
70. According to Rubin and Rubin, "Sandino . . . expressed a racialist anti-Americanism that was consistent with the most reactionary traditionalist forces in the region. His view of the United States as evil, innately aggressive, and inhumanly greedy made him identify all Americans as the enemy," in *Hating America,* 113.
71. Dozer, *Are We Good Neighbors?,* 16.
72. Rangel, *The Latin Americans,* 51.
73. D. Green in *The Containment of Latin America: A History of the Myths and Realities of the Good Neighbor Policy* (Chicago, 1971), 187, sees the Chapultepec Conference of 1945 as an anti-American milestone. See also M. Gurtov, *The United States against the Third World: Antinationalism and Intervention* (New York, 1974).
74. D. Cosío Villegas cited in Merrill, *Gringo,* 5.
75. On neglect, see Chile's C. Dávila, *We of the Americas* (Chicago, 1949).
76. Longley, *The Sparrow and the Hawk: Costa Rica and the United States during the Rise of José Figueres* (Tuscaloosa, 1997), 85.
77. An early socially realist novel was Chilean B. Lillo's *Sub terra: cuadros mineros* (Santiago, 1904). Among the hundreds that followed, the best-known are R. Gallegos, *Doña Bárbara* (Barcelona, 1929); H. Robleto, *Sangre en el Trópico: la novella de la intervención yanqui en Nicaragua* (Madrid, 1930); D. Aguilera Malta, *C.Z. (Canal Zone) (los yanquis en Panamá)* (Santiago, 1935); R. Marrero Aristy, *Over* (Santo Domingo, [1940] 1994); C. L. Fallas, *Mamita Yunai* (Santiago, 1949); A. Céspedes, *El metal del diablo* (La Paz, 1946); J. Gutiérrez, *Puerto Limón* (Santiago, 1950); B. Castro, *Un hombre por el camino* (Santiago, 1950); J. Beleño, *Luna verde* (Panama City, 1950), *Flor de banana* (Panama City, 1965), and *Gamboa Road Gang/Los Forzados de Gamboa* (Panama City, 1960); and M. A. Asturias, *El señor presidente* (Buenos Aires, 1948), *Viento fuerte* (Buenos Aires, 1950), *El papa verde* (Buenos Aires, 1954), *Week-end en Guatemala* ([Buenos Aires?] 1956), and *Los ojos de los enterrados* (Buenos Aires, 1960). Slightly later, Mexican author C. Fuentes made his major statement on the love-hate relationship between his nation and the United States in *La Muerte de Artemio Cruz* (Mexico City, 1962). G. García Márquez repeated the theme of US economic exploitation while departing dramatically from social realism with *One Hundred Years of Solitude* (Buenos Aires, 1967).

For scholarship on anti-US poetry and novels, see W. S. Stokes, "Cultural Anti-Americanism in Latin America," *Issues and Conflicts: Studies in Twentieth Century American Diplomacy,* ed. G. L. Anderson (Lawrence, 1959), 315–38; Monguió, "Nationalism and Social Discontent," 63–73; H. H. Orjuela, "Rafael Pombo y la poesía antiyanqui de Hispanoamérica," *Hispania* 45 (1962): 27–31; Toscano and Hiester, *Anti-Yankee Feelings;* and J. Skurski, "The Ambiguities of Authenticity in Latin America: *Doña Bárbara* and the Construction of National Identity," in *Becoming National: A Reader,* ed. G. Eley and R. G. Suny (New York, 1996), 371–402.
78. Rubin and Rubin agree that, "while Europe was the area of the world where anti-Americanism was most comprehensively developed, South America was the place more identified with that doctrine, especially between the 1950s and 1980s," in their *Hating America,* 101.

79. Rubin and Rubin, *Hating America*, 115.
80. Translated by author. Cárdenas cited in Rama, *La imagen*, 128.
81. Before the Cuban Revolution, other popular socialist writings included those of Cuba's N. Guillén and Argentine D. Ayres's *Estados Unidos: una mentira* (Buenos Aires, 1956).
82. Examples of socialists who focused on economics include J. E. Cuesta, *El imperialismo yanqui y la revolución en el Caribe* (San Juan, 1936) and V. Sáenz, *Hispano américa contra el coloniaje* (Mexico, 1949). Other critiques of US capitalism in Latin America are F. Morales Balcells, *La industria del cobre en Chile* (Santiago, 1946) and J. H. Hernández Cobos, *Crisis de la democracia: su preservación y defensa* (Guatemala, 1950). Scholarship on economic anti-Americanism includes W. S. Stokes, "Economic Anti-Americanism in Latin America," *Inter-American Economic Affairs* 11 (autumn 1957): 3–22; R. Vernon, ed., *How Latin America views the US Investor* (New York, 1966); and R. H. Swansborough, *The Embattled Colossus: Economic Nationalism and United States Investors in Latin America* (Gainesville, 1976).
83. Rama, *La imagen*, 36.
84. A. M. Dopico, "The 3:10 to Yuma," in *Anti-Americanism*, ed. Ross and Ross, 52.
85. T. Saraví, *Imperialismo y dominación cultural, por que pensamos y nos comunicamos "en extranjero"* (Buenos Aires, 1974).
86. On guerrillas in the 1950s and 1960s, see R. Gott, *Guerrilla Movements in Latin America* (London, 1970); T. C. Wright, *Latin America in the Era of the Cuban Revolution* (New York, 1991); and T. P. Wickham-Crowley, *Guerrillas & Revolution in Latin America: A Comparative Study of Insurgents and Regimes since 1956* (Princeton, 1992).
87. USIA poll cited in Rubin and Rubin, *Hating America*, 123.
88. "America Admired, Yet Its New Vulnerability Seen as Good Thing, Say Opinion Leaders," published 19 December 2001. Available at http://www.people-press.org, accessed on 15 March 2005.
89. Cited in "Take That, Gringos," *Newsweek*, 8 October 2001, 44.
90. Cited in G. Yúdice, "US *Prepotencia:* Latin Americans Respond," 69–84, in *Anti-Americanism*, ed. Ross and Ross, 75.
91. "Maioria dos brasileiros quer justiça, sem guerra," published 21 September 2001, and "90% dos brasileiros são contra ataques ao Iraque," published 6 April 2003, both available at http://www1.folha.uol.com.br/folha/datafolha, accessed 15 March 2005.
92. Argentina dropped furthest, by 16 points. Guatemala went up by 6 points. The polls are in "What the World Thinks in 2002," 4 December 2002, available at http://people-press.org, accessed 15 March 2005.
93. Latinobarómetro, "The Image of the United States in Latin America," paper presented at the *Miami Herald*'s Americas Conference, 30 September–1 October 2004, by M. Lagos.
94. "What the World Thinks of America," CBC News Special poll, available at http://www.cbc.ca, accessed 15 March 2005.
95. "Global Opinion: The Spread of Anti-Americanism," 24 January 2005, available at http://www.people-press.org, accessed 15 March 2005.
96. Cited in Tom Hayden, "Bolivia's Indian Revolt," *The Nation*, 21 June 2004, 18–22.
97. Cited in Radu, "A Matter of Identity," 160.
98. Cited in A. Solomon, "Porto Alegre Postcard: Artists Imagine Another World," *The Nation*, 21 March 2005, 18.
99. Grandin, "The Narcissism of Violent Differences," 27.
100. The fact that no Latin American scholar has contributed an essay was not a conscious decision by the editor. Some scholars from both Latin America and the Caribbean were asked, but declined for practical reasons.

Part I
NATIONAL NARRATIVES

Chapter 1

REDEFINING INTERVENTION
Mexico's Contribution to Anti-Americanism

John A. Britton

Anti-Americanism has a prominent place in Mexican history. The relatively harmonious relationship between the two nations in the 1990s and early years of the twenty-first century tended to obscure that fact that Mexicans have often been critical of the United States, especially concerning government and business policies that posed threats to the interests of Mexico. Anti-Americanism in Mexico, therefore, often manifested itself in arguments against specific policies and actions more so than the broad cultural and philosophical critiques of the United States typical of European anti-Americanism.[1] One purpose of this essay is to examine this theme in Mexican anti-Americanism in one of the most turbulent periods in Mexican history—the quarter century following 1917 when the epic Revolution followed its irregular and often unexpected trajectory that generated conflict with its powerful neighbor to the north.

A second major characteristic of Mexican anti-Americanism was its tendency, until recently, to appear mainly in the writing and speeches of the nation's political and intellectual leaders rather than in popular demonstrations and other forms of mass expression. Of course, there were cases of anti-American acts during the Mexican-US War of 1846–1848 and along the Mexican-US border in the 1910s, and moments when political statements aroused resounding public support, as in the case of President Lázaro Cárdenas's decision in 1938 to expropriate US and other foreign-owned oil properties. However, both calculation and spontaneity played their parts in the 1938 demonstrations. Historian Alan Knight has concluded that Mexican anti-

---

Americanism in this era was closely connected to politics and political leaders, and "that its popular roots were shallow" when compared to similar movements in other countries.[2] In this sense, anti-Americanism drew heavily on the ideas of politicians, political commentators, university professors, and other public figures who were often, directly or indirectly, employed by the national government. In the 1920s and 1930s, according to historian Enrique Florescano, such diverse groups "played an important role in the consciousness raising of the Mexican people, and this role has been undervalued in the past."[3]

President Vicente Fox's tenuous rapport with US President George Bush in the first few years of the new millennium testified to the importance of anti-Americanism in Mexican history. Fox initially chose to cultivate close relationships with his counterpart in the United States. He played host to the recently inaugurated US president in mid-February 2001 on his ranch in Guanajuato, where the two vowed to continue their open discussions of immigration, the drug trade, and other important issues. Mexican-US relations were so harmonious that both arch-conservative US Senator Jesse Helms and leftist Mexican Foreign Minister Jorge Castañeda found much to praise in this new spirit of friendship.[4]

The temporary nature of the Fox-Bush accord became obvious in February 2003 when the issue of intervention became the focal point in the relationship between the two leaders as the United States pursued a more aggressive policy in the Middle East. The distance between Fox and Bush was not apparent until the United States began to press for Mexico's vote in the United Nations Security Council in favor of a resolution to endorse the use of force in the removal of Saddam Hussein from power in Iraq. The Mexican public was decidedly opposed to military intervention in general and the US invasion of Iraq in particular, and the Fox administration followed this line.[5] Polls in Mexico cited a level of opposition to this war between 70 and 83 percent, and street demonstrations confirmed these results.[6]

The Fox-Bush discord touched historically based differences between Mexico and the United States on the issue of intervention. Among the nations with frequent and close interactions with the United States, Mexico underwent some of the most injurious experiences. In the War of 1846–1848, US military interventions resulted in Mexico's losing half of its national territory to its expanding neighbor to the north. The Mexican Revolution of 1910 spawned conditions that led to the US military occupation of Veracruz in 1914, a large incursion by the US Army into northern Mexico in 1916, and the threat of similar interventions for several years thereafter. These experiences and the "consciousness raising" of the Mexican proponents of anti-Americanism in the 1920s and 1930s contributed to the Mexican public's development of a sensitivity to the aggressive, intrusive exercise of power by the United States. A 1983 Gallup poll revealed that 74 percent of Mexicans believed that "a strong American presence around the world" increased the chance for war. The same poll asked 500 Mexicans to select "the characteristics most often associated with Americans." Those polled selected the following: "industrious," "intelligent," "decisive," and "greedy." The poll revealed a public wary of the neighboring nation that was quite willing to use its power for its own purposes.[7] Twenty years later, therefore, President Fox yielded to a citizenry whose historical conscience had been awakened.

Mexico's opposition to Bush's invasion of Iraq drew from important episodes in the history of Mexican-US relations. This chapter will examine the circumstances in which Mexico's political and intellectual leaders identified issues that, in their view, justified anti-American protests.

Military Interventions and Threats of Interventions

Anti-Americanism is rooted in Mexico's unfortunate relationship with the United States, first in the devastating war of 1846–1848, then in the interventions of 1914 and 1916. The 1846–1848 conflict began as a dispute along the Mexican-Texas border but expanded into a war of territorial aggression for the United States. Mexico suffered a major military defeat, the invasion of its capital, and a costly peace settlement. The 1914 intervention involved the occupation of Veracruz on the orders of President Woodrow Wilson. The 1916 intervention, directed by the same president, consisted of a so-called punitive expedition to track down Pancho Villa in response to his raid on Columbus, New Mexico. These events, spanning nearly three-quarters of a century, had a lasting impact in Mexico. US territorial aggrandizement in the 1840s and unilateral interventions in 1914 and 1916 inspired both resentment about the past and trepidation about the future. Mexico was the first country to face the dramatic reality that the US president, in command of one of the world's most powerful armed forces, could deploy naval and military contingents and then entice or manufacture public support for these operations in a polity and culture known for interventionist proclivities.[8]

The 1846–1848 war and the heavy-handed interventions of 1914 and 1916 were central to the anxious calculations of Mexico's leaders; but from 1917 to 1940 these leaders encountered new threats

from north of the Rio Grande. While the threat of military intervention turned out to be only rumblings and bluster, the new assertions
of power contained political and economic dimensions that, in their
own ways, also menaced Mexico's independence as a nation. Venustiano Carranza, the head of state who faced these new perils after
1916, also attempted to lead a large, diverse revolutionary movement
that stretched across the complex political and social landscape of
Mexico. Although there remains some debate about the nature of Carranza's government, a fair amount of consensus exists for the view
that he was a moderate among domestic revolutionaries and a nationalist vis-à-vis foreign powers. He fully recognized that Mexico's internal reforms, including the distribution of land to peasants and the
promotion of labor organizations, often aggravated and even alarmed
foreigners who owned property in Mexico. The United States in particular, with its record of aggressive action and its numerous citizens
with investments in Mexico, was the subject of much concern in the
Carranza administration.

These concerns intensified when the Constitutional Convention
of 1917 adopted Article 27 of the new constitution, which placed restrictions on private property. Pastor Rouaix, an engineer with an interest in the petroleum industry, led in the drafting of the article, the
content of which was disturbing for the US oil industry. Article 27
set the legal basis for several government policies from taxation to
regulation to nationalization. The oil companies objected strenuously
to the Mexican government and also turned to the US Department of
State for protection. When neither of these agencies responded to
their satisfaction, the oil representatives took their case directly to
the US public in a well-financed propaganda campaign. For example,
oil executive Edward L. Doheny announced that the "new constitution of Mexico is intended to confiscate or attack many vested rights
of foreigners." Doheny hired several journalists and academics, who
quickly added fuel to the propaganda campaign with their accusations that Bolshevism was emanating from south of the border.[9]

Faced with rising pressures from peasants and workers within
Mexico and hostile corporate critics from outside, Carranza and his
advisors expended much effort and energy to persuade other Latin
American nations to join with Mexico in opposing what they believed
to be an economic intervention that constituted a threat to the nation's sovereignty. Given the historical experience of the 1840s and
contemporary US military actions in the Caribbean as well as Mexico,
armed intervention was also a distinct possibility. Antonio Manero
and Hermila Galindo were among the activists who promoted the "Carranza Doctrine," which, in essence, asserted Mexico's right to imple-

ment Article 27 and denied the United States the option to use the defense of foreign-owned private property as a justification for military intervention.[10]

An insightful young diplomat named Isidro Fabela went beyond their glancing blows against the power bases in Washington and New York to produce a more penetrating critique. Fabela, entrusted with being Carranza's "confidential agent" in Europe during these troubled times, focused his analytical skills on the political leaders in Washington.[11] He employed an indirect but persuasive analytical device to make his case against the Wilson administration, one that has long been a standard in the repertoire of anti-US rhetoric. Instead of attacking by broad condemnation, he carefully drew a line between the US public and the nation's leaders in Washington. The people of the United States did not agitate for intervention and conquest, but chief executives and their high-ranking advisors who spoke so piously of democratic institutions at home could, at the same time, justify arbitrary, heavy-handed limitations on self-government abroad.[12] Fabela turned to recent Cuban history for evidence: US participation in the Spanish-American War in the name of "Cuba Libre" was followed soon thereafter by the imposition of the Platt Amendment on the nascent Cuban government. US intervention thereby became institutionalized in Cuba's internal affairs.[13] Fabela ranged through the recent history of Panama, the role of the United States in fomenting its break from Colombia, and the Hay-Bunau Varilla Treaty that guaranteed Washington's control over the fledgling nation's most valuable resource—the narrow isthmus between the Caribbean and the Pacific. More recent US interventions underscored how Washington's transparent idealism could not mask its thirst for imperial domination. Fabela drove home his point by citing the examples of recent US interventions in Haiti and the Dominican Republic: "Mr. Wilson, during the Great War, stated numerous times that he was a champion of law and justice, protector of the weaker nations . . . and that for him the liberty of a small nation was as sacred as that of the largest nation . . . . And yet what has Mr. Wilson done but abruptly eliminate the independence of Haiti and the Dominican Republic?"[14]

Fabela's sharp delineation of this gap between verbiage that sounded respectful of the rights of smaller nations and intrusive, unilateral actions that violated their sovereignty resonated well with *carrancistas* and other Mexicans across the political spectrum. But the downfall and defeat of Carranza in 1920 brought a new group to power, led by Alvaro Obregón. Fabela, like most *carrancistas*, left the center stage of politics, but his critique of US policy and its potential for harm in Mexico continued to have relevance. The new government's assertion of control over petroleum resources under Article 27 and also the division of large estates into small farms and communal lands *(ejidos)* as provided for in the same article created serious differences between the two nations. From 1921 to 1923, the administration of President Obregón wrestled with US President Warren Harding over the latter's refusal to extend normal diplomatic recognition, in part because of the uncertain status of US property. In the summer of 1923, the two nations finally signed the informal Bucareli agreements, which resulted in US recognition. Obregón faced sharp criticism from many Mexicans who insisted that he had "sold out" Article 27 and the national interest to open normal diplomatic relations with the United States. The public response to this perceived weakness in the face of pressure from Washington hurt Obregón's image at home and encouraged the abortive but disruptive de la Huerta rebellion in the fall of 1923.[15]

The new government of President Plutarco Elías Calles (1924–1928) was also caught in a difficult situation because Mexican agrarian and labor groups, aroused by the promises of the Revolution, demanded immediate reforms on a scale sufficiently large to affect US-owned property. In response to these internal pressures, Calles moved to enforce the laws pertaining to petroleum and agricultural lands. Such policies placed him on a collision course with the administration of President Calvin Coolidge. The pressure from Washington mounted. On 12 June 1925, Secretary of State Frank Kellogg proclaimed that the Calles government was "on trial before the world." The interventions of 1914 and 1916 and the diplomatic problems of Obregón left little doubt in the Calles administration that Kellogg's proclamation posed a threat to Mexico's sovereignty. Calles and his advisors resented threats by the Coolidge-Kellogg Department of State to withdraw diplomatic recognition, an action that would have encouraged domestic unrest in Mexico. There were additional concerns in Mexico City regarding US military intervention. Leading newspapers such as *Excelsior* saw ominous parallels with the Dominican Republic and Haiti, thereby echoing the warnings of Isidro Fabela.[16]

Calles's responses were less than diplomatic, including frequent public comments in which he asserted Mexican sovereignty, defended the Constitution, and criticized US politicians and businessmen for their efforts to block the Mexican government's domestic policies. For example, in 1926 he insisted that his government would enforce Article 27 for the benefit of the Mexican people and that he would not be intimidated by the threat of the withdrawal of US recognition. He blamed a "small group of American capitalists" for the uncertainties of diplomatic relations.[17]

Probably the most extensive anti-American analysis in these years came from the pen of Fernando González Roa in his book *Las cuestiones fundamentales de actualidad en México (The Fundamental Questions Concerning Current Conditions in Mexico, 1927).* Like the earlier work of Fabela, this publication was an appeal for support from other Latin American nations.[18] González Roa, one of his country's representatives at the Bucareli Conference, had the reputation of being an "erudite, cultured and hard-working lawyer" who was capable of impressive rhetoric and great verbosity.[19] *Las cuestiones,* he wrote, was intended to reply to misconceptions about economic and social policies in Mexico that resulted from false propaganda that had spread across North and South America.[20] From the perspective of most US observers, Mexico's experiments in land redistribution were violations of individual initiative and private property, and, in González Roa's words, "would be denounced as Bolshevik." He did not agree with the widely accepted definition of Bolshevism in the United States, which included a broad spectrum of government-sponsored reforms. González Roa, like Fabela, believed that the perception and motivation of the leadership in Washington were the crucial factors in Mexican-US relations. By the 1920s this confusion worsened to a large extent because of the muddled understanding of Bolshevism north of the Rio Grande. González Roa observed that, even though the Coolidge administration was already "totally supportive of large corporations, nevertheless, the tendency to promote commercial interests grows stronger every day. Under such circumstances, one cannot believe that the United States would permit the establishment among us [Mexicans] of a Bolshevik government. The establishment of Bolshevism in Mexico would not last twenty-four hours without being overthrown by foreign interests. We are not so stupid."[21]

In the fluid state of Mexican-US relations, however, the pointed anti-Americanism of González Roa soon seemed out of place. The arrival in late 1927 of a new US ambassador, Dwight Morrow, marked a turning point in relations between the two countries and a temporary abatement of public anti-Americanism. Morrow, a Wall Street banker with exemplary interpersonal skills, quickly developed a good working relationship with Calles. Through a series of convivial public appearances and negotiated arrangements, the two resolved the differences between their governments, at least for the short run. In this brief period of relative calm, Mexican anti-Americanism was dormant, but the contributions of Fabela and González Roa had added a new dimension to the definition of "intervention": the condemnation of US corporate and government policies intended to impede Mexico's efforts to carry out domestic social and economic reforms.[22]

Confrontations at Montevideo

The shattering consequences of the worldwide Depression of the early 1930s stimulated a revival of anti-Americanism in Mexico. Although historians disagree on the economic effects of the Depression in Mexico,[23] they do agree that political ideas and rhetoric shifted to the left. The anti-American fear of intervention would increasingly involve the premise that US influence was propagating the "disease" of capitalism.[24] Anti-American commentators were no longer preoccupied with Article 27, but turned to Mexico's foreign debt, 28.9 percent of which was owed to US banks.[25] This concern, however, was not exclusively a response to the demands of foreign creditors, but also found strength in the widespread acceptance of radical ideas among politicians, labor and agrarian leaders, and intellectuals in the wake of what seemed to be the demise of capitalism.

José Manuel Puig Casauranc, the minister of education in the Calles presidency, served as Mexico's ambassador in Washington from October 1931 until September 1932. Puig quickly grasped the importance of the new issues that came to dominate US-Mexican relations. A doctor by profession, a writer by avocation, and a politician by personal ambition, he earned the respect of Calles because of his cleverness and tenacity. In international economics, he found an issue through which he could maintain prominence in the popular press as well as the political elite. Sensitive to the public mood in the United States, Puig made use of his opportunities with an address in which he defended Mexico's Revolution (broadcast by the CBS radio network on 20 November 1931) and a speech in Springfield, Illinois the following February in which he praised Abraham Lincoln. He observed Franklin Roosevelt's successful presidential campaign and quickly grasped the public disillusionment with bankers, economists, and free enterprise doctrine in general. In a letter to Mexican President Pascual Ortiz Rubio, Puig reported from Washington that he avoided contact with bankers because of their disrepute and also because of his contempt for their past overzealous extensions of credit to unwary borrowers such as Mexico. Puig watched the US Senate Banking and Currency committee conduct its investigation of the nation's banking system at a time when the credibility of bankers was almost nonexistent.[26] Puig's May 1932 letter to Calles (who retained considerable influence in Mexican politics) contained severe criticisms of US economist Walter Kemmerer, a consultant to several Latin American countries in the 1920s. Puig saw Kemmerer as a proponent of the free enterprise doctrine that brought Mexico and other nations into deep indebtedness and to the brink of financial ruin.[27]

In 1932 and 1933, Puig formulated his policy ideas on how to deal with Mexico's financial crisis. An astute politician and a dynamic orator, Puig had more than held his own in the rough and tumble of Mexican politics. By March 1932 Puig asserted that economic problems were amenable to political solutions.[28] He observed that the disappointing results of the London Economic Conference of June and July of 1933 were largely caused by the failure of the delegates to consider the pressing economic issues of the day—especially international debts, which bore down so heavily on Mexico and other Latin American nations. Promoted to the position of Mexican foreign minister in October 1932, Puig gained an impressive endorsement from the *callista* leadership when President Abelardo Rodríguez appointed a special commission headed by the new foreign minister, Calles, and veteran politician and finance expert Alberto J. Pani to formulate Mexico's plans for the Seventh Pan-American Conference to be held in Montevideo in December 1933.[29]

Puig was determined to bring economic issues to the forefront. According to historian Friedrich Schuler, Puig wrought a major reorientation in Mexico's Ministry of Foreign Relations. The old methods that hinged on the niceties of formal diplomacy rapidly gave way to a more assertive approach that converted the ministry into "a modern economic intelligence service." The goal was to alert the government in Mexico City to international economic trends of importance for the nation. In September 1933, several months after the establishment of the agenda for the Pan-American Conference, Puig launched a campaign to place financial questions on the docket—especially the issue of foreign debts owed by Mexico and other Latin American nations. In a letter to the US ambassador to Mexico, Josephus Daniels, Puig insisted that the creditor nations held "the sword of Damocles" over the struggling governments of the debtor nations. He also circulated memoranda about his proposal to Latin American foreign ministers.[30] The outcome of his energetic campaign remained in doubt as the conference delegates departed for Montevideo.[31]

During a visit to Washington in mid-October, Puig met with both Roosevelt and Secretary of State Cordell Hull to explain the purposes behind his drive to place economic and financial issues on the agenda. Apparently the president and the secretary of state were noncommittal. The *New York Times* concluded that such discussions would probably embarrass the Roosevelt administration, which wanted to win friends through its disavowal of military intervention as part of the Good Neighbor Policy and hoped to avoid controversial issues such as international debts.[32] On his trip from Mexico City to Montevideo, Puig made frequent appeals for Latin American unity to secure support for his proposals.[33]

At the conference, Puig abandoned the language of diplomacy to initiate a verbal assault on the international banking system, much of which was based in the United States. Although he claimed he did not want to attack the larger aspects of capitalism, he lashed out at the "false science" of economics that created a "distortion of theory and of reality and of function . . . [which] the large corporations have converted into principles, into treaties, and into law." These "perverted legal formulas" thrust huge foreign debts upon the backs of the Mexican people. Puig called for "a new legal and philosophical conception of credit" that would take into account the debilities of nations in the early stages of economic development. This pattern of indebtedness would have serious repercussions on the "great masses of our [Latin American] nations for generations to come." He called for an "equation" in financial relations between creditor and debtor based on a sense of mutual obligation. He argued that bankers used deception in the extension of credit to nations with limited capital resources. His disdain broke through in his exclamation that "We do not want to continue to be deceived. We do not want to continue deceiving our people."[34]

The Mexican Revolution furnished Puig with justifications for his argument against the international credit system. In an appeal to Roosevelt, Puig emphasized the Mexican government's efforts to improve the lives of the poor and "its intention of raising the productive capacity of the common people." Puig claimed a sense of common purpose with the New Deal in his "opposition to the unjust interests and privileges of the few." The international credit system's "sword of Damocles" could easily smash these efforts to relieve human privation and to restructure Mexican society.[35]

Puig's presentation was couched in abstract, often moralistic terms and contained only one specific proposal on economic matters—a moratorium of the repayment of debts for "six to ten years." The main purpose of his presentation was to place the international debt situation on the agenda. In probably his most emotional plea he asked, "Are we to conform to an anachronistic, cowardly agenda . . . [to] a program incomplete in economic matters" that ignored the pressing economic issues of the day, especially the international indebtedness of the less industrialized nations such as Mexico?[36]

Puig's quest to place the debt issue before the conference was a procedural failure. Cordell Hull, who expected the attack, was nevertheless shaken by the Mexican's "long, fiery speech" to which the Latin American delegates "applauded wildly as he dramatized [the predicament] of the distressed debtors oppressed by conscienceless corporations in Wall Street." The wily Hull, with the help of Argentina's Carlos Saavedra Llamas, diverted Puig's proposal to a subcommittee removed from the purview of most delegates, where it died.[37]

Puig and Hull also clashed on one of the US secretary of state's sacrosanct policies: reciprocal tariff reduction. Hull believed that the massive economic contraction of the 1930s would be alleviated through the reduction of external tariffs that would stimulate international trade. Therefore, he proposed and the conference eventually adopted a "comprehensive economic resolution" that committed the signatory nations to negotiations for the reduction of tariffs.[38] Hull's reciprocity proposal elicited a pointed rebuttal from Puig. The Mexican diplomat again took up the cause of nations with what he termed "colonial type economies." He contrasted the predicament of these nations with the circumstances of the United States, the only country in the hemisphere to achieve an advanced stage of industrialization. Hull's reduction of tariffs could only harm the less developed nations because the cost of their imports (usually manufactured goods) generally exceeded the value of their exports (usually primary products). The resulting deficit was often made up through credit extended by banks in the United States, thereby pulling less developed nations further into debt, a situation Puig criticized in his earlier remarks. Puig wanted to minimize US control of the Mexican economy. Hull wanted to expand it by deeper, tariff-free trade.[39]

Puig argued that Mexico and other "colonial economies" should attempt to promote their own industrialization and that the policies of the wealthier nations such as the United States should not interfere in this process. He hoped to protect new industries from an inundation of manufactured goods from abroad.[40] Puig reminded the delegates of the human factor in the current crisis. "There is no real over-production" in the world economy, he insisted. Rather, the problem was under-consumption resulting from low wages and unemployment. The sad plight of "the great mass of producers, those who contribute through the effort of their muscles and . . . their minds resulted from the imbalance between capital and labor." He insisted that "the relationship between capitalist elements and productive elements is, in numerical terms, abysmal."[41]

Although Hull's resolution passed easily, Puig's forceful objections gained favorable responses from the Latin American delegates at the conference and the Latin American press corps.[42] Among the Latin American journalists to give extensive coverage to the Mexican foreign minister's remarks was Domingo Melfi of the Argentine newspaper *La Nación*. In Melfi's view, Puig spoke for the smaller, less advanced countries, which faced a bleak future under the economic domination of the larger, more powerful United States. Melfi observed that Hull shifted uncomfortably in his seat as Puig's orations grew in intensity and elicited enthusiastic applause from the Latin American delegates. Melfi saw Hull as the representative of "a country of 120 million inhabitants . . . , the greatest industrial power in the world . . . , a vast economic empire almost without limits" that pursued policies to benefit its own self-interest at the expense of weaker nations. Puig, on the other hand, called for a "correction of the excesses and failures of the economic aspects of civilization." Melfi obviously agreed with Puig in his demands "to adjust the [international] economy, to give it a sense of humanity because science, humanity, and well-being are eventually one in the same." Melfi's conclusion carried the essence of Puig's thesis: new policies are required "in order to save from their inevitable collapse those nations with scarce industrial potential and precarious economic systems."[43]

It would be poor history to place Puig's opposition to the US economic proposals at Montevideo in the dust bin for irrelevant, bombastic rhetoric as Hull, his delegation, and the US press corps tended to do.[44] Puig touched nerves in Washington and throughout Latin America when he elevated criticism of the US-led international economic system into the mainstream of inter-American diplomatic discussion at the very moment when Hull and Roosevelt hoped to win respect for the Good Neighbor Policy by their renunciation of military interventions as tools in their warehouse of hemispheric policies. In Puig's estimation, meddlesome bankers were more of a threat than bayonet-wielding Marines. Puig identified issues that could no longer be dismissed from the inter-American agenda.

The Expropriation

On 23 March 1938, the massive gathering of people in the Zócalo, the large public square in front of Mexico's National Palace, was a roiling sea of patriotic excitement. The crowd, estimated at two hundred thousand, dominated central Mexico City. The greatly anticipated event was a demonstration of support for the decision of President Lázaro Cárdenas, made five days earlier, to take control of the property of the multinational oil companies. Drawing from the Law of Expropriation of 1936, Article 123 of the Constitution of 1917 (the basis for the nation's labor code), and the notorious Article 27, Cárdenas announced his decision to expropriate, or to assume ownership of, foreign-owned oil properties, the largest of which were Royal Dutch Shell and Standard Oil.[45] Mexico would compensate the companies for their properties, but that was not the main point. In his explanation of this action, Cárdenas made clear that Mexico was in the process of defining itself as a nation by challenging the extensive power of the United States within Mexico. In this case, as in other manifestations of anti-Americanism during the early decades of the twentieth century, Mexican political leadership chose a specific target within the array of private businesses, governmental institutions, and cultural symbols of US power. In 1938, the target was no longer the banks, nor the Department of State, nor the armed forces, but multinational oil companies.

The president's comments were brief, a little over five hundred words long, but they made clear that the Mexican government was asserting the authority of the nation against the oil companies. Cárdenas criticized "the rebellious attitude of the petroleum companies," which brought into the open "the peril to our sovereignty." He seemed confident that US military intervention was not in the offing, but he warned Mexicans to prepare for "certain sacrifices" to be endured "in the face of danger." That danger lay in the economic and political ramifications of the expropriation, most of which would involve corporations with headquarters in the United States. He called upon his people to make voluntary contributions to "the liberation of our petroleum," a monumental step necessary "to safeguard the honor and dignity of our country."[46]

Cárdenas's radio announcement of 18 March 1938 was a surprise, but the mass demonstration on the Zócalo the following Wednesday involved careful planning. Taken together, they constituted one of the most important events in Mexico's political history. The chief of Mexico's Ministry of Communications and Public Works, Francisco J. Múgica, was the primary author of the first announcement and assumed control of the "public staging" of the expropriation. Múgica relied on labor unions, teachers' unions, and peasant organizations to assemble the mass demonstrations, which included not only the two hundred thousand in Mexico City but also crowds of about twenty thousand in each of the cities of San Luis Potosí, Monterrey, Tampico, and Guadalajara. Although the government planned these events, such political coordination did not diminish the emotional exuberance that characterized these mass meetings. The outpouring of public support was too extensive to be entirely orchestrated.[47] The boisterous crowd in the Zócalo spilled over for several blocks into the adjoining streets. The placards, banners, posters, and chants used by the celebrating marchers conveyed the values and ideas that supported Cárdenas. One banner was obviously connected with labor union organizers: "Sixty Thousand Railroad Workers Back Cárdenas." Following the approach furthered by Puig and other anti-American advocates, several posters identified the villains: "Oil Companies: You Can't Defy Mexican Laws," "Cárdenas Against Capital," "Down With Insolent Imperialism," and "We Demand Respect From Foreigners." Other messages were indicative of a generic anti-Americanism upwelling in the streets of Mexico City, particularly a chant that roughly translated as "One, two, three, four; down with the gringos." A more eloquent expression of nationalism appeared in a poster: "The Petroleum Expropriation Marks the Beginning of Our Independence."[48]

The petroleum issue quickly entered the realm of popular culture, where the rising young comedian Mario Moreno, known as Cantinflas, used it as material for his commentary on contemporary issues. Although often a critic of some members of the Cárdenas administration—especially radical labor leader Vicente Lombardo Toledano— Cantinflas supported the oil expropriation decision with his sarcastic, irreverent humor. Using absurdist parallels to belittle the powerful oil companies, Cantinflas compared their audacity and duplicity to the behavior of a stereotypical character well known to most Mexicans: the neighborhood milk vendor. In his mimicry of a pitch to potential customers by one of these street salesmen, Cantinflas mocked both him and Standard Oil by characterizing petroleum as one might describe milk, except for the last word: "the petroleum is pure, refined, substantial, expropriated." He further suggested through his loquacious milk vendor—always the salesman—that the companies should offer to pay Mexico for the petroleum instead of Mexico compensating the corporate giants.[49]

Moving the focus of attention away from the exuberant crowds on the Zócalo and Cantinflas's biting commentary, the international context presented an interesting and unexpected three-way relationship involving Mexico, the United States, and Great Britain. A narrow reading of the circumstances surrounding the expropriation might yield the conclusion that the British would be the greater threat to Mexican sovereignty because the giant British-Dutch firm Royal Dutch Shell and its Mexican subsidiary, El Aguila, were the largest producers and exporters of petroleum from the Mexican fields. By the spring of 1938, however, London faced an aggressive Nazi Germany in Europe and attempted to play the role of "buck-passer" in the expropriation— trying to convince the United States that it had the responsibility as a "great power" to intervene in Mexico.[50] The British overrated the willingness of the United States to intervene because they did not fully appreciate Washington's commitment to the Good Neighbor Policy.

Nor did the British grasp the ideological harmony between Roosevelt's New Deal and Cárdenas's social and economic program for Mexico. Roosevelt's propensity for experimentation in response to the needs of the unemployed paralleled Cárdenas's efforts in land reform and labor organization.[51] Mexico under Cárdenas also moved to help industrial workers, peasant farmers, and the lower classes in general. Puig, by this time on the sidelines of Mexican politics, as were most supporters of the former power broker Calles, testified to the current administration's movement in this direction in a trenchant discussion of Mexican history, *El sentido social del proceso histórico de México (The Social Meaning of the Historical Process of Mexico)*. The last pages of this book endorsed Cárdenas's plans to carry out the long-term goals of the revolution, the "social meaning" of Mexican history.[52]

Nevertheless, informed observers in both Mexico and Great Britain, obviously diametrically opposed on the expropriation, were in accord in their perception of an influential conservative interventionist tendency within the Roosevelt administration itself, as well as in sectors of the US public. Three relatively young, emerging figures in the Cárdenas administration expressed deep concern about the influence of the right wing within US politics and policymaking. This trio saw that the assertion of Mexican nationalism through the expropriation and the redistributive programs of the Cárdenas government ran the risk of eliciting a hostile reaction that could mobilize support in this powerful undercurrent that flowed within the US business community—especially the petroleum industry.[53] Francisco Múgica, a long-time friend of Cárdenas, served as the minister of communications and public works.[54] Ramón Beteta held the position of vice-minister in the Ministry of Foreign Relations and was also a close advisor to Cárdenas.[55] Jesús Silva Herzog, a dedicated leftist academic, had been a key official in several government agencies and was the central author of the crucial report on the oil workers' strike for the Federal Board of Conciliation and Arbitration.[56]

In addition to their leftist ideas, these three men shared a lingering distrust of the United States and harbored concerns that, in spite of the Good Neighbor Policy, the US government might attempt to discipline Mexico in order to protect the multinational oil companies. Múgica, Beteta, and Silva Herzog were aware that the programs they espoused—especially the oil expropriation—carried with them some of the "dangers" that Cárdenas had in mind in his speech of 23 March. Indeed, the oil companies led by Standard Oil engaged in extensive, virulent propaganda campaigns both in the United States and in Mexico. Their campaign in Mexico attempted to turn a significant portion of the population against the Cárdenas government; for the most part, it proved counterproductive. In the United States, however, oil company propaganda fed into a preexisting line of thinking, already expressed extensively in the press and conservative political forums, that Mexico had moved to the far left recently with the adoption of socialist and even communist policies that posed threats to US interests.[57] Múgica and Beteta monitored evidence of mounting anti-Mexican sentiment north of the border and sent their press clippings and analyses to Cárdenas and other officials in Mexico City. One volume in particular captured their attention. Burt McConnell, a former editor of the *Literary Digest*, assembled a volume of anti-Mexican editorials and articles from the US press for Standard Oil. Among the numerous quotations was an excerpt that contained exaggerated accusations concocted by Ray Moley of *Newsweek* in which the ex-New Dealer belittled Cárdenas and lambasted his government:

> Ambitious but vastly uninformed, [Cárdenas] proved to be an easy prey for the radical group which had been . . . controlled by Calles. Cárdenas appointed a puppet cabinet. Through his Autonomous Department of Press and Publicity, generally referred to in Mexico as the 'Dapp,' Cárdenas spread propaganda concerning his integrity and honesty of purpose. Everyone in Mexico knows, however, that the 'Dapp' is as strict a system of censorship as those in Russia, Germany, and Italy. Only that which will glorify Cárdenas and his Six-Year Plan is permitted publication.[58]

At this point, it is helpful to step back and examine the expropriation in order to gain further insight into how Cárdenas's action was the culmination of a lengthy disagreement between Mexican workers and the oil companies. Since the expansion of oil drilling along Mexico's gulf coast in the early twentieth century, the oil companies had maintained a segregationist enclave mentality and a two-tiered pay scale, both of which favored foreigners and left Mexican workers in disadvantaged positions. The surge in labor organization that swept across Mexico in the early and mid-1930s had a significant impact in the oil fields, where several small unions pulled together to form the powerful Union of Oil Workers in the Republic of Mexico (STPRM) in 1936. In turn, STPRM formed an alliance with the nation's largest and most politically influential labor body, the Confederation of Mexican Workers (CTM). The unionized oil workers demanded higher wages, shorter hours, and better working conditions. Management of the multinationals claimed they could not meet those demands and continue to operate profitably. The dispute festered for months as the workers took their case to Mexico's Federal Board for Conciliation and Arbitration, an agency established by law to settle labor disputes.[59]

The board, following standard procedure, appointed a commission of experts to examine the case. Of the three members of this commission, Jesús Silva Herzog was the primary investigator; he quickly assembled a staff of over one hundred researchers and writers to prepare the report. Silva Herzog and his staff compiled a large quantity of information—historical, economic, legal, and sociological—and produced a veritable tome over eight hundred pages in length. To reply to the criticisms in the US press and Congress, the Mexican government published an English translation of this report in 1940. This translation was the result of President Cárdenas's concerns about "the systematic publication of news, commentary, and editorials critical of Mexico," which were depriving his country "of the goodwill of the people of the United States." A large part of this printed onslaught resulted from the "bad intentions of the oil companies."[60] Silva Herzog and his colleagues voiced a resounding criticism of the workings of the multinational companies in Mexico. Standard Oil bore the brunt of this criticism as the authors scrutinized its burgeoning wealth and massive size. This volume, called *Mexico's Oil*, reported that the capitalized value of Standard Oil increased forty times from 1910 to 1930. The companies operating under the name Standard Oil paid their chief executives salaries of $100,000 per year (most Mexicans earned less than the lowest level of $500 for oil workers).[61] From 1915 to 1930, Standard Oil and other US oil companies accounted for approximately two-thirds of the world's oil production.[62] In short, Standard Oil's size, salaries, and its productive capacity reinforced the Mexican workers' demands.

Silva Herzog concentrated on financial issues, and one of the most glaring differences between oil policy in Mexico and the United States was in the area of taxation. According to *Mexico's Oil*, the petroleum companies in the United States in 1934 paid an average tax of $1.14 per barrel, the equivalent of 4.10 pesos in Mexican currency. In Mexico, oil companies averaged tax payments of 1,05 pesos, barely more than one-fourth of the tax rate in the United States. The Mexican government had, in a comparative sense, bestowed a significant tax break on the oil companies.[63]

And the oil companies made profits even during the Depression. Using figures from corporate financial records, Silva Herzog's team concluded that in the years 1934, 1935, and 1936 foreign oil companies in Mexico made healthy profits ranging from 16 to 18 percent return on invested capital.[64] The Mexican researchers also obtained information on the financial conditions for 1935 of the four main corporate entities that carried the name Standard Oil. Silva Herzog's group concluded that Standard Oil could well afford to provide better wages and working conditions for its employees in Mexico. Key figures for the Standard Oil companies are listed in Table 1.1.

Table 1.1 Financial Results for Standard Oil in 1935

	Net Profits ($US)	Return on Capital (%)
Standard Oil of California	18,594,330	4.17
Standard Oil of Ohio	2,690,647	7.82
Standard Oil of New Jersey	62,863,192	5.96
Standard Oil of Indiana	30,179,895	8.24
SOURCE: Government of Mexico, *Mexico's Oil* (Mexcio City, 1940) 511.		

Silva Herzog's team added another dimension to the case against the oil companies. *Mexico's Oil* made several references to Standard Oil's high-handed rejection of the Cárdenas administration's statements on the oil workers' dispute. This arrogance was amplified in the companies' propaganda against the Mexican government. The oil companies showed a "notorious lack of tact and good faith" in their propagandistic statements.[65] When the Board of Conciliation and Arbitration ruled against the companies and the Mexican Supreme Court upheld this ruling, the oil companies launched another publicity campaign against the Mexican government: "with the customary arrogance, the oil companies publicly stated that it was impossible for them to comply with the Award of the Labor Board" because they did not have the fiscal resources.[66] Silva Herzog saw this issue from an entirely different perspective.[67]

The lengthy introduction to *Mexico's Oil* contained a concise condemnation of the impact of the American oil companies and a celebratory farewell: "The oil companies, during the years of their operations in Mexico, earned enormous profits, on their departure they did not leave in the country a single work of any importance beneficial to the Mexican people. For this reason, the people not only did not regret their going but joyfully celebrated the event as the first firm step toward their [economic] independence."[68]

Resistance to US intervention, whether military or economic, was at the center of the often troubled relationship between Mexico and the United States in the first half of the twentieth century. One of the most salient and unique aspects of Mexico's contribution to anti-Americanism was its targeting those institutions and policies in the United States that posed the most immediate threats to Mexico, thereby asserting critical assessments of important elements in American national life while avoiding all-out confrontations with the powerful nation that had a track record of interventionism. In the years from 1917 to 1940, the focus of anti-American criticism shifted from military/ naval intervention to the assertions of power by the international banking system and multinational oil companies. In the first phase, Isidro Fabela and Fernando González Roa concentrated on what they saw as skewed perceptions and muddled thinking in Washington. For González Roa in the 1920s, the main problem was the widespread belief in Washington that Mexico had become a seedbed for Bolshevism, an exaggerated assumption that the Coolidge administration could have used to rationalize another intervention. In the Depression years, Mexico's anti-Americanism shifted its attention to the operations of multinational banks and oil companies. Puig's call for relief in dealing with Mexico's debt burden went unheeded and largely unnoticed in the United States, but Silva Herzog's indictment of the oil companies lay the groundwork for the 1938 decision by the Cárdenas administration to expropriate the property of multinational oil companies.

Mexicans did not express their arguments as broadly-based hostility toward the United States as a nation, nor did they direct animosity toward the North American people. Even the public demonstrations (both arranged and spontaneous) in support of the oil expropriation were interactions of popular culture and diplomacy in which attention for the most part focused on specific institutions, in this case the oil companies. Silva Herzog expressed his criticism of the petroleum companies in English in the pages of *Mexico's Oil* in order to reach an audience in the United States. The big oil companies and also the Coolidge-Kellogg State Department and the international banks were vulnerable to criticism within the United States as well as Mexico. In their statements to US diplomats and politicians, Calles, Puig, and Silva Herzog expressed their criticisms of these institutions in terms that were typical of current public controversies in the United States. In this sense, the Mexicans devised a type of anti-Americanism that reinforced their government's foreign policy by making use of the public debate inside the United States. In these discussions, Mexicans condemned the more threatening, aggressive aspects of American institutions and the darker, more ominous side of the American character and appealed to the potential for international good will that often lay dormant in their sometimes arrogant, sometimes friendly neighbor to the north.

Notes

1. T. Judt, "Anti-Americans Abroad," *New York Review of Books,* 1 May 2003, 24–27. See also M. Hertsgaard, *The Eagle's Shadow* (New York, 2002); J. Stiglitz, *Globalization and Its Discontents* (New York, 2002); and C. Prestowitz, *Rogue Nation:*

American Unilateralism and the Failure of Good Intentions (New York, 2003). For works that contain varied critiques of the United States from Mexican perspectives, see J. Ortega y Medina, *Destino Manifiesto: sus razones históricas y su raíz teológica* (Mexico City, 1972); A. Aguilar, *El Panamericanismo de la Doctrina de Monroe a la Doctrina de Johnson* (Mexico City, 1965), published in translation as *Pan-Americanism from Monroe to the Present: A View from the Other Side* (New York, 1968); L. Quintanilla, *A Latin American Speaks* (New York, 1943), and E. Meyer, *Conciencia histórica norteamericana sobre la Revolución de 1910* (Mexico City, 1970).

2. A. Knight, *U.S.-Mexican Relations, 1910–1940: An Interpretation* (San Diego, 1980), 23. For examples of anti-American incidents, see P. Foos, *A Short, Offhand, Killing Affair: Soldiers and Social Conflict During the Mexican-American War* (Chapel Hill, 2002); L. B. Hall and D. M. Coerver, *Revolution on the Border: The United States and Mexico, 1910–1920* (Albuquerque, 1988); T. J. Henderson, *The Worm in the Wheat: Rosalie Evans and the Agrarian Struggle in the Puebla-Tlaxcala Valley of Mexico, 1906–1927* (Durham, 1998); and F. Katz, *The Life and Times of Pancho Villa* (Stanford, 1998).

3. Cited in R. Camp, *The Intellectual and the State in Twentieth Century Mexico* (Austin, 1985), 65. For similar observations, see J. Vázquez, *Nacionalismo y educación en México* (Mexico City, 1970); and E. Llinás Alvarez, *Revolución, educación y mexicanidad: La búsqueda de la identidad nacional en el pensamiento educativo mexicano* (Mexico City, 1978).

4. *New York Times,* 2 April 2001, 17 April 2001, and 12 May 2001.

5. Ibid., 28 February 2003, 3, 8, 12, 13, and 17 March 2003, and *El Universal,* 16 and 17 February 2003, both available at http://el-universal.com, accessed 18 June 2003. See also *El Universal,* 17 February 2003 and *El Universal,* 4 March 2003, both available at http://el-universal.com, accessed 18 June 2003.

6. *New York Times,* 28 February 2003, and *El Universal,* 16 February 2003, available at http://el-universal.com, accessed 18 June 2003.

7. *Newsweek,* 11 July 1983, 44–50. This poll took place during extensive controversies about U.S. intervention in Central America. On this context, see R. Pastor and J. Castañeda, *Limits to Friendship: The United States and Mexico* (New York, 1988), 149–62. Also useful on the larger theme of Mexican public opinion is S. D. Morris, "Reforming the Nation: Mexican Nationalism in Context," *Journal of Latin American Studies* 31, 2 (1999): 363–97.

8. Katz, *Pancho Villa* and the same author's *The Secret War in Mexico: Europe, the United States and the Mexican Revolution* (Chicago, 1981); J. Vázquez and L. Meyer, *The United States and Mexico* (Chicago, 1985), 103–25; M. Gilderhus, *Diplomacy and Revolution: U.S.-Mexican Relations under Wilson and Carranza* (Tucson, 1977); and J. S. D. Eisenhower, *Intervention! The United States and the Mexican Revolution, 1913–1917* (New York, 1993).

9. A. Knight, *The Mexican Revolution,* 2 vols. (Cambridge, 1986), vol. 2, 435–527; B. Ulloa, *La Constitución de 1917* (Mexico City, 1983); D. Richmond, *Venustiano Carranza's Nationalist Struggle, 1893–1920* (Lincoln, 1983); Katz, *Secret War,* 387–578; and Gilderhus, *Wilson and Carranza.* On Pastor Rouaix, see Ulloa, *La Constitución,* 405–16; and Knight, *Revolution,* vol. 2, 474–75, 508. On oil company propaganda, see J. Brown, *Oil and Revolution in Mexico* (Berkeley, 1993), 242; and D. La Botz, *Edward L. Doheny: Petroleum, Power and Politics in the United States and Mexico* (Westport, 1991), 76–79. Quotation is from Brown, *Oil,* 242.

10. A. Manero, *México y la solidaridad americana: La Doctrina Carranza* (Madrid, 1918); and H. Galindo, *La Doctrina Carranza y el acercamiento indolatino* (Mexico City, 1919). Galindo incorporated the anti-American arguments of Argentine

Manuel Ugarte and Uruguayan José Enrique Rodó, among others. For valuable studies of *carrancista* propaganda, see P. Yankelevich, "En la retaguardia de la Revolución Mexicana: Propaganda y propagandistas mexicanos en América Latina, 1914–1920," *Mexican Studies: Estudios Mexicanos* 15, no. 1 (1999): 35–71; and M. Smith, "Carrancista Propaganda and the Print Media of the United States: An Overview of Institutions," *The Americas* 52, no. 2 (1995): 155–74.

11. I. Fabela, *Los Estados Unidos contra la libertad* (Barcelona, [1920?]), 11.

12. Ibid., 11–15, 82–85, 108–13, 218–25.

13. Ibid., 19–20.

14. Ibid., 138–62 and 164–309.

15. R. F. Smith, *The United States and Revolutionary Nationalism in Mexico, 1916–1932* (Chicago, 1972), 190–228.

16. C. J. McMullen, "Calles and the Diplomacy of Revolution: Mexican-American Relations, 1924–1928," Ph. D. diss., Georgetown University, 1980, 33–37, 46–63; Smith, *Revolutionary Nationalism*, 229–37; and J. Meyer, E. Krauze, and C. Reyes, *Estado y sociedad con Calles* (Mexico City, 1977), 7–38. On U.S. invasion plans, see S. T. Ross, *American War Plans, 1890–1939* (London, 2002), 68–76 and 134–37; and J. J. Horn, "Did the United States Plan an Invasion of Mexico in 1927?" *Journal of Inter-American Studies and World Affairs* 15 (1973): 454–71. For diplomatic assessments of the tensions see Manuel Téllez to Relaciones Exteriores, 16 January 1926 and (Foreign Minister) Aarón Sáenz to Téllez, 25 January 1926, both in AREM III/628 (010)/1L-E 552. See also "Propaganda Against the United States by the Mexican Government Since the Beginning of the Administration of President Calles," memorandum in the records of the U.S. Department of State, RG 59, 711.12/695, NA and Sáenz to Kellogg, 7 December 1925, AREM III 628 (010)/1-552-1. Many of Sáenz's public statements had a moderate anti-American content. For examples, see the *New York Times,* 29 December 1925, 1, 20, and 22 January 1926, and 24 and 30 November 1926.

17. *El Demócrata,* 7 February 1926, cited in P. E. Calles, *Mexico before the World,* ed. and trans. R. H. Murray (New York, 1927), 80. See other Calles statements in the Mexican press cited in Calles, *Mexico before,* 55–61, 86–89, 168–98. Calles's minister of education, J. M. Puig Casauranc, made similar statements in his *De nuestro México* (Mexico City, 1926), 149–53 and 171–93. For the views of other Mexicans on the problem of US power within Mexico see M. Sáenz, "Las inversiones extranjeras y el nacionalismo mexicano," *Publicaciones de la Secretaría de Educación Pública,* XII, no. 17 and "The Two Sides of Mexican Nationalism," *Current History* 24 (1927), 908–12; R. Nieto, *El imperio de los Estados Unidos y otros ensayos* (Japala, Veracruz, 1926); M. Téllez, "Mexico's Laws Against Foreign Land Ownership: Mexico Within Her Sovereign Rights," *Current History* 24 (1926): 338–40; and T. Esquivel Obregón, *México y los Estados Unidos ante el derecho internacional* (México City, 1926). See also A. Córdova, *La ideología de la Revolución Mexicana: La formación del nuevo régimen* (Mexico City, 1973), 379–401.

18. F. González Roa, *Las cuestiones fundamentales de actualidad en México* (Mexico City, 1927).   .

19. J. W. F. Dulles, *Yesterday in Mexico* (Austin, 1961), 163–64, 550.

20. González Roa, *Cuestiones,* 5.

21. Ibid., 11–85, 153–60, 192–98, 208–21. Quote from 251. González Roa was an authority on land reform. See his *El aspecto agrario de la Revolución Mexicana* (Mexico City, 1919).

22. N. Hamilton, *The Limits of State Autonomy: Post-Revolutionary Mexico* (Princeton, 1982), 67–103. Some proponents of anti-Americanism to the left of González Roa formed the Anti-Imperialist League (see DS 810.43 Anti-Imperialist League/

69-175) and joined with other Mexican radicals to accuse the United States of imperialism in the pages of *El Machete,* the newspaper of the Mexican Communist Party.

23. L. Meyer, *El conflicto social y los gobiernos del maximato* (Mexico City, 1978), and A. Córdova, *La clase obrera en la historia de México en una época de crisis (1928–1934)* (Mexico City, 1980), 81–88.

24. Meyer, *conflicto social,* 94–98; Córdova, *clase obrera,* 143–240; E. Krauze, *Caudillos culturales en la revolución mexicana* (Mexico City, 1976), 312–30; V. Lerner, *La educación socialista* (Mexico City, 1978); J. A. Britton, *Educación y radicalismo* (Mexico City, 1976), 2 vols.; F. Benítez, *Lázaro Cárdenas y la Revolución Mexicana,* 3 vols. (Mexico City, 1977), vol. 2; and T. Medin, *El minimato presidencial: historia política del maximato, 1928–1935* (Mexico City, 1982). For Puig Casauranc's account, see his *Galatea rebelde a varios pigmaliones* (Mexico City, 1938).

25. J. Bazant, *Historia de la deuda exterior de México, 1823–1940* (Mexico City, 1995), 201–11 and Meyer, *conflicto social,* 57–60.

26. Puig Casauranc to Ortiz Rubio, 7 January 1932, AGNM, Fondo Ortiz Rubio 24/390. On Puig as ambassador, see his *Mirando la vida* (Mexico City, 1933). On US economic conditions in the 1930s and the low esteem of bankers, see R. Sobel, *The Big Board: A History of the New York Stock Market* (New York, 2000), 262–92, and *Panic on Wall Street: A Classic History of America's Financial Disasters* (New York, 1988); and H. Bierman, *The Great Myths of 1929 and the Lessons to Be Learned* (Westport, 1991). On the US Senate Banking and Currency Committee, see S. E. Kennedy, *The Banking Crisis of 1933* (Lexington, 1973), 102–28; and F. J. Pecora, *Wall Street Under Oath: The Story of Our Modern Money Changers* (New York, 1939).

27. Puig to Calles, 17 May 1932, AGNM-OR 2/2254. On Kemmerer see P. Drake, *The Money Doctor in the Andes: The Kemmerer Missions, 1923–1933* (Durham, 1989).

28. Puig to Ortiz Rubio, 14 March 1932 and Ortiz Rubio to Puig, March 22, 1932, AGNM, Fondo Ortiz Rubio 84/1426.

29. F. J. Gaxiola, *El presidente Rodríguez* (Mexico City, 1938), 230–33.

30. F. Schuler, *Mexico between Hitler and Roosevelt: Mexican Foreign Relations in the Age of Lázaro Cárdenas, 1934–1940* (Albuquerque, 1998), 13–17. Quotation from 14. See also SRE, *Memoria general y actuación de la delegación mexicana,* 3 vols. (Mexico City, 1934), vol. 2, 3–40; and E. D. Cronon, *Josephus Daniels in Mexico* (Madison, 1960), 72–75. On the history of the Mexican debt, see Bazant, *La deuda exterior,* and C. Marichal, *A Century of Debt Crises in Latin America: From Independence to the Great Depression* (Princeton, 1989), 171–228.

31. *FRUS 1933,* 5 vols. (Washington, D.C., 1933), vol. 4, 147; *New York Times,* 19 October 1933; and S. Braden, *Diplomats and Demagogues* (New Rochelle, 1971), 114–15, 130–37.

32. *New York Times,* 19 October 1933.

33. Ibid., 28 October 1933, and 1 and 20 November 1933.

34. SRE, *Memoria . . . de la delegación,* vol. 1, 77–79. See also Enrique Jiménez D. to Puig, 23 October 1933, Eusebio Ayala to Puig, 23 November 1933, and Martin Fernández to Puig, 17 November 1933, all in AREM L-E 907.

35. SRE, *Memoria . . . de la delegación,* vol. 1, 81; and Puig Casauranc, *El sentido social y proceso histórico de México* (Mexico, 1936), 177–78.

36. SRE, *Memoria . . . de la delegación,* vol. 1, 80. For advisory reports sent to Puig, see Daniel Cosio Villegas, "Estudio sobre la creación de un organismo economico-financiero panamericano" in SRE, *Memoria . . . de la delegación,* vol. 2, 173–222 and Luis Sanchez Ponton, "El problema de las deudas," in ibid., 291–312.

37. C. Hull, *Memoirs of Cordell Hull* (New York, 1948), 335–36; *FRUS 1933,* 4: 159, 171, 174; and SRE, *Memoria . . . de la delegación,* vol. 1., 117–33, 472–73.

38. D. Steward, *Trade and Hemisphere* (Columbia, 1975), 1–30; E. Rosenberg, *Financial Missionaries to the World: The Politics and Culture of Dollar Diplomacy, 1900–1930* (Cambridge, 1999); T. F. O'Brien, *The Century of U.S. Capitalism in Latin America* (Albuquerque, 1999), 73–99, and SRE, *Memoria . . . de la delegación,* vol. 1, 437–65.

39. SRE, *Memoria . . . de la delegación,* vol. 1, 445–50.

40. Ibid., 462–83.

41. Ibid., 449.

42. Ibid., 117–24, 451–59.

43. Ibid., 282–87, 295–327, 435–39. For Melfi's article see SRE, *Memoria . . . de la delegación,* vol. 3, 283–87. See also C. Beals, *The Coming Struggle for Latin America* (New York, 1938), 269–70. *Excelsior* covered Puig's debt discussion on 5, 6, and 7 December 1933 and his opposition to Hull's tariff proposal on 13 and 15 December 1933. See also Pedro de Alba to Puig, 25 September 1934, AREM L-E 907.

44. *Nation,* 27 December 1933, 723–24, and 10 January 1934, 36; Ernest Gruening, "Pan-Americanism Reborn," *Current History* 39 (1934): 529–34, and *New York Times,* 17 December 1933. Journalist Carleton Beals was an exception among US observers who ignored Puig's remarks. See Beals, *America South* (New York, 1937), 500–509 and *Coming Struggle,* 251–74.

45. For various accounts of the announcement by Cárdenas, see A. Knight, "The Politics of Expropriation," in *The Mexican Petroleum Industry in the Twentieth Century,* ed. J. Brown and A. Knight (Austin, 1992), 103–20; L. González, *Los días del presidente Cárdenas* (Mexico City, 1981), 128–92; V. C. Millan, *Mexico Reborn* (Boston, 1939), 198–202; and A. Rodríguez, *El rescate del petróleo, epopeya de un pueblo* (Mexico City, 1975).

46. Mexican Government, *Mexico's Oil* (Mexico City, 1940), 881. This volume was a government translation of *El petróleo de Mexico: Recopilación de documentos oficiales del conflicto de orden económico de la industria petrolera, con una introducción que resume sus motivos y consequencias* (Mexico City, 1940).

47. Schuler, *Between Hitler and Roosevelt,* 115, and Knight, "Politics," 111–14.

48. Millan, *Mexico Reborn,* 198; F. Kluckhohn, *The Mexican Challenge* (New York, 1939), 121; Knight, "Politics of Expropriation," 106–109; González, *Los días,* 178–84; and Benítez, *Lázaro Cárdenas y la revolución mexicana,* vol. 3, 150–51.

49. J. M. Pilcher, *Cantinflas and the Chaos of Mexican Modernity* (Wilmington, 2001), 53; V. Prewett, *Reportage on Mexico* (New York, 1941), 123.

50. L. Meyer, "El ocaso británico en México, de las causas profundas a los errores políticos," *Mexican Studies/Esudios Mexicanos* 11 (1995): 25–43; the same author's *Mexico and the United States in the Oil Controversy, 1917–1942* (Austin, 1972), 149–228; and J. Mearsheimer, *The Tragedy of Great Power Politics* (New York, 2001), 234–333.

51. M. Parrish, *Anxious Decades: America in Prosperity and Depression, 1920–1941* (New York, 1992), 270–436; R. McElvaine, *The Great Depression, 1929–1941* (New York, 1984); and G. Jeansonne, *Transformation and Reaction: America, 1921–1945* (New York, 1994).

52. Puig Casauranc, *Sentido social,* 215–30.

53. Schuler, *Between Hitler and Roosevelt,* 38–40; I. F. Gellman, *Good Neighbor Diplomacy: United States Policies in Latin America, 1933–1945* (Baltimore, 1979), 51–56; and F. W. Marks, *Wind Over Sand: The Diplomacy of Franklin D. Roosevelt* (Athens, 1988), 217–50. On the right in Mexico, see D. J. Mabry, *Mexico's Acción Nacional: A Catholic Alternative to Revolution* (Syracuse, 1973), 1–49; H. C. Campbell, *La derecha radical en Mexico, 1929–1949* (Mexico City, 1976); and J. W. Sherman, *The Mexican Right: The End of Revolutionary Reform, 1929–1940* (Westport, 1997). On conservatism in the United States see J. T. Patterson, *Congressional*

Conservatism and the New Deal (Lexington, 1967); C. P. Weed, *The Nemesis of Reform: The Republican Party during the New Deal* (New York, 1994); and A. Brinkley, *The End of Reform: New Deal Liberalism in Depression and War* (New York, 1995).

54. Francisco J. Múgica, "Contestación al Cuestionario de *Todo*" 17 March 1939, Fondo Francisco J. Múgica, Caja 8, tomo XLVII, documento 47, CERMLC, Jiquilpan, Michoacán, México, and Múgica's response to Cuestionario sometido al General Múgica por J. C. Arnold *(Saturday Evening Post)*, undated, probably 1939, in Fondo Francisco J. Múgica, Caja 8, tomo XLVII, documento 52, also in CERMLC.

55. E. Llinás Alvarez, *Vida y obra de Ramón Beteta* (Mexico City, 1996), 17–36.

56. J. Silva Herzog, *Una vida en la vida de México* (Mexico City, 1975), 157–231.

57. J. A. Britton, *Revolution and Ideology* (Lexington, 1995), 128–53.

58. For example see Ramón Beteta to Raúl Castellanos (Cárdenas's executive secretary), 2 May 1938. Beteta received information from Francisco Castillo Nájera (Mexico's ambassador to Washington). See Castillo Nájera to SRE, 13 July 1938 and 8 August 1938; and Beteta to Castellanos, 27 April 1938, all in Fondo Lázaro Cárdenas 423.2/253-8, AGNM. See also Llinás Alvarez, *Ramón Beteta,* 23–34. For Múgica's work, see Múgica to Cárdenas, 9 May 1938, Fondo Lázaro Cárdenas 432.2/243-8 AGNM. Quotation, B. McConnell, *Mexico at the Bar of Public Opinion* (New York, 1939), 44–45.

59. J. C. Ashby, *Organized Labor and the Mexican Revolution under Lázaro Cárdenas* (Chapel Hill, 1967), 179–210.

60. Cárdenas to Castillo Nájera, 8 February 1939, Fondo Lázaro Cárdenas, Caja 28, CERMLC; Castillo Nájera to Cárdenas, 9 August 1939 AREM, 39-10-2 (1); and Castillo Nájera to Cárdenas, 4 June 1940, AREM 39-10-2 (10).

61. Mexican Government, *Mexico's Oil,* 58; Ashby, *Organized Labor,* 201–10; and Córdova, *La clase obrera,* 143–216.

62. Mexican Government, *Mexico's Oil,* 62.

63. Ibid., 78–79.

64. Ibid., 468.

65. Ibid., 511–14.

66. Ibid., "Introduction," xlii.

67. Ibid., xlvi.

68. Ibid., li. Mexico and the United States reached a settlement on the oil properties in 1942. The British settlement was not signed until 1946. See Meyer, *Oil Controversy,* 173–234, and the same author's "The Expropriation and Great Britain," in *Mexican Petroleum,* ed. Brown and Knight, 154–72. For an informative study of this episode, see C. Jayne, *Oil, War, and Anglo-American and British Reactions to Mexico's Expropriation of Foreign Oil Properties, 1937–1941* (Westport, 2000).

Chapter 2

"Bradenism" and Beyond

Argentine Anti-Americanism, 1945–1953

Glenn J. Dorn

In the summer of 2003, families facing eviction from their Buenos Aires apartment complex barricaded themselves in their homes and affixed to their makeshift defenses a sign reading "IMF Go to Hell." In the course of negotiations with the International Monetary Fund in 2002, an Argentine congressman placed a small US flag on the desk of another, implying that his colleague was a quisling for the United States. For more than a decade, Argentines have referred to the US ambassador in Buenos Aires as "The Viceroy," an emperor's representative in the colonies.[1] Clearly, symbols of the United States occupy a significant position in Argentine politics.

In the wake of the *argentinazo,* the economic collapse of 2001 that spawned riots that killed more than thirty people and toppled four presidents in two weeks, there was no shortage of domestic scapegoats. Nonetheless, blame was also foisted onto international actors as well. Among these stood out the "Washington model" of neoliberal austerity implemented in the 1990s that laid the foundations for the disaster, the IMF that encouraged these policies, and the international banking institutions and corporations that plundered the nation. While Argentines directed most of their attention to the domestic causes of the crisis, there obviously remained a significant if yet unfocused undercurrent of hostility toward globalization and international capital. The United States, of course, is intimately linked to both. This chapter examines a critical moment in Argentine history for evidence of the roots and contours of Argentine nationalists' close identification of the United States with the evils of global capital. Recent resentment can be traced directly to the catastrophic *argentinazo,* but should also be seen as a modern incarnation of an older anti-US sentiment that has persisted since Juan Perón offered his ill-fated challenge to US hegemony in the 1940s.

Although scholars have quite rightly focused upon the internal political, economic, and cultural factors that allowed for the emergence of Peronism as a unique populist movement in the 1940s, doing so neglects to some extent the role that anti-US nationalism played in shaping that evolution.[2] Indeed, *peronismo* emerged not only as a direct challenge to the oligarchy and its liberal capitalist economy, but also to the global capitalist order that appeared to consign Argentina to a secondary role. While it was therefore inevitable that Peronism would exhibit a certain amount of nationalism, overt US opposition to the movement in its formative stages at once helped to sharpen its anticapitalism, virtually invited retribution, and infused the movement with an exuberant confidence that it could challenge Washington. US diplomats were well aware that Perón sought at least some measure of cooperation with the United States, but their own actions almost ensured that his best prospects usually rested with the exploitation of anti-US nationalism. So although this chapter focuses primarily upon Argentine anti-Americanism, it also serves as an object lesson to US diplomats in the extent to which arrogant, shortsighted policymaking can exacerbate international crises.

Of all of the nations of the Americas, Argentina prior to World War II may well have had the least cause for open antagonism toward the United States. Theodore Roosevelt "took" no Argentine provinces, United Fruit did not spread its tentacles into the *pampas,* and US-Argentine relations regularly showed signs of amity, if not cooperation.

While this did not stop Argentine governments from posturing as a southern counterbalance to US power throughout the early twentieth century, it was Buenos Aires's neutrality during World War II that truly drew Washington's ire.[3] Secretary of State Cordell Hull, convinced that this neutrality was an expression of support for Nazi Germany, employed crippling economic embargoes, fierce rhetoric, and open political pressure in an effort to coerce Argentines to join the war against the Axis. Still, despite the debilitating effects of Hull's "hysterical" "moral embargo," to Argentines he remained a distant foe, quite unlike the man who was to become Perón's nemesis, Spruille Braden.[4]

A lifelong Republican, Braden nonetheless had served the Roosevelt administration for years and possessed a well-earned reputation for no-nonsense, heavy-handed diplomacy when he was dispatched as ambassador to Buenos Aires. He quickly identified Lieutenant Colonel Perón, the charismatic rising star of Argentine politics, as a serious threat to US interests and, as he put it, an "Al Capone with Nazi tendencies." Preaching economic nationalism and calling for industrialization through statist regimentation, Perón won the support of workers, their unions, his military colleagues, and the *descamisados* ("shirtless masses") through workplace reform, the promise of a welfare state, and cutting denunciations of the "decadent" elite. When he put forth his candidacy for the presidency in late 1945, Braden threw his considerable weight behind the Democratic Union (UD), the coalition that had emerged to derail Peronism.[5] He delivered powerful speeches and promoted Hull's embargoes as his embassy intrigued with anti-Peronists and may well have collaborated with revolutionaries seeking to cancel the election. Arguing that Perón "is on the ropes and could be dealt a finishing punch were there any leadership or initiative" within the UD, Braden attempted to provide both during the fateful election of 1946.[6]

For Perón and his backers, Braden's vigorous activities posed an obvious threat, but the ambassador's highly visible role also presented them a unique opportunity. *Peronistas* coined the term "Bradenism," which they eventually defined as "the penetration of Yankee imperialism through the great trusts and the native oligarchies."[7] Since Braden was acting as almost the de facto leader of the UD, which merged groups as disparate as conservative elites and the Communist Party, Peronists could argue that they were being besieged by the forces of both reactionary capitalism and radical communism, Wall Street and the Kremlin. This further allowed *peronistas* to brand their opponents as "country-selling traitors" allied to "wicked foreigners conspiring against Argentina." Perón, in contrast, cast himself as the valiant defender of Argentine sovereignty and "public enemy #1 of the imperialistic consortiums."[8] "Bradenism" thus referred not only to the "agents of the Cominform and the minions of Wall Street" who colluded "arm in arm" against an independent Argentina, but to Argentines of any political stripe who dared to oppose Perón.[9]

Braden only added credibility to these accusations when, weeks before the election, he released the infamous *Blue Book,* a catalogue of German documents and State Department commentaries that claimed to prove Peronist complicity with the Nazis. While some prophetic US diplomats urged against publication, warning that such blatant intervention would be "pounced on by [the] Perón clique as [a] clumsy effort to influence" the election, Braden, now assistant secretary of state, nonetheless ordered its release. As feared, Perón adroitly countered, announcing that voters' choice was simply "Braden or Perón," and that a vote for the UD was a vote for "anguish, misery, and disgrace," as well as the "evil oligarch-communist alliance."[10] By transforming the election into a referendum on "Wall Street Imperialism," the *Blue Book* may well have cemented Perón's victory and given Argentina's self-styled "Number One Worker" a weapon he would wield to good effect for years.

While this was undoubtedly his most famous employment of anti-US nationalism, it was hardly his last. The "Bradenism" discourse became far more than a rhetorical assault on an individual diplomat, but at once a fierce indictment of US capitalism and interventionism, and a vital tool for consolidating his hold on power.

Although Braden resigned from the State Department in 1947, all Perón had to do was link any rival with "Bradenism" to reincarnate the specter of "Yankee imperialism." For example, in 1947, he sought to rid the Argentine labor movement of popular leaders like Luis Gay, head of the powerful General Confederation of Workers (CGT), whose appeal among Argentine workers rivaled or even superseded his own. Unable to move directly against the widely-respected CGT boss, Perón took advantage of the visit of US labor unionists to paint Gay as a traitor. Claiming to have recorded conversations between Gay and members of an American Federation of Labor (AFL) delegation in Buenos Aires, Perón charged the CGT chieftain with "political high treason" and conspiring with Braden to "sell the Argentine workers to American imperialism."[11] The CGT, which only weeks earlier had lauded Gay, now echoed the denunciations of this plot to "separate Perón from the workers" and renounced the union chief.[12] It is difficult to envision another scenario whereby the CGT would have allowed Gay to be unseated without a bitter fight, but Perón knew well that nationalistic anti-US appeals virtually guaranteed him victory.

On other occasions, Peronists' use of "Bradenism" seemed to US diplomats to "constitute an open invitation" for "physical violence" against his opponents, foreign or domestic. When rumors of a plot to assassinate the Peróns surfaced in 1948, implicating one of Braden's old associates in the State Department, indignant *peronistas* responded with characteristic vigor. Mobilized by incendiary speeches by the president and his wife, Eva, as well as newspapers alleging an "order from the US to assassinate Perón," mobs "carrying scaffolds and nooses" descended upon the US embassy in Buenos Aires demanding the "downfall of the Yankees." Once again "in typical fashion and with little originality," blame was laid upon Braden, his "spies in the guise of foreign correspondents," and other assorted "agents of Wall

Street." While Perón and the US ambassador eventually defused the crisis, US personnel closed the embassy for days.[13]

Still, threats against US citizens were rare, unlike the intimidation that domestic opponents of *peronismo* faced. In June 1951, Perón urged sugar workers to suppress those who attended demonstrations against him so ruthlessly "that even their children would not dream of coming out again." In the days that followed, the Peronist newspapers *Democracia* and *Crítica* denounced a vague plot by the "nefarious" communists (acting in "close union with the oligarchy," and "once again moved by directives inspired from abroad") to deprive the working class of the benefits they had won under Peronism. The newspapers then published the names and addresses of Perón's domestic opponents who were allegedly connected with the conspiracy in what US diplomats considered crass intimidation and the creation of a "climate for political assassination."[14]

Not only did these tactics allow Perón considerable latitude when dealing with his domestic opposition, but they also forced Washington to alter its tactics. The State Department understood all too well after the *Blue Book* fiasco that any attack on Perón would boomerang. Thus, while the goal of US policy was to end the Peronist experiment in statist populism, as one US congressman succinctly noted, "the people of Argentina will take care of him if we don't make a national hero of him."[15] Hull's embargoes had to be abandoned as well. Not only did his brand of economic warfare fuel anti-US sentiment, but US leaders understood all too well that if the Argentine economy collapsed as a result of it, Peronists would not "bear the brunt of the blame," but would instead "shift it to our shoulders." So while the Truman administration remained committed to bankrupting Peronist Argentina, it was critical that this new stage of the "economic boycott" remain secret, lest Perón again employ "Bradenism" to save himself.[16] Put simply, US policy after Braden's resignation was an adroit and explicit effort to ignore Argentine provocations.

This was far from easy, especially when Perón launched his reelection campaign in 1951. He had taken to writing fierce anti-US critiques under the pseudonym "Descartes," and then went out of his way to reveal the identity of "Descartes" to US embassy personnel. State Department analysts concluded that "Perón wants us to take the attacks seriously enough to blow our tops and hit back." "If we are fairly sure that Perón wants us to do so, then we should be doubly cautious about doing it." He was already "looking for a substitute for Braden to serve him" in the upcoming election, and Peronists, who "would be overjoyed if we began beating up on Argentina," were already tentatively touting the campaign as "Truman or Perón." There-fore, US officials prudently determined to "withstand the onslaught without retaliation." In short, they refused to be baited despite the "melancholy fact" that Perón's anti-US propaganda had "reached a new height in intensity and a new low in content."[17]

Indeed, just as Perón was bolstered by attacks from the north, US silence or approval actually hurt him among his most nationalis-tic constituencies. For example, when the Export-Import bank granted him a $125 million credit in 1950 (in part to discredit and undercut his nationalistic appeal), he was forced to defend himself from Ar-gentines who claimed that "we are now moving, naked and on foot, along the road of dishonor like pitiful beggars for dollars." Similarly, when he urged ratification of the US-sponsored Rio de Janeiro Hemi-spheric Defense Pact and offered moral support of US troops in Ko-rea, his own followers joined his old enemies in rioting against him.[18] Thus, even when Perón attempted to extend olive branches to Wash-ington, he did so only at considerable risk. While US policymakers may have overestimated Perón's nationalism, the fact remained that Argentines, inflamed by Braden's interventionism, responded posi-tively when he gave a "kick in the pants to the foreigner" and pun-ished him for conciliatory gestures.[19]

The paradox of Perón's anti-Americanism, however, was that to fulfill his dreams of industrialization, he required US investment and technology. Therefore, he maintained that his quarrel was not with the people of the United States, but with Braden alone, as he urged US diplomats to ignore his public declarations. "Damn it," he pri-vately told one US ambassador, "can't people realize that certain things are said for domestic consumption"? He added that when he attacked capitalism, he referred to the "old extreme capitalism" that the United States had not practiced since the election of Franklin Roosevelt. Needless to say, this sort of "clarification" rarely found its way into his public rhetoric, and only appeared in his subsequent private apologies. Arguing that "it is sometimes politically wise and necessary to give the foreigners in general a small kick," Perón hoped to gain tacit US approval, while retaining the anti-imperialist creden-tials that guaranteed his political success at home.[20]

He never did achieve the former, of course. "It is all well and good for [Perón] to send me letters assuring me of his undying devotion to the cause of the United States (marked 'confidential')," Assistant Secretary of State Edward Miller noted in 1950, "but these are of small comfort to me when his public statements are inconsistent with his private protestations."[21] Whatever comfort the State Department might have derived if Perón had employed "Bradenism" solely for

' "domestic consumption," and it would have been small indeed, Peronists instead worked tirelessly to carry their fight against "Yankee imperialism" to the rest of the hemisphere.

Where Perón distinguished himself from other Latin American nationalists of his generation was in boldly disseminating anti-US propaganda to elevate Peronism as a rival to both capitalism and communism. *Peronismo* (or *justicialismo* after 1950) was a "Third Position" superior to both, he argued, because it harnessed the dynamic potential of capitalism for the good of all members of society through a powerful state apparatus and, at the same time, it avoided the repressive and sectarian aspects of communism. The "octopus of capitalism," Peronists claimed, spawned an anarchic "exploitation of the people" in the name of profit, while the totalitarian "octopus of collectivism" led only to "slavery" and "misery."[22] Although his professed anticommunism and repeated assertion that Peronism was actually an effort to redirect workers away from malevolent Bolshevism did shield him from red-baiting US statesmen and Latin American reactionaries, the vast majority of his rhetorical onslaughts were aimed against the "exploitation and abuses of capitalism," which he deemed to be "the great evil of the nineteenth and twentieth century." While US diplomats regarded *justicialismo* as little more than "polysyllabic fence-sitting," Perón nonetheless proclaimed that soon "the world will be rid of capitalism and rid of communism" as Peronism's "true democracy" rendered both obsolete.[23]

Therefore, it was in the field of inter-American relations, and not domestic policy, that Perón's "Third Position" truly challenged US-led globalization. *Peronistas,* recognizing that postwar US attention was focused upon the reconstruction of Europe, saw an opportunity to fulfill old Argentine dreams of continental leadership through the "Third Position." They hoped to exploit US negligence by offering loans to nations willing to repudiate the principles of liberal capitalism and had no qualms about utilizing coercive tactics against those hesitant to follow their lead. If successful, Perón would rectify what he believed to be the "incomprehensible error" by which the Southern Cone had been divided into separate nations and unify them under Argentine leadership. Still, Peronists understood that they could not truly challenge the United States economically, and therefore they dedicated more effort to a cultural and ideological contest for the hearts and minds of Latin American workers by advertising the gains that Argentine workers had won under Juan and Eva Perón. While foreign capital and sterile domestic oligarchies had warped South American development to suit their own needs, *peronistas* promised nothing short of the hemisphere's "emancipation."[24]

Adding updated condemnations of "Bradenism" to clichéd denunciations of "Wall Street Imperialism," Peronists launched an independent campaign to counteract the influence of the United States across the hemisphere. The CGT's *Boletín Latinoamericano,* distributed regularly by Argentine embassies, was one of the more effective means of "plucking the eagle's feathers."[25] The journal regularly featured political cartoons such as the one that depicted Harry Truman's face attached to the body of the Statue of Liberty with a black lynching victim hanging from the torch (see Fig. 2.1). Another portrayed Truman blithely fishing while two African Americans are lynched in the background. A third, entitled "Democratic Borders," showed Braden, fat and bloated, sitting alongside an emaciated Truman on a segregated beach. Across a fence stand trim, muscular African Americans, as a sign on the fence proclaims "Blacks and dogs forbidden" (see Fig. 2.2).[26]

Regular commentaries detailing US racism, anti-Semitism, exploitation of Latin American workers, and colonialism in Puerto Rico supplemented these editorial cartoons. But the *Boletín* was hardly the only medium through which propaganda flowed, as Argentine printers distributed pamphlets and entire monographs denouncing the United States. Two books distributed in Paraguay and elsewhere illustrate the trend. The first, *El principio del fin (The Beginning of the End),* gave detailed, highly unfavorable interpretations of US conflicts with Spain and Latin America dating back to the Louisiana Purchase and the occupation of Florida. Other chapters, again emphasizing the apparently limitless ambition of US expansionism, dealt with the "Dismemberment of Mexico," the "Occupation of Cuba and Puerto Rico," and the "Dismemberment of Colombia." The book concluded with US global dominance in the postwar period, and naturally, "Braden as the symbol of empire."[27]

The Argentine embassy in Asunción also distributed *La verdad periodística y la prensa amarilla (The Journalistic Truth and the Yellow Press),* which, after reaffirming that the Peronist press was "the purest journalism in the world," explained how "tons of paper are circulated each day to all the peoples of the world defaming us" at the behest of Wall Street. The *Washington Star, New York Times, Time,* and *Saturday Evening Post* were among the newspapers denounced as "cannibals of journalism" for their efforts to "poison the world against Argentina" through "sinister distortions of the truth." Peronists clearly hoped to erode the credibility of US journalism, again reinterpreting historical events to illustrate what they deemed to be the slavish devotion of the US press to the capitalist order.[28] Other titles included *The Rising of the Curtain,* a neutralist indictment of US

FRONTERAS DEMOCRATICAS

TRUMAN. — "¡No puedo ver ese espectáculo tan feo de los negros...!"
BRADEN. — "¡Yo tampoco comprendo cómo la naturaleza hace cosas así...!"

Figure 2.1
Truman: "I can't stand the revolting sight of those blacks!" Braden: "I can't understand how nature can produce such things!" *Boletín Latinoamericano de la C.G.T. Argentina,* September 1952.

Cold War policy, and *The Zero Hour of Capitalism,* a "smear" of "the
entire social and economic fabric" of the United States that, according to AFL diplomat Serafino Romualdi, "could have been signed by
a Communist."[29]

   Given the low literacy rates of the working class constituencies
that Peronists hoped to radicalize, literary propaganda was but one
facet of their campaign to stimulate *justicialismo* across the conti-

CONOZCA NORTEAMERICA

Figure 2.2

"Meet North America." Supporters of Juan Perón portrayed President Harry Truman as an upholder of Jim Crow racism. *Boletín Latinoameriano de la C.G.T. Argentina,* January 1952.

nent. Far more promising, it seemed, was for Peronist labor attachés and special ambassadors to make direct appeals to unions, workers, and populist organizations across the hemisphere. Within months of taking office, Perón started to "spread the revolution" by dispatching CGT members trained in a two-year program at the University of Buenos Aires, the *Curso de Elevación Cultural Superior Juan D. Perón,* as labor attachés to Argentine embassies. Their mission, which many pursued with almost missionary zeal, was to identify, strengthen, and forge ties with existing groups across South America that "could respond to our overtures for the formation of a bloc" against "Bradenism."[30] These included Víctor Raúl Haya de la Torre's American Popular Revolutionary Alliance (APRA) in Peru, Víctor Paz Estenssoro's Bolivian Revolutionary Nationalist Movement (MNR), Luis Alberto Herrera's Colorado Party in Uruguay, the Communist Party, and even US labor unions that might be won over to *justicialismo*. In short, Peronist embassies sought to circumvent traditional diplomatic channels and appeal directly to the masses of Latin America in order to forge nothing less than an international working-class alliance against "the penetration of the neighbors of the North."[31]

Their diplomatic offensive in Peru is instructive in this regard, as Peronists sought to foster an *"espíritu sanmartiano,"* recalling the Argentine-born hero of both Peruvian and Argentine independence, José de San Martín. Ambassador Hugo Oderigo, perhaps the most zealous *peronista* envoy, spearheaded the effort. While Peru had dutifully supported the "miserly and mercantile" United States throughout World War II, Washington had done almost nothing to reward that loyalty and was beginning to estrange even the most pro-US Peruvians. At the same time Truman was spending billions to reconstruct former Axis nations, the US Congress raised tariffs on Peruvian goods, and the State Department blocked Peruvian access to desperately needed private loans and credits. Although Oderigo understood that the Peruvian elite leaned toward supporting US-style liberal capitalism, increasing numbers of Peruvians were closely examining Peronism and the changes it had wrought in Argentina.[32]

Oderigo's embassy worked diligently to encourage Peruvians who believed that "what we need here is a Perón" and thereby to end Peru's "gravitation" toward the "Yankee colossus." It distributed Peronist books and pamphlets and broadcast radio programs, and Oderigo presented toys and clothes to Peruvian children.[33] Through these and other efforts, Peronists hoped to win the support of the powerful APRA, which shared with Peronism the search for a "new Latin American economic system based on the defense of the working class" and an anti-imperialistic track record.[34] While Oderigo was often unduly optimistic, even US embassy personnel lamented that "Argentine influence is on the increase both commercially and culturally" as Argentine magazines, books, movies, and music increasingly flowed across the Andes.[35]

Like Oderigo, Peronist emissaries in Bolivia, "the easiest place for the infiltration of Yankee imperialism," endeavored to use both paeans to Peronism and assaults on "Bradenism" to earn the support of Paz Estenssoro's MNR. While US fears that the MNR was "ideologically alongside of Argentina if not in its wake" were exaggerated, some MNR officials did endorse the concept of a "southern bloc" under Perón's banner, and at least one Bolivian revolutionary lauded Perón's Argentina as "the only country which has succeeded in saving itself" from the "loving care of the United States" and preserving "the rebellious and free spirit of South America."[36]

Estenssoro's organization, which like Perón had been featured in the *Blue Book,* had its own reasons to resent Braden and the "Bradenist plutocracy," whom it blamed for the 1946 revolution that had sent it into hiding. Peronists fed this perception, claiming to possess evidence that Braden plotted the downfall of both Perón and the MNR with the Bolivian tin barons in mid-1945. "Kill the dog, and the fleas will die," the cabal had apparently determined, suggesting that Braden would engineer the defeat of Perón. With the MNR's puppet strings cut, the oligarchs could oust it and regain control of government at their leisure. While these charges were never substantiated, the Argentine embassy in La Paz used them as one component of its own campaign to "penetrate" Bolivia and promote its own grudge against Braden. So while Paz Estenssoro bided his time in exile in Buenos Aires, Peronists hoped to hasten the day when he could return to his homeland and restore the MNR to power, presumably to their benefit.[37]

Although it was not uncommon for Argentine leaders to intrigue with one faction or another in South American politics, Perón managed to appeal to communists as well, despite his avowed anticommunism. In Chile, for example, communists for a time hailed his efforts to promote the establishment of an "anti-imperialist bloc." At various times, the Argentine and Brazilian Communist parties, and even the Soviet Union, endorsed aspects of Perón's battle against capitalism. Whatever doctrinaire differences existed between communists and Peronists, both shared an antagonism toward international capital in general and the United States in particular. Ambassador Claude Bowers explained that impoverished Latin Americans turned to communism "blindly and stupidly," understanding only that it "is something extremely opposite to the system under which [they] suffer" and "believing that nothing could be worse than [their] present state." In the eyes of US statesmen, the appeal of *justicialismo* was similar, if not more dangerous, because of the very real social and economic achievements that *peronistas* advertised so widely. So although communists had turned decidedly anti-Peronist by 1948, this did little to reassure US policymakers, who lamented that his propaganda still bore a disturbing resemblance in target, tone, and content to the Kremlin's.[38]

Still, communists were not the most unlikely allies that Perón sought to cultivate. He also hoped to carry anti-Americanism to America itself by forging an alliance with US unions against "imperialistic

Wall Street capitalism."[39] To this end, he invited both the AFL and Congress of Industrial Organizations (CIO) to send delegations to Buenos Aires in late 1946. Peronists hoped to impress their northern brethren with their "maturity" and believed that US workers would "find it easy to observe the contrast between our democracy and that of the *yanquis.*" Indeed, Argentine wages and benefits had increased substantially under Perón, and CGT members held posts in the Argentine national legislature and cabinet. In the United States, however, both "the government and the major political parties" promoted "anti-worker legislation designed to satisfy the imperialistic capitalists of Wall Street." As Truman was in the midst of his crackdown on labor leader John L. Lewis, and as the anti-union Taft-Hartley Act was working its way through Congress, the CGT fully expected to meet US unionists incensed at these betrayals.[40] Argentine labor attachés serving in Washington fed the belief that the time was ripe for *peronista* overtures, reporting that the United States was apparently heading for a record year of strikes. As Peronists introduced motions "rendering tribute to John L. Lewis in solidarity" in the *Cámara de Diputados,* they hoped US unionists might be willing to join with their Argentine brethren in an international labor alliance that repudiated the extremes of both capitalist plutocracy and communist totalitarianism. Internationally seasoned *peronistas* attempted to dissuade the CGT from issuing the invitation and hoped in vain that the "thing would fizzle out."[41]

The CIO immediately rejected the invitation. It had from the onset viewed Peronist Argentina as a "cancer" and an "outlaw in the family of nations," lamenting that CGT envoys comprised nothing less than a tireless "task force," dedicated to denouncing the United States.[42] Fearful that Perón was "sparing no effort or expense" to spread his ideology and undercut capitalism, CIO leaders had enthusiastically endorsed Braden's "taking up the cudgels for the cause of democracy" against Peronism. While some CIO members encouraged the idea of a visit to Buenos Aires to show Argentines that "there are not only 'Yankee Imperialists' in the US, but also honest and hard working people like themselves," they were clearly a minority. Instead, the CIO proudly announced that Perón "will not be able to use a CIO delegation to whitewash his fascist regime."[43] Their counterparts in the AFL accepted the invitation.

Not surprisingly, the AFL's visit ended in disaster with Romualdi concluding that "Perón hopes to gain control over Latin America by first taking over its labor movement," and the CGT countering that the AFL had come solely as a Trojan Horse for "the State Department's imperialistic plans of penetration." For Peronists, the episode made it clear that both the AFL and the CIO (like US journalists) had been suborned by Braden and his Wall Street allies.[44] Frustrated but undeterred, the CGT determined to resist AFL and CIO efforts to spread their tame brand of unionism to other nations. *Peronistas* eventually launched their own international labor federation to spread Peronist-style syndicalism and press their hemispheric battle against capitalism and communism. In short, Peronist unionists saw themselves as the vanguard of a "new consciousness," and rebels who had "produced a revolution which bore no resemblance" to any that had ever come before. They were nationalistic Argentines, but also considered themselves to be spokesmen for a united international working class, determined to "fight and die for democracy" against the "blood-stained talons and tentacles" of "Wall Street."[45]

While it is not surprising that Perón had little luck north of the Rio Grande, even his efforts and intrigues in Latin America never appear to have had the impact he intended. For example, Argentine diplomats made much of the fact that working-class Bolivian moviegoers openly applauded when newsreels showed Perón, but cultural successes of this sort rarely translated into more than moral victories.[46] For some Caribbean nations, the mere presence of Argentine propagandists in the region was a source of embarrassment, if not a direct threat. The Haitian government actually warned Peronist speakers to be "careful" and urged them to "not make public statements that could be misconstrued" by US leaders. Despite the admonition, "familiar" Peronist "catch phrases" nonetheless "made a very big hit in Haiti," US diplomats sadly reported. On the other hand, one Haitian labor leader claimed, most workers understood that the newspaper that published most Argentine propaganda only did so because "it is paid to do so by the Argentine embassy."[47]

In Rafael Trujillo's Dominican Republic, the US ambassador reported that Peronist "anti-American activities" also had "little if any effect," if only because workers and unions there were "so completely under governmental control that anti-US propaganda" could "be introduced only with the consent of the Dominican government." In this regard, Trujillo's repressive tendencies worked to Washington's advantage, as did El Salvador's ban on national labor organizations. Because the efforts of Peronists (or "anyone else for that matter") "must be dispersed among a large number of often quite unimportant labor groups," the US embassy in San Salvador reported, their effectiveness was "rather limited."[48] Therefore, Perón's anti-Americanism remained largely a South American affair.

But like their Central American and Caribbean counterparts, diplomats in the Southern Cone quickly came to view Perón's Argentina and its newfound international mission with alarm. Peruvian ambassadors across the continent reported that the real goals of Peronist diplomacy were nothing less than to supplant the United States and establish its own "political and economic hegemony" in the region. While diplomats from Bolivia, Chile, and Peru attempted to exploit US fears of Peronist expansionism by suggesting that they might be forced to align themselves with Argentina unless US aid was forthcoming, few seriously contemplated hitching their carts to Perón's volatile social upheaval. Instead, the governments of South America understood well that Perón was a "troublemaker" and that any dalliance with him risked Washington's ire.[49]

Moreover, Peronist tactics were often as counterproductive and heavy-handed as Braden's had been. The foremost of these was what Peruvians called the "stomach policy." Peronists discovered early on that by threatening either to cut off food exports to neighboring states or to dramatically increase their price, they could exert tremendous pressure. Peronists did utilize this form of "economic blackmail" against Brazil and Uruguay, and, it was widely suspected, Bolivia, Chile, and Peru. Despite early successes, this approach tended to backfire badly, as food shortages fell most heavily upon the working and lower classes that Perón hoped to unite. Even worse, the Truman administration could easily counter it by sending emergency shipments of wheat, flour, or meat, earning gratitude at Perón's expense.[50] Even when a government sympathetic to Perón came into power in Peru in 1948, its diplomats suggested that perhaps "the moment has arrived" to stop purchasing Argentine wheat entirely.[51] So while Perón hoped to be viewed as a benefactor, his own practices helped alienate even those predisposed to support his goals.

Indeed, Perón all too often found that the same populist movements he was working to suborn were just as determined to defend their independence from "short-term Argentine imperialism" as they were from the United States.[52] Víctor Raúl Haya de la Torre, legendary leader of APRA and an ally of the AFL, fiercely opposed Perón from the start, deeming *peronismo* to be wrongheaded and militaristic, if not totalitarian. Although Peronists intrigued to strengthen Haya de la Torre's supposedly pro-Argentine rivals within APRA against him, this was an effort doomed to failure.[53] Just as Haya de la Torre, the AFL, and the CIO saw Peronism as a threat to their efforts to secure the loyalty of the working class, so too did most communist parties in Latin America. A US diplomat in Guatemala claimed that Peronist efforts there had been fatally hamstrung by the fact that organized labor "is almost completely dominated by the Communists who are only slightly less hostile to Perón than they are to the United States."[54]

By 1952, Bolivia, Ecuador, Panama, and Uruguay were among the nations that had expelled Argentine labor attachés or ambassadors for their intrigues, illustrating well that *peronista* meddling was as every bit as unwelcome as the US variety.[55]

Even more daunting, Perón could never offer more than his North American rivals. The Eva Perón Foundation donated nine hundred packages of clothing and aid to "maimed and disabled" Bolivian war veterans in October 1949, but this amounted to little when Washington could simply pay higher prices for its massive tin purchases or send emergency flour shipments when hunger threatened. Argentine embassies in Central America could donate musical instruments to local orchestras and bands, sponsor baseball teams, and build schools in Managua, or donate corn threshers to Panamanian farmers "within artillery range of the Panama Canal," but these gestures could never compete with even the most minimal US aid. Peronists distributed pamphlets and buttons promoting Argentine-Chilean solidarity in Santiago, but again, Export-Import loans did far more to shape Chilean public opinion and foreign policy. While the *peronistas* hoped that their appeals to a "common noble Hispanic origin" could overcome US wealth and power, this was a contest they were doomed to lose and lose badly.[56] As often happened in the history of anti-Americanism, economic self-interest trumped pan-Hispanic solidarity.

Altogether, the impediments standing in the way of Perón's alliance-building were so formidable that quite possibly the only way he could have succeeded was to bait the Truman administration into retaliation. When Perón succeeded in signing a customs union with Chile in 1946, US journalists likened the pact to "the occupation of Czechoslovakia by Hitler and the Austrian *Anschluss.*" Argentines and Chileans quickly rallied to defend their actions. A Chilean diplomat dismissed the charge as "arbitrary and biased," and the Argentine response was even more venomous, contending that the "malicious and capricious" accusations were nothing more than the "nightmares of a sick mind." Little could have been calculated to better unite the two nations than attacks from the north that simultaneously accused Argentines of imperialism and Chileans of subservient acquiescence.[57] The lesson was not lost on US diplomats.

Just as they were incapable of refuting Peronist demagoguery within Argentina, US policymakers found themselves largely unable to respond directly to Perón's international propaganda offensive. They understood all too well that, at the first inkling of a US counterattack, he would rally Latin American nationalists to his cause with the cry of "intervention." The Truman administration, like its Peronist adversaries, had learned from Braden's experience that open assaults on Perón were "erroneous and counterproductive."[58] So although Perón expected, and probably hoped for, a rhetorical counterattack from Washington, the State Department refused to oblige him. On the contrary, it exercised "utmost tact" and "extreme delicacy" as it explicitly resolved to "not engage in any attacks" on Perón. Answering Perón, Miller concluded, would "allow the tail to wag the dog," and be "like a parent permitting his every action to be determined by a naughty child." While Miller did cryptically concede that covert steps would continue to be taken to ensure that Peronism never took root outside Argentina, any open action "would only further Argentine objectives." By "refusing to be drawn into a polemical exchange," US diplomats recognized Braden's errors and rejected the pointless bluster that had helped push Peronism onto the path of anti-Americanism in the first place.[59]

By 1953, it was clear that Perón's propaganda offensive was accomplishing nothing, even though four of his supposed allies—Paz Estenssoro in Bolivia, Getulio Vargas in Brazil, Gen. Carlos Ibañez in Chile, and Gen. Manuel Odría in Peru—had come to power. While such a line-up had ostensibly been Peronists' dream for years, none of these leaders had any interest in conflict with the United States, and in fact, each was seeking, or had already reached, his own accommodation with Washington. With his economy in shambles and no prospect of success through confrontation, Perón too sought rapprochement, and the election of Republican Dwight Eisenhower in 1952 presented him with the opportunity. The departure of the Democratic Truman administration, which would forever be tainted by "Bradenism" in Argentine eyes, granted Perón the freedom he needed for a rhetorical cease fire with Washington. Although necessity and desperation dictated his newfound amity toward the Yankee colossus, he was nonetheless able to claim a final, if somewhat hollow, triumph over "Bradenism."[60]

In the end, it should not be surprising that four years of Hull's economic coercion against Argentina and the blatant interventionist spirit that culminated in the *Blue Book* led triumphant *peronistas* to retaliate. What was noteworthy was how their indignation merged with revolutionary euphoria and traditional nationalistic aspirations to spark a bold anti-US campaign across the hemisphere. Perón always claimed that his goal was to fight communism by providing the social justice that capitalism had failed to deliver, but in the process, he not unwittingly unleashed a revolutionary fervor that he could not entirely control. Indeed, it seems that Perón found himself trapped between the role of revolutionary spokesperson for the working class that more ardent *peronistas* expected him to take, and that of an elected national leader charged with modernizing his nation by his more conservative constituents. Unable to balance these dual roles, he failed at both.

Washington also moved beyond "Bradenism" in its response. The speed with which Peronism had appeared was, for the State Department, an enlightening if frightening reminder of the volatility of Latin American politics. Its international appeal also seemed to appear from nowhere as it threatened to unite the disparate threads of South American nationalism in a way that communism had to that point failed to do. While the Truman administration did weather the storm, and did so rather handily, it never entirely unraveled the damage that Hull and Braden's campaigns had done to US-Argentine relations.

So although many parallels that could be drawn between 1945 and the present would be almost entirely superficial, Argentina once again faces a domestic economic and political crisis that overshadows, but should not entirely obscure, a powerful undercurrent of resentment toward the United States and the so-called Washington consensus. In this regard, sociologist Ernesto Laclau's analysis of Peronism remains quite pertinent. Laclau argued that the Great Depression and its aftermath shattered an old consensus centered upon traditional economic liberalism and democratic forms, making possible the emergence of wildly unpredictable new social phenomena such as *justicialismo*.[61] For more than sixty years, Peronism has, in one form or another, provided an outlet for Argentine discontent to find expression. In the 1990s, it again illustrated its protean nature by becoming "more a party than a movement." Indeed, when President Carlos Menem, a Peronist, implemented his famous austerity program based on privatization, foreign investment, and liberal orthodoxy— the "Washington consensus"—it was clear how far *justicialismo* had strayed from its nationalist roots. If indeed *menemismo* was "the end of Peronism as a popular movement," then it is not at all clear in what form Argentine social unrest will manifest and through what channels it will find expression in the twenty-first century.[62]

Prior to the *argentinazo* of 2001, Argentina had been one of the IMF's models for neoliberalism and an almost unqualified adherent to the "Washington consensus." In Argentina, as elsewhere, that consensus, if it ever truly existed, clearly broke down that year. While the political situation appeared to stabilize after the *argentinazo,* the crisis was in a number of ways more severe than even that of the 1930s. It was far from clear that the established political parties and national institutions could retain public confidence in the face of almost unprecedented economic deprivation. As of 2005, what was apparent was that the new president, Nestor Kirchner, faced a stiff test as he struggled to address Argentina's deep-rooted economic problems and ease the suffering of growing numbers of disenchanted and hungry Argentines. It could only be hoped that if he and his successors proved unable to tread the delicate line between the demands of his people and the dictates of the IMF, myopic and distracted ideologues in Washington would not again mismanage their response as they did in the 1940s.

Notes

1. N. Klein, "IMF Go to Hell," *Toronto Globe and Mail,* 19 March 2003; C. Denny, "IMF Rescue Plan Causes Fistfight among Argentinean Deputies," *The Guardian,* 11 May 2002.
2. It is not the intent of this essay to enter into the extensive and sophisticated debates regarding the origins of Peronism, but instead to examine the catalyzing impact that anti-US nationalism had on Argentine diplomacy under Perón. Two excellent synopses of the literature on Peronism are C. Buchrucker, "Interpretations of Peronism: Old Frameworks and New Perspectives," and M. Plotkin, "The Changing Perceptions of Peronism: A Review Essay," in *Peronism and Argentina,* ed. J. Brennan (Wilmington, 1998); see also C. Escudé, *Estados Unidos, Gran Bretaña, y la declinación argentina, 1942–1949* (Buenos Aires, 1983); M. Rapoport, *Gran Bretaña, Estados Unidos, y las clases dirigentes argentinos, 1940–1945* (Buenos Aires, 1980).
3. D. Sheinin, *Searching for Authority: Pan Americanism, Diplomacy and Politics in United States-Argentine Relations, 1910–1930* (New Orleans, 1998).
4. Escudé, *Estados Unidos, Gran Bretaña, y la declinación argentina;* and "US Political Destabilization and the Economic Boycott of Argentina during the 1940s," in *Argentina Between the Great Powers,* ed. G. Di Tella and D. C. Watt (Pittsburgh, 1990), 56–76; C. A. MacDonald, "The Politics of Intervention: The United States and Argentina, 1941–1946," *Journal of Latin American Studies* 12 (1980): 374–84; Rapoport, *Gran Bretaña, Estados Unidos, y las clases dirigentes argentinos;* R. B. Woods, *The Roosevelt Foreign-Policy Establishment and the "Good Neighbor"* (Lawrence, 1979).
5. A. P. Vannucci, "Elected by Providence: Spruille Braden in Argentina in 1945," in *Ambassadors in Foreign Policy: The Influence of Individuals in US-Latin American Foreign Policy,* ed. C. N. Romning and A. P. Vannucci (New York, 1987), 49–67; Bruce to Truman, 11 August 1949, Office Files, Argentina, HSTL.
6. Braden to Secretary of State, 17 July 1945, General Records of the Department of State, RG 59, 835.00, NA.
7. "Cooperacíon, Sí, Subordinacíon, No," *Democracia,* 17 February 1950.
8. Pool to Secretary of State, 18 June 1951, RG 59, 735.00, NA; *La Epoca,* 21 March 1951, 1; Pool to Secretary of State, 12 June 1951, RG 59, 735.00, NA.
9. *Democracia,* 17 June 1951, 1.
10. Cabot to Secretary of State, 4 December 1945, RG 59, 835.00, NA; Cabot to Secretary of State, 8 February 1946, RG 59, 835.00, NA; Perón quoted in C. Fayt, *Naturaleza de peronismo* (Buenos Aires, 1967), 146; see also C. A. MacDonald, "The Braden Campaign and Anglo-American Relations in Argentina, 1945–1946," in *Argentina Between the Great Powers,* ed. Di Tella and Watt (Pittsburgh, 1990), 137–53; G. Frank, *Juan Perón vs Spruille Braden: The Story Behind the Blue Book* (Lanham, 1980), 27–34.

11. *Periódico Seminal del C.G.T.,* 16 March 1947, Rollo 5, FSR; see also J. Page, *Perón: A Biography* (New York, 1983), 179–81; H. Gambini, *Historia del peronismo* (Buenos Aires, 1999), 206–8; J. C. Torre, *La vieja guardia sindical y Perón* (Buenos Aires, 1990), 95–102.

12. *Periódico Seminal del C.G.T.,* 16 January 1947, Rollo 5, FSR.

13. Embassy Buenos Aires to Secretary of State, 20 October 1948, RG 59, 711.35, NA; The episode is curious because once the US ambassador, James Bruce, convinced Perón that the US government had nothing to do with the plot (if one even existed), the two men joined together to calm tensions. Bruce suggested that he, General Matthew Ridgeway (who was "used to being shot at"), and their wives publicly join the Peróns in their box seats in the Teatro Colón where the assassination was supposed to take place. "That way," Bruce asserted, "if anybody is going to be assassinated, we can all be assassinated together." Perón agreed, took other steps that Bruce suggested, and actually worked with the US government to pacify his own followers. J. Bruce, *Memoirs* (Baltimore, 1997), 294–96.

14. Pool to Secretary of State, 18 June 1951, RG 59, 735.00, NA.

15. Baldwin to Truman, 13 April 1946, President's Secretary File, Foreign Affairs, Argentina, HSTL.

16. Bruce to Secretary of State, 21 January 1949, RG 59, 711.35, NA; Maleady to Secretary of State, 4 May 1949, RG 59, 711.35, NA; Escudé, *Gran Bretaña, Estados Unidos,* 322–30; see also C.A. MacDonald, "The US, the Cold War, and Perón," in *Economic Imperialism and the State: The Political Economy of the External Connection from Independence to the Present,* ed. C. Abel and C. Lewis (London, 1985), 410; G. J. Dorn, "Bruce Plan and Marshall Plan: The United States's Disguised Intervention against Peronism in Argentina, 1947–1950," *International History Review* XXI (June 1999): 331–51.

17. The son of the US Air Attaché in Buenos Aires came home from school and asked his father, "Daddy, who are you for, Truman or Perón?" Pool to Secretary of State, 25 June 1951, RG 59, 735.00, NA; Dearborn to Warren, 8 June 1951, RG 59, 735.00, NA; Mann to Messersmith, 22 March 1952, RG 59, Records of the Deputy Assistant Secretaries of State for Inter-American Affairs, 1945–1956, NA.

18. "Socialist Bulletin," May 1950, RG 59, 735.00, NA; see also US Embassy Monthly Summary, 18 September 1950, RG 59, 735.00, NA; Griffis to Miller, 20 July 1950, RG 59, 611.35, NA; M. Rapoport and C. Spiguel, *Estados Unidos y el peronismo: La política norteamericana en la Argentina, 1949–1955* (Buenos Aires, 1994), 87–93.

19. Messersmith to Braden, 20 August 1946, RG 59, 835.75, NA; Dearborn to Tewksbury, Woodward, Daniels, and Armour, 13 May 1948, RG 59, 711.35, NA; see also Pitts to Secretary of State, 13 May 1948, RG 59, 835.504, NA; J. Fodor, "Argentina's Nationalism: Myth or Reality?" in *The Political Economy of Argentina, 1946–1983,* ed. G. Di Tella and R. Dornbusch (Pittsburgh, 1989), 31–53.

20. Griffis to Miller, 1 August 1950, enclosure 1, RASS; Miller to Griffis, 5 August 1950, RASS; Dearborn Memorandum, 29 December 1950, RASS; Griffis to Miller, 31 August 1950, RASS; see also *Review of the River Plate,* 8 February 1946, 9.

21. Miller to Griffis, 5 August 1950, RASS.

22. *Democracia,* 17 December 1952, 1–3; Perón dismissed the threat posed by Argentine communism as irrelevant, as he "could stamp it out at a moment's notice." Flack to Secretary of State, 4 November 1947, RG 59, 724.35, NA.

23. Pool to Secretary of State, 21 December 1950, RG 59, 735.00, NA; *El Líder,* 29 December 1950, 1; Griffis to Miller, 31 August 1950, RASS; Griffis to Miller, 7 August 1950, RG 59, NA, RASS.

24. Norweb to Secretary of State, 10 July 1947, RG 59, 735.37, NA; see also A. Cafiero, *La política exterior Peronista, 1946–1955: sobre la falacia del "mito aislacionista"*

(Buenos Aires, 1996), 40–41; G. J. Dorn, "Perón's Gambit: The United States and the Argentine Challenge to the Inter-American Order, 1946–1948," *Diplomatic History* 26 (winter 2001): 8–9.

25. Cabot to Secretary of State, 9 January 1946, RG 84, Buenos Aires, NA.
26. *Boletín Latinoamericano de la C.G.T. Argentina,* January 1952; *Boletín Latinoamericano de la C.G.T. Argentina,* September 1952; Tittmann Memorandum, 13 September 1948, RG 59, 611.35, NA.
27. Although the book bore no publisher's mark, date, or author's name, US Embassy personnel concluded that due to the content, blue and white cover, and high quality paper, it was of Argentine origin. *El principio del fin: Latinoamerica despierta,* 1–76; Shaw to Secretary of State, 15 July 1952, RG 59, 611.35, NA.
28. Primer Congreso Nacional de Periodistas, *La verdad periodística y la prensa amarilla* (Buenos Aires, 1951), 14–45; Peronists also argued that what they deemed to be the "extreme left-wing press," including newspapers such as the *Daily Worker, New Republic,* and the *Chicago Sun* were essentially under Braden's control. Through this propaganda network, Peronist diplomats argued, Braden had managed to turn US public opinion against Argentina. Drago to Bramulgia, 6 December 1946, AMREC, EEUU 1946, Caja 8, Expediente 1; see also Luti to Ivanissevich, 11 June 1946, AMREC, EEUU 1946, 8, 1.
29. Romualdi, "Perón's Anti-American Network," Serafino Romualdi Papers, Archives of the International Ladies Garment Workers Union, Cornell University, 5459/11/11.
30. Kyne and Schwarz Report, 27 October 1949, James Carey Papers, Walter Reuther Archives of Urban and Labor History, Wayne State University, Detroit, Michigan; Rios Marmol a Bramulgia, 31 August 1948, AMREC, Bolivia 1948, 1, 2; Buitrago Carrillo, Memorandum, 28 November 1947, AMREC, Bolivia 1947, 1,2.
31. Esparue Memorandum, 16 October 1948, AMREC, Bolivia, 1, 1; see also Torcuato di Tella's analyses of these groups and movements, especially "Populismo y reformismo" in *Populismo y contradicciones de clase en Latinoamérica* (Buenos Aires, 1973), 58–70; and *Sociología de los procesos políticos* (Buenos Aires, 1985). Peruvian diplomats believed that Perón supported the Colorados not because of any philosophical common ground, but merely as a means to punish their rivals, the Blancos, for their ardent support of Braden. Rada a Ministro, 8 April 1946, AMRE, Lima, 5-1-Y/70; Rada a Ministro, 26 April 1946, AMRE, Lima, 5-1-Y/79.
32. Oderigo to Bramulgia, 21 March 1947, AMREC, Peru 1947, 12, 10; Oderigo to Bramulgia, 16 September 1947, AMREC, Peru 1947, 12, 1; Memoria Anual, 1947, AMREC, Peru 1947, 12, 5; Dorn, "Perón's Gambit," 18–19.
33. "Memoria anual," 1947, AMREC, Peru 1947, 12, 5; "Memoria Año 1949," undated, AMREC, Peru 1949, 28, 5.
34. Donnelly to Secretary, 10 June 1946, RG 84, Lima, NA; Oderigo a Bramulgia, 16 September 1947, AMREC, Peru 1947, 12, 1.
35. Memoria anual, 1947, AMREC, Peru 1947, 12, 5; Broderick to Donnelly, 19 June 1946, RG 84, Lima, NA.
36. Rios Marmol a Bramulgia, 31 August 1948, AMREC, Bolivia 1948, 1, 2; Buitrago Carrillo, Memorandum, 28 November 1947, AMREC, Bolivia 1947, 1, 2; Flack to Messersmith, 20 August 1946, RG 84, Buenos Aires, NA; Adam to Secretary of State, 1 May 1946, RG 59, 724.35, NA.
37. Foianini, "El libro azul y Bolivia," 27 February 1946, AMREC, Bolivia 1946, 1, 1; Flack to Secretary of State, 15 November 1946, RG 84, NA, Buenos Aires; "Memorandum sobre la situación de Bolivia," undated, AMREC, Bolivia 1946, 1, 1, Anexo II, Parte 1; Buitrago Carrillo, Memorandum, 28 November 1947, AMREC, Bolivia 1947, 1, 2.
38. Bowers to Secretary of State, 23 April 1946, RG 59, 625.3531, NA; Dearborn to Tewksbury, 23 December 1947, RG 59, Office of American Republics Affairs,

MRIC, Argentina, NA; Bowers to Secretary of State, 14 June 1945, Claude Bowers MSS II, Lilly Library, University of Indiana, Bloomington, Indiana; see also M. Rapoport, *Política y diplomacia en la Argentina: Las relaciones con EE.UU. y la URSS* (Buenos Aires, 1986), 24–28.

39. *Periódico Semanal de la C.G.T.,* 16 January 1947, Rollo 5, FSR; see also S. Romualdi, *Presidents and Peons* (New York, 1970); 52–53; Page, *Perón,* 176–81.

40. *Periódico Semanal de la C.G.T.,* 16 January 1947, Rollo 5, FSR; *Periódico Semanal de la C.G.T.,* 1 July 1946, Rollo 5, FSR; *Periódico Semanal de la C.G.T.,* 16 January 1947, Rollo 5, FSR; *El Trabajador de Carne*, January 1948, Rollo 55, FSR.

41. Ferrer, "Informe sobre el movimiento huelgista ocurrido en los EE.UU. desde 1940 a 1945," AMREC, EEUU 1946, 8, 3; Merle, "Nuevas actividades de John L. Lewis después de su derrota en la AFL," 11 December 1947, AMREC, EEUU 1946, 6, 50; Donoghue to Secretary of State, 22 January 1947, RG 59, 835.5043, NA; Messersmith to Braden, 30 August 1946, RG 59, 835.5043, NA.

42. Hoyt to Braden, Briggs, Trueblood, and Lyon, 13 January 1947, RG 59, MRIC, Argentina, NA.

43. Unsigned Memorandum, 16 August 1948, Carey Collection, AULH; Kyne and Schwarz, 27 October 1949, Carey Collection, AULH; Michanowski to Byrnes, 2 July 1945, James Byrnes Papers, Clemson University, Greenville, South Carolina; Jacob Potofsky Press Release, 19 January 1945, Carey Collection, AULH; Swayze to Mulliken, 13 November 1946, RG 59, 835.5043, NA.

44. Romualdi, "Anti-Americanism in the Americas," Romualdi Papers, 5459/11/11; *Periódico Semanal de la C.G.T.,* 16 March 1947, Rollo 5, FSR; they were to some extent correct. The major complaint of both the AFL and the CIO against Perón was that he had rendered the CGT subservient to the state. Ironically, the AFL delegation in Argentina reported directly the US embassy, while the CIO's George Michanowski phoned Braden's home four times in one day to determine "what should be done" with regard to the CGT invitation. Braden to Briggs, Mann, and Spaeth, 27 August 1946, RG 59, 835.5043, NA.

45. Juan Bramulgia, Luis Gay, and the CGT quoted in Fayt, *Naturaleza de peronismo,* 141–42, 148.

46. Torres a Ministro, 10 April 1946, AMREC, Bolivia 1946, 1, 1.

47. Norweb to Secretary of State, 10 July 1947, RG 59, 735.37, NA; Post to Secretary of State, 15 October 1952, RG 59, 611.35, NA.

48. Johnson to Secretary of State, 9 October 1951, RG 59, 611.35, NA; Donovan to Secretary of State, 9 October 1952, RG 59, 611.35, NA.

49. Garland a Ministro, 7 June 1946, AMRE, Lima, 5-7-Y/35; Cooper to Secretary, 28 March 1947, RG 84, Lima, NA; Ledgard a Ministro, 10 March 1947, AMRE, Lima, 5-1-A/117; see also Garland a Ministro, 30 December 1946, AMRE, Lima, 5-7-Y/65; Correa a Ministro, 23 December 1946, AMRE, Lima, 5-4-Y/50; Correa a Ministro, 29 December 1946, AMRE, Lima, 5-4-Y/52; Correa a Ministro, 2 January 1947, AMRE, Lima, 5-4-Y/1.

50. Correa a Ministro, 29 December 1946, AMRE, Lima, 5-4-Y/52.

51. Echecopar a Ministro, 3 February 1949, AMRE, Lima, 5-1-Y/5; Echecopar a Ministro, 18 January 1949, AMRE, Lima, 5-1-A/18.

52. *La Jornada,* cited in Ackerman to Secretary, 9 June 1947, RG 59, 823.00, NA.

53. Donnelly to Secretary, 10 June 1946, RG 84, Lima, NA; see also Oderigo a Bramulgia, 16 September 1947, AMREC, Peru 1947, 12, 1; Oderigo a Bramulgia, 21 March 1947, AMREC, Peru 1947, 12, 1.

54. Kreig to Secretary of State, 9 October 1952, RG 59, 611.35, NA.

55. State Department Memorandum, "Propaganda Campaign of the Argentine Government," 26 August 1952, RG 59, 735.00, NA.

56. Norweb to Secretary of State, 10 July 1947, RG 59, 735.37, NA; González, "Informaciones políticas," 26 October 1949, AMREC, DP, Bolivia 1949, 1, 1; Bernbaum to Secretary of State, 1 August 1947, RG 84, Buenos Aires, NA; Romualdi, "Perón's Anti-American Network," Romualdi Papers, 5459/11/11.

57. Simmons to Secretary of State, 13 December 1946, RG 59, 625.3531, NA.

58. Luti to Cooke, 30 January 1946, AMREC, EEUU 1946, 2, 2.

59. Griffis to Miller, 1 August 1950, RASS; Cabot to Secretary of State, 9 January 1946, RG 84, NA; State Department Memorandum, "Propaganda Campaign of the Argentine Government," 26 August 1952, RG 59, 735.00/82652, NA; Memorandum of Conversation, Miller, Nufer, Mann, Spalding, Fishburn, Atwood, Bennett, Randolph, and Dearborn, 23 June 1952, RG 59, 611.35, NA.

60. Rapoport and Spiguel, *Estados Unidos y el peronismo,* 161–80.

61. E. Laclau, *Politics and Ideology in Marxist Theory: Capitalism-Fascism-Populism* (London, 1977).

62. V. Palermo, "The Origins of Menemismo," in *Peronism and Argentina,* ed. J. Brennan, 149; see also A. Busso, "Menem y los Estados Unidos: un nuevo rumbo en la política exterior Argentina," in *La política exterior de Argentina del gobierno de Menem* (Rosario, 1994), 53–109.

Chapter 3

PATRIOTISM AND PETROLEUM
Anti-Americanism in Venezuela
from Gómez to Chávez

Darlene Rivas

Upon his election in 1998, Venezuelan President Hugo Chávez proclaimed a Bolivarian Revolution, identifying his policies with the legacy of the legendary Venezuelan hero and South American liberator, Simón Bolívar. Bolívar's legacy is subject to a variety of interpretations. To Chávez, Bolívar represented social equality and freedom for the poor and oppressed, as well as an independent foreign policy free from colonialism. References to this legacy appeared frequently in Chávez's rhetoric, including Bolívar's assertion that "the United States of North America seems destined by providence to plague America with misery on behalf of freedom."[1]

Chávez's perceived hostility to the United States gained attention, particularly in the wake of increased sensitivity to anti-Americanism after the terrorist attacks of 11 September 2001. To some international observers, Chávez appeared as a populist, using anti-American rhetoric in his bid to maintain political power by appealing to Venezuela's poor. Domestic conflict roiled Venezuela as Chávez challenged entrenched interests, including business and media leaders as well as the Confederation of Venezuelan Workers for the national petroleum corporation, Venezuelan Petroleum. Chávez identified his opponents as "fascist oligarchs" obeying "foreign masters."[2] As for his foreign policy, commentators and political pundits labeled it anti-American. Most egregiously, Chávez strengthened ties with US enemies, primarily Cuba's Fidel Castro (to whom he sold cut-rate oil), Iraq's Saddam Hussein, Libya's Muammar Qadafi, and, allegedly, narcotraffickers in Colombia. He led efforts to pursue multilateral arrange-ments designed to challenge US-dominated economic and political institutions, for example, by reinvigorating the Organization of Pe-troleum Exporting Countries (OPEC) and proposing a Humanitarian Fund for Latin America, an Andean alliance, and even a direct alter-native to the US-sponsored Free Trade Area of the Americas.[3]

The administration of George W. Bush implicitly acknowledged its agreement with this assessment of the anti-American character of Chávez's administration by leaping to approve an aborted coup against Chávez in 2002. Embarrassed, the administration then pro-claimed a "neutral" stance, supporting a democratic solution to in-ternal dissent in Venezuela by backing opposition efforts to hold a recall election. After a passionate speech in which Chávez angrily denounced President Bush, the "imperialist leader," for death and chaos in Iraq, Roger Noriega, assistant secretary of state for Western Hemisphere affairs, warned, "We obviously want to maintain normal relations, but it is difficult when [Chávez] continues in his very neg-ative . . . and irresponsible declarations about my country."[4] Anti-Americanism in Venezuela, the fifth largest petroleum exporter in the world and a country with the largest proven reserves of conven-tional oil in the Western Hemisphere, had the attention of foreign policy leaders in the United States.

This essay places Chávez's anti-Americanism in historical per-spective. While in some respects Chávez's Bolivarian revolution rep-resented a new phenomenon in Venezuela, his anti-Americanism also reflected traditional ambivalence toward the United States. Observ-ers noted that Chávez's actual policies belied his rhetoric, as petro-leum continued to flow to the United States, and he agreed to submit to the recall vote under international pressure. Despite Chávez's flir-tation with Castro, he did not follow a Cuban model of isolation from the United States. He encouraged private investment, particularly in the oil sector, and continued payment of the national debt (despite suggestions he might end these payments to relieve the poor). Al-though Chávez criticized U.S. policy in Iraq and denounced what he saw as efforts to undermine his government, he often deliberately personalized his antagonism by singling out President Bush and his administration as the culprits. To Chávez, it was the "cowboy" who pursued damaging policies in Iraq and failed to protect Americans in the wake of the devastating hurricane Katrina in September 2005. At a speech in Manhattan in September 2005, Chávez apologized for mistakes and claimed that "I tend to respond to any official from the government of Mr. Bush who verbally attacks Venezuela" and insisted "I love the people of the United States."[5] While his rhetoric was without question anti-American, his policies reflected an acceptance that even his Bolivarian Revolution required some accommodation with the United States.

This ambivalence is rooted in history. Anti-Americanism in Venezuela has occurred in the context of a political culture shaped by a shadow even more overwhelming than that of Bolívar—that of petroleum. In the twentieth century Venezuela developed a petroleum export-based political economy that brought close ties to the United States. The ever present foreign (mostly US) corporations fostered an almost constant static hum of anti-imperialist rhetoric and bolstered Venezuelan policies and attitudes designed to promote national identity and control over resources. Anti-imperialism in the Venezuelan context often did not mean challenging US power in general, even by members of the extreme left. Rather it meant confronting dangerous foreign economic concentrations that were tools of empire. Venezuelans came to believe that the nation, through the state, could and must protect Venezuelan interests by containing, yet not rejecting, large-scale foreign corporate interests, since a broad consensus held that the nation needed foreign capital to keep the petroleum industry productive. Petroleum revenues would finance state efforts to diversify the economy and advance social welfare. Given these conditions, anti-imperialist rhetoric was persistent while anti-American policies and popular responses were sporadic. Venezuelans often made distinctions between constant nationalist/anti-imperialist positions that advanced national interests and more threatening anti-US stances. In general, the US government and even petroleum companies understood this distinction. Still, dependence on US markets and frustration with specific elements of US foreign policy led to occasional, sometimes violent anti-American eruptions, often directed at representatives who symbolized American interests. When such anti-Americanism in Venezuela peaked, it did so at moments of intense domestic conflict in Venezuela and during periods of intense global anti-Americanism.

This chapter explores several cases of anti-Americanism in Venezuelan history to illuminate the tension between nationalism/anti-imperialism and anti-Americanism. In particular, it examines early responses to Nelson Rockefeller and his involvement in Venezuela, the angry reaction to Richard Nixon's visit in 1958, and the turbulence of the 1960s, culminating in violence prior to Rockefeller's planned trip to Venezuela as Nixon's emissary on a Latin American tour in 1969. Each of these cases represents bursts of anti-Americanism directed at individuals who represented the United States. Because I argue that the political culture of Venezuela has been anti-imperialist yet not predominantly anti-American, the essay places these events in the context of the development of national control over petroleum and partisan politics.

Venezuela's dependence on foreign capital emerged in the 1920s. US involvement in Venezuela grew dramatically after World War I, when US corporate interests participated in developing the oil industry. Companies such as British- and Dutch-owned Shell, Gulf Oil, and Standard Oil of Indiana—replaced at the end of the decade by Standard Oil of New Jersey—pursued concessions in oil-rich and politically friendly Venezuela. These years coincided with the dictatorial rule of Juan Vicente Gómez, a shrewd and determined leader who kept a tight rein on local opposition and a looser one on foreign oil companies. In fact, when multinational corporations shifted from Mexican to Venezuelan production in the 1920s, they did so in part because productivity of Mexican fields was declining and because political circumstances and anti-Americanism there made expansion difficult. With lower production costs than Mexico and, unlike Mexico, little internal market for petroleum, Venezuela emerged as a significant exporter.[6] By 1929, Venezuela was the second largest producer of petroleum in the world and the biggest exporter. Seventy-six percent of export earnings came from petroleum, and the government increasingly depended on revenue from the petroleum sector.[7]

The repressive Gómez permitted limited expressions of anti-Americanism primarily to increase his leverage in negotiations with the companies. Popular expressions of anti-American sentiment grew as US-based oil companies brought Americans to Venezuela, along with their customs, religion, and ways of thinking. The early concentration of American influence in the oil region around Lake Maracaibo, and later in the capital of Caracas, and the segregation of corporate officials from Venezuelan life bred resentment. Perhaps the most dramatic expressions of anti-Americanism were the attacks with poison darts thrown by Motilón Indians at oil workers. Indian attacks killed three employees—one Venezuelan, and two from the United States—of American Standard Oil of New Jersey. Written expressions of anti-Americanism focused on the disruption of agriculture, increasing racial tensions (due in part to the preference of the Americans for black laborers from the West Indies), and the physical and human consequences of drilling, as oil polluted the lake and conflicts between oil workers and Indians led to the killing of some natives.[8]

In an important sense, this anti-Americanism fostered the growth of Venezuelan nationalism. As historian Judith Ewell explains, "increased contact with United States citizens and business, added to

Gómez's authoritarian centralization, contributed to a stronger sense of Venezuelan national identity."[9] Gómez's authoritarian system incubated nationalist leaders, especially among university students who faced arrest and exile after criticism of his regime. Known as the generation of 1928, future politicians such as Jóvito Villalba, Rómulo Betancourt, and others would shape the political landscape for decades after Gómez died in 1935.

Anti-imperialist sentiment surged after Gómez's death. The relaxation of repression resulted in a release of pent-up tension, directed largely at the beneficiaries of his patronage and the idea that he had been more generous with foreigners than with Venezuelans. Mobs attacked Gómez family properties, and in the oil fields, workers also targeted the foreign-owned petroleum companies. After restoring order, President Eleazar López Contreras (1935–1941) used this popular sentiment, plus a wave of anti-imperialist rhetoric in Congress and the press, to support efforts to increase the Venezuelan share of oil wealth. Venezuelans hoped to use petroleum profits to "sow the oil," that is, to diversify the economy and improve social conditions. The 1936 Labor Law, which primarily benefited petroleum workers, required that companies allow collective bargaining and improve conditions, such as housing and health care. López Contreras's February Program was designed to improve the social and economic well-being of Venezuelans and also showed his skillful use of radio to rally popular support. As a small scale "New Deal," these moves gained the approval of the US embassy and the Franklin Roosevelt administration. López Contreras's success occurred in part due to changing international circumstances, namely, the nationalization of Mexican petroleum and Roosevelt's Good Neighbor Policy.[10]

Yet, dependent on demand in the international market for petroleum and upon foreign investors to develop and market the oil that was now the overwhelming basis of the national income, vulnerable Venezuela acted cautiously to "sow the oil." Overproduction (largely from East Texas) characterized the early years of the decade; the late 1930s and the early 1940s brought disruptions of the international market due to war. By the late 1930s, ninety percent of the value of Venezuelan exports came from oil. National leaders understood their dependence on markets in the United States. They also understood that, in a sense, the multinational petroleum companies were their allies in the face of challenges by independent oil producers and the US Congress to restrict petroleum imported to the United States.[11] Such concerns resulted in limits to Venezuela's demands on the oil companies. López Contreras also hedged radical demands by repressing a petroleum workers' strike and outlawing the Communist Party.

The communist left contributed to the growth of anti-imperialism in the 1930s, but a radical critique against foreign investment in petroleum never made much headway. This was true despite growing influence after 1931 of the Communist Party, which was legalized (briefly) in 1935. Repression of the party contributed to this lack. More significantly, the party divided often over the issue of alignment with international Communism, and many Venezuelan communists also agreed on the need for foreign investment in petroleum. Also, by the late 1930s the left's concerns over fascism and the consequent Popular Front strategy reduced the potential for vociferous anti-American sentiment.[12]

One communist, Rómulo Betancourt, left the party and emerged as a key nationalist, anticommunist figure in twentieth-century Venezuelan politics.[13] By the late 1930s, Betancourt's writings, disseminated through the periodical *Ahora,* included detailed suggestions for strengthening agriculture, diversifying industry, improving education and healthcare, and reforming politics, yet held surprisingly few complaints against Americans or US policy. There were some. When Nelson Rockefeller, grandson of Standard Oil founder John D. Rockefeller, traveled to Venezuela, Betancourt rebuked him as "Johnny Ten Cents" (a reference to John D. Rockefeller's habit of handing out dimes) who came to Venezuela claiming to want to help the poor but who left the nation no better off.[14] Betancourt also castigated the "imperialist" petroleum corporations. However, he praised Roosevelt's New Deal and Good Neighbor Policy. He believed that Venezuela needed to negotiate more advantageous terms with the oil companies, yet he argued specifically that nationalization was not a viable option in Venezuela. Even after nationalization, as in Mexico, foreign capital was necessary.[15] Despite his nationalism, Betancourt was keenly aware that Venezuelans "were hanging by the single thread of oil."[16]

Meanwhile, the multinationals that dominated the petroleum industry in Venezuela responded with mixed results to the growing anti-imperialist chorus. In part, they answered charges of imperialism by developing welfare capitalism. They generally complied with Venezuelan labor laws, for example, by building roads, housing, and hospitals. But the companies challenged the government's attempts to recover taxes by taking their cases to the Supreme Court (which often ruled in their favor) and actively hindered union organizing efforts. They successfully resisted Venezuelan proposals to build refineries in the country. The companies' continued investment in technological improvements and new drilling served to keep Venezuela competitive, thus satisfying Venezuelan government demands for ongoing revenues. Their continued resistance ensured ongoing anti-imperialist sentiment.

During this period of rising mass politics, limited welfare capitalism, and yearnings for economic diversification, a symbol of American imperialism emerged on the Venezuelan scene. Nelson Rockefeller, grandson of John D. Rockefeller, Sr., the consummate imperialist in Venezuelan eyes, acquired stock in the Venezuelan subsidiary of Standard Oil of New Jersey, Creole Petroleum, in 1935. When he visited the country for the first time in 1937, Venezuelan officials and Creole company personnel made sure that Rockefeller met the president, the entire cabinet, and at least four state governors. For Rockefeller, it was the beginning of a lifelong relationship with Venezuela and its people.[17]

Anti-imperialism and anti-Americanism made an impression on the young Rockefeller. He made connections between the two, which he believed might threaten American corporate interests and US interests in general if foreign firms ignored the social consequences of their presence. He articulated grave concerns with the segregation between Venezuelans and Americans in the oil industry and with the appalling conditions outside the walls of the oil compounds, where migrants in search of work lived in squalid conditions. Rockefeller encouraged Creole Petroleum managers to provide for workers' welfare and promoted corporate efforts to "sow the oil," approving Creole-built roads designed to make transport of food to cities less expensive and providing agricultural technical assistance to the government.

"Johnny Ten Cents" proved only a minor target for anti-American sentiment in the 1930s. The charismatic Rockefeller projected friendship. He learned Spanish and gave hearty *abrazos* to Venezuelan campesinos and labor leaders, as well as the social elite. Impressed by the possibilities of Venezuelan economic development through non-petroleum-related ventures, Rockefeller started a development company, which foundered with the outbreak of World War II. The company built the Hotel Ávila, the first luxury hotel in Caracas, but Rockefeller axed another major project, a comprehensive supermarket, in part because of concerns that it would lead to Venezuelan criticism of unfair competition.

Rockefeller soon busied himself with the project of improving inter-American relations, serving in the Roosevelt administration as coordinator of inter-American affairs (1940–1945) and assistant secretary of state for inter-American affairs (1945), while some of his associates, such as Robert Bottome and William Coles, stayed in Venezuela. They invested in business enterprises, raised families, and socialized with both the American colony and members of the Venezuelan business elite. Bottome was particularly integrated into the Venezuelan social elite through his marriage to Margot Boulton. Increasingly, members of the so-called American colony in Venezuela mingled with Venezuelans in ways that they had not done during the Gómez years. As the Venezuelan social elite embraced the Americans, the potential for anti-Americanism among them correspondingly decreased.

Pan-American solidarity reached a high point during World War II. This environment limited expressions of anti-Americanism. Venezuelans complained about restrictions on imports during the war years, but generally appreciated that these were lean times around the world. Some Venezuelans, like the Bloehm family of German background, were affected by the US-proclaimed list that targeted firms with potential Axis ties. The presence of US troops stationed in Venezuela to protect the oil fields concerned some critics, who compared their presence to that of the Marines who had occupied Caribbean nations in the early twentieth century. Others, however, welcomed the US presence. Margot Boulton, connected to the prominent Boulton and Uslar Pietri families, feared Germany might attack Venezuela to disrupt petroleum production and thus welcomed improved US-Venezuelan relations. Boulton contributed to closer ties to the United States with the 1941 creation of the *Centro de Información Cultural Venezolano Americano* (Venezuelan-American Cultural Information Center, later the Venezuelan American Center).[18]

Still, Venezuelan nationalism proceeded despite pan-American feeling. In 1943, President Isaías Medina Angarita (1941–1945) stirred the pot of popular opinion to Venezuelan advantage through the Petroleum Law. Medina took his anti-imperialist case to the people. The US embassy estimated that some fifty thousand people attended one public speech Medina made in Caracas.[19] Medina got what he wanted. The petroleum law consolidated previous conflicting petroleum legislation, reissuing concessions under a single set of rules. It authorized the government to receive higher royalties from petroleum profits. Critics in Congress, such as Juan Pablo Pérez Alfonso, disparaged the measure because it essentially gave amnesty to corporations accused of wrongdoing. The Communist Party of Venezuela (PCV), legalized by Medina, praised the law as advancing the national interest.[20] The Roosevelt administration, buoyed by the Good Neighbor ethos and the need to keep petroleum production high, encouraged the petroleum companies to concede to Medina. To the larger companies and the US government, the measure was nationalist, not anti-American.

Popular opinion, though, was clearly of increasing importance. Toward the end of the war, increased optimism about the prospects for social and economic change buoyed social democrats across the region, including in Venezuela. Pressure for a more open political process (the Venezuelan president was chosen by the Venezuelan senate) and for social and economic reforms financed by petroleum revenues grew in anticipation of the war's end. In general, the Roosevelt and then Truman administrations welcomed calls for greater democracy and did not appear threatened by increasingly open politics, which could mean greater criticism of US interests. In summer 1945, the US embassy, for example, made distinctions between then-political organizer/journalist Rómulo Betancourt's criticism of US-owned companies and anti-Americanism. Prior to a Betancourt visit to the United States, the embassy reported that his organization, Democratic Action (AD) was a "leftist, anti-administration, but also anti-Communist party which has not yet attained great political strength." Moreover, "in his writing and speeches he has shown himself violently critical of United States oil interests and other United States influence in Venezuela. However, he is considered more nationalistic, and anti-big business and foreign corporations, than anti-United States."[21]

Shortly thereafter, Betancourt and other such nationalists led the country as Venezuela entered a three-year period known as the *trienio.* In October 1945, Medina was toppled in a coup led by an alliance of young military officers and the leaders of the increasingly popular AD. The provisional Junta, led by Betancourt, promised a program of economic, social, and political reforms. Although widely perceived as populist because of its sympathy to labor and peasants, AD made special efforts to appeal to the elite of Venezuela by including leading citizens on a newly created Economic Council. The Junta by decree enforced a 50-50 revenue sharing plan they claimed was based on the Petroleum Law of 1943, but took care to assure the multinational corporations that they would discourage strikes and promote continued petroleum production by the companies. AD's foreign policy showed some independence but was hardly anti-American. The government opposed dictators that the US supported, severing Venezuelan relations with Spain, with Anastasio Somoza's Nicaragua, and Rafael Trujillo's Dominican Republic. Most anti-American and anti-imperialist rhetoric from AD accompanied their attempts to create a merchant marine, the *Flota Gran Colombia,* to compete with US-owned shipping.[22]

Some members of the American colony viewed AD policy as anti-American, in part because they could not forget or forgive Betancourt's earlier ties to communists and worried over his encouragement of labor organization. William F. Buckley, owner of Pantepec Oil, one of the smaller independent oil firms in Venezuela, was such a critic.

He had fretted about the 1943 law, complaining that the Venezuelan and US governments had cooperated to compel the companies to agree to its terms. As for AD during the *trienio,* Buckley was sure the party was communist-influenced, claiming that AD politicians "have used the vast dollar resources of the country to further Russian Communistic interests in the Western Hemisphere, and they have forced American capital to provide the money for this anti-American campaign."[23]

But representatives of the larger petroleum companies such as Creole, along with the American embassy and State Department, understood that AD policies were not hostile and that the government generally accepted the need for foreign, meaning largely US, investment in petroleum.[24] After all, the Venezuelan government enjoyed revenue six times greater in 1948 than in 1942, income it needed to carry out its ambitious agenda.

AD leaders saw themselves as staunch anti-imperialists. Yet AD soon received condemnation for opening a door to imperialism, for the government's acceptance of the so-called Rockefeller Plan. AD had development plans and petroleum revenues to finance them, but in the aftermath of World War II, US priorities of European recovery limited available supplies of items such as food and machinery. A rapidly growing population and long-term neglect of agriculture had made Venezuela highly dependent on food imports. Eager to increase the food supply as soon as possible and to develop Venezuelan agriculture, AD leaders negotiated a deal with Rockefeller, who hoped to spur development of what he called the "basic economy" of Venezuela through two new organizations. One, which generated little opposition, was the American International Association, a non-profit organization modeled after the US agricultural extension service and the New Deal's Farm Security Administration to provide technical assistance to small farmers and to improve health and nutrition. The other organization, the Venezuela Basic Economy Corporation (VBEC), designed to develop the food supply, proved a target of economic nationalist sentiment, even though it was formed with joint Venezuelan state and US private capital. VBEC subsidiaries, such as farms and supermarkets, provoked a backlash from Venezuelan commercial interests threatened by competition and from political opponents of AD.[25]

To established commercial interests, Rockefeller's wholesale company and chain of supermarkets (CADA) seemed to represent powerful and abusive trusts along the lines of the legendary Standard Oil. The Commercial Employers' Association opposed CADA because "a competitor like Rockefeller, with international political influence, with power to influence transportation of all kinds, with possibilities of investing millions even at risk of loss, cannot be resisted by *criollo* [Venezuelan] commerce."[26] A member of the Wholesale Trade Corporation worried, "Rockefeller can, with his immense means, with his planes, with his ships" provision the market cheaply, but the cost would be "the ruin of thousands of Venezuelans and the domination of the markets by foreign capital."[27] Even the conservative *Ultimas Noticias* editorialized that the government and the Wholesale Trade Corporation could supply the government without the help of foreign capital.[28] Since VBEC's farms and fishing company posed no threat to Venezuelan economic interests, little was said about Rockefeller's involvement in them.

Meanwhile, AD's political opponents charged that AD had embraced an imperialist Dracula, potentially capable of sucking Venezuela's lifeblood. In particular these sentiments were voiced by Jóvito Villalba, a member of the Generation of 1928, who had founded a leftist political party, the Democratic Republican Union (URD), and by members of the Communist Party. In a congressional debate on the Rockefeller Plan, political opponents variously called Rockefeller a gangster and a phantom as well as a blood-thirsty Dracula.[29] URD representative Alfredo Tarre Murzi told the story of John D. Rockefeller as robber baron, focusing on the rise of Standard Oil as a monopoly consuming its competitors. Nelson Rockefeller and his associates were "the inheritors of this international filibusterer," and the government was placing "the exploitation of agriculture, of livestock, of fish, and that which is most grave, the distribution and importation of food" in the hands of these dangerous men.[30] Villalba repeated this connection, calling Rockefeller "the incarnation of the financial forces that most gravely threaten us."[31] Despite avowals by AD representatives of their ability to contain Rockefeller through their deal with him, which required partial ownership of VBEC companies by the government-owned Venezuelan Development Corporation and called for increasing Venezuelan capitalization of the companies, Communist leader Juan Bautista Fuenmayor suggested such maneuvers with Rockefeller were like "boxing with Joe Louis."[32] The opponent was fully capable of a knock-out blow.

Betancourt, the party leader, had used similar tactics in the late 1930s, identifying Rockefeller with his grandfather, the oil baron. Now he found himself defending his embrace of a symbol of imperialism. One reason his position was vulnerable was because Betancourt believed Venezuela required US investment outside of the oil sector. He saw little hope that Venezuelan capitalists would participate in AD projects to diversify the economy, which could not promise risk-free, high returns on investments. "Compared with the Rockefellers, Morgans, Duponts, or the Deterdings, our capitalists are pygmies," he had earlier proclaimed. According to Betancourt, Venezuelan capitalists preferred to invest in commercial and real estate ventures guaranteed to succeed, rather than take risks in undeveloped areas of the economy, or "productive" investments.[33] Such views were common among Venezuela's political leaders.[34]

Betancourt was confident in Rockefeller's welfare capitalism and the conditions negotiated by the government, but many Venezuelans (including members of AD) were not. Sensitive to the dangers of imperialism, they feared that the oil companies' participation with Rockefeller and the Venezuelan Development Corporation opened the door for control of other aspects of the Venezuelan economy. Given other examples of US corporate investment, such as United Fruit's domination of Central American economies, such concerns resonated, even while they exaggerated Rockefeller's power. Ironically, Venezuelan nationalism and anti-imperialism had created conditions that insured that foreign investors, interested in gaining access to Venezuela, were more bound to act in what Betancourt defined as socially responsible ways than were Venezuelan interests. Venezuelans, on the other hand, could argue that it was they, as creoles, who were acting in the nation's interest, regardless of the nature of their investments.

The presidential election campaign of 1947, the first popular political election in Venezuela's history, yielded surprisingly little anti-Americanism, which was diffused in larger critiques of the AD-dominated government. Anti-imperialism was expressed primarily by communists and the URD. For example, at a colorful communist "victory parade" and rally on 5 December, led by some four hundred marching youth in red and black shirts and trousers with red berets, and including thirty-five to forty trucks and other vehicles, the main attraction was "a large truck bearing an octopus which was being killed by a worker." Each tentacle bore a label, such as "Imperialism, COPEI [the Committee of Independent Electoral Political Organization, or the Christian Democrats], *Latifundia* [large landholdings], Speculators, Petroleum Companies, Jesuits, etc." Prominent communist leaders Gustavo Machado and Juan Bautista Fuenmayor attended. According to the US Embassy, Fuenmayor "argued for agrarian reform, anti-imperialism, anti-Rockefeller . . . more schools, less university cities . . . and more houses for workers."[35] Almost a year later, observers of communist-sponsored strikes and demonstrations noted that strikers yelled "down with Yankee imperialism" and "down with [the] Rockefeller plan."[36] Verbal attacks that focused on AD's cooperation with Rockefeller fit within the anti-imperialist framework of Venezuelan rhetoric, yet they were hardly substantively anti-American (see Fig. 3.1).

Still, the communist parties did make the most significant challenges to US interests. The PCV platform called for Venezuela to "combat imperialism," nationalize the oil industry, increase state control of banking and insurance, protect Venezuelan interests in international trade, and oppose US foreign policies such as the Rio Treaty for hemispheric defense, among other things. The Progressive Republican Party, another communist party with less popular support,

Figure 3.1

Betancourt's agreements with Rockefeller led to criticism from the anti-imperialist left and right. This image portrays Betancourt as courting Yankee capitalism. *Ultimas Noticias,* 16 March 1948.

sought total revolution and attacked AD as an "instrument of Yankee imperialism."[37]

Indeed, the campaign generated relatively few anti-American appeals, and the strategy of calling AD policy imperialist proved ineffective. The US embassy reported that AD "conducted its campaign on a relatively high plane. There was no reported appeal by responsible party officials to popular prejudice by reference to the US "imperialism" or Venezuelan "colonialism."[38] The "high plane" referred to the lack of AD attacks on the United States, as the election did produce clashes, especially between supporters of AD and COPEI and strong verbal assaults on AD policy. Venezuelans overwhelmingly supported AD's candidate, the respected novelist Rómulo Gallegos, who won almost 75 percent of the vote to Caldera's 22 percent and Gustavo Machado's 3 percent (URD did not field a presidential candidate).

The military, encouraged by the political opposition and members of the elite, overthrew the Gallegos government on 24 November 1948.[39] The military junta, consisting of Lieutenant Colonels Carlos Delgado Chalbaud, Marcos Pérez Jiménez, and Felipe Llovera Páez, announced its reasons for the coup as the political turmoil of AD rule, the monopolistic control of offices by AD, its interference with the military, and its incitement to unrest of workers and peasants.[40] Villalba went further, and accused AD of trying to get US support in Venezuelan internal affairs through its agreement with Rockefeller. In contrast, he claimed URD was against "all penetration of foreign capital which does not respond to the necessities of the national economy and which menaces in an imperialistic manner the independence and development of Venezuelan industry and production."[41] Pérez Jiménez soon consolidated his control, through the arrest and political exile of AD and other opponents, the assassination of Chalbaud in 1950 (allegedly by the dictator's order), and fraudulent elections in 1952 that Villalba appeared likely to win.

Meanwhile, what Judith Ewell calls "the hydrocarbon economy and the American way of life" coalesced by the end of the 1950s. "Venezuela's new hydrocarbon society spawned a more complex group of political actors. These new actors—business associations, labor unions, industrialists, professional military officers, and middle-class professionals—often chose alliances with their counterparts, or complementary interests, in the United States over making common cause with their compatriots. . . . At the same time, many Venezuelans resisted and criticized what they perceived as the erosion of Venezuelan culture and the spread of the 'American way of life.'" Such disapproval appeared in the pages of *La Religión* in the

1950s, where Archbishop Monsignor Rafael Arías Blanco and later
Father Jesús Hernández Chapellin criticized the Protestant, materi-
alist influence wrought by the deluge of American television and
reading material that dominated Venezuelan information markets.
Such criticism made little difference as Venezuelans ate processed
foods with US brand names, celebrated Christmas with Santa Claus,
and watched films produced in Hollywood.[42]

Amid the increasing "Americanization," the seeds of ambivalent
anti-Americanism were sown in the 1950s. Proponents of democracy
resented Eisenhower's 1954 awarding of the Legion of Merit to dictator Pérez Jiménez. Ominously, US-independent oil producers renewed
efforts to reduce the flow of Venezuelan crude imported by the United
States even as Venezuelans grew increasingly concerned about competition from the Middle East. And Pérez Jiménez offered new petroleum concessions in 1956, an opening for criticism that he was soft
on US-based multinationals. On the other hand, exiles from Pérez
Jiménez's government found new allies in the United States during
the 1950s. Despite their frustration with the Legion of Merit award,
for example, AD exiles such as Betancourt knew that it was awarded
in part to appease Pérez Jiménez for the US refusal to support the
dictator's campaign to unseat the democratic leftist José Figueres of
Costa Rica. The Inter-American Association for Democracy and Freedom, made up of US and Latin American intellectuals, labor leaders,
and some Democrats, encouraged the exiles. Exiles communicated
with State Department officials, who were assured by Betancourt
that he remained staunchly anticommunist and opposed cancella-
tion of petroleum concessions. US policy was both to flatter Pérez
Jiménez and retain contact with his democratic political opposition.
Rockefeller, who maintained his business interests in Venezuela (many
of which failed), distanced himself as much as possible from the regime and kept a low profile relationship with Betancourt.[43]

To observers in the United States, 1958 brought arguably the most
traumatic single event in the history of anti-Americanism in Latin America, a violent assault on Vice President Richard Nixon's motorcade.
But to Venezuelans, the year is not remembered for anti-Americanism
but as a historical turning point. It began with the overthrow of the
dictator, and, after much turbulence and uncertainty, it ended with
the establishment of a political pact that endured until the early 1990s.
On 23 January 1958, widespread opposition to the Pérez Jiménez
dictatorship culminated in his overthrow by military officers, a group
of prominent civilians called the Patriotic Junta, and a broad array
of Venezuelans, including business elites, communists, the church,
and people in the streets. The January coup was violent, with fight-

ing on the streets and subsequent attacks on symbols of the Pérez Jiménez regime, especially his repressive and much despised security forces. Some nationalist sentiment resulted in attacks on foreigners, but they were Spanish, Portuguese, and Italians, who were seen as favoring the Pérez Jiménez regime. Little animosity was directed at Americans, and the mobs did not target the American colony. There were no attacks on American-owned businesses, including Rockefeller's supermarkets, although they did receive threatening phone calls. There was no criticism of Rockefeller or of his International Basic Economy Corporation in the press.[44]

Yet only a few months later, angry mobs attacked Nixon. Anti-Yankee feeling, it turned out, had been just under the surface as early as January. Jóvito Villalba felt obliged to assure the *New York Times* in January that, even though the United States had supported dictators, "US interests must be safeguarded," and two days later he reiterated that he had "deep amity" for the United States.[45] Venezuelan resentment of US relations with dictators intensified dramatically when the United States granted asylum to Pérez Jiménez and his reviled security chief, Pedro Estrada. Furthermore, in the heady atmosphere surrounding the fall of the dictatorship, youth activism, which had increased in the latter days of the Pérez Jiménez regime, increasingly took on an anti-American character. Some communist youth were growing frustrated by their elders' cooperation with reformist politicians. Underlying these sources of aggravation was another that brought nagging concerns. In 1957 and 1958, the US Congress introduced voluntary quotas on Venezuelan petroleum imports into the United States (see Fig. 3.2).[46]

The Eisenhower administration, hoping to stifle dissatisfaction with its Latin American policy of trade-not-aid and support for dictators, planned to send Nixon on a goodwill tour of Latin America following his attendance at the inauguration of Arturo Frondizi in Argentina. The goodwill tour began auspiciously, with friendly crowds and small protests. However, criticism and hostility toward the United States and Nixon grew, and students at San Marcos University in Lima even threw rocks at the vice president. His arrival in Caracas was set for 13 May 1958, a critical moment. Security was lacking, in part related to the transition from the dictatorship, as the hated security forces had been dismantled and the Junta had dismissed many police for firing on crowds during January protests. Elections were scheduled for December, but given recent history, their success was uncertain.

Then Nixon arrived. Soon after he and his wife, Pat, exited the plane, they were greeted by a hail of tobacco-laced spit, sprayed on

Figure 3.2

The late 1950s saw deepening resentment against the United States. Venezuelans viewed U.S. calls for friendly relations and support for their plans for social democracy as hypocritcal since they were accompanied by restrictions on petroleum to Venezuela's "first market." *Elite,* 14 June 1958.

them from a group of some five hundred protestors. Angry, Nixon still stood for the Venezuelan national anthem. The Venezuelan foreign minister, Oscar García Velatini, and twelve US secret service personnel hurried Nixon to his car. However, upon reaching Caracas, his motorcade ground to a halt. An angry crowd surrounded Nixon's vehicle, hammering it with sticks and steel bars and cracking the bullet-proof glass. A shard injured García in the eye. As the mob rocked the car back and forth, crying "Death to Nixon," the vice president restrained a secret service agent who considered using his gun. After twelve terrifying minutes, the driver finally found an opening and sped off, but Nixon and his wife, in separate cars, feared for their lives during the ordeal. Fortunately, they cancelled a planned trip to Bolívar's grave, where another crowd shredded the ceremonial wreath Nixon had planned to lay. The Nixons ended up spending the night in the American embassy.[47]

A furious Nixon lectured Venezuelan officials on the need for better security and the dangers of communist agitators, although he also acknowledged their resentment against US support of dictators. The Eisenhower administration responded by deploying airborne troops in the Caribbean, further angering Venezuelans, who saw the move as a threatened US intervention. This resentment proved wider than that of the angry crowds. The Venezuelan government demanded that Nixon deny the troop deployment, which he could not do. The press expressed outrage in editorials and cartoons. There was no need for the US military. Nixon rode back to the airport along barren streets, emptied of spectators in part through the use of tear gas. He was accompanied by Admiral Wolfgang Larrazábal, provisional president of the junta, with submachine guns, rifles, and tear gas canisters at their feet. Back home, a crowd of fifteen thousand, President Eisenhower, and the cabinet met Nixon's plane. The event resulted in much soul searching in the United States, as rising anti-Americanism befuddled a nation surprised at the vehement reaction to Nixon in Caracas.[48] While some Venezuelans expressed apologies, many others took exception to Nixon. His insistence on the communist origins of the attacks and his suggestion that Venezuela seek to extradite Pérez Jiménez seemed to minimize the sources of their resentment (see Fig. 3.3).

In Venezuela, the political pact that emerged in 1958 assured that anti-Americanism would continue its ambivalent character. The attack on Nixon strengthened the resolve of political leaders to develop a peaceful, stable, democratic system. The politicians who had returned to Venezuela in 1958, including Betancourt, Caldera, and Villalba, agreed in the Pact of Punto Fijo to reject "political cannibalism" and to work together to provide Venezuela with political options that would promote unity. They determined that Venezuela needed to follow a reformist policy that would promote gradual, nonrevolutionary change, in part based on lessons learned from the divisive politics of the *trienio*. In December elections, the staunchly anticommunist Betancourt won 47 percent of the vote, Larrazábal won 33 percent, and Caldera of COPEI won 16 percent.[49] The election confirmed popular support for change, with Betancourt's reformism and

Figure 3.3

Nixon's ill-fated Caracas trip in 1958 may have awakened the United States to the problem of anti-Americanism, but to Venezuelans, Nixon still did not "get it." *Ultimas Noticias,* 14 May 1958.

anticommunism dominating over Larrazábal's reformism but willingness to include communists in his coalition, and Caldera's more moderate Christian democracy trailing as the least popular alternative, perhaps associated as more to the right of the other choices. Venezuelans had opted for reform, not revolution, democracy, not communism, accommodation with the United States, not confrontation.

Betancourt's Venezuela soon emerged as a model of John F. Kennedy's vision for the continent, an anticommunist, anti-Castro, reformist social democracy. Betancourt's anticommunism and the inspiration of the Cuban Revolution resulted in the emergence of a guerrilla movement, which engaged in sporadic anti-US attacks. The government's criticism of "foreign" influence consisted of critiques of Cuban, not

US interference, while the US provided assistance in combating the insurgents. When President Kennedy visited Venezuela in 1961, anti-US violence did break out, but Betancourt ensured a peaceful visit by arresting possible agitators and using the military to provide security.[50]

The guerrillas, comprised of some members of the PCV and the Leftist Revolutionary Movement, a student-led splinter group from AD, formed the Armed Forces of National Liberation (FALN). They prescribed revolution for Venezuela and called for resistance against the United States as an obstacle to radical change. Their most vigorous activity was in the period 1962–1963, when they numbered as many as five hundred guerrillas and two to three hundred support personnel. The guerrillas sabotaged oil pipelines, kidnapped a Spanish soccer star, hijacked the steamer *Anzoátegui,* and stole and then returned a collection of French impressionist paintings.[51] On occasion, they hit nonpetroleum-related US targets. Guerrillas firebombed US Ambassador Theodore Moscoso's automobile in June 1961 and set off bombs at the US embassy in Caracas and the US consulate in Puerto la Cruz in 1962. On a few occasions, they attacked homes or cars of US embassy personnel and members of the US military mission. Guerrillas even kidnapped US military mission members. Each time, the US personnel remained unharmed, although one colonel suffered the indignity of being photographed in his underwear.[52] In a few cases, guerrillas targeted US-owned businesses: they bombed a Sears, Roebuck warehouse, started a fire in the Good Year tire factory, and hijacked two trucks owned by Rockefeller's CADA. Guerrillas distributed the contents of the CADA trucks in shanty towns as food "taken from the Imperialists and which belongs to the people."[53] In June 1963, at the high point of attacks on the United States, the US ambassador conferred with Betancourt over concerns about higher insurance costs.[54] Actual violence against US targets declined as the decade waned.

Betancourt's version of anticommunist nationalism proved more persuasive than the guerrillas' sporadic anti-Americanism and revolutionary option. The guerrillas did not win widespread support from Venezuelans, especially after the murder of several Caracas policemen. Venezuelans, regardless of social status, seemed to prefer Betancourt's reformism, which included labor and agrarian reform. General approval accompanied AD's nationalist policies. Venezuela's share of petroleum profits had increased to 60 percent in early 1959. The government also pursued protective measures to reduce reliance on imports, backed by growing nationalism among Venezuelan industrialists, as Venezuelan capitalists in the 1960s sought to limit US capital investment and win majority control in local ventures. A

1965 law required majority Venezuelan ownership of insurance companies, and a group of business leaders founded the Pro-Venezuela Association, which called for similar measures in other economic sectors.

Betancourt also articulated to some degree an independent foreign policy, particularly in his efforts to gain Latin American support to expel the dictatorships of Paraguay, Haiti, and Nicaragua from the Organization of American States. He was sharply critical of the US policy of exempting Canada and Mexico from petroleum quotas. Finally, his government, under the leadership of Minister of Mines Juan Pablo Pérez Alfonso, instigated talks with Arab petroleum-producing states to found OPEC. Still, Betancourt's anti-Castro stance meant general alignment with US foreign policy.

Venezuelan national politics in the 1960s reflected an anticommunist, antiguerrilla, anti-Castro consensus, with the United States an indirect issue only. Significantly, however, all the major candidates for president tended to promote state-sponsored industrialization and agrarian reform, financed by petroleum revenues. Candidates from either AD or the COPEI won every election, with AD's Raul Leoni winning in 1963 with 31 percent of the vote to Caldera's 19 percent. Anger over foreign influence was directed more at Cuba than at the United States, even after a "wave of national protest" in 1967 accompanied reports that the United States might make import restrictions permanent.[55] In 1968 AD's political rhetoric included the slogan, "Close the way to Fidel Castro in Venezuela." AD called for support for candidate Gonzalo Barrios "because he has confronted equally the anti-Venezuelan reaction and foreign communism."[56] A new political coalition, the Victory Front *(El Frente de la Victoria)*, charged COPEI's Caldera with having received money from German interests. "No Venezuelan loyal to Bolívar and his fatherland can commit the indignity of voting for a candidate who receives money from a powerful foreigner for his ostentatious company." Despite such efforts, Caldera broke the AD domination of the presidency, garnering 27 percent of the vote to Barrios's 26 percent.[57] Venezuelans voted for developmentalism, anti-Castroism, and anticommunism, which did not necessarily indicate they were pro-American, but it did mark them as fellow travelers.

Despite ongoing Venezuelan liberal developmentalist policies compatible with US priorities, the late 1960s also witnessed more anti-American incidents as criticism of US foreign policy as imperialist grew more widespread. This was particularly the case among a growing number of university students, who, like students across Europe and the Western Hemisphere including the United States, were increasingly dissatisfied with the commercialized, bureaucratized face of their societies. (Workers also participated in this criticism, except in the United States.) Buoyed by criticism of US policy in Vietnam, students increasingly faced off first against college administrators, national political and corporate elites, and, in Latin America, multinational corporations, which were viewed as part of a system of global capitalism that threatened democracy and freedom. For their part, Latin American political leaders were frustrated by what they saw as reduced interest in their welfare by the United States and were emboldened by the decline of US prestige.

Faced with Latin American criticism of US policy and the collapse of hopes for the Alliance for Progress, Richard Nixon, now president, promulgated a policy reminiscent of Eisenhower—trade rather than aid. Trying to package this change as a "new" policy, Nixon sent Nelson Rockefeller, now governor of New York, on a series of Latin American tours to solicit opinions, assess conditions, and promote goodwill. Instead, the tours were reminiscent of the worst aspects of the Nixon trip in 1958. Protests followed Rockefeller across the region, although dictatorial regimes in several countries suppressed anti-American protestors. Demonstrations targeted Rockefeller as an agent of an imperialist United States, and in some cases were accompanied by bombings of US-based multinationals such as the Bank of America and Xerox. In Argentina, fourteen of seventeen Rockefeller-owned supermarkets were bombed in a coordinated attack.[58]

Rockefeller's trip to Caracas threatened more violence, as it brought together two symbols of "US imperialism": Rockefeller and Nixon. Despite some embarrassment over the 1958 reception accorded Nixon, Venezuelans still viewed him in a harsh light. To express their displeasure after Nixon received the nomination for president in 1968, guerrillas dressed as soldiers had invaded Rockefeller's Venezuelan estate at Montesacro, stealing money and leaving behind painted revolutionary slogans.[59] Two weeks before Rockefeller was to arrive, violent student protests resulted in shooting deaths. The student wing of the FALN sent letters to the American embassy and consul in Maracaibo, insisting that the diplomats tell the "agent of Yankee imperialism" to stay away. The embassy also received reports that FALN planned to cooperate with other leftist movements in staging a large anti-Rockefeller protest and possible attacks on Rockefeller's investments in Venezuela.[60]

At first, the Caldera government continued to make plans for the visit, adjusting security measures. Nixon's announcement of trade over aid did not dismay Caldera, because Venezuela had traditionally sought to enhance trade more than aid, relying on increasing petroleum revenues to promote economic development.[61] However, Caldera could not escape the controversy over the Rockefeller visit. At press conferences in May, Caldera responded to questions about his agenda for discussions with Rockefeller and about his plans for Rockefeller's safety by reiterating his focus on increasing the petroleum trade as a means to enhance development. He expressed confidence that Venezuelans would treat the presidential envoy with dignity and respect, in a sense trying to encourage good behavior by appealing to the "Venezuelan tradition" of receiving foreign emissaries. He conveniently overlooked the reception afforded Nixon in 1958.[62] Perhaps Caldera hoped that the reaction to Rockefeller would be figurative rather than dangerous. After all, in February a group of guerrillas had declared an innocuous "symbolic seizure" of Rockefeller properties.[63]

As the scheduled visit neared, Caldera did worry, as did US representatives who relied on intelligence reports that suggested Rockefeller's visit would be a target of anti-American demonstrations. An embassy assessment in late May concluded that "student unrest, while not as dramatic as last week, continues to percolate. Rockefeller visit will provide an inviting target for leftist agitators to channel unrest into anti-US protest. . . . Hopefully, Gov [sic] determination both to protect governor Rockefeller and control demonstrations (without undue harshness) will prevent serious incidents."[64]

Faced with previsit demonstrations and violence, and unsure of the government's ability to ensure a peaceful trip, Caldera in early June "asked" Rockefeller to defer his visit. (It was soon cancelled.) For Caldera, the decision itself was not anti-American, but it avoided an anti-American outburst he could not control. When asked about his choice, he insisted that the decision was in the interest of the higher purpose of Rockefeller's travels—to enhance good relations. At a 5 June press conference, reporters aired a variety of theories regarding the decision—that it was initiated by the United States, that it showed the "debility of the national government" against the extreme left, or that it was a wise and sensible decision. A reporter for TASS, the Soviet news agency, after praising the independence and power that the decision demonstrated, suggested that perhaps the United States would retaliate with sanctions. Caldera responded forcefully that there was no reason to believe the White House "is going to take an attitude of aggression, of enmity, of attack." Caldera reiterated that his choice was not an "act of enmity," one of "independence" certainly, but also an "act of friendship."[65]

Caldera's policies were in keeping with the Venezuelan government's handling of anti-Americanism, emphasizing independence of action, friendship with the United States, and the necessity of pursuing diversified economic development through enhancing petroleum production, particularly by enhancing trade with its major market. Most likely, Caldera hoped to prevent a recurrence of the reception given Nixon, and no doubt he anticipated that Rockefeller's visit would spark an even more divisive incident, with domestic, not just international, consequences. Venezuela could ill afford to alienate the United States, the major market for its petroleum. Nor was Caldera willing to risk either fanning flames of popular protest that could turn against the government or demonstrating government weakness in the face of violence.

Rockefeller and the Nixon administration had little choice but to agree with Caldera's decision. Rockefeller put a positive spin on the decision in public, but privately felt wounded because of his long relationship with Venezuelans. From his perspective, he had spent decades countering anti-Americanism by demonstrating his concern for Venezuelan economic and social development and had enjoyed good relations with the country's reformist political leaders. The furor soon died down. In 1974, when Rockefeller was nominated for the vice presidency of the United States, the *New York Times* reported on his Venezuelan connections, observing that he was remembered more for his "three decades of quixotic business failures and successes" than as a symbol of a capitalist family or as a politician.[66]

While the 1970s were a period of relative crisis of confidence for the United States and decline in its international prestige, Venezuela benefited from rising prices for petroleum and an emerging sense of the power held by "southern" states, particularly those with petroleum reserves. Venezuelan governments pursued an independent foreign policy, including increased efforts at international multilateral cooperation, as in OPEC, the Andean Pact, and the Latin American Economic System, which challenged the global economic system the United States had built after World War II. The nation restored ties with Cuba and began to offer foreign aid to poorer nations.

Nationalism and a more assertive anti-Americanism peaked in the 1970s, yet even then, Venezuela's policies were not overly confrontational. During the 1973 Arab oil boycott, Venezuela continued to export petroleum to Europe and the United States. When the Ford administration slapped punitive trade restrictions on Venezuela along with other oil producing nations because of "excessive" profits, Venezuelans were outraged at what they saw as ingratitude. Already, over many years, government policy had increasingly "Venezuelanized" the petroleum industry. Laws required the hiring of Venezuelans for managerial positions and increased Venezuela's share of profits. The Hydrocarbons Act of 1971 initiated the nationalization of the petroleum industry, originally to be accomplished by 1983. As petroleum output declined and the petroleum companies had no incentive to develop new reserves, the process was accelerated. Popular opinion overwhelmingly supported the early 1976 nationalization of oil (and iron in 1975). Some critics of the nationalization, like Juan Pablo Pérez Alfonso, wanted even greater control by Venezuela. They opposed the contract system by which foreign corporations provided technical support and marketed petroleum in the United States and elsewhere. The international petroleum companies maintained a Venezuelan presence because of these contracts. Venezuelan nationalism, more than anti-Americanism, was significant in the nationalization of Venezuela's oil. Moderation marked what could have been seen as the ultimate rejection of US influence.

Venezuelan leaders celebrated nationalization because it seemed to enhance the nation's position as a social democratic, consumer-based Western society within the international capitalist system, not because it represented an anti-American act. President Carlos Andres Pérez could say, "oil is the weapon used by the Third World countries which belong to OPEC to force the industrialized countries into a new kind of dialogue which might make it possible to set up a new economic world order," yet also remind his hearers, "Of course we do not mean to underestimate the contribution which foreign technical experts will still make."[67] Celebrating nationalization as a patriotic act and Venezuela's avoidance of a "distorted, submissive and humiliated colonial mentality," Betancourt warned that Venezuela "can't hope to make it work if we don't realize that myths about self-sufficiency and autarky reminiscent of Robinson Crusoe are quite out of place today. We live in an interconnected world, in which nobody can hope to make purely national decisions; so nationalism is not incompatible with internationalism."[68]

Some Venezuelan social critics expressed concerns about the effects of reliance on petroleum and the developmentalist model. In part buoyed by government patronage made possible because of petroleum revenues, the arts flowered in Venezuela in the 1960s and 1970s, when art, film, literature, music, and theater explored political and social criticism that on occasion implicated US interests in lamenting the extreme contrast between affluence and poverty and the alienating effects of rapid urbanization. The literary politico, Arturo Uslar Pietri, and the "father" of OPEC, Juan Pablo Pérez Alfonso, also decried the effects of petroleum. Pérez Alfonso deplored rampant consumerism and the environmental and social costs that the "devil's excrement" had wrought.[69]

But for most Venezuelans, the 1970s were a time of optimism. President Pérez (AD) celebrated, "It's our oil and we now have the chance to show that we are competent to run the industry. If we are confident in our ability, oil will help to bring democratic development together with social justice. [Oil] will take us a long way toward the fulfillment of our destiny. There is no more fitting place to say this than in the presence of Simón Bolívar, who taught us to believe in our people, and fought to show what we are capable of."[70] Indeed, high 1970s oil prices brought immediate benefits, and the government went on a spending spree.

The Bolivarian "destiny" did not come to fruition. An oil glut and low prices in the 1980s resulted in economic depression, debt, increasing disparity in wealth, and mounting internal conflict. Pérez (in a second, nonconsecutive term) initiated neoliberal policies, which in 1989 led to violence in the streets. He faced two coup attempts (one by Hugo Chávez) in 1992 and charges of corruption that led to his resignation. The political stability Venezuelans had wrought unraveled, leading to the 1990s collapse of the virtual two-party system, the election of Chávez in 1998, and the political polarization that culminated in the emergence of fierce opposition to him.

As anti-imperialists, Venezuelans decried the effects of foreign capital, made eloquent speeches about its distortions of their economy, and more substantively, took control of the industry. Still, since Venezuela depended on the export of petroleum to pursue modernizing goals, Venezuelans had incentive to keep anti-Americanism at a minimum. A relatively wide Venezuelan consensus shaped Venezuelan political culture: the country needed foreign capital and the goodwill of the United States. Nationalist anti-imperialism and even an independent foreign policy (within limits) did not necessarily threaten either. Even after nationalization in 1976, Venezuela sought foreign investment and technical expertise to keep the industry competitive and to foster continued exploration and development. Chávez's policies, in the early twenty-first century, continued to reflect this reality. Whether Chávez will break with this historic pattern is uncertain, despite his self-identification as a revolutionary and his pursuit of a boldly independent foreign policy.

From its inception, the nature of the Venezuelan petroleum industry and the nation's dependence on it brought persistent anti-imperialism yet limited anti-Americanism. As the case of Nelson Rockefeller in the 1930s through the 1950s shows, the rhetoric of anti-imperialism served two purposes. It insured the development of policies that protected Venezuelan interests, and it served as a

weapon against political opponents. Yet, anti-imperialism rarely resulted in violent attacks on US interests or persons. The attack on
Nixon in 1958, the sporadic anti-American actions of guerrillas in the
1960s, and the violence preceding Rockefeller's visit in 1969 are aber-
rations in Venezuelan history. They reflect a period of deep internal
crisis and global criticism of US foreign policy, ominously, one not
unlike the early twenty-first century. These occasional violent outbursts of anti-Americanism have focused primarily against representatives of the United States, who served as symbolic targets against
whom to vent frustration against US policies, especially if they seemed
to directly threaten petroleum exports or Venezuela's project of social democracy. What is most remarkable about Venezuelan social
critiques is that responsibility for the country's political and social
ills has been directed internally as much as or more so than externally. Perhaps this is best expressed by one of the veterans of the
guerrilla movement of the 1960s, Teodoro Petkoff, who in the 1970s
launched a new strategy and a new party, Movement Toward Socialism, proclaiming, "the anti-imperialist struggle in Venezuela does
not consist of a declaration of war against the United States, but a
very real confrontation with our own dependent capitalism and its
political power."[71] While poverty and lack of access to healthcare
and education continued to plague the nation, Venezuelans tended
to place primary blame on Venezuelan politicians and oligarchs for
malfeasance, corruption, and greed even as they maintained hope in
petroleum's promise.

Notes

1. M. Harnecker, *Hugo Chávez Frías: un hombre, un pueblo, entrevista de Marta Harnecker* (Havana, 2002).
2. *The Economist,* 12 June 2004, 36.
3. For further discussion of the Chávez administration, see D. Hellinger and S. Ellner, eds., *Venezuelan Politics in the Chávez Era: Class, Polarization, and Conflict*
   (Boulder, 2003).
4. *New York Times,* 15 April 2004, A5.
5. "Chavez: Sometimes 'Gone Too Far with Words,'" 18 September 2004, available
   at www.cnn.com (last visited 19 September 2005).
6. J. C. Brown, "Why Foreign Oil Companies Shifted Their Production from Mexico
   to Venezuela during the 1920s," *American Historical Review* 90 (April 1985):
   383–85; 375–81. See also B. S. McBeth, *Juan Vicente Gómez and the Oil Companies in Venezuela, 1908–1935* (New York, 1983); E. Lieuwen, *Petroleum in Venezuela: A History* (Berkeley, 1954); S. Rabe, *The Road to OPEC: United States
   Relations with Venezuela* (Austin, 1982); J. Salazar-Carillo, *Oil in the Economic
   Development of Venezuela,* (Westport, 1976).
7. D. Yergin, *The Prize: The Epic Quest for Oil, Money, and Power* (New York, 1991),
   236.

8. Lieuwen, *Petroleum*, 41, 51–52; J. Ewell, *Venezuela and the United States: From Monroe's Hemisphere to Petroleum's Empire* (Athens, 1996), 115–18.

9. Ewell, *Venezuela and the United States*, 115–18.

10. Ibid., 146–47.

11. Yergin, *The Prize*, 434.

12. S. Ellner, "The Venezuelan Left in the Era of the Popular Front," *Journal of Latin American Studies* 11, 1 (May 1979): 169–84.

13. Ibid.; see also S. Schwartzberg, "Rómulo Betancourt: From a Communist Anti-Imperialist to a Social Democrat with US Support," *Journal of Latin American Studies* 29, 3 (October 1997): 613–65.

14. "Nelson Rockefeller está en Venezuela," *Ahora*, 23 February 1939, cited in R. Betancourt, *Problemas venezolanos* (Caracas, 1940), 48.

15. "Hacía la explotación nacional de nuestro petróleo," *Ahora*, 24 and 25 January 1939, 38–40; "La expropriación petrolera mexicana y las perspectivas de un arreglo con las Compañías yanquis," *Ahora*, 20 March 1939, both cited in Betancourt, *Problemas venezolanos*, 124–26.

16. R. Betancourt, *Venezuela's Oil*, 31.

17. See D. Rivas, *Missionary Capitalist: Nelson Rockefeller in Venezuela* (Chapel Hill, 2002).

18. M. Boulton de Bottome, *Una mujer de dos siglos* (Caracas, 1992), 70–77.

19. Corrigan to Secretary of State, 23 January 1943, *FRUS 1943*, 6: 809–12.

20. Ellner, "The Venezuelan Left," 174–75.

21. Embassy to Rockefeller, Assistant Secretary of State, July 6, 1945, "Visit to Washington of Romulo Betancourt, prominent Venezuelan politician and journalist," RG 59, 831.00/7-645, NA.

22. Rabe, *Road to OPEC*, 94–116; D. Hellinger, *Venezuela: Tarnished Democracy* (Boulder, 1991), 58–64.

23. Cited in Yergin, *The Prize*, 435, 437, and in Schwartzberg, "Rómulo Betancourt," 658.

24. Rabe, *Road to OPEC*, 94-116; Yergin, *The Prize*, 436.

25. See Rivas, *Missionary Capitalist*.

26. *Gobierno y época del presidente Rómulo Gallegos: la opinion política a través de la prensa* (Caracas, 1992), doc. 1170; *Ultimas Noticias*, 12 March 1948.

27. *Gobierno y época*, doc. 1171, *El País*, 13 March 1948.

28. *Gobierno y época*, doc. 1175, *Ultimas Noticias*, 14 March 1948.

29. *Gaceta del Congreso de los Estados Unidos de Venezuela*, 29 October 1948, 1014, 1029, 1051.

30. Ibid., 1007–9.

31. Ibid., 1029.

32. Ibid., 1049.

33. "Tendencias parasitarias del capital nacional," *Ahora*, 21 May 1939, in Betancourt, *Problemas venezolanos*, 343–46. Also see R. Betancourt, *Venezuela, Oil and Politics* (Boston, 1979), 275–77.

34. A. Avendaña, *Arturo Uslar Pietri: entre la razón y la acción* (Caracas, 1996), 213.

35. Memorandum, "Conclusion of Communist Election Campaign," Embassy to State, RG 59, 831.00/12-1847, NA.

36. Donnelly to Secretary of State, 28 October 1948, RG 59, 831.00/10-2848, NA.

37. "Report on the Dec. 14, 1947 Venezuelan Elections" 26 December 1947, Thomas Maleady to Secretary of State, RG 59, 831.00/12-2647, NA.

38. Embassy dispatch, 12 December, 1947, "Report on the Dec. 14, 1947 Venezuelan Elections," 26 December 1947, Thomas Maleady to Secretary of State, RG 59, 831.00/12-2647, NA.

39. W. Burggraaff, *The Venezuelan Armed Forces in Politics, 1935–1959* (Columbia, 1972), 116–38; Rabe, *Road to OPEC*, 112–16; Schwartzburg, 613, 663–65.

40. *Documentos oficiales relativos al movimiento del 24 de noviembre de 1948* (Caracas, 1949), 72.
41. Memo, "URD Platform and Officials," May 17, 1949, Ambassador to State, RG 59, 831.00/5-1749, NA.
42. Ewell, *Venezuela and the US,* 167.
43. Rivas, *Missionary Capitalist,* 103–6.
44. B. Coles to L. Boyer, n.d., RAC, J. Camp Papers, 1:5; B. Jofre to NAR, 15 March 1958, RAC, RG 4, Countries, 69:592, NA.
45. *New York Times,* 27 January 1958, 11; 29 January 1958, 1.
46. B. Jofre to NAR, 23 May 1958, RAC, RG 4, Countries, 69:592, NA.
47. Memo of Telephone Conversation Among Min-Counselor of Embassy in Venezuela (Burrows), Assistant Secretary of State for Inter-American Affairs (Rubottom) in Caracas, and the Deputy Director of the Office of South American Affairs (Sanders) in Washington, 13 May 1958, *FRUS 1958–1960,* 5: 226–27; R. Nixon, *Six Crises* (Garden City, 1962), 215–18, 226–27. A. McPherson, *Yankee No! Anti-Americanism in US-Latin American Relations* (Cambridge, 2003), 28–30.
48. Ibid., Memo of Telephone Conversation Between Rubottom in Caracas and Acting Secretary of State (Snow) in Washington, 13 May 1958, *FRUS 1958–1960,* 5: 232–33.
49. A. Alvarez, *Estrategías de propaganda electoral* (Caracas, 1994), 48–74.
50. See *New York Times,* 8–18 December 1958; Nixon, *Six Crises,* 223.
51. T. Petkoff, "The Crisis of the Professional Revolutionary, Part I: Years of Insurrection," by N. Gall, available at http://www.normangall.com/venezuela_art4.htm.
52. *New York Times,* 15 June 1961, 2; 23 January 1962, 11; 15 April 1962, 15; 16 June 1963, 32, 2 November 1963, 10, 28 November 1963, 1; 10–14 October 1964; 6 May 1965, 4.
53. B. Jofre to NAR, RAC, 16 February 1963, RG 4, Countries, 67:574, NA. Petkoff, "The Crisis."
54. *New York Times,* 30 June 1963, 27.
55. Betancourt, *Venezuela's Oil,* 63.
56. Alvarez, *Estrategías,* 123.
57. Ibid., 155.
58. Rivas, *Missionary Capitalist,* 208. For Latin American criticism of the tours, see G. Selser, *Los cuatros viajes de Cristóbal Rockefeller con su informe al Presidente Nixon* (Buenos Aires, 1971).
59. *New York Times,* 30 September 1968, 15.
60. Student Unrest 2481 and Student Unrest 2510, 23 May 1969, RAC, RG 4, Washington, D.C., Presidential Mission to Venezuela, box 101, NA.
61. Press Conference, 10 April 1969 in R. Caldera Rodríguez, *Habla el Presidente: diálogo semanal con el pueblo venezolano,* 20 March 1969 to 5 March 1970, 1: 39–40.
62. Caldera, *Habla,* Press Conferences, 22 and 29 May 1969, 129–30, 133–34, 137–38.
63. *New York Times,* 26 February 1969, 10.
64. Rockefeller Visit Security, 28 May 1969, RAC, RG 4, Washington, D.C., Presidential Mission to Venezuela, box 101, NA.
65. Caldera, *Habla,* Press Conference, 5 June 1969, 145–47, 149–50.
66. *New York Times,* 24 November 1947, 7.
67. Pérez speech in Betancourt, *Venezuela's Oil,* 201–2.
68. Betancourt, *Venezuela's Oil,* 42–43.
69. Yergin, *The Prize;* also J. P. Pérez Alfonso, *Hundiéndonos en el excremento del diablo* (Caracas, 1976), 335.
70. Pérez speech in Betancourt, *Venezuela's Oil,* 210.
71. Quoted in N. Gall, "Carnival in Caracas," *New York Review of Books,* vol. 20, no. 18, 15 November 1973.

Chapter 4

THE MAKING OF
AN ECONOMIC ANTI-AMERICAN
Eduardo Frei and Chile during the 1960s

Jeffrey F. Taffet

Anti-Americanism in Latin America was a growing concern in Washington as John F. Kennedy assumed the US presidency in 1961.[1] Vice President Richard Nixon's horrendous Latin American goodwill trip in 1958, and more significantly, Fidel Castro's success in Cuba, clearly indicated that many in the region were angry about US international behavior.[2] Policymakers in Washington feared anti-Americanism because they understood that it could be an important factor in helping communists take control of Latin American governments. In response to this problem, Kennedy introduced a massive economic aid program he called the Alliance for Progress. The logic behind this program was a belief that, if the United States could improve Latin American economies, communists would lose their appeal. A rising middle class, US policymakers reasoned, would not support Marxist agendas.[3] As important, the Alliance for Progress would demonstrate that the United States was not a neo-imperialistic evil empire, as the communists argued, but rather a force for good in the hemisphere.[4]

Chile became one of the key targets for the Alliance for Progress. The country had the most powerful Marxist parties in Latin America, and in 1958, Salvador Allende, representing these parties, narrowly lost the presidential election. The Marxists had consistently argued that US influence in Chile stifled national independence and kept the country relatively poor by limiting the government's ability to take advantage of the nation's natural resources.[5] Looking at this situation, US policymakers feared that the regional growth in anti-

Americanism would help the Chilean Marxists enough to allow them to win either the 1964 or 1970 presidential elections. In response, the US government, over the course of the 1960s, sent roughly $760 million to Chile to improve both material conditions for the Chilean people and public perceptions of the United States. This money helped the Chileans enact broad reform programs, spend money on social programs, and finance the construction of schools, roads, housing developments, medical facilities, and electrical generation stations. Throughout this period, aid to Chile was among the highest for any country in Latin America, and most years it was among the top ten aid recipients around the world. In Latin America, only Brazil and Colombia, both significantly larger countries, received more money between 1961 and 1969 (see Table 4.1).[6]

Even the briefest examination of the course of Chilean history suggests that this funding, and the ultimate US plan, were not successful. Allende, after losing for a second time in the 1964 presidential election to the center-left Christian Democrat, Eduardo Frei (1964–1970), won the presidential election in 1970. Notably, Allende's campaign platform called for the elimination of US influence over Chilean soci-

Table 4.1 Total US Loans and Grants to Latin American Nations and Other Major Recipients from 1961 to 1969 (in US $ millions)

Brazil	1925.7	India	5725.3
Colombia	801.5	Vietnam	3257.6
Chile	*758.7*	Pakistan	2462.4
Dominican Republic	402.4	South Korea	1928.6
Bolivia	322.9.	Egypt	654.0
Peru	279.1	Indonesia	516.1
Argentina	191.5	China (Taiwan)	409.7
Ecuador	181.7	Israel	399.4
Venezuela	181.3	Philippines	273.1
Panama	176.7		
Mexico	153.9		
Nicaragua	118.4		
Guatemala	115.0		
Costa Rica	111.2		
El Salvador	108.8		
Paraguay	84.4		
Honduras	81.0		
Uruguay	80.9		
Haiti	56.1		

Source: Office of Statistics and Reports, Agency for International Development, *Economic Assistance Programs Administered by the Agency for International Development and Predecessor Agencies, April 3, 1948–June 30, 1971* (Washington, 1972).

ety.[7] Given this outcome, an important question is why US aid programs failed.

This paper will suggest a basic problem in the way the United States attempted to use money to counter anti-Americanism. US policymakers envisioned foreign aid as a tool to control Chilean political and economic change. During the mid-1960s, US government officials consistently tried to make their Chilean counterparts change their policies to reflect Washington's vision of what Chile should become. This process created a great deal of anger and frustration. Chilean leaders wanted economic support, but did not necessarily want to accept the demands that accompanied aid programs. As a result, rather than improve bilateral relations, economic aid programs strained them. In the Chilean case, the US government alienated key centrist political leaders, which in turn made them less willing to counter rising anti-Americanism.

This case is important because many of the dynamics of US-Latin American relations in the 1960s have become global. Anti-Americanism, which emerged as a force in the 1950s and 1960s in places such as Chile, has become, perhaps, *the* global problem for the United States in the first decade of the twenty-first century. For the US government, dealing with anti-Americanism is as difficult as ever. As in the 1960s, one of the few possible tools for countering anti-Americanism remains spending money to develop economic aid programs, to make loan guarantees, or to execute nation-building schemes. In the first decade of the twenty-first century, US policymakers continue to believe that international development assistance has the ability to "fix" or "build" countries, and that this will lead to friendlier relationships between the United States and people around the world. As the Chilean case demonstrates, using aid in this way does not guarantee results. This does not suggest that aid programs are always doomed to failure. US programs in Europe and Japan following World War II were relatively successful at helping to rebuild national economies and create strong bilateral relationships. But successful implementation of aid programs requires, at the least, a great deal of planning and a healthy dose of humility. During the 1960s these were in short supply as the United States approached Latin America.

Anti-Americanism in Chile in the 1960s: The Context for Giving Aid

Washington's fear that intensely negative visions of the United States would lead to long-term political problems were understandable given the evidence about anti-Americanism in Chile in the 1960s. As the 1960s progressed, many Chileans became increasingly vocal in expressing their anxieties about US power. There are many reasons for these growing sentiments. Some Chileans saw the Vietnam War as a case study in US arrogance. Others focused on local concerns about the power of US-owned businesses in Chile or western cultural domination. It is important to note that there was not necessarily an increase in Marxist strength because of these sentiments. Allende's percentage of the national vote in the 1964 and 1970 presidential elections remained relatively constant.[8] Nevertheless, Chileans with anti-American sentiments did become more aggressive, active, and perhaps more sophisticated.

One of the clearest anti-American movements in Chile developed in opposition to the Vietnam War. Many young Chileans, like their counterparts around the world, empathized with the victims of US aggression and organized protests in the late 1960s.[9] In Chile these protests were generally peaceful, and as elsewhere peaked in 1967 and 1968. Among the most notable was a highly publicized 187-kilometer "Peace March" from Valparaiso to Santiago. On 8 June 1967, roughly one thousand marchers took five days to reach Santiago, where large crowds met them for a peaceful rally. Though reports claimed that most marchers received generous help from trucks along the way, the march and the news coverage gave the protesters a national platform for attacking the war. Other protests were less organized and less ambitious. Some were apparently spontaneous, such as a near riot at a ceremony in which the University of California announced the gift of laboratory equipment to the University of Chile. In this protest, also in June 1967, students disrupted speeches with fifteen minutes of chanting slogans such as "Cuba Yes, Yankees No," "Cuba and Vietnam Together Will Win," and "Neighbor Johnson, Fascist and Murderer."[10]

Anger about the US role in Vietnam was secondary to concerns about the US economic role in Chile. Throughout the 1960s leftist leaders argued that US-owned copper companies dominated the national economy and kept Chile from being truly independent. Inspired by dependency theorists such as Raúl Prebisch, many Chilean Marxist politicians believed that allowing foreigners to control Chile's most valuable resource kept the country from reaching its potential. Because of copper, the US government was able to treat Chile as part of its Latin American empire.[11]

It is impossible to determine exactly how many Chileans accepted this vision of the US role, or how this translated to anti-Americanism in the 1960s. But there is substantial evidence that suggests anti-

American sentiments were widespread and that they were connected to fears about US power in Chile. Perhaps the most telling source about the extent of anti-American sentiments is the polling data that the US government funded.

One of the largest polls taken in Chile during the 1960s was a study of over 3,700 Chilean university students from August 1964. This poll, taken just before the presidential election in September, was designed to help the US government determine the likely outcome of the election and to discern its meaning. The questions plainly indicated that the United States had a real problem with Chilean youth (see Table 4.2).[12] More than 60 percent had a favorable opinion of socialism. Almost 57 percent expressed a negative opinion about capitalism, while

Table 4.2 August 1964 Survey of Chilean University Students (in percentages)

Question: "What is your opinion of Socialism?"*	
Very Good	20
Good	40.9
Neither Good nor Bad	28.5
Bad	8.5
Very Bad	1.3
Don't Know	0.8
Question: "What is your opinion of Capitalism?"	
Very Good	1.3
Good	13.7
Neither Good nor Bad	27.5
Bad	39.0
Very Bad	17.9
Don't Know	0.6
Question: "Are you for or against foreign-owned industries being expropriated by the government?"	
For	68.9
Against	29.2
Don't Know	1.9

*In Chile, one of the two major Marxist parties, along with the Communists, was the Socialist party. Often the Socialists adopted more aggressive platforms on reform and revolution than the Communists. As a group linked to the USSR, the Communists were often advised to tone down their rhetoric and work with the bourgeois parties. Though many Socialists supported Castro and others adopted a pro-Beijing line after the Sino-Soviet split, they were independent. The question is unclear about whether it is asking about the Socialist party or Socialism as a theory.

SOURCE: Study of Chilean University Student Opinions: Marplan, August 1964, USIA CI6402, Student Attitudes, Part I, USIA file, Box 20, RG 306, NA.

only 15 percent said it was either good or very good. As dramatically, just under 69 percent of all students supported the expropriation of foreign-owned companies.

In questions from a broad 1965 Latin American poll, the results from Chile also demonstrated that problems existed for the United States (see Table 4.3). By the largest margins, residents of Santiago supported socialistic ideas and had the least significant objections to communists taking power.[13] Unfortunately, this kind of poll was not taken at regular intervals and Chilean institutions did not sponsor polls, so determining changes over time is difficult. In addition, there is not necessarily an exact correlation between anti-Americanism and

Table 4.3 1965 Multi-City Survey of Public Opinion (in percentages)

Question: "In general, which do you prefer—government ownership or private ownership of major industries?"

	Government	Private	Don't Know
Mexico City	41	50	9
Caracas	22	57	21
Buenos Aires	28	54	18
Santiago	63	23	14
Rio de Janeiro	35	36	29

Question: "All things considered, would you say that it is a good thing or a bad thing for (survey country) to have US companies operating here?"

	Good Thing	Bad Thing	Don't Know
Mexico City	55	37	8
Caracas	53	29	18
Buenos Aires	50	31	19
Santiago	39	43	18
Rio de Janeiro	35	32	33

Question: "Do you think it would be a good thing or a bad thing if people sympathetic to communism came to power in (survey country)?"

	Good Thing	Bad Thing	Don't Know
Mexico City	5	87	8
Caracas	4	69	27
Buenos Aires	6	79	15
Santiago	17	70	13
Rio de Janeiro	4	67	29

SOURCE: Omnibus Study of Public Opinion: International Research Associates. S.A. and C.V., ZP 6501 World Survey III, Multi-Latin America, Part 3, Box 20, RG 306, NA.

support for socialist economics or expropriation of foreign properties. But other evidence combined with these polls supports a conclusion that a large number of Chileans held negative visions of the United States and its role in Chile. Editorial cartoons in Chilean papers, for instance, suggested that Chileans had increasing concerns about the role of the United States as the 1960s progressed. Early in the 1960s, cartoonists generally portrayed the United States and the Alliance for Progress as dedicated to helping the Chilean people. But by the late 1960s, cartoonists were much more likely to draw negative images. Some suggested the United States was using aid programs as a front for covert operations and that it was run by particularly stupid individuals (see Fig. 4.1).[14]

Figure 4.1

This multi-image cartoon focusing on Peace Corps activity suggested both that the program was run by particularly stupid individuals, but also that it was designed to spy on Chileans. In one frame a Peace Corps volunteer, or as he refers to himself, Agent X-81, is about to be attacked by natives yelling "Go Home." The agent reports to the CIA the good news that the natives understand a little English. In another, two Americans, who are plainly out of place and surrounded by a group of Chilean men in mustaches believe that the fact they also have mustaches allows them to blend in with the crowd. Other frames make fun of a belief that the Peace Corps was paying people to bring them political news, and one even suggests that the unmanned satellite to Mars, Mariner 6, was part of a Peace Corps spying mission. *Topaze,* 29 August 1969.

Editorial cartoons also increasingly reflected concerns about US copper companies and their exploitation of Chile's most valuable resource. One cartoon, using some rather suggestive puns, pointed to the long-term Chilean frustration with Anaconda, one of the two largest US copper firms active in Chile. In a city scene, two poor men look out across the street and watch as an American flirts with an attractive buxom woman with the word Anaconda written across her chest. One of the Chilean figures said, "Yes, in Chile we have many attractive women. The bad thing is that they are exploited by the gringos." The idea was unmistakable: that the United States was taking the best of Chile and keeping it from the Chilean people. The Spanish text of the short caption suggested a deeper meaning. The phrase used for "attractive woman" was *"guena mina,"* which referred to a woman who was voluptuous and perhaps close to being a prostitute. But "mina" also translates to mine, as in a copper mine. Thus, the American could extract pleasure from exploiting the woman or the mine. In either case, the Chilean male (or the Chilean nation) was not part of the process (see Fig. 4.2).[15]

Finally, editorial cartoons from the late 1960s also indicated a concern with US support for right-wing politicians such as Jorge Alessandri, the Chilean president from 1958 to 1964 and a presidential candidate in 1970. In one cartoon, a befuddled Chilean examined an Alessandri campaign poster with the slogan, "Vote for an Independent." However, the sponsor of this poster, and presumably Alessandri's campaign, was a fictional "American and International Company" based in New York (see Fig. 4.3). This image clearly expressed frustration about perceived US influence over Chilean life and institutions.[16]

More disturbingly, as the 1960s progressed, there were a series of attacks against US interests in Chile. Some incidents were minor, such as the vandalism of property owned by US-based companies such as Ford and Citibank, or the destruction of automobiles owned by US government officials. However, as the antiwar protests began to gain publicity, the size and scope of these attacks increased. In early September 1967, roughly seventy people rushed the US consulate in Santiago and threw paint on the front steps of the building. In October 1967, at a Santiago fair, a crowd hurled rocks, eggs, tomatoes, tar, and ink at a US government display. An assault in early 1968 was more serious. On 12 March, a black powder bomb detonated in the ladies' bathroom on the second floor of the US embassy in Santiago. Fortunately no one was in the room at the time. Pieces of metal were embedded into the woodwork in adjoining offices, and the embassy reported that anyone in the vicinity certainly would have died.[17] There were still more attacks at US facilities. On 20 Feb-

Figure 4.2

In this cartoon two poor Chileans watch as an American picks up an attractive woman representing the Anaconda copper company. They complain that although there are many attractive and available women in Chile (or *Muy Guenas Minas*) they are taken by Americans. The cartoon has a double meaning because *Minas* could also refer to a copper mine. Thus, the caption could also suggest that although there were many valuable resources in Chile, they were being exploited by the foreigners. *Topaze,* 23 May 1969.

ruary 1968 and on 11 March 1968, assailants bombed the US–Chile cultural centers in Santiago and Rancagua. The March bombing in Rancagua was especially powerful and destroyed almost the entire facility. As in the embassy bombing, no one was hurt in these attacks.[18]

The existence of some Chileans who hoped to use violence against the United States was not, in itself, evidence of widespread anti-Americanism. Most observers believed that two small extremist left-wing parties that had become popular among Chilean university students in the late 1960s were responsible for the attacks, though there was little evidence supporting this theory.

The far bigger problem for the United States was that few Chileans, including those in government, were willing to denounce the attacks. Only the conservative-establishment paper, *El Mercurio,* and its tabloid

Figure 4.3

This image, drawn before the 1970 presidential election, indicated a concern that Jorge Alessandri, the candidate of the political right, was controlled by the United States. A confused citizen looks at an Alessandri poster with his slogan, "vote for an independent," but the poster also notes that he is being funded by the fictional American and International Corp. of New York, USA, thus he is not truly independent. *Topaze,* 29 August 1970.

production, *La Tercera,* condemned the bombings.[19] The most important politicians in the Frei administration failed to criticize the violence. This problem was significant for the United States because it meant that the government, at some level, agreed with the notion that US influence in Chile was problematic and that steps taken to counter that influence were acceptable.

Frei, Aid, and A Positive Vision of the United States

The Chilean government's failure to stand up to rising anti-Americanism in 1967 and 1968 was notable because of President Frei's extremely positive statements about the United States as he took office. In the 1964 presidential election campaign, Frei repeatedly made speeches in which he called for a closer relationship with Washington and the implementation of US economic aid programs as part of the Alliance for Progress. Frei's positive vision of the United States stemmed in part from an expectation that Washington would support his government and help him improve the national economy. Frei feared the rise of Marxist parties and understood that Washington did also. Thus he knew that there was significant room for a mutually beneficial partnership.

In comments before his inauguration, Frei explained that although Chile had "spiritual and geographic" connections to other Latin American countries, its most important relationship needed to be with Washington. Close ties with the United States, Frei explained, were vital because they would lead to the advancement of liberty and economic development in Chile. In talking about aid programs and the relationships with the United States, Frei claimed that he had been inspired by Kennedy. To Frei, Kennedy understood "the different evolution, and the creation of distinct communities" in Latin America, but he also appreciated "the need to readjust international commercial mechanisms to help underdeveloped countries accelerate their economies." Frei claimed that Kennedy believed that this would be the "one way that democracy could be defended" in Latin America. Kennedy understood that police or military action could not protect democracy, but that it was ensured through an "internal conviction of the people that they exist in the one system that permits a rational life and can lead to their own liberation."[20] In other words, Frei knew that the United States would lend money to the Latin Americans on generous terms to fight communism and protect democracy.

In November 1964, just two months after Frei's election, the US government offered Chile $33 million in debt relief and $106 million in economic aid programs.[21] The US program, in the view of the State Department and Agency for International Development (AID) apparatus, represented a major US government commitment to Chilean development. In December, the United States announced that Chile was to receive one of the most significant Alliance for Progress aid packages in the calendar year 1965.[22] AID administrators claimed in an internal memo that the

> decision to extend substantial support . . . [to] Chile was based . . . on [that] government's commitments to comprehensive programs aimed at increasing internal resource mobilization, improving balance of payments, substantially reducing [their] rate of inflation, and removing bottlenecks to production in [the] private sector. An important element in [the] US decision was [the] belief that [the Chilean government was] sincerely dedicated at [the] highest levels to self-help and reform and [is] making [its] best efforts to mount integrated programs designed to correct basic distortions in their economies.[23]

As a result of the financial support, the relationship between the United States and Frei was positive throughout late 1964 and most of 1965. The United States was happy with Frei's efforts, and Frei was pleased that the Johnson administration had followed through on Kennedy's Alliance for Progress and had offered significant support.

As early as April 1965, just months after the initial set of loans, the Frei government again looked to the United States for more money. In a number of meetings in Santiago between US Ambassador Ralph Dungan and Frei's top advisors, the Chileans requested a series of interim loans beyond the 1965 aid package. In these meetings the Frei government asked for an additional $30 to $35 million from the US government and Washington's support for loans of between $30 and $40 million from major New York banks.[24] In a similar set of meetings between Radimiro Tomic, Frei's ambassador in Washington, and Secretary of State Dean Rusk in August 1965, Tomic argued that the loans were necessary because Frei's program "could not succeed without the understanding and support of the United States."[25] Tomic and other Chilean representatives argued that the Frei government had initiated school construction and housing development programs and had boosted production levels, but that further progress in these areas would need the support of the United States over the coming years.[26] According to the Chileans, their government was going to have a $130 million shortfall in its balance of payments for 1965. The Chileans hoped that the United States would help meet that gap by providing a loan of $100 million.[27]

Though the United States did not provide an emergency or supplemental loan in 1965, the requests set the State Department apparatus in motion to begin to consider a loan for 1966. In September and October 1965, AID officials looked at Chilean needs and identified what would be possible from the US standpoint. In early November 1965, this study led to a State Department suggestion that the United States propose a loan of $80 million for the coming year. Ambassador Dungan strongly supported this figure as high enough to give the United States significant leverage over the Chilean development program but low enough to require significant Chilean self-help efforts.[28]

The $80 million figure may have had less to do with Chilean needs than political considerations in Washington. In a memo to National Security Advisor McGeorge Bundy in the White House, Under Secretary of State for Economic Affairs Thomas Mann explained that his support for the $80 million loan "took into account the fact that the Chilean government was most uncooperative in the Dominican crisis." Following the US intervention in the Dominican Republic in April 1965, which had been driven by Johnson administration fears about instability in that country, Frei made a series of public comments expressing concerns about a new era of big stick diplomacy. Mann now recommended that the United States explain to Frei that "we expect cooperation to be a two way street and that we are very disturbed about the Chilean government's attitude toward the Dominican crisis." Mann even hoped to insert a clause into the 1966 agreement "to the effect that US obligations are contingent on our balance of payments position, and then add that this is to be interpreted by him [Frei] as meaning we will not continue to make heavy sacrifices to help Chile unless the Chilean government will cooperate with us on matters we consider vital to hemisphere security." Mann's memo suggested that he hoped to reduce the loan amount even further because of the Chilean positions on international issues.[29] This became one of the earliest suggestions in 1965 that aid should be used as a political tool to get the Chileans to change their policies in return for receiving US aid.

David Bell, the AID administrator, agreed that a major loan was necessary, though in terms more in line with the logic behind the Alliance for Progress. In a memo to President Lyndon Johnson, Bell explained that the program loan and "increased Chilean self-help efforts, would make possible a significant increase in investment, a continued deceleration of inflation, and the undertaking of important reform actions." Frei needed support to enact his development program; otherwise Chile might face serious economic and social disturbances, which would then play into the hands of the left. The US national interest, wrote Bell, "rests on the pivotal role Chile can play in demonstrating to Latin America and to the world the validity of the concept of the Alliance for Progress that economic and social progress can be achieved rapidly within a system of democratic liberty."[30] Success in Chile would clearly demonstrate the power of economic aid programs as a foreign policy tool.

At the same time, however, Bell argued that the United States should use the loan to ensure that Frei's development program was in accord with Washington's determinations about what types of changes would be necessary in the Chilean economy. Bell argued that the United States should require the Chileans to commit to a series of reforms, including passage of land reform legislation and adjustment of exchange rates. The US government should require "a substantial increase in the share of the public investment program financed from the government's own domestic revenues" and the "establishment of the government's finances on a sounder basis by the elimination of inflationary government borrowing from the Central Bank."[31] In making this case, Bell expressed a central change in policy toward Chile. Before this point, concern with the Marxists winning the presidential election in 1964 and then exuberance about Frei's victory had made US policymakers hesitant to push for Chilean reforms that might lead to short-term economic hardship.

By late 1965 the Johnson administration began to think that it did not need to lavish Frei's government with unconditional generous aid packages. This change in policy came, in part, from the employment of a strict calculus about what was important to the United States. The highest international priority for the US government remained stopping countries from falling to the communists in the near term. This was a constant from Kennedy to Johnson. However, by late 1965, White House officials began to think that Asian threats were more pressing than Latin American ones. No Latin American country had followed Cuba's example. The fears of the early 1960s seemed to have been blown out of proportion. The Chilean situation appeared, at least to Washington, to have settled. Chile, simply put, was less important to the US government in 1965 without an immediate communist threat. The next presidential elections would be in 1970, so there was no urgency to deal with Chilean problems. Frei was moving forward with a reform program and attracting support from the moderate left. The outlook in Chile seemed good. Therefore, it required less attention and, interestingly, less financial support. This perception led Johnson administration policymakers to become less responsive to Chilean concerns and to use significantly more heavy-handed tactics in dealing with Frei. US policymakers failed to understand that this policy might lead Frei to question his positive vision of the United States.

The Problem of Copper Prices

As the US government considered new loans for Frei, global copper prices began to rise dramatically. This development would decisively impact the Chilean loans. The price increases were a result of a mounting problem of growing international consumption without expanding supply. This problem was exacerbated by the US military's need for copper-based products in Vietnam. On the supply side, labor strikes in Chile and conflicts in other leading copper producing nations created fears about a global shortage.[32] Higher international prices encouraged Frei to order the two major mining companies active in Chile, Anaconda and Kennecott, to raise their prices from 36 to 38 cents per pound. This change would bring millions in additional revenue to the Chilean government. Following this action, companies in the United States then raised their prices and passed on the higher costs to consumers.[33]

Although they helped Frei, price increases in copper were dangerous for Johnson. Perhaps the major threat, according to Gardner Ackley, the Chair of the Council of Economic Advisors, was the likely effect on inflation. Ackley argued in 1965 that price increases in copper had "contributed significantly to the rise in the index of wholesale industrial prices in the past year" following "several years of complete stability." The result of continually increasing prices for copper would be more and more pressure on prices throughout the economy, which would ultimately drive increases in the cost of living, and potentially lead to an inflationary spiral.[34]

One solution, or at least part of a solution, would be to get US producers to roll back their prices. However, the price increase was due to the increase in the Chilean price. If the US government could induce the Chileans to move back to 36 cents, the companies would have no excuse but to follow. Thus, getting Chile to act became an important US goal. Johnson decided to send Ambassador W. Averell Harriman and Deputy Assistant Secretary of State Anthony Solomon to Santiago on a secret emergency mission to pressure Frei to lower prices.[35]

On 15 November 1965, Harriman and Solomon arrived in Chile. In their initial meeting with Frei, reported immediately in detail to Johnson and top White House officials, the US envoys made the case for a Chilean price rollback. They started by stressing to Frei that "Johnson had personally sent [the] mission" and then explained US fears about inflation and the possible repercussions to the global economy. Harriman and Solomon explained that "President Johnson feels Chile [is] the bellwether: If Chile brings [the] price back to 36 cents [a] price rise can be prevented." They further explained that Johnson was asking directly for Frei's cooperation to help protect the world economy. To help make Frei change his policy, they explained that they were "authorized to discuss ways of compensating Chile for [the] short-term loss involved." The US presentation, according to Harriman, impressed Frei, who responded that "naturally" some consideration of the issue would be necessary because Johnson had sent a special mission asking him to help. But Frei explained that "the problem is not easy." He argued that the Chilean price rise was not the only factor in the price of copper. More to the point, he explained that his domestic political situation made a rollback tough. All of the Chilean political parties were attacking him for not raising the price higher, many suggesting 50 cents a pound. Frei explained that not only opposition parties felt this way; his own cabinet was "unanimously in favor of increasing the Chilean selling price even further." Frei claimed he had been alone in arguing against more price rises, confessed that a plan to raise the price to 40 cents in January seemed inevitable, and indicated that all members of his own cabinet felt that 40 cents was still too low.[36]

Frei did not like the idea of having policy dictated by the United States, and certainly worried about what would happen if the story hit the Chilean press. Any suggestion that he had allowed the US government to dictate Chilean copper policy would be perceived by the public, understandably, as surrendering a key piece of national sovereignty. Copper was Chile's most important natural resource and Frei understood that any leak indicating that he was allowing the United States to control the resource would be a political disaster. At the same time, Frei understood that Chile's financial future was linked to economic aid from the United States and that, with cooperation from the Johnson administration, making economic development programs successful was far more likely. Ultimately, Frei had no real choice. He agreed to roll back the price of copper. The Chileans would agree to allow Anaconda to sell roughly 110,000 tons of copper to the United States at the 36 cent price. The United States, in turn, would add $10 million onto the 1966 program loan, to total $90 million. The deal would also remain secret until January 1966 when the shipments would begin, which hopefully would shield Frei from accusations he had caved to US pressure.[37]

Harriman, betraying an understanding of the pressure he had brought to bear, wrote to Johnson that "Frei agreed to [the] copper price roll back in spite of serious domestic political difficulties because he clearly appreciates [the] importance to Chile and himself of [the] good will of the President of the US. But beyond that, he clearly has solid respect for you as the leader of the free world. Although Chile has independent views on some subjects, he [Frei] is realistic enough to know that Chile's future depends on [the] US."[38]

While Harriman and Solomon were in Chile, State Department officials had been successful in putting pressure on Anaconda, ensuring that if the Chileans changed their policies, this would result in a move back to 36 cents. With news of the success of the Harriman and Solomon mission, Anaconda kept its word and moved the price back by two cents. Following this step, the other major copper companies in the United States reduced their prices back to 36 cents, marking a major victory for the Johnson staff.[39]

The US government was also relatively successful, at least at first, in keeping the deal quiet. Harriman, in Santiago, gave a misleading press conference, claiming that the purpose of his mission was to confer with Chilean government officials prior to upcoming inter-American meetings in Rio de Janeiro. Asked point-blank about copper negotiations, Harriman claimed it "was discussed in passing."[40] However, the story did leak into US papers. On 23 November, *The Washington Post* reported, based on a leak from State Department officials, that US government officials had been discussing the possibility of a copper price rollback with the Chileans. The paper explained that Harriman and Solomon made a "quiet visit" and that there was "little reason to doubt that Mr. Harriman and Mr. Solomon . . . explored the possibility of a rollback of the copper price increases ordained by Chile." This report, until the recent release of highly classified documents, was the only suggestion to the public that Harriman and Solomon traveled to Chile to negotiate the copper price deal.[41]

Though the close of the Harriman-Solomon mission to Chile solved the US problem of rolling back the copper price in the United States, the problem of obtaining the program loan for the Frei government remained. Rather than note Frei's extraordinary goodwill in allowing Harriman and Solomon to dictate terms of Chilean national policy for an additional $10 million in aid money, the Johnson administration quickly forgot the incident and followed a policy of commanding strict terms for the program loan. Rather than allowing Frei to sign the loan on easy terms in appreciation for his action, or perhaps more crassly, to sign the loan as a payoff, the United States insisted on forcing concessions to promote a vision of Chile's ideal economy conjured up in Washington.

To that end, in the weeks following the Harriman-Solomon mission, US aid administrators began arguing that the Chileans would have to make dramatic changes in their budget plan for 1966, and indeed in the entire structure of their reform programs.[42] In correspondence with the State Department, US officials in Santiago negotiating the loan argued that their position was to "recommend against compromising" with the Chileans on budgetary issues. The United States would only sign the program loan when the Frei government "adapts its program to conform with minimum [US-dictated] conditions," which included cutting spending for government agencies and "spending in less essential investment sectors, such as housing." Dungan explained that this approach ran the "possible risk of provoking a sharp Chilean reaction, which could include reconsideration of their part of the copper arrangements made during the Harriman/Solomon visit," and that a hard line on the program loan negotiations ran the risk of becoming a public issue.[43] But officials in the State Department in Washington ignored Dungan's warnings and agreed that the United States should take a firm stand.[44]

US policymakers did not consider Chilean leaders' ideas about their own economy as relevant. In meetings in Washington, for example, Ambassador Tomic was forced to plead for a "better understanding of and appreciation of the uniqueness of the Chilean experiment as it affects the rest of Latin America and the United States." Tomic explained that "he and key members of his government were concerned that there was not a true understanding within the US government of the significance of what was happening in Chile and the fact that negotiations for the program loan had not been concluded increased this concern." Tomic argued at length that the United States was not paying attention to the dramatic achievements and self-help programs the Frei government had undertaken that proved "the sincerity and singleness of purpose" in its commitment to reform. Tomic explained that the Chilean sacrifices on copper prices showed a willingness to bend over backwards to accommodate Washington, but negotiations seemed to be a one-way street.[45] Frei, in Chile, also argued that not only was the United States program not in the best interests of his country, but that it was impossible. US criteria for reduced government spending and a limitation on borrowing from the Central Bank would lead to serious political problems, including unrest in the military as wages fell behind inflation.[46]

The problems in finding a compromise position stalled the program loan negotiations, forcing the Frei government to create a budget that the US government would find more appealing. After almost a month of considering the figures, in late December the Chilean government produced a new budget that increased public sector savings but did not eliminate Central Bank borrowing. These changes were not enough however. For the United States, ending Central Bank borrowing was absolutely vital. The Frei team again argued that such a restriction in 1966 was simply not possible if it hoped to keep its reform programs on track.[47]

Frei was forced to plead with Dungan for some understanding by the United States government. In meetings in early January, Frei made the case for a more liberal loan policy. Frei complained to Dungan that the US government was not looking at his problem with sufficiently broad vision or allowing for the complexities he faced. In quite dramatic fashion Frei became emotional about his plight and the lack of compassion coming from Washington. Dungan reported that at one point Frei addressed him gravely and said, "I hope that no President of Chile ever is in the position in which I find myself. I speak to my country about our dignified position though small and weak, but in my heart I know this is not true." Frei continued, "I have no dignity. I am mendicant." He then went on to speak about the Socialist Senator Carlos Altimirano who "talked about the US having its knees at the throat of Chile." Frei empathized with this position. He could not understand the hard line on the loan requirements and claimed that "certainly no politician in Chile could . . . [appreciate] why the US should be inflexible on [a] program loan with a small democratic country trying its best to follow commonly agreed economic policies." To Frei, the Chileans were doing their part by "following reasonable policies with respect to copper prices in the interests of others" but this flexibility was not returned by the United States.[48] Ultimately Frei compromised on the issue of Central Bank borrowing and received the loan in January 1966, but the negotiations had created a great deal of animosity.[49]

Frei's Nationalist Response

Although Frei was angry with the United States, initially he was powerless to do anything about the relationship because of his reliance on aid. However, through 1966, as copper prices remained high, the Chilean leader took steps away from the United States.[50] Frei began to sound far more nationalistic themes because of the increasing revenues coming from sales outside the Harriman-Solomon agreement.

In a speech in early October 1966, in which his government announced the creation of a company that would own 51 percent of Kennecott's Chilean holdings, Frei chose to ignore the fact that US foreign aid made the transaction possible. Instead, harkening to themes in his country's struggle for independence from Spain, Frei exclaimed, "Just as the Chileans who were in the Plaza of Rancagua . . . took care of the threats they faced, the peoples of today have been challenged to conquer their new liberty and their new independence." Frei continued, "When shall we be independent? When we don't have to ask for loans for our development."[51]

Frei understood that copper would be the means to create this independence. In a telling speech made in December 1966 during a reception for Kenneth Kaunda, the president of Zambia, Frei argued that copper was the instrument for the liberation of both nations and their hope for economic development. Part of Frei's intent in working with Kaunda was to develop some type of price and production control over the world market. Frei had come to realize that he could not allow the United States to dominate discussions on prices. His nation and the other major copper producing nations, Zambia, the Congo, and Peru, had a joint interest in keeping prices stable and high. In this speech Frei positioned himself as the spokesman for Latin American, African, and Asian nations in opposition to the industrialized North Atlantic world. Partnership with the United States and Europe would not lead to development, Frei argued. Only a recognition of the value of exports could change centuries of relative poverty.[52]

Frei's most dramatic statement suggesting the need for economic independence came in his Christmas radio message of 1966. Frei explained that, because of strong prices in copper, his government would renounce aid from the United States. While on this occasion Frei was clear that his country might need loans in the future, he argued that the strain on development in Chile because of foreign debt was simply too strong. Chile, if it were to develop true economic independence, needed to set its own budget priorities. Although Frei did not fully explain that the United States had essentially vetoed his budget, an understanding of the loan negotiation processes makes the reasons for the speech clear.[53]

Copper prices certainly emboldened Frei to sound more nationalistic messages, but these were a response to his perception of the problems in the aid process. These ideas became clear in an article Frei penned for the April 1967 *Foreign Affairs,* "The Alliance That Lost Its Way." Though asked by the editor, Hamilton Fish Armstrong, to write about his philosophy of his government in early 1965, and repeatedly pressured through intermediaries for an article, Frei only decided in November 1966 to make a statement to the American public.[54] However, Frei chose not to explore the tenets of Christian Democracy, but to explain the failures in the Alliance for Progress. Not surprisingly, the problem with aid relationships Frei found most disappointing was the lack of mutual cooperation. He wrote, "It is unnecessary to point out names and dates, but at some stage the imaginative, dynamic commitment of countries united in a common ideal was gone." Aid programs were not coordinated between states with shared goals in large part because there was no guidance or leadership behind the Alliance for Progress. Frei reserved some blame for Latin American leaders who only hoped to receive dollars from the United States without making structural changes in their societies. However, to a reader familiar with Frei's efforts in areas such as land and tax reform, the problem in his case had to be with the United States. To the very few readers familiar with the ugly history of the 36 cent copper deal and the subsequent loan negotiations, referring to a lack of "clear ideological direction" was obviously a slap at the Johnson administration's machinations.[55] Ultimately Frei again needed to ask the United States for economic aid in the late 1960s, but his attitude toward those loans and the United States in general had changed. In late 1965 and early 1966 he had come to realize that the United States was not a friend but a powerful nation that had to be handled carefully and without sentimentality.

Though the fear of Marxists taking power in Chile was remote in 1965 and 1966, as the decade wore on, and as the 1970 presidential elections neared, Chilean politics again became a concern in Washington. However, in the late 1960s, the United States could not count on Frei and the Christian Democrats for active support. Frei's party moved leftwards, becoming as anti-American in rhetoric as the Marxist left. While Frei was not always at the vanguard of his party's aggressive calls for complete independence from the United States, Frei did continue to call for more local control over Chilean natural resources and financial institutions. He no longer served as a force for defending the role of the United States in his country. This does not suggest that Frei's change of position vis-à-vis the United States led directly to Allende's election. However, it did ensure that the political rhetoric of Chile's most powerful centrist political figures sounded quite similar to that of the Marxists. Rather than countering Allende's nationalistic and anti-American rhetoric, or taking a stand against attacks on US interests, Frei's rhetoric often echoed themes popular with the Marxists.

This shift may have had a significant role in the Allende victory in 1970. Frei's changing position certainly explains why he accepted

Radimiro Tomic as the Christian Democratic party's nominee for the presidency in 1970. Tomic came from the left-leaning wing of the party, and on most important matters, including the US role in Chile, he held views almost indistinguishable from Allende. Yet Allende was far more popular and better known for his anti-American views as a result of the 1958 and 1964 elections. This meant that the Christian Democrats essentially failed to give the Chilean people a centrist alternative in 1970 and, in so doing, may have helped Allende win. Frei's perceptions of US power are thus important for understanding the course of Chilean history in the 1960s.

Aid was employed not for what it would do within the recipient country, but for what it would buy the United States. By the middle of the 1960s the US government had forgotten the basic logic of the Alliance for Progress. Kennedy had developed the program to ensure that Latin American economies would develop and, as importantly, that relations between the United States and its neighbors would improve. This element of the program, using financial aid to counter growing anti-Americanism, got lost as concerns with the US economy and the war in Vietnam shifted US priorities. The United States continued to send money to Latin America throughout the 1960s, but exactly what that money was supposed to do became muddled.

Throughout this period, the United States did not act as a friend or partner of the Chileans. Instead, simply put, the Johnson administration acted as an imperialistic nation, expecting the Frei government to forgo its own resources for the benefit of a dominant power. These actions, quite clearly, were contrary to the best interests of democracy in Latin America and created new antagonism toward the United States. Frei came to understand that his country, while tied to the aid apron strings of Uncle Sam, was not, and could not, be truly independent. This revelation, and a greater flexibility coming from high copper prices, turned Frei in late 1966 to declare his "second independence." The independence of 1966 was not from Spain, but from the United States.

How the United States has employed foreign aid programs must receive a prominent place in understanding how anti-Americanism can develop even from policies meant to prevent it. Certainly, Central Intelligence Agency involvement and support for coups d'état and military regimes throughout the region cannot be ignored as actions contrary to the best interests of democracy. However, the US government did not hesitate to use all of the tools it had available to ensure control of Latin American destinies during this period, including foreign aid spending. In Chile, the efforts to dominate the political process through foreign aid programs became an end in itself. As a result, the Johnson administration failed with the grander policy goals of keeping Marxists at bay and dealing with anti-Americanism. There is a lesson here for the makers of foreign policy today. Economic aid programs that have the dual goals of improving bilateral relations and controlling the internal workings of a foreign government will not succeed. Using aid to control foreign countries will not promote good relations; it will instead lead to more antagonism. To be effective in stopping anti-Americanism, the United States needs to do more than send money to poorer nations. The US government needs to consider carefully how it helps.

Notes

1. As a faculty member at the United States Merchant Marine Academy, I am an employee of the US government. However, the views expressed in this paper are solely my own and do not necessarily reflect those of the US government. The views expressed in this paper also do not necessarily reflect those of the generous people who have commented on drafts of this essay, but who deserve thanks for making it better. These people include David Painter, Alan McPherson, Glenn Dorn, William Walker, Judith Ewell, Stephen Rabe, Heather Gold, and members of my spring 2004 seminar in the history of US-Third World relations at the United States Merchant Marine Academy (Ian Stewart, John Hammond, Tormod Engvig, Adam Rapacki, Sean Russell, Bradley Griffin, David Dwyer, Matthew Lynch, Alex DePalo, and Max Scafidi).
2. M. R. Zanhiser and M. W. Weis, "A Diplomatic Pearl Harbor?: Richard Nixon's Goodwill Mission to Latin America in 1958," *Diplomatic History* 13 (1989): 163–91; A. McPherson, *Yankee No!: Anti-Americanism in US-Latin American Relations* (Cambridge, 2003), 9–37.
3. See W. W. Rostow, *The Stages of Economic Growth: A Non-Communist Manifesto.* (Cambridge, UK, 1960); M. Latham, "Ideology, Social Science, and Destiny: Modernization and the Kennedy-Era Alliance for Progress," *Diplomatic History* 22 (1988): 199–229; M. Latham, *Modernization as Ideology: American Social Science and "Nation Building" in the Kennedy Era* (Chapel Hill, 2000); N. Gilman, *Mandarins of the Future: Modernization Theory in Cold War America* (Baltimore, 2004).
4. See S. G. Rabe, *The Most Dangerous Area in the World: John F. Kennedy Confronts Communist Revolution in Latin America* (Chapel Hill, 1999), for a good recent analysis of the Alliance for Progress.
5. F. G. Gil, *El Sistema Político de Chile* (Santiago, 1969); C. Caviades, *The Politics of Chile: A Sociogeographical Assessment* (Boulder, 1979); G. U. Valenzuela, *Historia Política de Chile y su Evolución Electoral: Desde 1810 a 1992* (Santiago, 1992).
6. J. F. Taffet, "Alliance for What?: US Development Assistance in Chile during the 1960s" (Ph.D. diss., Georgetown, 2001).
7. Unidad Popular, *Programa Básico de Gobierno de la Unidad Popular* (Santiago, 1969), 5, 6–7, 20, 24–25, 33.
8. In 1958 Allende took 28.8 percent of the vote in a four-person race, in 1964 he polled 38.9 percent in a two-person race, and in 1970 he took 36.3 percent in a

three-person race. In other words, his share of the vote actually dropped between 1964 and 1970. However, Radimiro Tomic, who ran as the candidate of the Christian Democratic party, also ran on an anti-American platform in 1970 and took 27.8 percent of the vote. Caviedes, *Politics of Chile,* 206, 222–31, 253–58.

9. M. Kurlansky, *1968: The Year that Rocked the World* (New York, 2003).
10. R. Fuentealba, "En el torno a la via violencia," *Política y Espíritu* 22 (1967): 41–58; Dean to State, 10 June 1967, Pol 23-8 Chile, Central Foreign Policy Files 1967–1969, Box 1999, RG 59, NA.
11. P. Donner, *Cambios Sociales y Conflicto Político: El Conflicto Político Nacional Durante el Gobierno de Eduardo Frei* (Santiago, 1984); A Fontaine Aldunate, *Todos Guerían la Revolución: Chile, 1964–1973* (Santiago, 1999).
12. Study of Chilean University Student Opinions: Marplan, August 1964, Student Attitudes Part I, USIA CI6402, Box 20, RG 306, NA.
13. Omnibus Study of Public Opinion: International Research Associates. S.A. and C.V., World Survey III: Multi-Latin America Part 3, ZP 6501, Box 20, RG 306, NA.
14. *Topaze,* 29 August 1969. J. F. Taffet, "Selling the Alliance: US Propaganda vs. Chilean Editorial Cartoons during the 1960s," *International Journal of Comic Art* 6 (2004): 163–90.
15. *Topaze,* 23 May 1969.
16. *Topaze,* 29 August 1970.
17. *El Mercurio,* 13 March 1969; *Clarín,* 13 March 1968; Dean to State, 12 March 1968, Pol 23-8 Chile, Central Foreign Policy Files 1967–1969, Box 1999, RG 59, NA; Dean to State, 16 March 1968, Pol 23-8, Central Foreign Policy Files 1967–1969, Box 1999, RG 59, NA.
18. *Vea,* 21 March 1968; Dean to State, 18 March 1968, Pol 23-8 Chile, Central Foreign Policy Files 1967–1969, Box 1999, RG 59, NA.
19. Study of leftist Chilean papers such as *El Siglo* and *Última Hora* during 1967 and 1968 reveals that the issue of anti-American violence was not reported. Even in more moderate papers such as *Clarín,* or the government-controlled *La Nación,* reports on the incidents were not made.
20. Frei interview with J. Dubois, cited in *El Pensamiento de Eduardo Frei,* ed. O. Pinochet de la Barra (Santiago, 1982), 155.
21. Solomon to Mann and Bell, 13 November 1964, AID (US) 8, Central Foreign Policy Files 1964–1966, Box 541, RG 59, NA; *New York Times,* 26 November 1964; Solomon to Mann and Bell, 11 November 1964, FN 1, Central Foreign Policy Files 1964–1966, Box 842, RG 59, NA; Del Canto to the Managing Director, 22 December 1964, Chilean Debt Renegotiation 1964–1971, Chile Files, IMFA.
22. *New York Times,* 4 December 1964.
23. Palmer and Bloomfield (Solomon) Circular Memo, December 8, 1964, AID (US) Chile, Central Foreign Policy Files 1964–1966, Box 541, RG 59, NA.
24. Del Canto and Zassenhaus to Robichek, 13 August 1965, C/Chile/810 Mission - July 1965, IMFA.
25. Memorandum of Conversation, Rusk, Tomic, Sayre, Williams, 6 August 1965, Pol Chile-US, Central Foreign Policy Files 1964–1966, Box 2030, RG 59, NA; on Chile's general position in mid-1965, see E. Frei, "Los Fundamentos de Nuestra Acción: Primer Mensaje del Presidente de la República de Chile, 21 May 1965," (Santiago, 1965), 5–11; R. Fuentealba, "Nuestro país está en crisis, pero el Presidente Frei no se quedara de brazos cruzados frente a la oposición," *Política y Espiritu* 19 (1965): 3–11.
26. Memorandum of Conversation, Rusk, Valdes, Magnet, Vaughn, Williams, Topping, 25 September 1965, Pol 2 Chile, Central Foreign Policy Files 1964–1966, Box 2020, RG 59, NA.
27. Memorandum of Conversation, Valdes, Tomic, Molina, Vaughn, Sayre, Palmer, Bronhiem, Robinson, Williams, 7 October 1965, Pol Chile-US, Central Foreign

Policy Files 1964–1966, Box 2030, RG 59, NA. Williams (Vaughn) to Santiago, 12 October 1965, Aid (US) 9, Central Foreign Policy Files 1964–1966, Box 541, RG 59, NA.

28. Palmer (Vaughn) to Ambassador, 3 November 1965, Aid (US) 9, Central Foreign Policy Files 1964–1966, Box 541, RG 59, NA; Dungan to Vaughn, 3 November 1965, Aid (US) 9, Central Foreign Policy Files 1964–1966, Box 541, RG 59, NA; Dungan to Vaughn, 9 November 1965, Aid (US) 9, Central Foreign Policy Files 1964–1966, Box 541, RG 59, NA.

29. Mann to Bundy, 10 November 1965, Chile, vol. IV, Memos, 10/65–7/67, NSF Country File, Box 13, LBJL.

30. Bell to Johnson, 6 November 1965, Chile, Vol IV, Memos, 10/65–7/67, NSF Country File, Box 13, LBJL. In a earlier memo to Johnson, Bell wrote, "the Frei government is a democratically elected reform-minded government of exactly the kind we hope to see emerge gradually in more and more Latin American countries." Bell to Johnson, 21 October 1965, Document 44, *FRUS 1964–1968,* IX, available online at http://www.state.gov/www/about_state/history/Vol_IX/index .html.

31. Bell to Johnson, 6 November 1965, Chile, vol. IV, Memos, 10/65–7/67, NSF Country File, Box 13, LBJL; See also, Schultze to Johnson, 10 November 1965, CF Oversize Attachments [Materials on Copper], 1 of 2, WHCF, Box 161, LBJL.

32. *Wall Street Journal,* 16 November 1965; *American Metal Markets,* 1 July 1965; *Wall Street Journal,* 3 November 1965; *American Metal Markets,* 27, 28, and 29 October 1965, 8, 9, and 18 November 1965, 1, 2, and 3 December 1965; Dungan to State, 25 October 1965, Inco-Copper Chile, Central Foreign Policy Files 1964–1966, Box 2 – TS, RG 59, NA.

33. *Wall Street Journal,* 10 November 1965; Dungan to State, 20 October 1965, Inco-Copper Chile, Central Foreign Policy Files 1964–1966, Box 2 – TS, RG 59, NA

34. Ackley to Attorney General, 14 November 1965, Copper 11/12/65–11/17/65, Legislative Background, Copper Price Increases, November 1965, Box 1, LBJL; Dungan to Rusk, Mann, Vaughn, Harriman, Solomon, and Califano, 4 December 1965, Inco-Copper Chile, Central Foreign Policy Files 1964–1966, Box 2 – TS, RG 59, NA; Ackley to Attorney General, 14 November 1965, Copper 11/12/65–11/17/65, Legislative Background, Copper Price Increases, November 1965, Box 1, LBJL; Califano to Ackley, 14 November 1965, Copper 11/12/65–11/17/65, Legislative Background, Copper Price Increases, November 1965, Box 1, LBJL; Memorandum-Why Stability of Copper Prices, 14 November 1965, Copper 11/12/65–11/17/65, Legislative Background, Copper Price Increases, November 1965, Box 1, LBJL; Ackley made these points in brief form to Johnson in a memo dated 8 November 1965, Document 296, *FRUS 1964–1968,* IX, available online at http://www.state.gov/www/about_state/history/Vol_IX/index.html.

35. Mann to Johnson, 13 November 1965, Copper - After 11/17/65 Folder II, Legislative Background, Copper Price Increases, November 1965, Box 1, LBJL.

36. Harriman to Johnson, Ball, McNamara, Califano, and Bundy, 15 November 1965, Copper Problems, NSF Subject File, Box 7, LBJL; Solomon to Ball, Mann, McNamara, and Califano, 16 November 1965, Copper Problems, NSF Subject File, Box 7, LBJL; also see Inco-Copper Chile, Central Foreign Policy Files 1964–1966, RG 59, NA; Mann to Harriman and Solomon, 15 November 1965, Inco-Copper Chile, Central Foreign Policy Files 1964–1966, Box 2 – TS, RG 59, NA.

37. Harriman to Johnson, Ball, Mann, McNamara, Califano, 19 November 1965, Trips and Missions: Latin America File, W. Averell Harriman Papers, Box 547, Manuscript Division, LOC; Califano to Johnson, 21 November 1965, Folder of Material Sent by Califano, [2 of 2], WHCF, CF, Oversize Attachments, Box 161, LBJL. On the $10 million loan see, Palmer to Solomon, 8 March 1966, Copper File, Papers of Anthony M. Solomon, Box 2, LBJL.

38. Harriman to Johnson, 19 November 1965, Trips and Missions: Latin America File, W. Averell Harriman Papers, Box 547, Manuscript Division, LOC.
39. *New York Times,* 20 November 1965; *New York Times,* 21 November 1965; *Wall Street Journal,* 22 November 1965; News Conference Text, McNamara, 17 November 1965, CM Copper, WHCF CM, Box 2, LBJL; *Wall Street Journal,* 18 November 1965. See also Telephone Transcript, McNamara, Ball, 17 November 1965, Chile [5/12/64–11/18/65], Box 2, Papers of George Ball, LBJL; Telephone Transcript, Mann, Ball, 18 November 1965, Chile [5/12/64–11/18/65], Box 2, Papers of George Ball, LBJL; *New York Times* 18 November 1965.
40. Dungan to Harriman and Rusk, 23 November 1965, Trips and Missions: Latin America File, W. Averell Harriman Papers, Box 547, Manuscript Division, LOC.
41. *Washington Post,* 23 November 1965; Dungan to Rusk, Mann, Vaughn, Harriman, Solomon, and Califano, 4 December 1965, Inco-Copper Chile, Central Foreign Policy Files 1964–1966, Box 2 – TS, RG 59, NA; Merriam to Rusk, 21 November 1965, Inco-Copper Chile, Central Foreign Policy Files 1964–1966, Box 2 –TS, RG 59, NA.
42. Dungan to State, 27 November 1965, FN 1-1 Chile, Central Foreign Policy Files 1964–1966, RG 59, NA; Dungan to Vaughn, 30 November 1965, FN 1-1 Chile, Central Foreign Policy Files 1964–1966, Box 842, RG 59, NA; Dungan to State, Commerce, Treasury, and Federal Reserve, 4 December 1965, Aid (US) 9 Chile, Central Foreign Policy Files 1964–1966, Box 541, RG 59, NA.
43. Palmer and Dungan to State, 4 December 1965, Aid (US) 9 Chile, Central Foreign Policy Files 1964–1966, Box 541, RG 59, NA.
44. Bloomfield (Bell) to Palmer, 7 December 1965, Aid (US) 9 Chile, Central Foreign Policy Files 1964–1966, Box 541, RG 59, NA.
45. Memorandum of Conversation, Vaughn, Tomic, Bronheim, Sternfield, Morris, Bloomfield, 10 December 1965, Aid (US) 9 Chile, Central Foreign Policy Files 1964–1966, Box 541, RG 59, NA.
46. Dungan to State, 9 December 1965, Aid (US) 9 Chile, Central Foreign Policy Files 1964–1966, Box 541, RG 59, NA.
47. Dungan to State, 27 December 1965, FN 1-1 Chile, Central Foreign Policy Files 1964–1966, Box 842, RG 59, NA; Staff Memorandum to Ambassador, 5 January 1966, Inco-Copper 17 US-Chile, Central Foreign Policy Files 1964–1966, Box 2 – TS, RG 59, NA.
48. Dungan to State, 14 January 1966, Inco-Copper Chile, Central Foreign Policy Files 1964–1966, Box 2 – TS, RG 59, NA; Dungan to State, 19 January 1966, Aid (US) 9 Chile, Central Foreign Policy Files 1964–1966, Box 541, RG 59, NA.
49. Dungan to State, 14 January 1966, Inco-Copper Chile, Central Foreign Policy Files 1964–1966, Box 2 – TS, RG 59, NA; Palmer to Santiago, 17 January 1966, Inco-Copper Chile, Central Foreign Policy Files 1964–1966, Box 2 – TS, RG 59, NA; Palmer to Santiago, 19 January 1966, Inco-Copper Chile, Central Foreign Policy Files 1964–1966, Box 2 – TS, RG 59, NA.
50. Dungan (Daniels) to State, 22 July 1966, E 2-2 Chile, Central Foreign Policy Files 1964–1966, Box 701, RG 59, NA; Dungan (Morehead) to State, 19 August 1966, E 2-2 Chile, Central Foreign Policy Files 1964–1966, Box 701, RG 59, NA.
51. Frei's Rancagua Speech, 2 October 1966, copy from Guenther (Weintraub) to State, 7 October 1966, Pol 15-1 Chile, Central Foreign Policy Files 1964–1966, Box 2029, RG 59, NA; The "second Independence" language of Frei's plans became a shorthand political justification of the later copper nationalizations. See "El Cobre: Entre la Gran Estafa y un Segundo 1810," *Panorama Económico* 246 (1969): 3–10.
52. Frei speech to Kenneth Kaunda, 17 December 1966, cited in E. Frei, *América Latina Tiene un Destino* (Santiago, 1967): 93–105; Frei made a similar point in a

speech to a meeting of his Christian Democrats on 4 November 1966. See E. Frei, "Nuestra revolución en libertad," *Política y Espíritu* 20 (1966): 32–46.

53. *Clarín,* 22 December 1966; *El Siglo,* 22 December 1966; *Última Hora,* 22 December 1966; *La Nación,* 22 December 1966; Frei speech cited in Dean to State, 28 December 1966, Pol 1 Chile, Central Foreign Policy Files 1964–1966, Box 2020, RG 59, NA.

54. H. F. Armstrong to E. Frei, 1 March 1965, Hamilton Fish Armstrong Papers, Correspondence File: Frei, Eduardo, Box 29, MUDD; H. F. Armstrong to E. Frei, 28 May 1965, Hamilton Fish Armstrong Papers, Correspondence File: Frei, Eduardo Montalva, Box 29, MUDD; P. W. Quigg to R. Dungan, 28 May 1965, Hamilton Fish Armstrong Papers, Correspondence File: Frei, Eduardo Montalva, Box 29, MUDD; P. W. Quigg to R. Dungan, 1 September 1965, Hamilton Fish Armstrong Papers, Correspondence File: Frei, Eduardo Montalva, Box 29, MUDD; H. F. Armstrong to R. Dungan, 7 December 1965, Hamilton Fish Armstrong Papers, Correspondence File: Frei, Eduardo Montalva, Box 29, MUDD; H. F. Armstrong to R. Tomic, 26 September 1966, Hamilton Fish Armstrong Papers, Correspondence File: Frei, Eduardo Montalva, Box 29, MUDD; R. Tomic to H. F. Armstrong, 6 October 1966, Hamilton Fish Armstrong Papers, Correspondence File: Frei, Eduardo Montalva, Box 29, MUDD; H. F. Armstrong to E. Frei, 27 October 1966, Hamilton Fish Armstrong Papers, Correspondence File: Frei, Eduardo Montalva, Box 29, MUDD; H. F. Armstrong to R. Tomic, 4 November 1966, Hamilton Fish Armstrong Papers, Correspondence File: Frei, Eduardo Montalva, Box 29, MUDD.

55. E. Frei, "The Alliance That Lost Its Way," *Foreign Affairs* 45 (1967): 427–48; Frei's article provided the inspiration and title for J. Levinson and J. de Onis's text, *The Alliance That Lost Its Way* (Chicago, 1970).

Chapter 5

BATTLE FOR THE HEART OF THE HEAVYWEIGHT
Anti-Americanism in Brazil

Kirk Bowman

The first sign of anti-Americanism in Brazil in 2003–2004 surfaced rather dramatically to arriving passengers in the shops of the country's international airports, where Michael Moore's bestseller *Stupid White Men* was ubiquitously displayed. Given the worldwide success of Moore's book, this was no surprise. What was unusual was the title. While Spanish-speaking Latin America used a literal translation of the title *(Estúpidos hombres blancos),* as did Portugal for its Portuguese edition *(Brancos estúpidos),* in Portuguese-speaking Brazil, Moore's book spent nineteen weeks on the bestseller list as *A Nation of Idiots (Uma nação de idiotas).*[1] In the rest of Moore's world, only a small sector of the United States was stupid; but for Brazilians, all Americans were idiots.

The book title did not represent an anomaly or isolated case of intense anti-Americanism in contemporary Brazil. Rather, anti-US sentiment in Brazil was widespread and potent as the largest nation in Latin America entered the twenty-first century. Most commentators argue that this resulted from a long series of discrete events, including the exhaustion of the so-called Washington Consensus on neoliberalism, the presidential election of Luiz Inácio "Lula" da Silva in 2002, Brazil's quest for regional hegemony in South America, the US refusal to sign the environmental agreements that emerged from the 1992 Rio de Janeiro Earth Summit, the George W. Bush administration's apparent snubs of Brazil, the treatment of Brazilians as they traverse immigration at US airports, the trade wars, US unilateralism in foreign affairs, and the war in Iraq. The combination of these factors has been important. Unfortunately, an emphasis on random world and domestic events conceals additional and more systematic causes. In fact, there is a powerful systematic account of the decline of US support throughout the hemisphere, including Brazil, based on changes in power relations and interests. The end of the Cold War brought an end to a fundamental incentive (waging the war on communism) for US and Brazilian elites to cooperate. At the same time, the emergence of transnational activist networks empowered grassroots critics of the hemispheric hegemon. This chapter uses the Brazilian case to illustrate this structural explanation for anti-Americanism.

The chapter proceeds as follows. I first highlight the most commonly cited immediate causes of disenchantment with the United States, arguing that these explanations are discrete and often ad-hoc. Borrowing from Johan Galtung's models of imperialism and Margaret Keck and Kathryn Sikkink's work on transnational advocacy networks, I provide a more systematic analysis of the increase in anti-Americanism. I then provide a brief overview of Brazil-US relations over the period 1950–2000, while at the same time using the historical record to flesh out our structural model of anti-Americanism. The final section details contemporary anti-Americanism in the country, using both anecdotal and survey data.

To better understand the recent rise in anti-Americanism, I conducted over 120 interviews in Brazil over a nine-week period in June, July, and September 2003 and March 2004. I interviewed journalists, academics, attorneys, university students, businesspeople, and taxi drivers. This was not part of a random survey, but rather a series of open-ended discussions. I would ask if anti-Americanism was growing and why, allowing for open response. In addition, I read the *Folha de São Paulo* and other publications each day during the nine weeks, and consulted secondary sources.

Before proceeding to the description of the current state of anti-Americanism in Brazil, it is important to briefly define the concept in order to understand some important, unique characteristics of Brazil. Anti-Americanism is, in fact, a confusing term. One simply does not come across the level of antipathy, resentment, or anger against "Americans" that is often palpable to even casual visitors to Central America. In fact, Brazilians are very friendly with American citizens. Anti-Americanism in the Brazilian context is a negative reaction to things associated with the United States (which could include policy, government, diplomacy, culture, sports, or products) and not directly to citizens.[2]

In international affairs and diplomacy, size matters. In contrast to the Central American republics, the islands of the Caribbean, and the smaller countries of South America, Brazil is nearly equal to the United States in size and population. The country is slightly larger than the continental United States and has a total population of approximately 180 million. Brazil sees itself as a potential major player (belittled by some as the perpetual "country of the future"), wanting a permanent seat on the United Nations Security Council, organizing trade blocs, and winning five World Cups. As a giant country with a large population and abundant natural resources, Brazil is a major consumer market and industrial power. The gross domestic product of a medium-sized Brazilian city like Curitiba, the capital of the southern state of Paraná, is larger than the entire gross domestic product of many Latin American countries, such as Bolivia, Honduras, or Nicaragua. Like many large countries (including the United States), exports and imports comprise a much smaller part of the economy than in smaller countries such as Chile and Costa Rica. Brazil is less trade dependent, allowing the country to pursue a more autonomous course, at least in principle and rhetoric.[3]

Due to the self-perceived correlation between country size/population and prestige/international muscle, Brazilians see a much greater need to demand equal treatment from the United States than do others in the hemisphere.[4] Indeed, Brazil is regularly willing to sacrifice material benefits rather than give the perception of submission to the United States. When the United States began charging Brazilians $135 for tourist visas, Brazil responded by charging US citizens the same, in spite of the potential damage to the tourism industry. When the United States in 2004, ostensibly due to security concerns, required fingerprinting and a photo of all Latin Americans entering the United States through international airports, only Brazil responded in kind to the United States.[5] This response undermined Brazil's renewed efforts to increase tourism, yet it was widely popular in the country. Brazilian size and national prestige demands reciprocity. This heavyweight tit-for-tat is a point of national pride, and is only somewhat approximated by Latin America's other large country in terms of population, Mexico. This factor alone may lead one to expect more anti-Americanism in Brazil than in other countries, where people may accept US slights, snubs, or unilateral actions as the burden that small countries must bear.

Discrete Explanations for the Growth of Anti-Americanism

Why is anti-Americanism so pronounced and growing in contemporary Brazil? A 2003 poll conducted by Zogby International and the

University of Miami School of Business found that only 19 percent of Latin American elites rated President Bush's performance on Latin America as positive. Yet these figures were even lower in Brazil, where only 2 percent rated Bush's performance as positive, and a remarkable 98 percent viewed him negatively.[6] From my interviews and an October 2001 Datafolha survey, the most common reason given for antipathy toward the United States dealt one way or another with the view that the country in general and Bush in particular were arrogant, imperious, or swaggering. These can be broken down into two general categories: international events that have some repercussions in Brazil, and incidents that mainly touch Brazil.

On the international stage, Brazilians reacted unfavorably to what they perceived as unilateral, imperialist, and arbitrary US policies. The war in Iraq (as well as the perception that the United States brushed off the United Nations in prewar diplomacy) was only one of several issues. Interviewees specified global environmental policy (particularly the US refusal to comply with the agreements made at the Earth Summit in Rio de Janeiro), the drug war, and the US rejection of the International Criminal Court as issues that marked Brazilian attitudes. While US willingness to exercise unilateral power has irked people throughout the hemisphere and the world, it has been particularly abrasive in Brazil for specific reasons. Many of the interviewees mentioned that President Luis Inácio "Lula" da Silva was the first Latin American leader to openly criticize the US-led invasion of Iraq and strenuously and publicly opposed the use of Brazilian troops in the conflict. Second, many Brazilians were outraged when, in October 2002, just days before the landslide democratic election of Lula (who—as many Brazilians told me—won 3 million more votes than did Bush), influential Illinois Congressman and House International Relations Committee Chairman Henry Hyde wrote a letter to Bush calling Lula a terrorist and announcing "a real prospect that (Cuba's) Castro, (Venezuela's) Chávez, and (Brazil's) Lula da Silva could constitute an axis of evil in the Americas which might soon have nuclear weapons and ballistic missiles."[7] After watching US threats and pressures on the original "axis of evil" countries— Iran, Iraq, and North Korea as labeled by Bush in his 2002 State of the Union speech—it is no surprise that many Brazilians viewed their inclusion into the Latin American axis of evil club with great trepidation.

Brazilians also regularly identified US trade policy as a source of conflict. US antidumping rulings and the Bush administration's steel tariffs, which were eventually ruled illegal by the World Trade Organization (WTO), were widely acknowledged as prejudicial toward

Brazil and an example of US hypocrisy. It was, after all, the Washington Consensus and US pressure that led to financial, currency, and trade liberalization in Brazil in the latter part of the twentieth century. The United States was the principal cheerleader of these changes, which, when enacted, did not pay off in greater economic growth or better jobs in Brazil. This combined disenchantment with Washington Consensus prescriptions and arbitrary US trade policies left Brazilians with a sour taste.

Unlike Chile and Costa Rica, which largely exported products that complemented US products, Brazil's export product mix placed it on a collision course with the United States. By 2003, Brazil was the world's top exporter of coffee, citrus, sugar, soy products, beef, and chicken, as well as a major grain producer. One of the great success stories of recent years was a rapid and remarkable modernization of Brazilian agro-business for export, with a stunning increase in productivity. Brazilians cried foul, therefore, as the United States, Europe, and Japan collectively subsidized agriculture by some $1 billion per day. The inability to include meaningful subsidy reform in WTO talks in Cancún in late 2003 led to Brazil organizing the G-21, a group of countries that resisted progress of the Doha Round of WTO trade talks unless the wealthy countries paid greater attention to the concerns of the developing world. The fiasco in Cancún led US Trade Representative Robert Zoellick to publicly blame Brazil for the collapse of the talks.[8] Brazil's foreign minister and organizer of the G-21, Celso Amorín, was welcomed back to Brazil from the Cancún debacle as a national hero.

Brazil also emerged as the counterweight to the United States in the negotiations over the Free Trade Agreement of the Americas (FTAA), again demanding that agricultural subsidies, quotas, and tariffs be included in any negotiations. Brazilian leadership against the US version of the FTAA and the Cancún talks was expected, given the country's heavyweight status. Brazil's endless demands on the United States led *Veja* to publish a cover story titled "Brazil stands up to the US in the FTAA: Courage or Stupidity?"[9]

Brazilians want to be respected as a large and important country, and are loathe to forgive and forget national slights, whether real or perceived. When President Bill Clinton visited in 1997, Brazilians were still reeling from President Ronald Reagan's toast "to the people of Bolivia" during a 1982 visit to the Brazilian capital city of Brasilia.[10] This public gaffe by Reagan was trumped by a widely reported private gaffe by President George W. Bush in a meeting with then Brazilian President Fernando Henrique Cardoso in March 2001. Bush reportedly asked Cardoso, a highly regarded sociologist, "Do you have blacks,

too?" National Security Advisor and African-American scholar Con-
doleezza Rice allegedly intervened when the question left Cardoso
open-jawed and speechless, rescuing Bush by noting that Brazil has
more people of African descent than does the United States.[11] Other
administration comments and actions have frustrated Brazilians. At
the top of the chart is the comment by former US Treasury Secretary Paul O'Neill that the International Monetary Fund should not
lend money to Brazil because all of the money would end up in Swiss
banks. His spokesperson later clarified the comment, adding that
the treasury secretary was only referring to Argentina and Uruguay,
and not to Brazil.[12]

A Structural Model for Anti-Americanism

While there are many discrete explanations for anti-Americanism in
Brazil, I contend that there are more systematic explanations based
on class and interests. The main argument is that the international
system and transnational networks previously favored alliances between important Brazilian sectors with strong ties to the United
States and incentives to encourage pro-US sentiment at home. In recent years, however, many of these ties have weakened, and elite
segments that formerly had incentives to build pro-US sentiment in
Brazil now have incentives to encourage anti-Americanism. In particular, the end of the Cold War and the ensuing US unilateralism eliminated many important incentives for political alliances between the
United States and Brazil. At the same time, marginalized progressive
groups in both the United States and Brazil have been united through
the development of non-materialist transnational activist networks.
These groups are most likely to critique US policies, culture, globalization, and multinationals. The simultaneous deterioration of US
support by elite segments in Brazil and the expanding ability of formerly marginalized sectors to critique the United States have resulted in a net increase of anti-Americanism not only in Brazil but
throughout the region. This shift is not mere conjuncture, but represents a paradigmatic and long-term shift where previous US policies
of coercion and incentives no longer function.

In 1971, Johan Galtung offered a structural non-Marxist theory of
imperialism based on relationships between collectivities. "Imperialism is a system that splits up collectivities and relates some of the
parts in relations of *harmony of interest*, and other parts in relations of
disharmony of interest, or *conflict of interest*."[13] For Galtung, there are
relationships or collectivities of core (center) countries and periph-

eral countries. Each country in turn has its own center and periphery sectors. There exist, in turn, relationships between sectors in both the core and the peripheral countries. Often, a harmony of interest develops between the central or elite sectors of both the center and peripheral countries. The harmony of interest implies a positive sum game where both can simultaneously benefit. However, there is a disharmony of interest between the periphery of the center country and the periphery of the periphery country. This disharmony of interest is a zero sum game (jobs moving from a textile mill in South Carolina to Haiti benefit the capitalist class in both countries, but among the workers there are clear winners and losers). The overall relationship between a peripheral country and a core country is dependency. Brazilian sociologists Cardoso and Faletto[14] developed a theory of dependency and dependent development similar to that of Galtung, in which they include the regional core and periphery within Brazil.

Let us take an example of collectivities dealing with current issues of the means of production: high-tech outsourcing. In our hypothetical case, the high-tech corporation IBM decides to dismiss 4,000 software engineers, each of whom makes $50 per hour in California, in order to replace them with 4,000 software engineers making $8 per hour through a company in Southern Brazil. Galtung explains a powerful harmony of interest between IBM and the Brazilian outsourcing company. Both benefit financially: the relationship is positive sum, and both sides are voluntarily participating as active players. Between the periphery of the center (high-paid software engineers) and the periphery of the periphery (low-paid software engineers), there is a disharmony of interest, and the collectivity relationship is zero sum. It is hard to imagine how the workers would organize for mutual benefit. There emerge clear winners and losers, with the workers in the core resisting the move, and the workers in the periphery hoping that the jobs shift from Silicon Valley to Porto Alegre. The core in both the center and the periphery (IBM and the Brazilian outsourcing company) has incentives to maintain or even further the relationship. This can be done in advertising, through media relationships, legislation, and other core networks. A positive sum game or harmony of interest between the cores in Brazil and the United States also implies that there is a group of influential elites in Brazil who benefit from the success of their American partners and who may have incentives in promulgating or facilitating pro-American attitudes.

Galtung described five types of imperialism: economic, political, the repressive apparatus of the state (military and police), communication, and cultural. In each of these domains, the core sectors in both the core and periphery countries are characterized by a harmony of interest. The peripheries of both the core and the periphery, in contrast, are unable to identify or organize around common interests.

What Galtung does not account for is the great oscillation in relations between core groups. In practice there is not always a harmony of interest between the core sectors in core and periphery countries, for example, between the Brazilian and US military or between the heights of capital in both countries. As the Brazilian case study presented here clearly shows, the country's political and military sectors sometimes have harmonious positive sum relations with US counterparts and sometimes have conflictual zero sum game relations.

The most important collectivity or type of imperialism for shaping sentiment toward the United States is political, as political discord can color a wide range of attitudes. A single influential administration or individual can temporarily alter the contours of relations between US and Brazilian elites (a point that will be explored in more detail below). When considerable harmony of interests exists, pro-US sentiment increases. When disharmony dominates at a political level, anti-Americanism tends to grow at all other levels.

A lot has changed, however, in periphery-periphery relations since Galtung's article. According to Keck and Sikkink,[15] one major change has been the emergence of transnational activist networks to create a harmony of interest between periphery sectors in core and periphery countries; for Galtung, there was only disharmony of interest where the marginalized sectors in core and periphery countries had neither the shared interests nor the means to join forces. In recent years, transnational activist networks emerged in sectors such as human rights, the environment, women's rights, animal rights, and antiglobalization. Periphery groups have been empowered by advances in communication and networking, and the emergence of positive sum postmaterialist issues (the environment or human rights instead of jobs). This shift in networking and empowerment amongst formerly atomized groups has fundamentally altered power relations, with Brazil's World Social Forum a prominent exemplar that will be discussed below.

A well-publicized recent event helps to illustrate the Keck and Sikkink model. In the early 1990s, the Mexican government and the Japanese conglomerate Mitsubishi agreed to partner and build the world's largest salt plant on the Sea of Cortéz. The Mexican government and Mitsubishi had a harmony of interest: profit. The local community of fishermen that would be displaced had a disharmony of interest with the Mexican government, as did local environmentalists who wanted to protect the last pristine breeding grounds of the California Gray Whale. It seemed impossible that a small group of local fishermen and environmentalists could stop the Mexican government and a major multinational (with some $230 billion in annual revenues) from constructing the salt facility. Fortunately for the local community, they shared a harmony of interest with well-organized environmentalists in the United States, Europe, and Japan. Using the Internet, faxes, cellular phones, and the global reach of transnational environmental nongovernmental organizations (NGOs), the Mexican opponents to the salt facility gained support from US politicians at the federal and state levels (in California, for example), from intergovernmental organizations such as the North American Free Trade Agreement (NAFTA) commissions and Organization of American States (OAS) and United Nations officials, and from the media. The combined peripheries brought considerable pressure to bear on Mitsubishi and the Mexican government, who eventually abandoned the project and lost a sizable investment.[16] This simply could not have happened a few decades ago.

A second major change since Galtung's 1971 article is the end of the Cold War and the emergence of US global hegemony. The harmony of interest that often existed between the political sectors of the United States and Latin America involved simple trade-offs. The dominant US interest from 1950 to 1989 was halting the spread of Soviet influence. It was usually in the interest of the Latin American political class to be a partner. It could regularly exchange Cold War support for military aid, developmental assistance, grants, loans, and other support. Perhaps more importantly, a Latin American leader who sought a more autonomous position could be punished. US involvement in the overthrow of Jacobo Arbenz in Guatemala, João Goulart in Brazil, Salvador Allende in Chile, Cheddi Jagan in Guyana, and others in the region had a powerful demonstration effect. As political scientist Lars Schoultz argued, the United States chose to combat communism in Latin America with friendly dictators and economic development.[17] Peter Smith described the US strategy in the region as "making friends" with money and "crushing enemies" with force.[18] With the end of the Cold War, however, the stakes have fallen dramatically. Latin American leaders have far fewer incentives for aligning with the United States (with the exception of Colombia, US assistance to other countries has virtually dried up)[19] and far fewer disincentives for publicly opposing US policy (it is no longer a viable option to force out leaders who do not agree with the United States through a military coup).

In Brazil, these two changes have had a major impact. First, the rise of transnational activism of formerly marginalized groups (who focused on the environment, human rights, globalization, workers' rights, trade, gender issues, imperialism, war, genetically modified foods, among other issues) has magnified the voice and power of sectors long critical of US policies. Indeed, through 2003 and again in 2005, Brazil's Porto Alegre created and hosted the World Social Forum, the principal global meeting of transnational peripheral groups. These groups were overwhelmingly critical of US power, policies, culture, and multinationals. These transnational alliances have been remarkably sophisticated and successful in organizing and publicizing their critique of the United States throughout Brazil, influencing the level of anti-Americanism in the country.

Second, the end of the Cold War has made the United States less willing to make concessions or threats to keep its allies. As political scientist Joseph Nye argues, instead of using the "hard power" of coercion and force as in the Cold War, the United States must now lead through "soft power" or the attractiveness of a country's culture, political ideas, and policies.[20] In the Brazilian context, the United States has not effectively exercised soft power. Pro-US sentiment by Brazilian elites has declined, while the visibility and organization of the anti-US peripheral sectors has grown. The election of Lula was only one manifestation of this massive structural shift in anti-Americanism in Brazil.

Historical Overview of Anti-US Sentiment in Brazil

Brazil-US relations long showed a potential for the structural shift we are now witnessing.[21] During the Cold War period from 1945 to 1989, anticommunism disciplined the relationship and tempered potential anti-Americanism in Brazil. During times of stress, therefore, the elites' shared concerns over communism maintained Galtung's core-core harmony of interest. At the same time, however, organized anti-Americanism from below emerged, a process that gained strength with the World Social Forum in the late 1990s.

Anti-Americanism became a political and social force as Brazil first became aware of its dependence on the United States. The 1929 global economic crisis severely impacted Brazil. Commodity prices crashed, and Brazil's principal agricultural exports, such as coffee, floundered, dragging the economy down with it. This in turn led to a surge in protectionist and nationalist sentiment, as well as a widespread desire to increase economic autonomy, alter the laissez-faire economic policies of the past, and rely less on commodities and more on value-added products. Since that time, a great deal of Brazilian economic, political, and military policy has responded to the challenge of finding a balance between autonomy and insertion into the modern capitalist world.

With the Revolution of 1930, Brazil under Getúlio Vargas began a new developmental course, one that would sometimes complement and sometimes challenge US economic and political interests. Rather than being content with producing primary products and importing industrial goods, Brazil adopted the Economic Commission for Latin America (CEPAL) proposals of import substitution industrialization (ISI), with the most visible results being the nationalization of petroleum and steel. Whereas in 1919 industry accounted for some 21 percent of the national economy, by 1939 this expanded to 43 percent. In order to protect these infant industries and the industrial jobs that they supplied, Brazil, like other developing countries, erected barriers to imports. These barriers could both contribute to tensions with the United States (when American products were discriminated against) or could contribute to a harmony of interest between Brazilian and US elite sectors (when General Motors and Brazilian partners produce automobiles in Brazil behind the import barriers).[22]

Trade and investment gained importance in US-Brazilian relations after 1929, revealing areas of joint interest in Brazilian and US core sectors. The Good Neighbor Policy of President Franklin Roosevelt increased US investment in countries such as Brazil. In 1936, Brazil and the United States signed a reciprocal agreement of most favored nation status, which included Brazilian access to the US coffee and cocoa markets and a reduction in Brazilian tariffs on industrial products such as heavy equipment and steel.

The United States partly entered into this agreement because it feared stronger Brazilian ties to Germany. Vargas was playing both sides of the Atlantic, signing agreements with both countries and bartering coffee and cotton for German electrical generators and other heavy equipment. Within the diplomatic corps, Oswaldo Aranha stood out as the strongest supporter of tying Brazil's fortunes to the United States. Aranha held many high positions in the foreign ministry and abandoned Vargas and the role of minister in 1944 to occupy the vice presidency of the *Sociedade Amigos de América* (Society of Friends of America). Brazil tried to remain neutral in World War II. After the war cut off exports to Germany, Brazil aligned itself with the Allies. Its participation with the United States in the war led to an important shift in Brazilian attitudes. Bilateral relations gained strength in economic, military, and cultural domains. US participation in a new steel company in Volta Redonda, military arms and equipment sales, the creation of joint military commissions, and Brazilian armament benefits under the Lend-Lease program deepened cooperation and linked important sectors in a harmony of interest.[23]

While much of Latin America supported the Allies, Brazil went much further. It allowed the construction of an airbase in northeastern Brazil, which facilitated Allied operations in North Africa. Brazil was also the only country in the region to send troops to fight and die in Europe. The country expected to amplify its international image and even play a prestige-generating role in the wartime conferences. At the end of World War II and the beginning of a bipolar division of the world, Brazil was firmly implanted in the West.[24] In the period 1947–1950, nearly 60 percent of Brazilian exports were destined for the US market.[25] Positive proactive US policies could have capitalized on the wartime alliance to bring the largest country in Latin America into a very special relationship with the United States.

Unfortunately, Brazil never received the expected benefits of supporting the allies. Its hope for a permanent seat on the UN Security Council was rebuffed, and Washington began to retreat from its alliance with the Getúlio Vargas regime, which it considered insufficiently democratic. Vargas was deposed in a coup in October 1945. While discourse during the war gave Brazil hope that the United States would actively assist industrial development in Brazil, the 1947 Marshall Plan revealed that US promotion of industrialization would be focused in Europe. As early as the 1945 Inter-American Conference in Chapultepec, Mexico, the United States made clear that it considered Latin America's postwar importance reduced.

General Eurico Gaspar Dutra was elected president after the fall of Vargas, ushering in a period of modern political democracy in Brazil and a pragmatic Cold War-friendly Brazilian posture. Dutra faced the daunting task of exerting the influence that a large and growing country like Brazil deserved in an increasingly bipolar world. While Brazilian intellectuals continued to debate the possibilities of autonomy, Dutra aligned with the United States in the fight against communism while trying to leverage the relationship to enhance the Brazilian armed forces and expand domestic industrialization. By 1947, the Communist Party was formally barred from political activity, and a heavy persecution of the left ensued. A wide range of political actors and groups in Brazil received financial and other support from the Central Intelligence Agency and other US agencies in the battle against communism, even as the Soviets aided their potential allies in the country.[26]

There were cracks in the alliance early on, however. Brazil's support for the United States in the Korean conflict was not unequivocal. The United States pressured Brazil to authorize the commitment of troops in the conflict, but this was too much during an election year. While the Brazilian masses had not yet developed an identity that could result in protests of government policies, they could punish unpopular measures at the ballot box.[27] The Korean conflict continued to reverberate in Brazil after Vargas came back and won the presidency in the 1950 elections. Vargas's nationalist rhetoric and ISI developmental model worried US leaders. And while Vargas continued to resist sending troops to Korea, Brazil and the United States signed a military agreement in 1952 that assured the continued supply of Brazilian strategic raw materials. The Brazilian Workers' Party (PT) and some sectors in the Brazilian military opposed such cooperation with the United States, revealing a polarization between pro-Americans and anti-Americans in the country.

Anti-Americanism coalesced more strongly in the late 1950s. One reason was the election of Juscelino Kubitschek as president. After his election in 1955, Kubitschek embarked on an ambitious "Fifty Years in Five" developmental program, centered on industrialization (particularly automobiles) and the moving of the capital from Rio de Janeiro to Brasilia. General Motors, along with European producers such as Volkswagen, Renault, and Fiat, were lured by the market potential of the region. The fact that Kubitschek liberally employed tariff barriers did not mean that US actors were shut out. There were ample opportunities for direct investment and financing of the often pharaonic projects.

Another reason is that 1959 witnessed both the Cuban Revolution of Fidel Castro and increased commercial relations between Brazil and the Soviet Union, with the former trading coffee for wheat and petroleum products. The overthrow of Fulgencio Batista in Cuba horrified the United States and energized the region's leftists. The stakes for direct US intervention were perceptively higher, and the failed Bay of Pigs invasion stoked the flames of anti-Americanism throughout the hemisphere.[28]

The governments of Janio Quadros (1961) and João Goulart (1961–1964) experimented with a new policy of "Independent Foreign Affairs" *(Política Externa Independente)* for Brazil that challenged the United States at the same time that the United States was implementing the Alliance for Progress, a multibillion-dollar aid program for Latin America. While Alliance for Progress funds did assist Brazil, local critics argued that the program's real purpose was to maintain the established socioeconomic structure and to buy government and political support for US interests.[29]

Relations between the two countries became quite tense when Brazil voted against the US-sponsored blockade of Cuba at the 1962

Punta del Este conference. Months later, however, Brazil voted with the United States at a meeting of the OAS for the somewhat softer embargo of Cuba. Not only was Brazil unstable in its international affairs but also in its domestic politics. By 1963, Goulart was facing increasing pressures. Finally, he was deposed in a military coup in April 1964, an unconstitutional play that was applauded by the majority of the Brazilian media and by the government of Lyndon Johnson. The media likely soon regretted their euphoria, as the new military government closed congress, banned political parties, and strongly censored the media. Washington, however, was relieved to have the tensions with Goulart over and a strong ally in the military in charge in Brasilia.

In terms of Brazilian attitudes toward the United States, 1964 was a complex year. While the extent of US involvement in the coup was only verified in 2003 upon the release of previously confidential government files, rumors of US participation ran rampant in Brazil. The perception on the streets generated anti-US sentiment among urban sectors and university students, particularly after the military waged a dirty war against the left. That year also marked the escalation of US involvement in the Vietnam War. A strong antiwar and anti-American movement in Brazil took shape as, for the first time in history, Brazilian youths organized and protested in large numbers. When university students rebelled against the Institutional Act Number 5 in 1968, which hardened military rule in the country, it was also a rebellion against the Vietnam War and US support of military rule in Brazil.

In the 1960s for the first time, it was hip to be anti-American. An important antiestablishment cadre of university students, bohemians, intellectuals, labor leaders, and others came of political age in the turbulent 1960s, a decade marked by the Vietnam War abroad and the collapse of democracy and the rise of authoritarianism at home. Many of these same individuals stepped into the political and intellectual elite in the 1990s and beyond.[30] During the administration of George H. Bush, many elite Brazilians who became politically active in the 1960s advanced anti-Americanism in the country. Even with new political restrictions after the 1964 coup that deposed Goulart, a new and important alternative weekly was launched in 1964, *O Pasquim*. This journal combined rebellion with satire and humor, and featured a large number of political cartoons. *O Pasquim* targeted young Brazilians with an irreverent and hard-hitting commentary that criticized the military regime, condemned colonialism, and disparaged the United States.[31]

By the mid-1970s Brazilians no longer wanted to be automatically aligned with the United States, but preferred a "special relationship."

In February 1976, Secretary of State Henry Kissinger and Minister of Foreign Affairs Antônio Azeredo da Silviera agreed to a special status for Brazil, which included semiannual meetings of foreign ministers. Of all the countries in the developing world, only Saudi Arabia had such an agreement with the United States. This was a clear victory for Brazil's heavyweight ambitions. Brazilian national pride and resentment toward US interference arose for very different reasons during the US administration of President Jimmy Carter. Carter's emphasis on human rights did not sit well with the generals, and US opposition to the transfer of nuclear technology from Germany angered many Brazilians.[32]

In the 1990s, the liberalization of the economy and the slow but steady retreat of the military from politics[33] produced a strong harmony of interests among economic elites in the United States and Brazil. Privatization brought huge investments from US and European companies, and many elites benefited. At the same time, Brazil continued a policy of protection of certain sectors, such as the computer industry. The United States attempted to pry open Brazilian markets, eventually applying commercial restrictions to Brazilian products in 1988. Despite the commercial tensions, the end of the military regime in 1985 and the partial adoption of the Washington Consensus brought expanding economic partnerships with the United States. Total trade between the two countries grew from $9.6 billion in 1985 to $16.7 billion in 1994.[34]

The return to civilian governments in 1985 led to the expansion of civil society and gave greater voice to critical sectors in Brazil. Students, intellectuals, and union members, among others, wanted the full transition to democracy to accelerate. This push resulted in the important Campaign for Rights Now! *(Campanha Diretas Já!)*. The timing was such that Brazil witnessed the increased importance of critical sectors of the population just as the Cold War was winding down. The ascension of organized constituents for human rights, workers' rights, and women's rights would eventually result in transnational ties and the founding of the World Social Forum (WSF).

The organizers of the WSF enlisted support from the PT-governed city of Porto Alegre, and the first Forum was held in 2001. Over twenty thousand participants showed up that year, followed by fifty thousand in 2002, and over one hundred thousand in 2003. The number of official delegates grew from 4,700 in 2001, to 12,274 in 2002, and 20,763 in 2003, hailing from 123 countries.[35] The WSF emerged as a counter-hegemonic project to the World Economic Forum of Davos, Switzerland. Envisioned as a space for reflection, for debate of new proposals, and for offering critical responses to the unbridled enthusiasm for free markets and globalization, many of the goals of the WSF directly contradicted US policies on war, global warming, intellectual property rights, the International Criminal Court, the FTAA, the WTO, and the Tobin Tax, which proposed a surcharge on all international financial transactions in an effort to slow currency speculators and the portfolio capital flight that can throw developing economies into crises.

The impact of the WSF on Brazil has been considerable. Even Brazilians who do not consider themselves as progressives view the forum as a point of national pride. More importantly, the WSF represents a powerful link between Brazilian NGOs and transnational activist networks. It empowers domestic agencies and groups, actors highly critical of the United States.

Bush, Iraq, and the Future

With the Cold War well over and the recent rise of connected progressive transnational activists in Brazil, as of this writing, the Bush administration would have to positively engage Brazilians in order to build pro-Americanism. Brazilians have not accepted the War on Terror as an interest-shaper in the same way they accepted the war on communism. With the WSF lambasting the Americans every year, and Washington unwilling to provide economic aid or other substantial assistance to the country, the United States would have to make a consistent proactive effort to undermine anti-Americanism.

In many arenas, the opposite has occurred. The Bush administration increased US farm subsidies and placed tariffs on Brazilian steel, hurting important export and industrial sectors. In addition, various US officials such as Paul O'Neill have publicly criticized Brazilian policies in a tone that could easily be construed as demeaning, and US immigration policies have been taken as a personal affront to Brazilians wealthy enough to travel to the United States. Anyone who has recently lived in Brazil and has followed the local media cannot but be impressed by the failure of the United States in winning the war of public opinion and forging harmonies of interest with elite sectors. "The entire mainstream Brazilian media, without exception, is anti-American, anti-Bush. . . . Everybody in [the] Brazilian media commenting on September 11 was unanimous in attributing to the United States several different degrees of responsibility for the evil that was done to them. . . . Brazilian public opinion is massively persuaded that the United States is in a full-fledged imperialistic campaign to subjugate Brazil economically, destroy it culturally, and finally, to occupy with troops at least part of its territory."[36]

The terrorist attacks of September 2001 and the subsequent war in Iraq triggered an outpouring of hostile sentiment. The public evidence of heartfelt anger of Brazilians against the United States was astonishing, particularly in response to the 11 September attacks. Prominent Brazilian economist Celso Furtado charged in the Brazilian media that the attack was likely a provocation carried out by the US right wing to justify a takeover of the government. Brazilian theologian Leonardo Boff complained in Rio de Janeiro's daily *O Globo* that only one airplane crashed into the Pentagon; he would have preferred twenty-five.[37] The ubiquitous anti-US clatter resulted in a 3 October 2001 cover article in Brazil's most important newsmagazine, *Veja*, entitled "The Anti-USA Virus: The demagoguery that blamed the victim" *(O Vírus Anti-EUA: A demagogia que transformou a vítima em culpada).*

In the wake of 11 September 2001, Osama bin Laden emerged as a triumphal hero not only to public intellectuals but to a surprising number of Brazilians. For the poor, there was a vividly painted mural of Osama along the walls of Rio's largest ghetto.[38] For the elites, a private Rio de Janeiro high school soccer team wanted to change its name to "Osama bin Laden," but was overruled by the school's administration.[39]

When the war in Iraq began in spring 2003, the most important newspaper in the country, *Folha de São Paulo,* headlined every front page article dealing with the war with "The Attack of the Empire" *(O Ataque do Imperio).*[40] This daily headline had a double meaning. The first was that the United States was emerging as a dangerous imperialist power. The second cleverly morphed the United States into the evil empire of the Star Wars film series. The overmatched Iraqis represented the underdog rebels, and the technologically superior United States the Evil Empire (the Empire had the Death Star, while the United States had smart bombs). For *Folha de São Paulo* and many Brazilians, Defense Secretary Donald Rumsfeld represented Darth Vader.

Bush did not fare any better than Rumsfeld (see Fig. 5.1). Seemingly everywhere one looked, he was compared to Adolf Hitler. On the sunny beaches of Balnerario Camboriú, in the southern state of Santa Catarina, souvenir shops hawked T-shirts featuring the caption "Wanted" and a picture of Bush with a Hitleresque moustache. The highly respected progressive journal *Caros Amigos,* in an article titled "George W., but He Could be called Adolf H.," argued that the Bush doctrine of preemptive war was stolen from the ideas of Hitler.[41] Bush, finally, appeared on the cover of *Veja* as a Roman emperor.

In 2003–2004, Brazil's suspicions of US intentions in the future remained sky-high. Both the left and right publicly stated that the United

Figure 5.1

Anti-Bush poster seen at Landless Movement land invasion site in São Paulo state, Brazil, 2003. Photo by Kirk Bowman.

States might invade the Amazon region. *Caros Amigos* postulated in the April 2003 edition that today, the United States invaded Iraq, tomorrow Venezuela, and after that Brazil's Amazon. Elements in the Brazilian military had the same fears: "In the frontier bases, many officers and soldiers are already dedicated to the study of the works of Ho Chi Minh and General Giap, aiming to assimilate the Vietcong war techniques for future combat against the North American invaders."[42] Brazilian paranoia reached a new high when it was insinuated that the Americans subverted Brazil's most recent failure in its rocket launching program: "Brazilian authorities say they are not dismissing the possibility that the accident that killed twenty-one Brazilian space technicians in the Alcântara Space Base was an act of sabotage. Who would benefit from this crime? The US and its allies. No one has the right to think Brazil is a county of inept technicians."[43]

The Internet has also spawned a rich arena for anti-Americanism in Brazil. A keyword search in January 2003 returned 1,560 Portuguese language hits for "Anti-EAU" and another 1,640 Portuguese language hits for "anti-Americanismo." One site spelled out "death to the USA" in its URL (morte.aos.eua.vilabol.uol.com.br/) and featured a detailed plan for invading, conquering, and dividing up the United States by Brazil, Cuba, Mexico, China, Iraq, Iran, and Russia. Other addresses included "GetoutUSA" (forausa.vila.bol.com.br/) and "Anti-USApage" (www.paginaantieua.hpg.ig.com.br/).

One may dismiss these examples as biased anecdotes and not representative of Brazilian attitudes. Yet, more objective survey data reinforces the anecdotal evidence. A September 2001 Datafolha poll[44] found that 79 percent of Brazilians unequivocally opposed any US military action in response to the 11 September attacks. Perhaps surprisingly, wealthier Brazilians were more opposed (83 percent) than were the poor (78 percent). A separate Datafolha poll at the end of October 2001 revealed that 45 percent had a lower image of the United States after the attacks, and only 2 percent had a more positive image.[45] The number one reason for this negative opinion was US "arrogance," and again the wealthy and best-educated were most likely to hold such views. In addition, a growing number of Brazilians were averse to visiting, working, or studying in the United States. Sixty-one percent of Paulistanos (inhabitants of São Paulo) responded that they would refuse a scholarship to study in the United States, and 60 percent stated that they would refuse a job offer there, despite a severe employment crisis in Brazil.

These numbers were indeed new. While in 2000, 18 percent of Brazilians had a negative image of the United States, this number more than doubled to 37 percent by November 2003.[46] While the perception of the United States had deteriorated in recent years, the image of President Bush has plummeted. The Bush administration not only lost the battle for public opinion in difficult places like Jordan and Morocco, but had failed in Christian and western Brazil.

Given Brazil's heavyweight status, Brazilians' perceptions of the United States are shaped by a demand for reciprocity and equal treatment. Under President Lula, this insistence on being a respected regional power and active member of the emerging club of large developing countries (along with China, India, and South Africa) has enhanced the tit-for-tat strategy of Brazilian foreign policy. During the Cold War, the war against communism was the highest priority for many political and military elites in both countries. The US nourished support in Brazil and throughout Latin America through military assistance and economic aid. A strong and influential bloc of support for the United States always existed in Brazil, a force that would temper periods of discord and anti-Americanism. Center-center harmonies of interest were strong, and elite cooperation largely operated within a positive sum arena. Once the logic of anticommunism disappeared, elite harmonies of interest declined, and support for the United States within Brazil depended much more on US policies and diplomacy, along with the perception of respect for Brazil. Brazilians do not join US officials in the belief that antiterrorism is the new universal cause to rally behind. In fact, the Brazilian military publicly rebuked US Defense Secretary Donald Rumsfeld's late 2004 demand for a greater role for the hemisphere's armed forces in domestic police activities and dismissed allegations that terrorists train in the triple frontier region of the country. In addition, traditional critics of the United States have been empowered through transnational activist networks in general and in the World Social Forum in particular.

The Clinton administration did far better than the current Bush administration in portraying respect for and cooperation with Brazil in the post-Cold War era, with Clinton's successful forty-five-hour trip to Brazil generating considerable goodwill. The Bush administration has engendered anti-Americanism through both substance and style. Policies on trade and immigration have disappointed traditional allies and supporters of the United States. And a series of belittling and demeaning comments by government officials have caused a spike in anti-American sentiment.

The disappearance of the anticommunist paradigm and the emergence of postmaterialist values and transnational activists networks turned Galtung's model on its head. Suddenly (at least in the domain of postmaterialist issues), a harmony of interest is stronger between the periphery groups in Brazil and the United States than between elite groups. This structural shift and decline in US support is not only apparent in Brazil, but throughout the region. Without considerable effort and incentives by the United States, anti-Americanism is likely to remain strong in Latin America for some time. There still exist incentives for cooperation and progress between Brazil and the United States. Clearly, development, trade, cultural, human rights, and other issues could create harmonies of interest. However, without a paradigm like the Cold War to bind the relationship, and with the United States focused on the "war on terror," it is unlikely that the United States will be willing to make the effort necessary to successfully deploy soft power and enhance its image in the region.

Notes

1. Available at http://vermelho.org.br/diario/2003/1023/michael_moore.htm. Published in Brazil by Francis Books, 2003. (All web addresses cited in this chapter were last accessed on 27 April 2004.)
2. See A. McPherson, *Yankee No! Anti-Americanism in US-Latin American Relations* (Cambridge, 2003), 4–8, for an excellent treatment of the concept of anti-Americanism.
3. Time series trade data for Latin America for the second half of the twentieth century is available through the Penn World Table project. Available at http://pwt.econ.upenn.edu.
4. See C. Lafer, *A identidade internacional do Brasil e a política externa Brasilera,* (2001), chapter 2, for a full discussion of continental size, population, and the formation of Brazilian national identity.
5. After the United States began photographing and fingerprinting arriving passengers from most countries including Brazil, a Mato Grosso federal judge took offense, describing the US policy as "worthy of the worst horrors of the Nazis" and ordered that all Americans arriving in Brazil be subjected to the same treatment. These rules infuriated tourism officials in Rio de Janeiro, who feared the loss of millions of dollars from the negative publicity of nine-hour waits for the new bureaucratic hassles. US treatment of arriving Brazilians has been a high profile topic ever since the Brazilian foreign minister was forced to remove his shoes at the Miami International Airport. At first, it appeared that the Lula administration would quickly end the measures, but the fingerprinting and photographing of American tourists has been so popular among Brazilians, the government decided instead to maintain the reciprocal action during a period of study. Some critics, such as *Folha de São Paulo* editor Gilberto Dimenstein, posited that "We Brazilians must have very low self-esteem to see this as a motive for patriotic celebration" (12 January 2004).
6. The Zogby poll is available at http://www.zogby.com.
7. Available at http://www.insightmag.com/news/308706.html.
8. *Financial Times,* 22 September 2003.
9. *Veja,* 15 October 2003. *Veja* is Brazil's most important news weekly.
10. J. Epstein, "How to Win Over a Country in 45 Hours," *Christian Science Monitor,* 17 October 1997.
11. This was reported in a 28 April 2001 column in *Estado de São Paulo* headlined "An Overwhelming Ignorance," by Brazilian journalist and Cardoso friend Fernando Pedreira. Shortly after the meeting with Bush, Cardoso publicly warned Brazil and Latin America that they should not look to the United States for partnership and cooperation, as the US leadership knew very little about the region. See

also A. Kamen, "What Did He Say and When Did He Say It?" *Washington Post,* 5 June 2002.

12. P. Blustein and A. Faiola, "Brazil To Get Record Loan," *Washington Post,* 8 August 2002.

13. J. Galtung, "A Structural Theory of Imperialism," *Journal of Peace Research* 8 (1971): 81–117.

14. F. H. Cardoso and E. Faletto, *Dependency and Development in Latin America* (Berkeley, 1979).

15. M. Keck and K. Sikkink, *Activists Beyond Borders: Advocacy Networks in International Politics* (Ithaca, 1998).

16. Available at http://www.cnn.com/EARTH/9804/17/baja.whales/. For more on this important case, see C. Lazaroff, "Whales Win Out Against Mitsubishi's Salt Plans," *Environment News Service,* 3 March 2000; P. Franco, "Gray Whales Face New Threat," *InterPress Service,* 6 April 1999; C. Lazaroff, "Money Talks in Campaign to Save Gray Whale," *Environment News Service,* 22 October 1999; and "Battle over Baja Salt Factory Rages On," *Environment News Service,* 18 November 1999.

17. L. Schoultz, *Beneath the United States: A History of US Policy Toward Latin America* (Cambridge, 1998), chapters 17 and 18.

18. P. Smith, *Talons of the Eagle: Dynamics of US-Latin American Relations* (Oxford, 2000), 143–89.

19. For example, US assistance to Central America fell from $1.2 billion in 1985 to $167 million in 1966, and military aid fell to virtually nothing (Schoultz, *Beneath,* 366).

20. J. Nye, *The Paradox of American Power: Why the World's Only Superpower Can't Go It Alone* (Oxford, 2003); and J. Nye, *Soft Power: The Means to Success in World Politics* (New York, 2004).

21. For a detailed examination of Brazil-US relations through 1998 see the two volumes of M. Bandeira, *Relaçóes Brasil-EUA no contexto da globalizacáo* (São Paulo, 1997 and 1999); and S.P. Guimarães, *Estados Unidos: visões brasileiras* (Brasilia, 2000).

22. B. Sallum, *A condição periférica: O Brasil nos quadros do capitalismo mundial (1945–2000)* (São Paulo, 2000), 411.

23. This harmony of interest is described with different language in a classic work on bureaucratic authoritarianism, G. O'Donnell's *Bureaucratic Authoritarianism: Argentina 1966–1973 in Comparative Perspective* (Berkeley, 1988).

24. Sallum, *Condição,* 412–13.

25. These data are available at http://www.mre.gov.br.

26. T. Skidmore, *Brazil, Five Centuries of Change* (New York, 1999), 132.

27. F. Weffort, *O populismo na política brasileira* (Rio de Janeiro, 1980).

28. An excellent discussion of the effect of the Cuban Revolution on US-Latin American relations is T. Wright, *Latin America in the Era of the Cuban Revolution* (New York, 1991).

29. See *Política Externa Independiente,* 1 (May 1965): 126.

30. One excellent example is Lula's chief of staff and the principal strategist of the PT, José Dirceu. Dirceu was a bohemian, musician, and leftist during the 1960s, who was arrested by the military government in 1968 and freed after his companions kidnapped then US Ambassador to Brazil Charles Elbrik in 1969. He fled to Cuba for guerrilla training and plastic surgery on his nose to alter his appearance, and returned to Brazil with a false identity in 1975 and married. His wife did not know his true identity until 1979, when he resurfaced as José Dirceu after the decree of a general amnesty (he took this opportunity to leave his wife). He is now considered by many to be the most powerful person in the government (http:www.brazzil.com/p14nov02.htm).

31. S. Bertol, *Tarso de Castro: editor de "O Pasquim"* (Passo Fundo, 2001).
32. Skidmore, *Brazil: Five Centuries.*
33. T. Skidmore, *The Politics of Military Rule in Brazil, 1964–1985* (New York, 1988).
34. Bandeira, *Relações* (1999), 182.
35. Information on World Social Forum available at http://www.forumsocialmundial .org.br.
36. O. de Carvalho "Our Enemy, the USA: What every American should know about anti-Americanism," December 2002. Available at http://www.Brazzil.com.
37. K. Maxwell, "Anti-Americanism in Brazil," *Correspondence: An International Review of Culture & Society* 9 (spring 2002).
38. M. Taves, "Observing Globalization's Discontents in Brazil," *The Hoya,* 8 November 2002.
39. *New York Times,* 28 October 2001.
40. See http://www.miami.com/mld/elnuevo/news/columnists/andresoppenheimer/ 5458894.htm for a strong critique of the *Folha de São Paulo* headline.
41. J. Arbex, Jr., *Carros Amigos,* 17 (June 2003): 16–17.
42. Carvalho, *Our Enemy.*
43. C. Chagas, "Who Sabotaged the Brazilian Rocket?" August 2003. Available at http://www.Brazzil.com.
44. Available at http://www1.folha.uol.com.br/folha/datafolha/po/guerra_eua_ 092001.shtml.
45. Available at http://www1.folha.uol.com.br/folha/datafolha/especiais/ecos_ guerra_102001a.shtml.
46. A. Oppenheimer, "La Imagen del Tío Sam." Available at http://www.elnuevoherald .com.

Part II

COMPARATIVE AND TRANSNATIONAL APPROACHES

Chapter 6

DIASPORA AGAINST EMPIRE

Apprehension, Expectation, and West Indian Anti-Americanism, 1937–1945

Jason Parker

In the early summer of 2003, amid a global surge of anti-American sentiment, the residents of Jamaica felt that surge reach a particularly high crest. Far from the geopolitical spotlight—indeed, arguably not even inside the theater, let alone on stage—Jamaica's economy experienced a jarring episode. In a proverbial perfect economic storm, several trends of US trade and monetary policy coincided with a trough in fluctuations of the island's currency, which were then unexpectedly exacerbated and produced a whipsawing Jamaican dollar. In the space of three weeks, that currency went from trading at 40 cents to the US dollar to 70 cents, and back again. The fluctuation was as painful as it was beyond the control of any one force or factor. The crisis, although brief, nonetheless produced familiar frictions: lamentation of its impact on the island's most vulnerable, resentment at US indifference to that plight, and a measure of resignation to forces that, though ostensibly American in origin, were in most respects beyond American control.[1] The dynamic is well-known in inter-American affairs, one consistent with a regional history of resistance to—and relative powerlessness to stop—the extensions and repercussions of US power abroad.

Several factors, though, set Jamaica and the rest of the West Indies apart within the hemispheric tableau. Principal among these factors are a largely insular geography, recent experience of European imperial rule, and populations of predominantly, though not exclusively, African derivation.[2] These factors, combined with the often-decisive disparity in power between the United States and its neighbors, complicate the comparative regional picture by diffusing potential and actual West Indian resistance to the American colossus. They also help to explain more than just the particular character of West Indian anti-Americanism. When a crucial additional element—the West Indies' ultimately ambivalent attitude toward the US mainland—is introduced, the final formula also helps to explain why, in its dealings with the New World, the United States tends to get its way.[3]

Recent scholarship on inter-American relations reveals this ambivalence to be present far beyond the West Indies.[4] Shared elements of political anti-Americanism, for example, combined with a love-hate relationship to *Yanqui* culture, present certain commonalities between the British Caribbean and its hemispheric neighbors. These, however, have been little explored because of the more striking differences between the two. Indeed, those differences account for the West Indies' general absence from the literature on inter-American relations, much of which simply ignores the British territories.[5] This historiographical misfortune is replicated in other areas of scholarship as well. As in inter-American relations, the West Indies do not easily "fit" into the burgeoning literatures on the Cold War, race and US foreign affairs, and decolonization.[6] Major works in those fields make little or no reference to the British Caribbean, which thus tends to fall through the cracks of each one. Despite the obvious reasons—history, demography, insularity, language, culture, and most of all the diasporan element—to sustain such an exclusion, there are insights to be gleaned from overcoming it. Chief among these is the interplay of subnational and transnational racial-ethnic networks as an undercurrent in relations. Analyzing the particulars of West Indian anti-Americanism, with an eye not only to what sets it apart from its neighbors but also what it shares with them, helps to explain why even though much hemispheric resistance to the hegemon has deep roots, in practice it also tends to have weak branches.

However, West Indian ambivalence displays a unique cast. Thanks primarily to currents in race relations, West Indians have historically seen "America" in three particular ways: as the homeland of Jim Crow; as a source of anticolonial leverage against British rule and for economic development and external security; and finally as the crucible of a diasporan activism potentially able to exploit the second aspect while battling the first. The cumulative result might be characterized as a distinctively West Indian "ambivalent anti-Americanism," to adapt the title of Cary Fraser's study. As Trinidadian Eric Williams described it in 1944, "the people of the Caribbean take an intense interest in the United States. This might take the form of apprehension [but] more generally it takes the form of expectation."[7]

This thread runs brightly visible through Anglo-American-Caribbean affairs during the transformative years of World War II. The shocks of depression and war had brought the West Indies to a point of intense crisis. Social unrest throughout the 1930s, combined with the rise of pan-African movements across the diaspora, called into question the future of the colonies' relationship to the British metropole. External factors, most of all Nazi victories in Europe and the consequent isolation of Britain, exerted a geopolitical gravity that drew the United States increasingly into Caribbean affairs at the precise moment when British authority was ebbing. Leaders of the embryonic West Indian nationalist movement, though wary of America's racial and imperial record, saw that the extension of US power could serve their agenda. "In the field of foreign relations," Jamaican reformer W. Adolphe Roberts argued in 1938, "Jamaica's chief concern is, and always must be, the United States of America."[8] An increased American presence brought on by internal chaos and external danger could, in short, assist in evicting the British empire—albeit at the risk of simply taking its place.

This essay explores the question of how the West Indies reacted to the rise of American, and the decline of British, power in the Caribbean. It examines how West Indian nationalists both welcomed and dreaded the American advance and British retreat into the islands, and how they sought—with some success—to turn that advance to their advantage. The story begins with the wave of labor unrest in Trinidad and Jamaica in 1937 and continues throughout the war years. It focuses on those islands because the two offer the ideal loci for tracing the themes that drive this study: the importance of the islands to US security arrangements; the close diasporan ties linking the islands to the black mainland, especially to New York City; the surprising influence of these ties on American efforts to reform the colonial Caribbean regime; the way in which this transnational race factor differentiated West Indian from other regional reform and anti-American movements; and finally the ability and determination of West Indian nationalists to play the American hegemon off the British metropole—and off each other—in their effort to effect change, even as they feared the racial, social, and long-term repercussions of a greater US presence.

Backdrop: Race, Labor, War, and the Caribbean Sea-Change

The transnational connection linking the island and mainland nodes of the diaspora was as central to the nationalists' strategy as it is to our understanding of the varied nature of West Indian ambivalence. A brief review of events of the 1920s and 1930s provides an essential background to that transnational link and its role in the flux years of 1937–1945. From the first stirrings of post-World War I West Indian nationalism, its proponents, though relatively few in number, realized that the West Indian expatriate presence on the US mainland constituted an important asset to their cause. Many residents of the British Caribbean migrated to the mainland only temporarily or episodically in the decades after 1900, but even so, by the end of the 1930s, mainland-resident West Indians and their offspring numbered almost one hundred thousand. Their numerical importance grew from their geographical concentration. Most found their way to the urban archipelago of the northeast, especially to New York City. There, one-fourth of Harlem's black population during the renowned Renaissance was of British-Caribbean derivation, including most notably Marcus Garvey, who spread black consciousness broadly among his new neighbors in black America.[9]

This transnational connection meant that events in the islands would resonate on the mainland, and vice versa. When long-simmering labor, racial, and colonial crises boiled and merged during the 1930s, this interlinked diaspora lit up. Beyond Garvey's well-known call for pan-African unity and racial pride, for example, a similar consciousness—one rooted in class oppression rather than race solidarity—soon exploded on the islanders' home-grounds. With the onset of the Great Depression, peripheral areas such as the West Indies fell into dire circumstances. Beginning in 1934, violent, labor-based unrest broke out on a more or less yearly basis. By 1939 such disturbances had erupted in almost every corner of the British Caribbean, leaving trails of blood and ash from Trinidadian oil fields to Jamaican cane fields.[10] Disturbances in Trinidad in 1937 and Jamaica the following year, because they involved the most populous and prosperous of the colonies, together formed a watershed in post-emancipation Caribbean history.[11] Although the unrest had its specific roots in anger over labor conditions, it grew more generally, and thoroughly organically, from the grinding misery of day-to-day West Indian life. Moreover, the disturbances coincided with nascent middle-class support for reform of the British colonial regime.[12] Rage—over riots, and their causes and implications—fueled West Indian activism at home and in the United States. In the months afterward, Jamaican activist W. A. Domingo noted the disturbances had changed the debate by incubating "the germ of nationalism" among regional writers and intellectuals.[13]

This diasporan connection drew further strength from events well beyond the Caribbean. The 1935 Italian assault on Ethiopia and consequent exiling of Emperor Haile Selassie had outraged blacks across the New World.[14] African Americans and West Indians who were centuries removed from the African motherland breathlessly watched the emergency.[15] The Ethiopian crisis spurred what one scholar called the "making of the politics of the African diaspora," and its repercussions included the founding or radicalization of several race-based groups devoted to various anticolonial and pan-African agendas.[16] The crisis fired racial consciousness, and more-over, as historian Ken Post observed, combined with the decade's labor unrest to solidify the bonds between African Americans and US-resident West Indians.[17] Although racial and colonial oppression in Africa garnered impassioned attention across the diaspora in the 1930s, it held a special urgency to expatriate West Indians who feared for their homelands and who, thanks to their physical presence in Harlem, were able to place the Caribbean at center stage of the struggle.

The convergence of labor, racial, and colonial turmoil in the West Indies left the longevity of British rule there very much in question. In addition, the transnational black nexus connecting mainland and island, as well as the geographic proximity of the United States, meant that American influence of various kinds would powerfully affect the answer. Two particular aspects of the US role in the subsequent regional flux stand out. The first extended beyond the Caribbean alone: the post-World War I eclipse of Great Britain by the United States in global economic and strategic spheres. The ebb of British power in the Caribbean, and the flow of American in its place, escaped no one. Activists in the aforementioned "Harlem Nexus"—the second notable aspect of the US role—were not alone in grasping the shift. Top military and civilian officials in the Roosevelt administration realized both that the strategic balance had begun to change and that labor unrest—which struck American as well as British holdings in the Caribbean—represented a regional security threat that respected no single nation's flag.[18] But the activists were among the first to grasp the Atlantic power shift and to make sure others did, too.

Both aspects—the US eclipse of Britain and the rise of transnational diasporan activism—merit at least brief attention as contributors to West Indian ambivalence regarding the United States, but their greater importance arguably lies in how they affected the subsequent course of decolonization. The political space that America—

and specifically black America—provided was indispensable to early efforts at promoting reform of the colonial regime. This was the case despite the fact that that space consisted of little more than pockets of the urban US north in a society marbled with racial oppression. However, those pockets furnished activists with a relatively greater freedom than was available at home. The first group, for example, to splice budding Jamaican nationalism to a demand for greater self-rule organized itself in Harlem before expanding operations to Kingston. The Jamaican Progressive League (JPL), founded 1 September 1936 in New York, was one of more than ten such expatriate leagues to promote similar agendas.[19] The existence of such transnational ties through Harlem meant two things. First, that Jim Crow was not the last word in New World race relations; and second, that Western-Hemisphere dialogue about black liberation frequently had a Caribbean accent. These two elements combined to feed West Indian ambivalence about the actual and potential "American" role in seeking colonial reform. More important, they made such a role indispensable to a movement that would later move from an agenda of reform to one of nationalist independence.

The Year 1940: From Harlem to Havana and Back

When war came to Europe in 1939, its repercussions deepened both the American role in the Caribbean and West Indian ambivalence about it. The "phony war" following the Nazi invasion of Poland gave way in the spring of 1940 to the quick conquest of Western Europe. This opened the possibility that French and Dutch possessions in the Caribbean might become Axis outposts, leaving first the weakly defended British holdings and then the American continent vulnerable to possible attack. The strategic perimeter of the hemisphere had, in effect, been redrawn through the heart of the Caribbean. The events of 1940 revealed this changed and changing landscape. Three developments during that year show most clearly the West Indian determination to use the new status quo, and in particular the expanded US presence in the Caribbean, to advance the reform of the colonial regime.

The first development, the Havana Declaration, came close on the heels of the successful Nazi blitz through Western Europe. The Declaration held potentially great import for the West Indies, but despite this, as Jamaican socialist and proto-nationalist leader Norman Manley put it, "the wishes of the colonies [were] never ascertained" regarding the document.[20] In response to the June 1940 capitulation of

France, US Secretary of State Cordell Hull convened the hemisphere's foreign ministers in Havana, Cuba, to address its geostrategic consequences. Their meeting produced the Havana Declaration, which drew a multilateral line sealing off the European possessions in the western hemisphere from Nazi penetration. This unified stance was the fruit of the Good Neighbor Policy's economic relations.[21] As Hull put it, "the political lineup followed the economic lineup."[22] Regarding the geopolitically less significant matter of who was to decide the future of Europe's regional possessions, however, the Havana Declaration demonstrated that—not for the first time—it would not be the residents of the European West Indies, a fact Manley blasted in a column delineating what he saw as the act's more ominous implications.[23]

This omission was not, however, for lack of West Indian effort. Expatriates in the United States had perceived that the Havana meeting—and the fact that the Nazi onslaught now threatened the metropole—presented a strategic opportunity, and they sprang into action. West Indian émigrés, and JPL veterans, W. A. Domingo, Richard B. Moore, and H. P. Osborne, established the West Indies National Council (WINC) in New York.[24] WINC set out to use the crisis and its consequent US expansion in the Caribbean to seek Washington's help in securing West Indian interests, including self-rule.[25] The group sent a delegate to Havana, albeit one without official standing, to make that case. Moore later claimed that, if not for WINC's delegate, the United States would have bullied the Latin Americans into affirming US annexation of the West Indies.[26] Domingo lauded his organization's efforts as influencing the language of the declaration itself, which "constitute[d] a substantial political gain for the colored race in the Western world."[27]

As Moore hinted, though, the Havana Declaration might simply effect the exchange of one imperial master for another. Here, then, the particular challenge of West Indian anti-Americanism took form: to use US hegemony as a strategic counterbalance to British rule, yet not to succumb to the former in turn. Moore declared in his "Reply to Cordell Hull" that "in the name of justice and democracy, this Committee must firmly oppose any plan whereby the [American] Republics, at the behest of the United States, shall act as custodians, receivers, and bailiffs for European Empires now tottering, bankrupt, or definitely fascist."[28] An American-Caribbean empire in place of the British one was arguably a more immediate threat than was Nazi incursion in the region.[29] While Moore's fears about US designs, and about the extent of WINC's influence on them at Havana, actually overestimated both, his organization's actions nonetheless demonstrated its determination to play a role in the unfolding Caribbean transition. West Indian activists knew that the greater US presence had equal potential either to help or to hurt their agenda. Yet, even years before the war began, they had discerned the shifting balance of power and resolved to use the expanded American presence however they might, even at the expense of their erstwhile British landlords.

The Bases-for-Destroyers Deal of 2 September was the second development of 1940 to show the changing calculus of Caribbean reform. In some respects, this deal merely formalized the obvious; the ongoing eclipse of British by American influence in the colonies was plain to see. Since World War I, mainland voices from the *Chicago Tribune* to the US Congress had periodically called for acquisition of the West Indies as repayment for Britain's war debts. While the bases deal fell far short of such an arrangement, it did make official the transfer of security responsibility at a moment of intense crisis. According to the terms of the deal, aging American warships were sent to London in exchange for leases on military base-areas in Western-Hemisphere British possessions. Like the Havana Declaration, the deal paid little heed to opinion in those possessions. However, the deal also extended the declaration's logic in ways that were potentially both useful and dangerous to efforts at West Indian reform: it acknowledged the growing eclipse of British sovereignty by American influence, but gave no guarantees that the American expansion would stop at the base fences.

This second development in the crucial year of 1940 led to a third event: the November tour of the region by the Roosevelt administration's chief Caribbeanist, Charles W. Taussig. Although American observers knew that the recent labor unrest had left the region in a state of political flux, few had any sense of how this would affect the new security arrangements that would grow from the newborn bases deal. Taussig wrote to the president and Hull regarding the need for an updated survey of the region.[30] His subsequent tour confirmed the shifting state of the Caribbean landscape. Taussig knew the region very well, and indeed had met with Roosevelt three years earlier to warn him of the growing crisis there.[31] In addition, as a New York Democrat, Taussig was familiar with the diasporan crossroads in Harlem. Before leaving, he consulted with diasporan scholars and activists familiar with Caribbean trends. These included representatives of the African-American professorate and contacts in greater Harlem.[32]

Taussig's tour deepened his conviction that, now that America had taken over the West Indies' external security, Washington would now have to address its internal insecurity as well—lest the next round of social unrest be directed at US power.[33] His trip convinced him that joint allied efforts at improving Caribbean conditions were thus a security necessity. This conviction would later father the Anglo-American Caribbean Commission (AACC), itself emblematic of US determination to bring socioeconomic and, by extension, political progress to the region.[34] Yet Taussig found during his mission, during which he met with West Indians from a broad spectrum, that while they welcomed American support for such reform, they remained wary of larger American designs of regional domination.

This, Taussig surmised, would produce West Indian attempts to play the United States and Britain off one another. He confirmed that before the bases deal was announced, rumors had held that Washington would acquire bases in Britain's hemispheric holdings. At that time, "West Indian negro leaders vigorously opposed the idea. Now that it is an accomplished fact, they have changed their policy."[35] The head of Trinidad's Workers' Union, Adrian Rienzi, asserted to the Taussig Mission that Trinidadians welcomed the US arrival in hopes that it would lead to a temporary American takeover and soon thereafter to independence. Taussig detected the same attitude in other colonies, as well; it seemed a "well-discussed and studied policy [directed at] breaking the ties with the British Empire . . . They feel that it would be easier to acquire their ultimate freedom from the United States."[36] Indeed, as Taussig wrote to Under Secretary of State Sumner Welles, "The general attitude . . . toward the US is extremely friendly. So friendly in fact that under certain circumstances it could prove embarrassing. For instance: the important negro labor leaders in Trinidad told us that they felt that the people of the West Indies would be better off under the American flag than under the British. In the event of any serious disturbances, which we do not expect, it would not be surprising to see a substantial movement on the part of West Indian masses for the US to annex [the colonies]."[37]

Undoubtedly this was, to some degree, mere flattery. Certainly, island activists realized that this stance, invoking a principle of anticolonialism ostensibly shared by both islands and mainland, could give them some measure of political leverage against the British. Yet there was more than principle in play. There was a practical asset as well, which Taussig noted: "even a casual investigation [shows] that there is definite campaign in the West Indies for federation and self-government [whose] headquarters [are] in New York City."[38] The existence of such a campaign suggested that island—and expatriate—activists viewed the American role instrumentally, within the pursuit of their larger objectives, and thus that pro- or anti-American sentiment would fluctuate accordingly.

The Taussig mission, and the American bases and the AACC that followed it the next year, reflected the changed power realities in the

Caribbean. The new context was inescapable: British power, bleeding heavily since 1914, was nearing its nadir. However unpalatable to old-line British enthusiasts of empire, American assertion in its own neighborhood was in London's interest, a truth that cooler British heads grasped.[39] Those battling for West Indian change saw the same scenario, but from a different angle. As Manley put it—in agreement with colleagues further left than he—"America will decide our future status . . . when we have to face America and not Britain there won't be any empire and 'self-government' will mean independence."[40] His somewhat less sanguine comrade Ken Hill extended the point: "For good or ill, our future destiny is interlocked with the United States."[41] In an article in a British journal, Roberts perceptively noted that the events of 1940 had left America preeminent, and Britain nearly irrelevant, in the Caribbean.[42] This, Roberts feared, gave Britain an excuse to shirk the responsibility, which it had only acknowledged in the wake of the labor unrest, to provide for the West Indies' welfare and development. Such a costly obligation might well be abdicated if British disengagement were to continue and deepen. Worse still, the same trend led to the possibility of US annexation, which many West Indians suspected was already underway.[43] As late as July 1942, expatriates held a public Harlem meeting to address the subject: "Will United States [*sic*] Take Over the West Indies?"[44]

Roberts thought not. Given the American racial record on one hand and the Good Neighbor Policy on the other, he argued, Washington would not annex the colonies. US reluctance to increase its black population, and the certainty that the "more articulate colonies" would continue to call for self-determination, foreclosed that prospect. However, Roberts also perceived that the changed dynamics of power in the region also entailed a shift in the dynamics of race, in at least two ways. One—the transnational race-based cooperation of which Roberts was an avatar—now had the Americans' ear, thanks to the bases in the islands and to Taussig's Harlem connections.[45] The other was the specter of Jim Crow. The American racial regime was well-known in the West Indies, and the fear that it would accompany the new US bases there was arguably the single biggest contributor to island anti-Americanism in 1940 and after.

Race Feeling, Mixed Feelings: Intimacy and Contempt

These two faces of the race question in the new Anglo-American-Caribbean dispensation interacted to nearly contradictory effect, simultaneously reinforcing anti-American sentiment and deepening its ambivalent character. On the one hand, the diversity of diasporan reformist organizations—including both West Indian groups and their African-American allies, notably the National Association for the Advancement of Colored People (NAACP)—ensured a fractious diversity of opinion regarding both tactics and strategy in the crusade for black freedom in the hemisphere. On the other, hostility to American racial practices had a unifying effect, as all parties agreed that, as part of that crusade, Jim Crow must not be exported to the Caribbean. This consensus included Taussig and Roosevelt, who designed US policy in the islands accordingly and more or less successfully. The range of black opinion at the moment of Caribbean shift, when contextualized alongside US efforts at turning race and reform into assets in its regional expansion, sketched the instrumental—and equivocal—West Indian view of the hegemon.

For example, while diasporan activists in Harlem sought to employ the United States' Caribbean role as a tool to evict the British empire, Barbados-born Chicago lawyer Bindley Cyrus imagined a variation on American empire in Britain's place. His vision indicated the range and variety of diasporan opinion in the wartime window of opportunity. Between the Havana Declaration and the bases deal, Cyrus sent a long proposal to Navy Secretary Frank Knox and to Roosevelt. Havana, he argued, opened up "opportunities for the expansion of American economic and political power. The Guianas . . . should be acquired [immediately] and [militarily] developed, and for purposes of colonization . . . by the Negro population of the US which is sadly in need of the increased opportunities, [and which] should colonize and control the new territory."[46] The black colonizers would extend and protect US power in the hemisphere: "There is no opportunity for the well-trained Negro in the United States . . . White Americans have lost the propensity for adventure such as is found in colonizing new lands. Negroes should be encouraged to cultivate this desirable trait and bring glory to themselves and the great Stars and Stripes . . . and [later] establish an independent nation known as the Republic of Guiana."[47]

Carrying such an imperial flag abroad as a means of creating black opportunity and proclaiming black patriotism was not an especially new idea. Garvey, for example, had draped his call for black departure in imperialistic finery.[48] Brenda Gayle Plummer has pointed out that prominent African Americans such as Channing Tobias served on the board of the American Colonization Society into the 1950s.[49] What was notable was the context in which the idea resurfaced. The turmoil of depression and especially war now excited anew American-tinted visions of black exodus. African Americans could escape US racism while widening US influence—while serving US hemispheric expansion. Cyrus insouciantly urged annexation and colonization as solutions for racial problems at home and geopolitical problems abroad, with nary a glance at the opinions of the present inhabitants of the Guianas.[50]

Guianese and other West Indians, of course, were at that moment expressing their wishes to audiences in Harlem. It is unclear what portion of the mainland or island population would have supported Cyrus's position, though other letters in State Department files—apparently unconnected to his—second the motion of African-American colonization.[51] Still, the existence of such a position indicates the diversity of black thought on international issues, even those involving race and colonialism. It reveals, in short, the range of impulses in diasporan thought, and the ambivalence necessary to formulate a proposal that attacked American racism by carrying abroad the US flag.

That range of analysis persisted throughout the war, and opinions often differed based on the degree to which the speaker believed American racism undercut America's usefulness in the anticolonial fight. A Howard University conference on the Caribbean in mid-1943 brought these differences to the surface.[52] All attendees agreed on the certainty of a growing US role in the devolution of the imperial status quo. But the course of that devolution sparked debate. African-American attendees, such as Howard professor Rayford Logan, by and large shared the conviction that the United States could be used at least to reform and at most to remove British rule.[53] West Indian and African conferees tended to disagree. The consequent clash of views, as summarized in Logan's diary, suggested the limits of transnational black unity.

At a dinner of the black intellectuals running the conference, a casual debate between Logan and Kwame Nkrumah—future first premier of an independent Ghana—uncovered the fault lines. The latter argued for independence for imperial Africa well-nigh immediately. Logan took what he termed a "more practical" approach: "How would Africans be able to develop if European science and capital were withdrawn? [Also], Europeans were not going to withdraw of their own accord, and Africans are not strong enough to expel them."[54] Logan, for his part, and the future first prime minister of an independent Trinidad, Eric Williams, clashed over the politics and economics of decolonization: sugar versus self-sufficiency, immediate versus gradual independence. Logan took the latter stance in each case.[55] This left him a relative conservative, although he bowed to no one in his distaste for colonialism.[56] His diaries suggest that all parties shared a strong anticolonial commitment, but the disputes among them turned on fundamental questions of immediate versus gradual, and intellectual versus material, independence.[57] As Logan put it at the conference: "I do not believe that home rule or independence will necessarily mean better living conditions for the masses."[58]

Despite differing on means and specifics, though, African Americans and West Indians from Cyrus to Roberts to Logan could agree on two things. One was that, regardless of differences, transnational black ties were of paramount importance. At the June 1943 conference, Jamaican Dr. Charles Petioni stated that "the movement for independence of the British West Indies would have to find its leadership among colored British West Indians in the US," in part because of their connections to African-American institutions such as Howard University and the NAACP.[59] In part, too, it was expected that the two groups would have even closer relations as a result of the war and would continue working together for an end to empire.[60] The second point of consensus was the need to monitor the Roosevelt administration's partially successful effort to prevent Jim Crow practices at American facilities in the West Indies. Some feared it was too late; Howard sociologist E. Franklin Frazier argued that "there had been no real problem of Negro-White conflict in the Caribbean but now that North Americans were carrying their prejudice there the problem was beginning to arise."[61]

The racial situation in the islands was historically delicate and complex, and the Roosevelt administration and Taussig in particular knew that whether or not Frazier was correct about the origins of race problems in the Caribbean, he was undoubtedly right about the risks that race could pose to American plans. A Jim Crow regime, even if strictly limited to US base areas, would upend social customs and arrangements in the islands, as well as indelibly stain the American reputation. Fears of such a prospect had quieted enthusiasm for the Yanks' arrival. Taussig reported that, during his mission, native West Indian leaders were wary of the racial implications of the US presence and strongly hoped that the worst of these could be prevented.[62] The British colonial secretary concurred on all points, reporting that West Indians "are yet most apprehensive of the [US] arrival. This is due partly to a deep-seated loyalty and attachment to British traditions, and not less to the fear that American treatment of the Negro and colored population will follow the lines notorious in the [US] South."[63]

Taussig shared many of these concerns, and they shaped his design of US Caribbean policy. He emphasized to Roosevelt that American officials had to be specially chosen for their racial sensitivity.[64] The president agreed and so directed his secretaries of Navy and

War.[65] The American bases would, in a sense, be ground zero for a West Indian variation on the Good Neighbor Policy. The United States would neutralize its racial faults locally in the conduct of its military presence, publicly join with the British to pursue shared interests, and at the same time compete with them for the sympathies of West Indians. This last objective took the public form of the AACC, meant to embody the joint effort to improve the islands' economies.[66] For many in the islands, the creation of the commission made clear the economic balance of power: "The existence of the [AACC]," wrote a Jamaican commentator, "more than suggests that the economic future of Jamaica [and] the West Indies, Self Government or no Self Government, is linked to the United States. There is no questioning that."[67] However, Washington perceived another essential consideration. Welles spelled out the regional and domestic rationales to British Ambassador Lord Halifax: "conditions in the West Indies are likely to become difficult [in case of war], and the Negro population in New York are likely to become troublesome in that event."[68] American support for reform, that is, was meant not only to improve colonial welfare or to redeem American racism, but also—in doing both—to win diasporan affections on both island and mainland.

Although this approach—of good racial behavior around the bases and support for reform across the colonies—on the whole showed more success than Frazier or Logan, or even Taussig, might have expected, it proved insufficient to resolve fully the contradictions of America in West Indian eyes. These continued to find expression as the regional war wound down following the Allies' spring 1943 victory in the Battle of the Atlantic. They often did so as the unintended fruit of American attempts to win West Indians' allegiance. While some of these attempts demonstrated good faith on the part of the United States to either end (or both ends) of the Harlem-Caribbean axis, others tended instead to reinforce lingering West Indian suspicions of the United States' real motives and ultimate designs.

The AACC's inaugural West Indian Conference, for example, contrasted competing US and British colonialisms and their reform efforts. The conference, held in March 1944 at Barbados, divulged more about the geopolitical than the racial dynamics of the Anglo-American-Caribbean situation.[69] However, those two dynamics converged at particular points, in large part because, thanks to Taussig and his diasporan connections, American prescriptions more often than not corresponded with those of diasporan activists. Partly as a consequence, race never moved far offstage at the conference, from neither the white nor West Indian perspectives.

Racial dynamics did, however, influence the proceedings in some-times unexpected ways. American observers, both white and black, for example, expressed surprise at the divisions among the West Indians. Whatever regional unity could be detected by American eyes seemed more negative—that is, anti-British—than positive in char-acter. The popularity of the United States also came as a surprise. During one of the few conference events that brought working-class Barbadians into the picture, the American delegates noted that "the United States is looked upon as a 'Great White Uncle' [to which] West Indians look . . . not only for benefits such as emigration permits, etc., but as a moral force for improving Caribbean conditions."[70] It is unclear from the conference record whether the specter of Jim Crow made more than a passing appearance, but mainland comparisons were at least at the back of US minds. After a speech by a light-skinned West Indian, reported the American delegation, "[a] sophisticated American Negro audience [would have] thrown chairs at him; the Barbadians showed no resentment, but . . . a good deal of respect."[71]

Beyond such efforts within the region, the war years offered an-other way for West Indians to get acquainted with the "Great White Uncle" as well, one that sought again to meet mutual American and Caribbean needs. It did so, but in one important sense at least, this came at a cost. At the urging of Taussig and Jamaican proto-nation-alist leader Norman Manley, the Roosevelt administration and the British Colonial Office negotiated a migrant farm-labor program to bring West Indian guestworkers to farms and fields in the eastern United States. The program had long been a pet project of Taussig, Manley, and other reformers from Harlem to Kingston. In 1944 the program was expanded, in an effort to relieve island unemployment and the mainland workforce deficit. Ongoing US labor shortages throughout the war made the program politically saleable, and in its first year, ten thousand West Indians worked fields from Florida to Connecticut.[72]

Success in meeting wartime labor needs, however, obscured the public relations risks of the program. Exposing working-class is-landers to the American racial regime risked alienating West Indians who were historically less suspicious of the United States than was the island middle class. Nor were black Southerners, themselves fight-ing for jobs, sure to embrace the migrants. A British observer wrote of the migrants' foodless, submarine-chased passage, after which they faced a quarantine "so they will not go into [town] and cause unpleasant incidents with the native negroes."[73] As a result, back home Manley's People's National Party (PNP) reversed its support for the program, instead using the farmworkers' US experience to blast the sincerity of Anglo-American "progress."[74] Roosevelt administration analyst Henry Field noted this, while pointing out the limited effectiveness of the PNP's appeals even to those who had fresh and personal experience with Jim Crow: "The thousands of laborers reported back . . . in full concerning the [racial] practices in American restaurants, railroads, theaters, and stores. On the whole the reaction of the Jamaicans to the US was friendly—the good wages and steady work outbalanced the racial discrimination, and when a new call for laborers was issued in 1944, the recruiting offices were swamped. . . . Nevertheless, the knowledge of race discrimination in our Southern states turned some Jamaicans into bitter critics of this country."[75]

Race was never far from the center of US-West Indian relations, nor from a leading role in the American reputation abroad. Most working-class West Indians—who did not have the luxury of letting resentment over Jim Crow foreclose an economic opportunity—recognized race as only one of several concerns affecting US-Caribbean affairs. Yet for them, as well as for many of their most active compatriots in the push for Caribbean reform, race was a decisive factor preventing the formation of any sort of pro-American consensus among West Indians. This was the case, it seemed, almost regardless of any efforts Taussig and other American officials made to build such a consensus— efforts that always had equal potential to undermine it instead.

Even sensitivity to racial dynamics at ground-level around the bases, a sensitivity ordered at Taussig's suggestion and Roosevelt's command, proved insufficient to change the pattern. Despite occasional violence between West Indian workers or locals and American military or civilian personnel, and despite less-infrequent gaffes such as a USO "whites-only" help-wanted ad, race relations around the bases went more smoothly than almost anyone had dared hope. The static that did occur, that is, was much less than Taussig, Manley, and others had feared. Nonetheless, such friction took its toll on the American reputation: "One [Trinidadian] said recently: 'when the Americans first came, they were welcomed, and most of us would have preferred American to British rule. Today, after years of contact with American racial attitudes among the troops, we would prefer the rule of almost any other nation to that of the US'"[76] As Field succinctly put it, the "[West Indian] intelligentsia are consistently anti-Britain, anti-imperialist, and frequently anti-American because of race discrimination in the US."[77] By war's end, discrimination by the United States in the islands themselves had on balance—in spite of the Roosevelt administration's best intentions—reinforced this judgment.

West Indian apprehension about the United States during the window of wartime flux flowed from two sources: the uncertain scope of ultimate American designs, and the certain stain of American racial practices. The British flag had hitherto shielded the West Indies from the interventions, occupations, and annexations that had historically marked US conduct in the circum-Caribbean. World War II effectively brought that era to a close. The islands were now much more vulnerable than before—though still less so than their neighbors—to American appetites. West Indians seeking reform and self-rule could take some comfort in Roosevelt's Good Neighbor Policy. But they could not be certain of avoiding the fate of Puerto Rico—or more recently, the formerly Danish Virgin Islands—should circumstances so incline Washington. As for race, West Indians knew that their transnational diasporan connections with expatriates and African Americans could be a valuable asset in staving off any unpleasant fate involving that subject. But even this might be of little use against the extension of Jim Crow; West Indians' first- and secondhand experience with it had left them with a visceral distrust of the United States.

Whatever the depth of West Indian hostility and suspicion of the United States, however, colonial and expatriate reformers grasped the hegemon's importance in the new power equation, and they looked for ways to exploit it. Seismic change was afoot in the West Indies—as Field put it, "revolt against the imperial system is evident everywhere"—and the question was not whether the United States would play a role in that revolution but rather what that role would be.[78] Activists on both island and mainland understood this inevitability. It gave them a strong incentive both to make provisional peace with American imperfections and to overcome their suspicions enough to leverage the US presence to their benefit. West Indian apprehension about ultimate US designs and racism, in short, balanced against a tactical determination to use the irrevocable rise of US influence in the British West Indies to counter crown rule. West Indians thus had an ability to "triangulate" in that effort, an asset that few other peoples in the colonial world—or for that matter in Latin America—could claim.

From this conclusion, three larger implications stand out. First, anti-Americanism is rarely uncomplicated, and any true picture of the phenomenon must account for the ways in which it could coexist with a prima facie pro-American stance. Second, the mix of official and nonstate actors in inter-American affairs mandates attention to factors often glossed over—racial, cultural, and regional interactions, for example—in formal diplomacy. This brings to light not only the extent of transnational activism in Anglo-American-Caribbean relations, but also the points at which the agendas of various alliances—

the United States and Britain, and New York-based and island-based activists, to name two—came into unexpected conflict. Finally, this study suggests that the intellectual and historiographical separation of the British Caribbean from its neighbors rests on a half-truth. The West Indies are, in ways that matter, rightly not seen as part of Latin America thanks to accidents of history, demography, language, and economy. However, it is an error to exclude them from studies of inter-American relations. The islands are geostrategically indistinguishable from their Spanish-speaking neighbors. They were considered as such by US strategists, and West Indian nationalists used that consideration in their attempts to manipulate the American hegemon to their advantage.

While West Indians often found that these attempts were of only limited effectiveness, the larger theme of ambivalence regarding the United States adds depth to our understanding of inter-American relations. It helps to explain US success in achieving American objectives in the hemisphere, and the somewhat more limited success of its neighbors—whose ambivalence prevented their forming a fully united front—in achieving their own. In addition, this equivocal anti-Americanism reflects the ways in which Caribbean actors could harness US power to their own agendas, even as they dreaded the possibility of being ultimately dominated by that power in unexpected ways. Mixed feelings about the United States among West Indians—simultaneously loving Harlem and hating Jim Crow, for example—were nothing new; but in the late 1930s and early 1940s, events gave those feelings a role in diplomacy, and West Indians showed underappreciated agency in acting on them. The consequences shaped subsequent US-Caribbean relations leading up to the ultimate achievement of West Indian independence twenty years later. Eric Williams in some ways embodied this; having written in the 1940s of apprehension about and guarded hopefulness for the US presence, he would in the years just before independence wage a somewhat calculated anti-American crusade only to embrace a pro-Western stance once independence was achieved.[79] Indeed, although rooted in the decolonization years, regional ambivalence has endured well beyond that era into present-day relations that are equal parts disputatious, amicable, expedient—and resigned to being all three.

Notes

1. *Daily Gleaner,* Kingston, Jamaica, 22 May 2003.
2. The British Caribbean is conventionally defined to include, along with the insular Anglophone areas in the arc from Jamaica to Trinidad and Tobago, the main-

land states of Belize and Guyana. This paper, however, will concentrate on the former category for reasons cited below.

3. C. Fraser, *Ambivalent Anti-Colonialism: The United States and the Genesis of West Indian Independence, 1940–64* (Westport, 1994).

4. See especially A. McPherson, *Yankee No! Anti-Americanism in US-Latin American Relations* (Cambridge, 2003).

5. See, for example, L. Langley, *The United States and the Caribbean in the Twentieth Century*, 4th ed. (Athens, 1989), and S. Rabe, *The Most Dangerous Area in the World: John F. Kennedy Confronts Communist Revolution in Latin America* (Chapel Hill, 1999).

6. For example, little or no reference is made to the Caribbean in T. Borstelmann, *The Cold War and the Color Line: Race Relations and American Foreign Policy since 1945* (Cambridge, 2001); J. Meriwether, *Proudly We Can Be Africans: Black Americans and Africa, 1935–1961* (Chapel Hill, 2002); and B.G. Plummer, *Rising Wind* (Chapel Hill, 1996). However, the efforts of US-based race reformers to connect with activists abroad, in the Caribbean and elsewhere, have begun to attract scholarly attention. See, for example, Meriwether, *Proudly*, and J. Rosenberg, *How Far the Promised Land? World Affairs and the American Civil Rights Movement from the First World War to Vietnam* (Princeton, 2005).

7. Williams to Johnson, 21 September 1944, EWMC, folder #019.

8. K. Post, *Arise Ye Starvelings: The Jamaican Labor Rebellion of 1938 and its Aftermath* (The Hague, 1978), 223. Other activists, such as Jaime O'Meally, concurred on the importance—for good or ill—to Jamaica's future of the "capitalist colossus." Ibid., 230.

9. W. James, *Holding Aloft the Banner of Ethiopia: Caribbean Radicalism in America* (New York, 1996), 12.

10. The sequence of unrest ran as follows: 1934: British Guiana (later Guyana), British Honduras (later Belize), Trinidad; 1935: Jamaica, St. Kitts, Trinidad, British Guiana, St. Vincent, St. Lucia; 1936: British Guiana; 1937: Trinidad, the Bahamas, Barbados; 1938: Jamaica; 1939: Antigua, British Guiana.

11. The story of the riots has been well told elsewhere. See O. N. Bolland, *On the March: Labor Rebellions in the British Caribbean, 1934–1939* (Kingston, 1995); Post, *Arise;* R. Thomas, ed., *Trinidad Labor Riots of 1937: Fifty Years Later* (St. Augustine, 1987); R. Hart, *Toward Decolonization: Political, Labor and Economic Developments in Jamaica 1938–1945* (Bridgetown, 1999) and *Rise and Organize: The Birth of the Workers and National Movement in Jamaica, 1936–1939* (London, 1989); T. Holt, *The Problem of Freedom: Race, Labor, and Politics in Jamaica and Britain, 1832–1938* (Baltimore, 1992), 382–88.

12. T. Munroe, *The Politics of Constitutional Decolonization: Jamaica 1944–62* (Mona, Jamaica, 1972), 21. To a degree, the crown agreed on the need for reform. A royal commission under Lord Moyne recommended a more active British stewardship of island welfare and development, the first such stance in three centuries of the British-West Indian relationship. The Moyne Commission's recommendations informed parliament's passage of the 1940 Colonial Welfare and Development Act, which appropriated—at least on paper, since at the time the royal exchequer was all but empty—millions of pounds in aid. However, these actions fell short of any serious political reform. For an overview of the Moyne findings, see Fraser, *Ambivalent*, 42–49.

13. "Retreat From Phantasy," W. A. Domingo, *Public Opinion* (Kingston, Jamaica), 12 November 1938, NLJ, MS 234 - JPL.

14. Plummer, *Rising Wind*, 40–43; J. Harris, *African-American Reactions to War in Ethiopia, 1936–1941* (Baton Rouge, 1994), 34–38.

15. African-American anger over Ethiopia was concentrated in the string of growing black communities between Washington and Boston. However, blacks across

the country expressed interest in the crisis. W. R. Scott, *The Sons of Sheba's Race: African-Americans and the Italo-Ethiopian War, 1935–1941* (Bloomington, 1993), 100–101.

16. P. Von Eschen, *Race Against Empire: Black Americans and Anticolonialism, 1937–1957* (Ithaca, 1997), 11, 17. These included Britain's League of Colored Peoples, and the 1937 establishment in London of both the International African Service Bureau under the leadership of Trinidadian George Padmore, and in New York of the ICAA, the precursor of the Council on African Affairs. West Indians were prominent in these groups, with Padmore helming the IASB. Winston James points out the particular importance of Caribbeans to mainland radicalism and black nationalism in the United States. James, *Banner*, 184.

17. Post, *Arise*, 167–70.

18. The handoff of security responsibility began taking shape in military minds in 1938. "The Anglo-American Naval Staff Talks of 1938–39, [a result of events of the previous two years], helped to define a new defense framework for the Caribbean." F. Baptiste, *War, Conflict, and Cooperation: The European Possessions in the Caribbean, 1939–1945* (Westport, 1988), 3. In this regard the geographic context is also key. David G. Haglund emphasizes the importance to US strategy during the Roosevelt years of a "whole," defensively unified Western Hemisphere. D. Haglund, *Latin America and the Transformation of US Strategic Thought* (Albuquerque, 1984), 2, 16. The European colonies were thus potential Achilles' heels.

19. See Post, *Arise*, 221–24. Hart, writing many years later, agreed regarding the key role of the "intellectual ferment" in New York. Hart, *Rise*, 23. For more in this connection, see J. Parker, "'Capital of the Caribbean': The African American-West Indian 'Harlem Nexus' and the Transnational Drive for Black Freedom," *Journal of African American History (JAAH)* 89, 2 (2004): 98–117.

20. *Public Opinion*, 14 September 1940, University of the West Indies Main Library—West Indiana & Special Collections, Mona, Jamaica, microfilm reel #2682.

21. See L. Gardner, *Economic Aspects of New Deal Diplomacy* (Madison, 1964).

22. C. Hull, *The Memoirs of Cordell Hull*, vol. I (New York, 1948), 365. Haglund records that Adolf Berle confided to his diary his amazement at the broad, "blanket authority" scope of the Havana document. Haglund, *Transformation*, 219.

23. *Public Opinion*, 14 September 1940.

24. Hoover to Berle, 15 February 1944, 844.00B/1; Hoover to Berle, 31 May 1944, US, RG 59, 844D.00B/2, box 4928, NA. The group first called itself the West Indies National Emergency Committee (WINEC) but soon made the name-change to WINC in an effort to broaden its base and appeal.

25. Ibid.

26. Hoover to Berle, 31 May 1944.

27. Domingo to Walter White, 6 November 1940, LOC, NAACPP, folder "Labor - British West Indies – 1940–49," box A332.

28. R.B. Moore, "Reply to Cordell Hull," in *Richard B. Moore: Caribbean Militant in Harlem, Collected Writings 1920–1972*, ed. W. Burghardt and J. Turner (Bloomington, 1988), 267–68.

29. This threat of "American imperialism" lingered throughout the war, especially by the PNP, which singled it out as a danger once the Nazi submarine offensive had been beaten back. In the same document, however, the PNP held out the hope that America's better angels—such as FDR's "Four Freedoms"—would help the West Indies and the world construct a "just world order." Report, PNP, 21 August 1943, NLJ, MS 126a - PNP Pamphlets vol. 1.

30. Taussig to FDR and Hull, "Memorandum Concerning the Caribbean Area," 12 September 1940, FDRL, CWTP, Taussig Caribbean Files (TCF), folder "Caribbean

Commission - US Section [Taussig] - Report: Committee on British West Indies, 1940," box 35.

31. Taussig to Roosevelt, 25 February 1937, FDRL, folder "President's Personal File (PPF) 1644 [Charles Taussig]."

32. White to Reid, 15 October 1940, LOC, NAACPP, folder "British West Indies, 1940–49," box A155.

33. "Memorandum Concerning the Caribbean Area," 12 September 1940.

34. On the AACC, see Fraser, *Ambivalent*, 63–71 and 76–79; C. Whitham, *Bitter Rehearsal: British and American Planning for a Post-War West Indies* (Westport, 2002); and Parker, *Brother's Keeper: The United States, Race, and Empire in the British Caribbean, 1937–1962* (forthcoming), chapter 2. See also H. Johnson, "The United States and the Establishment of the Anglo-American Caribbean Commission," *Journal of Caribbean History* 19, 1 (1984): 26–47; and Johnson, "The Anglo-American Caribbean Commission and the Extension of American Influence in the British Caribbean, 1942–1945," *Journal of Commonwealth and Comparative Politics* 22, 2 (1984): 180–203.

35. Report of Taussig Mission, December 1940, FDRL, CWTP, TCF, folder "Caribbean Commission - US Section [Taussig] - Report: Committee on British West Indies, 1940," box 35.

36. Ibid.

37. Taussig to Welles, 4 December 1940, Attached as Appendix to Report of Taussig Mission, December 1940.

38. Report of Taussig Mission, December 1940.

39. This did not translate to British acquiescence to all American demands. Churchill, most notably, defended the empire throughout the war. See W. R. Louis's magnificent *Imperialism at Bay: The United States and the Decolonization of the British Empire, 1941–1945* (New York, 1978).

40. Manley, cited in Post, *Strike the Iron: A Colony at War: Jamaica, 1939–1945*, vol. I (Atlantic Highlands, 1981), 259.

41. Hill, cited in Post, *Iron*, 260.

42. Article Manuscript, attached to Amidon to Taussig, 6 March 1941, FDRL, CWTP, TCF, folder "Caribbean- General - Manuscripts - Correspondence," box 36.

43. Ibid.

44. Handbill, "Will United States [*sic*] Take Over the West Indies?" American-West Indian Association on Caribbean Affairs, 1 July 1942, in fiche #005,732-1, SCCF.

45. For more on the Harlem connections, see Parker, "Capital."

46. Cyrus to Roosevelt, 29 August 1940, RG 59, 844B.52/20, box 4710, NA.

47. Ibid.

48. Von Eschen, *Race*, 10.

49. Plummer, *Wind*, 224.

50. Neither did Washington tend to take said wishes into account; the State Department reply to Cyrus's letter notes only that "the Department is not informed . . . that the British, French, and [Dutch] *governments* are interested in the alienation of their respective territories in question" (emphasis added). Culbertson to Cyrus, 6 September 1940, RG 59, 844B.52/20, box 4710, NA.

51. Thomas to Hull, 15 April 1941, 844B.52/21; Stewart to Hull, 6 December 1940, RG 59, 844B.014/5, box 4721, NA.

52. The Howard community, thanks to connections to the Roosevelt administration, played an often-overlooked role in keeping racial concerns on the administration's diplomatic agenda. See C. Muse, "Howard University and US Foreign Affairs During the Franklin D. Roosevelt Administration, 1933-1945," *JAAH* 87, no. 4 (winter 2002): 403–16.

53. Entries 9 and 11 February, and 9 May 1943, LOC, Logan Papers, Rayford Logan Diary, box 4, diary 2.
54. Entry, 11 February 1943.
55. Entry, 9 May 1943. Logan, of course, was only one member of the Howard faculty; Williams's position coincided with that of African-American professors such as E. Franklin Frazier and Ralph Bunche. K. Janken, *Rayford W. Logan and the Dilemma of the African American Intellectual* (Amherst, 1993), 205. The larger point, however, is the intellectual diversity—and hence somewhat circumscribed solidarity—on the race and colonial questions.
56. Entries, 9 February 1943, 5 January 1944, LOC, Logan Papers, Rayford Logan Diary, box 4, diary 2.
57. Logan's emphasis on material progress as a prerequisite to independence may have made him a relative conservative next to Williams and Nkrumah, but this in no way endorsed colonialism, especially the British variety. After a day spent with a British writer, Logan sums up their exchange in his diary: "Almost too casually he asked 'what do you people think of the British?' 'Not very much,' I replied. 'Because of British imperialism?' he queried. 'Yes.' I said. Nothing more was needed on that subject." Entry, 5 January 1944.
58. Entry, 9 May 1943.
59. Entry, 27 June 1943, LOC, Logan Papers, Rayford Logan Diary, box 4, diary 2.
60. *Jamaica Gleaner*, 31 July 1943, cited in Report of Henry Field and Paul Blanshard, December 1944, FDRL, Henry Field Papers.
61. Entry, 27 June 1943.
62. Report of Taussig Mission, December 1940. This confirmed what Walter White had been saying for some time. In his writings and speeches, White sought to alert the country to the damage done to its reputation by American racial policies. Jim Crow undermined the Good Neighbor policy, White pointed out, needlessly sowing suspicion in Latin American and West Indian minds. White to Cabot, 8 January 1941, LOC, NAACPP, folder "staff - Walter White - Good Neighbor Policy 1940–41," box A609.
63. Colonial Secretary to War Cabinet, 27 December 1940, PRO, Foreign Office, 371/26152.
64. Report of Taussig Mission, December 1940.
65. Roosevelt to Knox and Stimson, 19 March 1941, FDRL, OF-4101, "Naval Bases 1940–43."
66. Report of Taussig Mission, December 1940.
67. *Public Opinion*, 9 May 1942.
68. British Embassy-Washington (Edwards) to Churchill, 14 April 1941, and Martin to Mallet, 7 May 1941, both PRO, Foreign Office 371/26175.
69. For more on the conference as an arena of said "competing colonialisms," see Parker, *Brother's Keeper*, chapter 2. For another view, see Whitham, *Bitter Rehearsal*.
70. Report to the President and Secretary of State on the First West Indian Conference at Barbados, March 1944, Under Auspices of the AACC, by Taussig, 13 May 1944, FDRL, Franklin D. Roosevelt Papers, PSF Subject File, folder "Taussig at 1st West Indian Conference 1944," box 166.
71. Ibid.
72. See C. Hahamovitch, *The Fruits of Their Labor: Atlantic Coast Farmworkers and the Making of Migrant Poverty, 1870–1945* (Chapel Hill, 1997).
73. Halifax to Eden, with Daiches report, 7 July 1944, PRO, Foreign Office 371/38536.
74. Post, *Strike the Iron: A Colony at War: Jamaica, 1939–1945*, vol. II (Atlantic Highlands, 1981), 461–62.

75. Report of Henry Field and Paul Blanshard, December 1944. Earlier in the year, Williams had warned the administration of this danger: "more and more [American-West Indian] contact [via the farm-labor program and the bases] raises the possibility of race discrimination," with difficult consequences for relations. Williams to Hastie, 15 February 1944, EWMC, folder #028.

76. Report of Henry Field and Paul Blanshard, December 1944.

77. Ibid.

78. Report of Henry Field and Paul Blanshard, December 1944.

79. On Williams's 1940s apprehension, see T. Martin, "Eric Williams and the Anglo-American Caribbean Commission," *JAAH* 88, 3: 282. On his crusade, see Fraser, *Ambivalent,* 147–59; J. Mordecai, *The West Indies: The Federal Negotiations* (London, 1968); and Parker, *Brother's Keeper,* chapters 4–5.

Chapter 7

CONTRASTING HOSTILITIES OF DEPENDENT SOCIETIES

Panama and Cuba versus the United States

Alan McPherson

In their relations with the United States, Panama and Cuba have long shared a number of similarities. Geographically, both are small nations close to US shores. Cuba is roughly the size of Pennsylvania and, famously, 90 miles from the Florida Keys, while Panama is farther away and smaller (slightly smaller than South Carolina). Strategically, both have been crucial to the defense of the Caribbean: Cuba, by hugging the Windward Passage, and the Isthmus of Panama, by providing a hub of transportation not only after the opening of the Panama Canal in 1914 but also prior to then, by offering the quickest way between the oceans by canoe, mule, and train. Finally, they both have also been the target of significant US economic penetration: Cuba on the eve of its Revolution in 1959, wrote Louis Pérez, Jr., "operated almost entirely within the framework of the economic system of the United States"; in Panama, meanwhile, although US dollars were not as numerous as they were in Cuba, they dominated a smaller economy, so much so that one scholar concluded that Panama in the mid-twentieth century was the most US-dependent country in the world.[1]

Why, then, did Cuba sustain a successful rejection of US power from 1959 on while Panama largely remained a US client after its independence from Colombia in 1903? How can attitudes toward the United States be so different in societies that are of roughly equal dependence? This essay asks these questions through a comparative, long-term, culturalist approach to anti-Americanism. It does so neither by focusing on structural factors, whether external or internal, nor by comparing the immediate political conditions that encouraged anti-US democracies or dictatorships in the era of the Cuban Revolution. Both of these approaches, to be sure, have borne fruit.[2]

Yet they have somewhat neglected the more subtle yet deep-rooted and lasting differences in cultural assumptions and consequential political practices that can be summed up as political culture. This definition of political culture, influenced by anthropological approaches to the history of US foreign relations, assumes that politics operates within webs of meaning that bring comfort in the form of making intellectual sense and giving emotional satisfaction. It also assumes that shared values and behavior in a given environment are at once internally and externally conditioned as well as superficially adaptive while fundamentally consistent.[3]

Less easily assumed is the *impact* of political culture on US-Latin American relations. As Roland Ebel, Raymond Taras, and James D. Cochrane argued over a decade ago, while in Latin America the impact of political culture on domestic affairs has long been studied, political culture "has received little or no such attention in the study of Latin American foreign policy."[4] Partly for this reason, when scholars claimed causal relations between anti-US political cultures and their impact on Latin American policy toward Washington, they resorted to unpackaged generalizations. In 1974 for instance, a Cold War-influenced textbook on political culture, citing "anti-imperialism" as a major principle of Latin American political culture, explained that "anti-imperialism, which in reality came to be merely anti-Americanism, . . . influences the foreign policies of Latin American governments. It provides a platform for demagogues and a scapegoat for militaristic and social elites. Also, anyone not wholly in agreement with an anti-imperialistic group runs the risk of being labeled an 'accomplice of imperialism.' During the Cold War, the communists spread ideological fears and portrayed all who criticized the Soviet Union or its diplomacy as allies and lackeys of the United States."[5] However much they may have rung true, such statements nevertheless failed to link the impact of anti-Americanism on foreign relations to social trends in Latin America. They also did not foresee what might happen to anti-Americanism after communism lost its appeal as a shared topic of interest (as it largely did in the Western Hemisphere after the Cold War). Vectors of political culture are not unchanging, to be sure, but they do tend to survive pivots in geopolitics such as the beginning and the end of the Cold War.

This essay explores the contrast in political cultures between Cuba and Panama and assesses the impact on each country's anti-

US strategies. To do so, it joins two apparently highly distinct eras, the nineteenth and the twenty-first centuries, thus jumping over the well-known twentieth. Why the jump? To see if the twentieth century distorts. Taking the *longue durée* approach allows a broader perspective in which Panama and Cuba were freer from US power than they were in the mid-twentieth century, or at least less in the sights of the White House as crisis-ridden nations.[6] Looking at the two countries outside the twentieth century thus minimizes external pressures on political culture and allows a freer expression of self-definition vis-à-vis the United States.[7]

In Cuba, from José Martí to Fidel Castro, anti-Americanism was marked by what could be called nationalist radicalism, an often idealistic—but politically feasible—uprooting of foreign influence while emphasizing the oneness of Cubans and the importance of social justice. In Panama, meanwhile, anti-Americanism emerged from what may be termed outward-oriented collaboration. From the mid-nineteenth-century days of statesman Justo Arosemena, when Panama was not yet a republic, to the handover of the Canal from US to Panamanian hands at the turn of the twenty-first century, a political culture far more open to global influences but far more internally fractious shaped relations with the colossus of the north. In both nations, patterns of political culture set forth in the faraway past contain profound implications for present and future relations with the United States.

The Nineteenth Century: Contrasting Founding Fathers

In the nineteenth century, Cuba and Panama displayed strikingly dissimilar visions of the Yankee, even as the United States began in both a similar process of brushing aside European powers and installing itself as the main hegemonic foreign presence. From 1850 to 1877, for instance, as more and more US ships sailed in and out of Cuban ports, the US share of Cuba's exports rose from about one-third to over four-fifths, displacing British but especially Spanish markets. US investments in the island reached $50 million by the end of the century.[8] Meanwhile, in Panama, a more sudden change brought about US displacement of British and French imperialists. Before a railroad crossed the continental United States, one in 1855 connected both ends of Panama (to be sure, a smaller feat at forty-eight miles). The railroad benefited from being ensured by the Clayton-Bulwer Treaty between the United States and Britain and financed by New York City bankers.[9] The United States therefore became the dominant power in the two soon-to-be nations even if Spain formally held on to Cuba, and Colombia, independent from Spain since 1821, held on to its own department of Panama.

Partly because of the shaky formal political oversight they faced, Creole leaders in both Cuba and Panama increasingly imagined their impending political independence and, soon thereafter, their economic one. Cubans first expressed nationalist radicalism toward the United States, while Panama shaped its more cautious outward-oriented collaboration in this context. José Martí in Cuba and Justo Arosemena in Panama, each a "founding father" or intellectual-political leader, shaped his future nation-state's identity partly in reference to the newly dominating northern neighbor. Contrasting their writings, actions, and allies offers a first glimpse into variations in anti-US identities and strategies: Martí's were ambivalent and intimate but ready for revolution; Arosemena's were more prudent, distant, and dedicated to global service.

José Martí came from a social group that expressed both significant admiration and resentment toward the increasing US presence. "At the core of the ideology of the Cuban Revolution," wrote scholar Richard Fagen, "lie two intertwining themes: the theme of *lucha,* or struggle, and the theme of utopia, or the millennium." Fagen wrote these words about the Castro era, but remarked that Martí's colleagues had shared the two themes.[10] And strange as it may seem today, many nineteenth-century Cubans of property and commerce identified these themes with the United States. Some even considered annexation to the United States because they admired the US ability to maintain a democracy yet not abandon slavery—unlike Spain, which made the former impossible, and England, which abolished the latter. "We admire your institutions, your laws, and your form of government; we see that they procure your prosperity and your happiness," explained two pro-annexation Cubans presenting the case of elite planters to US Consul William Shaler in 1810. These men saw annexation, however, not as a way to subordinate their nation to a more powerful one but as the safest route to self-determination and a way to preserve their power against slaves and Spain simultaneously.[11]

Creole Cubans notably imagined themselves particularly fit for industrial capitalism and democracy. According to Pérez, "Cubans shared with North Americans some basic values, including performance, organization, and instrumental rationality, all of which more than adequately lent themselves to North American production methods."[12] From notions of gender equality to brands of cigarettes to the passions of baseball, Cubans who came in contact with US norms consistently chose them over others' and eventually incorporated them into Cuban nationality.[13]

From this intimacy came a paradox—the conviction that Cubans more than other Latin Americans earned the right to criticize the United States. To be sure, some merely resented any Protestant influence on Catholic Cuba. Others such as José Antonio Saco realized that US designs, as expressed in the 1854 Ostend Manifesto, were either to purchase Cuba or to take it by force. Others still resented the US government for rejecting annexation on the racist grounds that Cuba had a large population of African descent. And finally, combining fears of class and race oppression, Cuban workers living in the US South grew wary of the racism and anti-labor tendencies in US society.[14]

José Martí (1853–1895) would bring these anti-American views into the sharpest focus and transform them into the most effective political strategy. Founder of the Cuban Revolutionary Party (PRC), Martí lived most of the last fifteen years of his life in the United States. As a correspondent for Latin American newspapers, he commented on everyone from Walt Whitman to Grover Cleveland and on everything from social customs to international relations. He demonstrated a detailed knowledge of US achievements, especially political and literary.[15]

Martí expressed forward-looking but ambivalent views of the United States. He held certain aspects and leaders of the country in the highest regard. His eulogies of US citizens were admiring. He also grew personally attached to the United States as a haven for immigrants. "I feel obligated to this country," he conceded, "where the unprotected always find a friend. A kind hand is always outstretched to those looking for honest work. Here, a good idea always finds welcoming, soft and fertile ground."[16] Martí imbibed progressive US ideas and promoted class and gender consciousness by allying with workers and women in the United States as well as in Cuba.[17]

But he also felt confident enough in his knowledge of the United States to be highly critical. On 18 May 1895, the day before he died, Martí wrote, "I lived within the monster and I know its entrails; my sling is that of David." This remark more than any other, wrote scholar Howard Wiarda, made Martí "famous for his anti-Americanism." Martí certainly set a precedent. He was the first to refuse all help from the US government in achieving Cuban independence. He felt that US observers stubbornly saw an "essential baseness" and an "irredeemable incompetence" among Cubans, and he warned that US officials with such prejudices would never let Cuba be free. Finally, he feared that the rampant materialism of US society—he called it the love of "interests"—led to a rapacious, untrustworthy, uncharitable use of US power abroad. Summarizing his compatriots' nationalism and radicalism, he wrote, "The Cubans admire this nation, the greatest ever built by freedom, but they distrust the evil conditions that, like worms in the blood, have begun their work of destruction in this mighty Republic."[18]

In a fascinating gendered rendering of Cuba's anti-Americanism, Martí concluded that his own up-and-coming nation appeared tragically "effete" in the eyes of US policymakers. He proposed that, in relations with the US government, Cuba walk the line between femininity and effeteness, between pride and deference, authenticity and imitation, "Cuban" and "North American." "They who think us weak should see us at all times alert and virile. Nations and men go around this world sticking their finger into other people's flesh to see if it is soft or firm; we must make our flesh resistant to the touch, so that it may reject insolent fingers."[19]

Martí also perceived an international division of labor and saw Cuba at a disadvantage in it. Precocious in his economic thought, he foreshadowed theories of dependency by warning that "the nation that buys, commands. The nation that sells, serves." The repression of US workers following the Haymarket Square riots of 1886 also convinced Martí that greater US influence over Cuba would in no way ensure fair treatment for Cuba's poor. Wiarda observed that Martí "became disillusioned by the growing gap between rich and poor in American society" and "believed the United States had sold its soul for the sake of greed and aggression." Martí felt that the notion of *Cuba Libre* should include working-class compatriots and *ex*patriates like him. He actively sought the support of the émigré proletariat along the US eastern coast. He got that support from Cuban cigar workers in Florida, who pledged a voluntary 10 percent of their salary to Martí's PRC in the 1890s.[20]

Martí helped sow the seeds of Cuba's nationalist radicalism by preparing its multifaceted identities and strategies that Cubans would later unleash when resisting US power. For instance, he perceived a "good" people in the United States led into imperialist ventures by "bad" governments and vowed that Cuba would never succumb to such schizophrenia. He also fully understood the political subservience that might emerge from economic dependence. As if Martí's goal of an independent Cuba were not idealistic enough, he defined another goal as defending continental self-determination in the name of "our America," a Latin America united across national and class lines and free from US or any other extra-hemispheric influence. The ambitious yet ambivalent stance was a heavy burden to bear for a small dependent country, a burden that could crack the back of a Cuba that was not fully dedicated to a nationalist, radical anti-Americanism.

Panama's Justo Arosemena (1817–1896) was not only of an earlier generation than Martí's but also of a social group that was, while perhaps equally patriotic, less concerned with self-determination and social justice. Panama's nineteenth-century leaders developed a more restrained anti-Americanism as a way to preserve their power over other Panamanians and to fulfill the national destiny expressed in the soon-to-be national motto "service to the world" *(pro mundi beneficio)*.

Panama's place as a hub of world transportation shaped its political culture to be open to foreign influences and its collaborative anti-Americanism. On one hand, trade gave the elite its privileged status; on the other, it had to protect that status by criticizing the US administrators who made trade flow. As a result, ruling families in Panama long suffered a crisis of identity to the point where historians have debated whether there existed an oligarchy at all. There were very few elite families—eight or ten—but they were less grounded in landed wealth and more so in commercial ventures than were oligarchs in surrounding countries. Compared to the elite in Central American countries (with the partial exception of Costa Rica), Panama's was more diverse, more inclusive, and more commercially oriented.[21] After Spain began shipping around Cape Horn in the late eighteenth century, Isthmians championed the coming of a "hanseatic state" (after a medieval trading guild), and in the nineteenth century tried repeatedly to secede from Colombia.[22] One of the results of this turn away from Spanish economic models was a growing attraction to US shipping.[23] By the mid-nineteenth century, therefore, Panama was already a unique experiment in Latin American political culture.

Oligarchs did worry about growing US power, however. Both in Colombia and on the Isthmus, wealthy Latin Americans feared the social havoc and cultural degeneration that produced events like the Watermelon Riot. The riot occurred on 15 April 1856, when one US traveler outside Panama City refused to pay a vendor for a slice of watermelon. The two fought, and poor bystanders and Panamanian policemen joined in. The fighting killed two Panamanians and fifteen US travelers and injured dozens more. The attackers were most probably West Indians, who had recently arrived to build the US-financed railroad and who had doubled the population of Panama City. In their response to this migration, leading white Panamanians faced a classic anti-US dilemma in Panama: while they needed poor West Indian laborers to finish the US railroad, they now had to contend with riotous masses as a constant threat, which made ordinary

Panamanians hate the United States.[24] Leading Panamanians increasingly worried that their love of things foreign had been excessive and that yet-unborn Panama would never acquire but the shallowest of autochthonous identities.

Their best and brightest representative was Justo Arosemena. In many ways the Thomas Jefferson of Panama, Arosemena was an accomplished jurist, statesman, economist, journalist, and philosopher. One Panamanian historian called him "the most eminent person on the Isthmus."[25] Arosemena garnered such praise because he expressed a clear social and political vision of national identity rather than peremptory patriotism. As a loyal Colombian but an advocate of a loose federal structure that would benefit his beloved department of Panama, Arosemena was torn, and it showed in his attitudes toward the United States. On one hand, he fully embraced the Benthamite utilitarianism in vogue among the commercial oligarchy of the Isthmus. He admired the democracy and capitalism in the United States. He hailed US federalism as a model for a free Panama within a strong Colombia and presided over the establishment of one such scheme, a "Federal State" in Panama. Such a political arrangement would have lowered tariffs for imported goods and thus allowed Panama to be truly responsive to its leading class, the merchants. The plan proved ill fated but nevertheless set a precedent for later independence.[26]

On the other hand, Arosemena was an early *antiyanqui.* His devotion to his department of Panama was unassailable. He warned during the construction of the US railroad from 1850 to 1855 that sudden wealth and uprooted migrants to the Isthmus would give free rein to mass licentiousness and greed. And as president, Arosemena attempted to tax the railroad and shipping companies for a right of passage. Historian Ricaurte Soler saw Arosemena in the vanguard of Panama's "social realism," the tendency on the Isthmus to reject US influence not based on the abstractions of nineteenth-century romanticism but on day-to-day observations of "social fact."[27]

A July 1856 speech conveyed not only Arosemena's openness to the outside world but also his criticism of fellow elites who tended to be a bit too complacent and collaborationist. Its title, to be sure, beseeched Latin Americans to unite "Against US Colonial Expansion." But Arosemena also berated Colombia for "sleeping" while the United States appropriated the Isthmus in all but legal title, and he reproached Latin America for not keeping up with US political stability and social dynamism. "We, sons of Spain," he said, "can and must emulate our adversaries, inhabitants of the north and descendants of the impersonal Breton." As historian Walter LaFeber has noted,

what concerned Arosemena most was that the United States was taking away in practice what geography had given Panama in theory—
its *own* manifest destiny.[28]

As the 1856 speech suggested, Arosemena proved even too independent of US power for Panama's leading families. The Watermelon
Riot took place a few months after conservatives deposed Arosemena
as president of the Federal State. Arosemena had warned compatriots against letting their guard down against "such restless neighbors"
from the north.[29] After the riots, he could only protest that the US
government had shown "by its acts of provocation the most insolent
disregard for the institutions, customs, authority and race of the Isthmus."[30] A decade later, Arosemena himself fully accepted the premise that Panama's future lay in the promise of an interoceanic canal,
and in 1868 he served as a member of a Colombian commission to
negotiate the building of one by the United States.[31]

Martí and Arosemena both died a few years before the United
States inaugurated its century of dominance in Latin America with
the War of 1898 against Spain and Cuban nationalists. In that century, the United States intervened in Cuba and Panama several times.
Eventually it developed more subtle mechanisms of control: pup-
pets replaced Marines, investment replaced forced expropriation,
and cultural exchange replaced censorship. Throughout, new nationalist leaders in both countries marshaled the memory of Martí and
Arosemena to guide them in pursuing strategies that varied widely
in their political culture. Fidel Castro, for instance, described his
eradication of US industry and landowning from the island as finishing the work that Martí had started a generation before. And Panama's nationalists revived Arosemena as a "Latin Americanist anti-
Yankee" in their insistence that Panama should regain control of the
territory in which the canal now ran—even that it should claim ownership over the waterway itself.[32] It appeared to most that nationalism—or "anti-imperialism"—was thus cut from the same cloth in both
societies, and that if it was different at all that difference was due to
Cold War distortions imposed upon these struggles by the United
States.

Few noticed, however, that anti-US leaders in Cuba and Panama
were operating in societies that held widely differing images about
the United States: Cuban political culture portrayed US power as un-
interested in social justice and eager to trample on sovereign rights
of nations; Panama's political leadership, more outwardly oriented
and self-interested, saw itself more attuned to material progress and
remained more open to collaboration provided it was mutually
beneficial.

The Twenty-First Century: Contrasting Independences

It was perhaps over a century later that these differences between Panama and Cuba returned most clearly. As the twenty-first century dawned, US relations with both countries demonstrated the underlying continuity, respectively, of radicalism and reticence in anti-Americanism. There *were* major changes that could have altered anti-US political cultures in each country. Most importantly, the Cold War ended, which somewhat relaxed US pressures on small Latin American countries to purge themselves of socialism. In Cuba, however, pressures increased: the end of Soviet subsidies sparked a 40 percent contraction of the economy from 1989 to 1994. In response, the Cuban government enacted the "special period," austerity measures coupled with limited free-market initiatives and the use of US currency. Panama, meanwhile, finally could call the canal its own as of noon on 31 December 1999, when the United States handed back the waterway as it said it would in the Panama Canal treaties signed in the 1970s. By the turn of the century, in other words, Cuba had stultified into an authoritarian, decades-old regime relatively secure in its immediate future while Panama was poised to thrive or collapse as a once-and-for-all independent but anxious hub of world commerce.

Yet little changed in each country's fundamentals of anti-Americanism: Castro, relying on the support of the *duros,* or hardliners in his government, remained hostile as a matter of policy, and Panamanian leaders remained quiescent, even obsequious clients of the United States.[33] In preserving the status quo of anti-Americanism, political culture seemed to weigh as much as did immediate external or internal changes. Events in each country illustrated the lasting legacy of political culture.

In Cuba, the nationalist radical tenor of anti-Americanism found its most emotional expression in the Elián González affair of 1999–2000. The crisis began at the eve of the turn of the century, in November 1999, when US fishermen found González, a six-year-old Cuban boy, clinging to an inner tube off the coast of Florida. The makeshift vessel on which he and other Cubans were escaping the island had capsized, drowning Elián's mother and ten others. The boy's father, Juan Miguel González, divorced from his mother and still in Cuba, was ecstatic to know his son was alive and insisted that he be returned to him in Cárdenas. Fidel Castro, too, wanted the boy returned. Meanwhile, in the stridently anti-Castro community of Little Havana in Miami, Elián's more distant relatives refused to turn Elián over to the US Justice Department. As a standoff ensued, Miami-based cousin

Marisleysis González pleaded in vain, "Let's not turn this into a political thing."[34]

Her request was not that naïve. The case did not have to become so political because the US government agreed with Castro for perhaps the first time since 1959. US immigration law clearly stated that surviving parents in foreign countries had the right to have their children repatriated. Despite the father's suspicion that the courts would not rule thusly, they did. Following the rulings, after a six-month standoff, in April 2000 the Justice Department forcibly snatched Elián from his Miami relatives. Castro and Attorney General Janet Reno made for strange bedfellows, to be sure. Nevertheless, within days, Reno had the boy reunited with his father, who flew into Washington for the occasion.[35] Before his return to Cuba, Juan Miguel González expressed optimism about the bilateral relationship: "Despite all my family's suffering, I think that this has allowed me to meet very beautiful and brilliant people in this country," said González. "And I hope in the future, this same impression I took from this country, can become true between Cuba and the United States."[36]

Yet throughout the crisis, and following its resolution, Castro was so taken with unlimbering a radical anti-Yankee stance that he foiled a real opportunity to help end the US embargo on Cuba and other policies that, as Castro himself said repeatedly, drove people such as Elián's mother to hop on barely buoyant ships in the first place.[37] Castro understood the public sympathy that ordinary Cubans held for the boy and his father, and he encouraged a rhetoric not designed to end the US impoverishment of Cuba but more likely to keep him and his government in power. These two historically competing desires of Castro's—social justice and personal power—were clashing, and the latter was, again, winning.

Cuban revolutionaries enlisted millions of their country's citizens in breathing new life into Cuba's anti-US political culture as they put together rituals that emphasized the oneness of Cubans and the evil of US social injustice. During the crisis, the government organized mass demonstrations of children and others in front of the US Interests Section in Havana.[38] They even built a sprawling stage there—called Dignity Plaza—to hold the demonstrations. To mark the momentousness of the event, speechmakers drew numerous links between Elián, the Revolution, and Martí. One warned against US imperialism and then noted, "Martí was able to appreciate the size of that threat, denounce it, and organize patriots to face it. Today, we denounce the kidnapping, the torture, and the imprisonment of the Cuban boy Elián González."[39] The Cuban state also revved up its propaganda machine. Official newspapers such as *Granma* produced special editions detailing every development in the story. The street where the Gonzalezes lived, where tourists and journalists were sure to visit, was repainted. So was Elián's schoolhouse, where a hole in the boy's desk was repaired. Castro had notably gone to his school during his absence and inscribed its guest book with the greeting, "For Elián's Liberty, Motherland or Death."[40]

Cuban television programs also invited child specialists—psychologists, sociologists, educators, and so on—to discuss the harm being done to Elián in Miami. One psychologist decried the "overstimulation" that Elián must be undergoing, surrounded by so many US toys. "They are symbols of a different culture. . . . One loses the affective tie, which becomes replaced with mere objects." More than one US cartoonist had fun with the same concept (see Fig. 7.1). The expert could only imagine, in contrast, the pain that a withdrawal from the objects representing *Cuba* must do to a child: "we Cubans are a coat of arms, a flag, my school—above all my school—my teachers, and in many instances, the bust of Martí also is a patriotic

Figure 7.1

U.S. cartoonists made light of what they read as Cuban hypocrisy in trying to dramatize the cultural dislocation that young Elián González was undergoing while surrounded by an abundance of material culture—and, in this instance, popular culture slogans—while in the United States. Cartoon by Jake Fuller, *The Gainesville Sun* (Florida). Used with permission of Jake Fuller.

symbol."[41] The great Colombian writer Gabriel García Márquez, long a sympathizer of the Revolution, chimed in that Elián was undergoing a dangerous "cultural uprooting."[42] As one sociologist explained, "Here [in Cuba] we see a society that finds its identity in the boy, that finds in the boy a way to express itself, that is moved by him."[43]

On 19 February 2000, while Elián's fate was still unsure, Castro prepared his post-crisis strategy to take advantage of a newly stoked Cuban nationalist radicalism. He called forth a massive "Free Elián" rally in Baragua. There, he took a nationally televised oath that declared war on the panoply of US policies on Cuba. The oath named enemies—the Miami "mafia" and certain members of the US Congress—and called the Bill Clinton administration "impotent." The battle to get Elián back, it declared, "has become the first episode in a much more prolonged struggle."[44]

Elián's return to Cuba also presented an opportunity for Castro. Upon the boy's arrival (at José Martí Airport), on national television a cartoon voice-over said, "Welcome, Eliancito," and exclaimed, "Now we have to keep the battle against the Cuban Adjustment Act [a 1966 act that offers exile status to political refugees], the blockade and the foundation" (i.e., the anti-Castro Cuban-American Foundation)[45] It was a bizarre instance of radical indoctrination through children's culture. Castro was himself absent from the boy's welcoming party, but soon enough he anointed Juan Miguel González with one of Cuba's top civilian awards for his "heroic behavior." Castro also donned athletic shoes to lead what state-run media claimed were one million Cubans in denouncing the US blockade—the largest march in Cuban history. The crowd proceeded past a statue erected during the crisis: it featured José Martí clutching a little boy. As journalist Ann Louise Bardach described it, "Although officially designated as Martí's son, the sculpted boy's visage has an undeniable resemblance to Elián González." What's more, "Martí's free arm is pointing accusingly straight ahead at the US Interests Section."[46]

More than a year after the boy's return, Elián's trials still inspired Castro to make them Cuba's trials. While making his annual speech before hundreds of thousands under the older, better-known towering statue of Martí in the Plaza de la Revolución, Castro stood with Elián's father again. The Cuban leader not only denounced the embargo but warned against "annexation of Latin America to the United States" under the Free Trade Agreement of the Americas. "There was no truce after the return of the boy," thundered Castro. "That is when the battle began."[47]

The concept that most turned the Elián affair into an expression of Cuba's nationalist radical anti-Americanism was that of family.

The fighting of two families—one in Miami, one in Cuba—over the future of a little boy perfectly encapsulated the emotional core of Cuba's anti-Americanism. Castro himself had often made young Cubans central to the Revolution, partly because of their energy and idealism, but also partly because they represented the renewing of a pure, uncorrupted Cuba free of US influence. "In a Communist society," the Cuban leader said in 1968, "man will have succeeded in achieving just as much understanding, closeness, and brotherhood as he has on occasion achieved within the narrow circle of his own family. To live in a communist society is to live without selfishness, to live among the people and with the people, as if every one of our fellow citizens were really our dearest brother."[48] In so defining the political value of youth, Castro used the metaphor of family as shorthand for unity, loyalty, and sacrifice.

Castro reiterated these associations during the Elián crisis. He emphasized the incompleteness of Cuban youth as long as Elián was missing from his school desk. He allowed Elián's grandmothers to visit the boy while in the United States. A Cuban TV host spoke of the grandmothers as "our grandmothers." "I say *our* grandmothers because they have begun to be a part of—we are all a part of—one big family: the family of all good Cubans on this island." Her comment not only reasserted the parallel between the unity of family and that of nation, but also assumed the existence of "bad" Cubans, defined as those in Cuba whose loyalty to the Castro regime was in question.[49]

Ann Louise Bardach explained in her account of the Elián affair that the "prism" of the "broken family" clarified the Cuban Revolution, especially after the Cold War. She recalled the little-known fact that Castro himself, when he began his guerrilla struggle in the mid-1950s, had felt alienated from his own six-year-old son, Fidelito, who remained in the United States with Castro's estranged wife Mirta Díaz-Balart.[50] Transforming an interfamilial matter into an international one, therefore, was fully in line with Cuba's—and especially Castro's—political culture of anti-Americanism.

The rhetoric of radical struggle, when added to the change from the more accommodating Clinton administration to the more confrontational one of George W. Bush, led to an intensifying crisis in US-Cuban relations. The Bush administration acted partly out of its own beliefs that Cuba was an unacceptable dictatorship in the hemisphere but also out of the need to secure the Cuban-American vote in tight contests for Florida's electoral votes in 2000 and 2004, which it won both times. The White House increased the isolation of the Castro regime from the outside world while multiplying those who subverted the regime from the inside. In 2001, for instance, the Bush administration apprehended five Cubans in the United States accused of spying and handed down sentences ranging from fifteen years to life in prison.[51] In Havana, James Cason, Bush's new chief of the US Interests Section, provoked the regime by hosting encounters with dissidents at the residences of US diplomatic personnel. Between 2000 and 2004, too, the National Endowment for Democracy quietly pumped almost $5 million to dissidents in Cuba.[52] In January 2004, Bush closed all channels for dialogue and appointed a Commission for Assistance for a Free Cuba to recommend "an expeditious end of the dictatorship" and a plan for "a post-dictatorship Cuba." In 2004 and 2005, the Departments of State and of the Treasury tightened the screws on the embargo of US farm products to Cuba and on visits to and from Cuba for family members, academics, students, and artists.[53]

The Cuban response was in keeping with the political culture that Castro and his revolutionaries had perfected to the point where it left no alternative. First, Castro unleashed a wave of repression. In March and April 2003, the Castro regime arrested a group of seventy-eight Cuban critics of the government, charged them with sedition, tried them hurriedly, and sent them to prison with an average sentence of twenty years. The regime claimed it was acting to protect the Revolution from what *Bohemia* called a "clear imperialist offensive." The Cuban government claimed that "known CIA agents" had been doling out cash to Cuban opponents of Castro. This was a cardinal sin in Cuba. To be a constructive, internal critic of the regime was one thing: it followed the political culture of idealism and self-determination for Cuba. To take US money, however, was another matter altogether: it denoted materialism and self-interest. "From the Cuban perspective," scholar William LeoGrande explained, "US aid marks a dividing line between patriots and traitors."[54]

As in the Elián affair, Castro seemed to relish Martí's notion of *lucha*. At yet another "million-man" rally, Castro plainly stated that the Bush administration's war on terrorism had Cuba in its sights: "In Miami and Washington they are now discussing where, how and when Cuba will be attacked or the problem of the revolution will be solved," said Castro. "It might turn out to be the last of the administration's fascist attacks, because the struggle would last a very long time."[55]

By 2004 and 2005, US-Cuban relations were arguably more unstable than they had been since the 1962 Missile Crisis. In retaliation for tightening the embargo, Castro took out US dollars from circulation, closed down all stores that sold goods in US dollars, and ordered

Cubans to cut off contacts with tourists unless absolutely necessary for their jobs. In February 2005, Castro made a five-hour speech in which he said he looked into the face of Bush during the president's second inaugural address in January and saw there "the face of a deranged person." Decreeing economic asceticism and abusing confrontational rhetoric, Castro once again retreated into the depths of a radical anti-Americanism. "This country is heaven, in the spiritual sense of the word," he claimed. "And I say, we prefer to die in heaven than survive in hell."[56]

While Cuba's actions fully matched its rhetoric in heated crises in the early twenty-first century, Panama's newfound independence from the United States, while real, competed with the country's lingering collaborationism. On the eve of the 1999 handover, Panama faced a potentially bright future. Nationalists had once and for all defeated the US proposal to establish a multinational counterintelligence center in Panama, which would have allowed two thousand US troops to remain under the guise of anti-drug operations.[57] Panamanians looked forward to converting the territory surrounding the Canal into prime real estate, shopping centers, civilian airports, tourist resorts, and learning institutions—all told, a $5 billion value.[58] And of course, Panamanians now constituted 93 percent of the nine thousand Canal employees and were fully trained to operate the locks, which still ushered through fourteen thousand ships per year. Panamanians were sharply aware of the opportunities to fulfill their historic mission of *pro mundi beneficio* and were proud to have fought for that opportunity.[59] One West Indian-Panamanian worker, who had put in seventy-one years on the Canal by 1999, looked back with pride on "my canal." "I am glad we Panamanians now have the canal, and we will run it as well or better than the Americans did."[60] Around the same time, former student activist Oydén Ortega struck a similar note of pride as he reflected on his years fighting for the canal. The stoic nationalist pledge to "live off sovereignty" and refuse total subservience to the United States instead of living off the scraps given to Panama under US control of canal revenues had been worth it, said Ortega. In 1999, "there was no anti-North American sentiment."[61]

In fact, Panamanians expressed *increased* collaborationism along with their openness. Beginning in 1991, polls indicated that majorities ranging from 60 to 80 percent of Panamanians favored keeping US bases and troops in Panama after the canal transfer.[62] Researcher Mark Falcoff reviewed twenty-nine of these surveys and noted that not one of them indicated that a majority rejected the US presence.[63] Panamanians also expressed surprising gratitude to the George H. W. Bush administration for its invasion of their country in 1989 to capture General Manuel Noriega. "My reaction was, 'Thank God, at last,'" said an opposition spokesman. "I don't know how patriotic that sounds, but the situation had gotten very nasty recently." According to a CBS poll taken shortly after the invasion, 92 percent of Panamanians agreed with the action (in contrast, the members of the Organization of American States disagreed twenty to one).[64]

In keeping with an outward-oriented political culture, the final months of 1999 witnessed concerns over fears of losing US protection. One of these concerns was the specter of China. The Hong Kong-based company Hutchison-Whampoa secured twenty-year contracts for container ports at both ends of the Canal, apparently giving the Chinese Army the potential to block the entrance of US ships. In this context, the facts that two-thirds of all of the Canal's cargo traffic remained US-originated or US-bound, that the transfer of the Canal still allowed for US intervention to protect its neutrality, and that US investments remained more important than those of any other country all seemed a consolation to Panama rather than a burden.[65] On the literal eve of the handover, one Panamanian newspaper reported that fully seven of ten Panamanians believed their country was unable to defend either the Canal or the border with Colombia.[66]

Panama's traditional gulf between elites and ordinary people had not diminished under US tutelage. In fact, from the mid-1990s to 2000, Panama went from having the third-worst income distribution in Latin America to having the second-worst.[67] This upper crust felt not elated but rather isolated as the handover loomed; it was they who could profit most from the new responsibilities and riches but it was also they who would be blamed if anything went wrong. Suggesting this disconnect between power and public opinion even after the regime of Noriega, one scholar called Panama "a kind of elite-directed democracy."[68] Writer Guillermo Sánchez Borbón also suggested that disconnect. "The gringos are going," he explained, "and if anything goes wrong we have to fix it. And people are terrified. They don't trust the Panamanian government. They don't trust themselves."[69] Polls indicated that "political, economic, and social leaders" were both more concerned with sovereignty and nationalism but also more willing to see the US presence in a positive light.[70] Years before the handover, the *Washington Post* described how the loss of "16,000 jobs and $330 million in wages and sales" was already prompting elite Panamanians to suggest privately to US counterparts how that presence could remain. Like many other US observers, the *Post* interpreted this ambivalence as "a ritual dance with the truth."[71]

As the ceremonies for the handover rolled around, Panamanians expressed anxiety and wistfulness at the departure of US troops and hurt feelings at what they saw as the disdainful way the handover occurred. Two decisions of the US government exacerbated Panama's anxiety by signaling the lack of remorse that the United States felt in its imperial endeavors on the Isthmus.

The first decision was the foot-dragging on environmental clean-up. According to the Canal treaties of the 1970s, the United States was to leave military and other installations in an environmentally sound state to the extent "practicable." To Panamanians, the bases had long represented such US insouciance in the face of dangers faced by Panama. From 1979 to 1996, for instance, twenty-one Panamanians had been killed on or near military ranges. The United States had "moral commitments" to leave the Isthmus a safer place, said Panamanians (see Fig. 7.2). Yet post-Cold War demobilizations at home and throughout Europe stretched the military's budget and made those environmental clean-ups less "practicable." To ease its own fiscal burden, the Pentagon ordered local commanders to pay for detoxification through their own budgets. In Panama, US personnel faced massive problems, from high levels of lead in the water to leaking underground fuel tanks to the storage of depleted uranium.[72] There was little for which the local budget could pay. One US deputy reported told Panamani-

Figure 7.2

This Panamanian cartoon, published days before the handover of the Canal from U.S. into Panamanian hands, highlighted some of the contradictions in the event: on the left, the fact that Uncle Sam is washing his hands of unexploded ordnance in his shooting ranges while holding on to a right to intervene after his departure; and, on the right, the fact that a "united fatherland" prohibits demonstrations against the U.S. presence. Cartoon by Julio Breceño in *La Prensa* (Panama City), 30 December 1999, 50A. Used by permission of Julio Breceño.

ans: "Whatever you find after the transfer is your problem." What they found, among other things, were 100,000 pieces of unexploded ordnance.[73] In 2004, when Secretary of Defense Donald Rumsfeld visited Panama City in November, he called the cleaning up of firing ranges on San Jose Island a "closed case," but immediately, Panama's Justice Minister Hector Alemán shot back that the issue was still "pending."[74]

The second US decision that hampered a smooth devolution was the failure to send high-ranking representative to the handover ceremonies. In late fall 1999, freshly inaugurated President Mireya Moscoso traveled to Washington to invite Clinton to attend them but the president was noncommittal. When it became apparent that no US official wanted to spend the day before millennium celebrations in Panama, the Panamanian government moved up the ceremonies from 31 to 14 December. Still, a few days before that new date, Secretary of State Madeleine Albright announced she would not attend as planned. She would instead send a delegation headed by former President Jimmy Carter, who had signed the handover treaties in the 1970s.

Panamanians were crestfallen. Whatever the real reason Albright was staying in Washington—to attend Middle East peace talks, as she claimed, or to appease conservative resentment at giving away the Canal, as others suspected—Panamanian commentators interpreted Albright's reversal as typical US insensitivity. "This is part of the lack of respect and attention the United States pays to the region," commented Foreign Minister José Miguel Alemán.[75] "It shows that the United States has lowered their estimation of us even more," agreed Ricardo Arías Calderón, a former vice president. "The special relationship between Panama and the United States is disappearing."[76]

Yet in the longing for economic collaboration at least, the relationship remained. A few weeks into 2000, Albright did visit.[77] And, after 2000, many Panamanians begrudgingly looked to the outside world—and the United States—for further development. Independence had not brought immediate rewards. Developers around the former Canal Zone claimed that they were unable to sell former US military properties and were losing millions simply to keep them up. Rich and poor Panamanians in 2002 lobbied for the return of thousands of US troops and civilians. One union leader, nostalgic for $10-an-hour jobs, even declared that "the United States has always been on the side of the poor. . . . Ninety-eight per cent [of Panamanians]— I'll bet on it—want the gringos back."[78]

That may have been, but they wanted the gringos back in a way that would also accommodate Panama's anti-Americanism—its fear of "selling out" in exchange for commerce and security. As a result, Panamanians now spoke of *inter*dependence the way Jose Arosemena had a century and a half earlier. First, the Panamanian government openly sought a bilateral free trade agreement (FTA) with the United States, spending as much as $1.5 million on Washington lobbyists in complex, multiround negotiations. (In early 2005, the two countries were very close to a deal.)[79] Also in early 2005, the Canal's board of directors planned to expand traffic through the Isthmus. After doubling the waterway's income and reducing the rate of accidents, it was on the verge of proposing a $5 billion investment in a set of locks parallel to the existing ones to accommodate giant cargo ships.[80]

Panama also increasingly welcomed US retirees and tourists. Because senior citizens found the low taxes, cheap housing, and cool climate of the mountains attractive, the number of foreign retirees in Panama doubled almost every year after 2000. By early 2005, Panama had issued foreigners a total of 2,500 pensioner visas, which made retiring there easier. Those vacationing in Panama also increased, doubling from 1993 to 2003 and then again in 2004, when they reached 1.6 million. The government of Panama's tourism budget multiplied in response, to $24 million in 2004. As cultural officials explained, tourism offered the possibility of a more reciprocal relationship with the United States, which was still fraught with resentment from the colonial past. "When America controlled the Panama Canal, they thought of us as a military base, like Cuba, but not as a country," said a manager for Panama City. "When they invaded us in 1989, they got rid of the hated Noriega, but they made us an occupied country, which was humiliating. We are trying to show . . . that we are a real country with a real culture."[81]

On security matters, Panamanians also increasingly saw eye-to-eye with US counterparts. In late 2004, Secretary Rumsfeld toured Central America and informed Panama that Al Qaeda trainees had been spotted in the region, perhaps targeting the Canal. Washington also warned against incursions of guerrillas from neighboring Colombia and made the improvement of security at Panamanian ports an integral part of all free trade negotiations.[82] Understandably, an increase in security measures prompted some Panamanian fears of a return to US militarization. The military presence along the border with Colombia was being beefed up, and newspapers reported that Panamanian police forces were training in the United States. Yet Panama's justice minister vehemently dismissed fears of a "return to militarism," a view that, to him, was "part of the past." "Just as society has become globalized, crime has become globalized as well," he said. "Panama cannot be an island. . . . I am sure that the people understand this."[83]

In all these endeavors, Panamanians were more than ever trying to treat the United States as they would any other powerful foreign country. Perhaps the best illustration of this normalization was that Panamanian farmers blocked the Pan-American Highway in 2004 to protest negotiations of the bilateral trade pact. In their physical, grass-roots, class-based protest against neoliberalism, they imitated other protests around Latin America and helped soften the uniqueness of anti-US hostility in Panama.

In 2005, Cuba and Panama were perhaps as different as any two countries in Latin America. To be sure, several noncultural factors were responsible for this state of affairs. Yet the distance between the two was also partly a result of long-term differences in how each country's population had imagined its identity and its relation with the outside world, especially the United States.

Panamanians, living on the slimmest slice of territory between the Atlantic and the Pacific, had long accepted the positive possibilities inherent in their geography. From the nineteenth century to the twenty-first, they had developed an outward-directed collaborationism vis-à-vis great powers ranging from Spain to the United States that brought Panama independence from Colombia, security from its neighbors, and commercial advantages for the merchant elite. Collaborationism restrained anti-Americanism but also brought more US citizens and imperial subjects to the Canal Zone, reinforcing a periodical rejection of foreigners. This mixture created an ambivalent political culture expressed not only in great speeches but in riots, protests against the US army, and the courting of US tourists.

Cubans, meanwhile, developed a more protective yet also more idealistic anti-Americanism. Uniquely dependent on the United States for not only their standard of living but for their national identity, Cubans from José Martí to Fidel Castro developed their nationalism in tandem with a fervent pursuit of a radical vision of independence and social justice. This particular political culture swung Cuba's political pendulum most dramatically, from intimacy with the United States in the late nineteenth century to a regime in the early twenty-first that at times defined itself blindly as whatever the United States was not. The intensifying crises since the Elián González affair in 1999 demonstrated the resilience of nationalist radicalism but also its self-destructiveness.

Drawing such admittedly broad links between national political culture and political expressions of anti-Americanism (or the lack of it) is bold. Hopefully the comparison between Panama and Cuba lends credence to the argument that each has a unique style of hostility as well as it suggests that other Latin American nations have theirs, too. Hopefully, too, this way of blending various types of evidence and asking long-term questions may lead those of us interested in the past of anti-Americanism to explore further the intersections between culture and international history in the making of anti-American politics. This chapter self-consciously uses a disciplinary mixture of evidence—from traditional high-level diplomatic documents and political speeches to the voices of ordinary workers and poll respondents to the symbolism found in riots, marches, and media campaigns—to suggest that the recipe that blends political and cultural sources may best produce the rich, thick substance of political culture that nourishes the growth of anti-Americanism.

Notes

1. L. Pérez, *Cuba: Between Reform and Revolution,* 2d ed. (New York, 1995; orig. 1988), 13; N. Richardson, *Foreign Policy and Economic Dependence* (Austin, 1978), 94–111. O. Pérez writes: "no country in [Latin America] has been more influenced by the United States than Panama," in "Public Opinion and the Future of US-Panama Relations," *Latin American Politics and Society* 41 (fall 1999): 1–33.
2. On comparative US-Latin American relations and Latin American revolutions, see C. Blasier, *The Hovering Giant: US Responses to Revolutionary Change in Latin America 1910–1985* rev. ed. (Pittsburgh, 1985); T. C. Wright, *Latin America in the Era of the Cuban Revolution* (New York, 1991); T. P. Wickam-Crowley, *Guerrillas & Revolution in Latin America: A Comparative Study of Insurgents and Regimes Since 1956* (Princeton, 1992); J. C. Castañeda, *Utopia Unarmed: The Latin American Left After the Cold War* (New York, 1993); C. J. Ayala, *American Sugar Kingdom: The Plantation Economy of the Spanish Caribbean 1898–1934* (Chapel Hill, 1999).
3. Gabriel Almond and other political scientists in the late 1950s first developed the modern concept of political culture. It usually referred to accepted ideas, institutions, and practices relating to politics in a society. Sociological, anthropological, and psychological insights influenced its proponents. See Y. C. Kim, "The Concept of Political Culture in Comparative Politics," *The Journal of Politics,* 26 (May 1964): 313–36; L. W. Pye and S. Verba, eds., *Political Culture and Political Development* (Princeton, 1965); and E. L. Pinney, ed., *Comparative Politics and Political Theory: Essays Written in Honor of Charles Baskervill Robson* (Chapel Hill, 1966). While this definition seemed generally accepted among social scientists in the 1960s, it lost much of its appeal and saw its use drop significantly by the 1970s, as political scientists themselves, along with other scholars, argued that political culture thus defined seemed to offer little explanation of change through time and also described dominant, national practices that left little room for alternative politics. H. Eckstein, "A Culturalist Theory of Political Change," *American Political Science Review* 82 (September 1988): 789–804. Some of these debates took place within Latin Americanist circles. On Latin American political culture, more essentialist "political culture" approaches include R. R. Fagen, *The Transformation of Political Culture in Cuba* (Stanford, 1969); R. H. Fitzgibbon and J. A. Fernandez, *Latin America: Political Culture and Development,* 2d ed. (Englewood Cliffs, 1981; orig. 1971); P. Smith, "A View from Latin America," 3–27, in *The New History: The 1980s and Beyond,* ed. T. K. Rabb and R. I. Rot-

berg (Princeton, 1982); and H. J. Wiarda, *The Soul of Latin America: The Cultural and Political Tradition* (New Haven, 2001). Fitzgibbon and Fernandez notably provide an implicit comparison of Cuba and Panama by titling their Cuba chapter "The Politics of Revolutionary Development" while that on Panama is called "The Politics of Artificiality."

Recent studies of non-dominant approaches include D. H. Levine, ed., *Constructing Culture and Power in Latin America* (Ann Arbor, 1993); and especially S. E. Alvarez, E. Dagnino, and A. Escobar, eds., *Cultures of Politics, Politics of Cultures: Re-visioning Latin American Social Movements* (Boulder, 1998). While I share this latter work's constructionist approach, it necessarily places more emphasis on non-state leaders, ethnic groups, or women's cultural politics.

4. R. H. Ebel, R. Taras, and J. D. Cochrane, *Political Culture and Foreign Policy in Latin America: Case Studies from the Circum-Caribbean* (Albany, 1992), quotation from 2; definitions on 6–10.

5. L. K. Harris & V. Alba, *The Political Culture and Behavior of Latin America* (Ohio, 1974), 106–7.

6. For a study of that mid-twentieth century anti-Americanism, see A. McPherson, *Yankee No! Anti-Americanism in US-Latin American Relations* (Cambridge, 2003).

7. Other works on political culture in Latin America have largely focused on the twentieth century and the Cuban Revolution. See Fagen, *Transformation.*

8. Pérez, *Cuba: Between Reform and Revolution,* 83–84, 13.

9. W. LaFeber, *The Panama Canal: The Crisis in Historical Perspective* (Oxford, 1977), 12.

10. Fagen, *Transformation,* 1, 9.

11. Cited in L. Pérez, *Cuba and the United States: Ties of Singular Intimacy* (Athens, Ga., 1990), 36–37. See also 5–7, 13–14, 34–36.

12. L. Pérez, Jr., *On Becoming Cuban: Identity, Nationality, and Culture* (Chapel Hill, 1999), 25; C. A. Montaner, "The Roots of Anti-Americanism in Cuba," trans. N. Durán, *Caribbean Review* 13 (March 1984): 13–16, 42–46.

13. Pérez, *On Becoming Cuban,* 47, 75, 85–86; A. Padula, Jr., "The Fall of the Bourgeoisie: Cuba, 1959–1961" (Ph.D. diss., New Mexico, 1974), vii.

14. S. Liss, *Roots of Revolution: Radical Thought in Cuba* (Lincoln, 1987), 5–15. Saco's writings have been gathered in *Contra la anexión,* ed. F. Ortiz, 2 vols. (Havana, 1928). For more on Saco see J. Suchlicki, *Cuba: From Columbus to Castro,* 2d ed. (Washington, 1986), 59, and Pérez, *Ties of Singular Intimacy,* 50–52, 73.

15. Martí, *Martí on the USA.,* ed. and trans. L. Baralt (Carbondale, 1966).

16. Cited in E. Roig de Leuchsenring, *Martí Anti-imperialist* (Havana, 1967), 10.

17. Cited in Roig de Leuchsenring, *Martí Anti-imperialist,* 10; see also 7, 9. On Martí's ambivalence, see also B. Karras, "José Martí and the Pan American Conference, 1889–1891," *Revista de History de América* 77–78 (1974): 77–99. Suchlicki, *Cuba: From Columbus to Castro,* 76, 77; Pérez, *Ties of Singular Intimacy,* 77.

18. Cited in Roig de Leuchsenring, *Martí Anti-imperialist,* 17; Wiarda, *Soul,* 184; cited in Suchlicki, *Cuba: From Columbus to Castro,* 77.

19. Roig de Leuchsenring, *Martí Anti-imperialist,* 18.

20. Pérez, *Ties of Singular Intimacy,* 79; Roig de Leuchsenring, *Cuba no debe su independencia a los Estados Unidos* (Havana, 1960; orig. 1950), 36; Wiarda, *Soul,* 185. See also Pérez, *Ties of Singular Intimacy,* 77–78; and Pérez, *On Becoming Cuban,* 46.

21. Fitzgibbon and Fernandez, *Latin America: Political Culture,* 90. Interpretations of the oligarchy that do not define it rigidly include M. Conniff, *Panama and the United States: The Forced Alliance* (Athens, 1992), 80–81, and R. M. Koster and G. Sánchez, *In the Time of the Tyrants: Panama: 1968–1990* (New York, 1990), 48–49. Around 1967, of the sixty largest companies in Panama, forty-five dealt with

commerce, fifteen with manufacturing. About twenty families held almost all economic power in Panama, based on import-export businesses: M. A. Gandásegui, Jr., *La concentración del poder económico en Panamá* (Panama City, 1967), 7, 11; LaFeber, *The Panama Canal*, 92.

22. R. Soler, *Formas ideológicas de la nación* (Panama City, 1971), 27–28; Conniff, *Panama and the United States*, 8, 12–13; LaFeber, *The Panama Canal*, 25. Panamanians first rebelled against New Granada in 1830.

23. A. Figueroa Navarro, *Dominio y sociedad en el Panamá colombiano (1821–1903)* (Panama City, 1978), 215–37 passim.

24. M. Chen Daley, "The Watermelon Riot: Cultural Encounters in Panama City, April 15, 1856," *Hispanic American Historical Review* 70 (February 1990): 85–108, offers the most complete description and analysis of the riots; see also Conniff, *Panama and the United States*, 24–39, and *Frank Leslie's Illustrated Newspaper*, 17 May 1856, 1.

25. J. P. Fábrega, *Justo Arosemena y el Estado Federal de Panamá* ([Panama City?], n.d.), no. 49 in *Panama Canal Zone Library Pamphlets*, microfilm, LOC.

26. I. García S., *Historia de la literatura panameña* (Panama City, 1986), 34–37; R. Soler, *Pensamiento panameño y concepción de la nacionalidad durante el siglo XIX* (Panama City, 1971), xvii, 63–68, 92–93; J. Arosemena, *El Estado Federal de Panamá* (Panama City, 1979), 11, 12. First published in Bogotá in 1855, *El Estado Federal* has been reissued throughout the 20th century. Figueroa states that *El Estado Federal* is "the masterpiece of nineteenth-century Panamanian nationalism," in his *Dominio y sociedad*, 320; C. Andrés Araúz, *Panamá y sus relaciones internacionales: estudio introductorio* tome 15, vol. 1 (Panama City, 1994), 56, 65, 66. See also Fábrega, *Justo Arosemena y el Estado Federal*.

27. N. Castro, *Justo Arosemena: antiyanqui y latinoamericanista* (Panama City, 1974), 20, 39; D. J. Chávez, *Autonomía, nacionalidad y antiyanquismo en Justo Arosemena* (Panama City, 1997), 17; R. Soler, *Estudios sobre historia de las ideas en América* (Panama City, 1979), 45–46. Panamanians in the 1970s revived Arosemena's anti-US side: N. Castro, *Justo Arosemena*, 7, 8, 9. Castro writes of Arosemena that "when the anti-Yankee component is missing, there is a mutilation that is not unlike a castration." Chávez, in *Autonomía*, argues that intellectuals like R. Soler and N. Castro revived Arosemena and made possible the "rescue of the anti-Yankee vision," 1. *Tareas* in the 1970s, with Soler as its editor from 1960 to 1994, proclaimed itself the "re-discoverer" of Arosemena.

28. Emphasis in original; Arosemena, *Panamá y nuestra América* (Mexico City, 1981), 157, 159; LaFeber, *The Panama Canal*, 25–26.

29. Arosemena cited in Araúz, *Panamá y sus relaciones internacionales*, 66.

30. Arosemena cited in Castro, *Justo Arosemena*, 44.

31. "Justo Arosemena," available at http://www.pancanal.com/eng/history/proceres/arosemenaj.html. Accessed 16 November 2003.

32. Castro, *Justo Arosemena*. The essay was published by the Panama Ministry of Government and Justice.

33. J. Corrales, "A Stubborn Cuba and a Stubborn America," *New York Times*, 1 January 2001.

34. Cited in R. Bragg, "Playing Geopolitics With a Tiny Prop," *New York Times*, 12 December 1999. Scholarly and journalistic overviews of the case can be found in M. Morley and C. McGillion, *Unfinished Business: America and Cuba After the Cold War, 1989–2001* (Cambridge, 2002), 158–63, and A. L. Bardach, *Cuba Confidential: Love and Vengeance in Miami and Havana* (New York, 2003).

35. R. Bragg, "Cuban Boy Seized by US Agents and Reunited with His Father," *New York Times*, 23 April 2000; D. González with L. Alvarez, "Havana Welcome," *New York Times*, 29 June 2000.

36. Cited in González with Alvarez, "Havana Welcome."
37. Editorial, "Strenghtening Mr. Castro's Hand," *New York Times,* 23 December 1999.
38. The Interests Section came out of the need to conduct limited diplomatic relations with Cuba after full diplomatic relations were severed in 1961. In 1977, Cuba and the United States agreed to set up these mechanisms in each other's capitals. In Havana, US personnel re-occupied the old US embassy and were accredited to the Swiss Embassy.
39. C. Martínez Blanco cited in "Contundente denuncia a la mafia y sus secuaces en el seno del imperio, en la Tribuna Abierta frente a la Oficina de Intereses de Estados Unidos, el 23 de February del 2000," *Granma,* 23 February 2000, 2.
40. Bardach, *Cuba Confidential,* 17; D. González, "The Boy, 6, From Cuba: So Missed," *New York Times,* 30 December 1999.
41. *Granma* and *Juventud Rebelde* published articles, speeches, and transcripts of TV roundtables together as *Batalla por la liberación del niño cubano secuestrado Elián González,* 16 December 1999–3 July 2000. Cited is Dr. A. García, "¿En qué tiempo puede cambiarse la mentalidad de un niño?" *Juventud Rebelde,* 16 December 1999, 13, 7.
42. G. García Márquez, "Náufrago en Tierra Firme," editado por *Juventud Rebelde,* 21 March 2000, 6.
43. T. Moulian of Chile cited in "Las denuncias, cuando son serias, hacen justicia," *Juventud Rebelde,* 1 May 2000, 13.
44. Oath cited in M. Fineman, "Elián Battle Won, Castro Looks to a Bigger Fight," *Los Angeles Times,* 30 June 2000.
45. Cited in "Havana Welcome." See also D. González, "After Boy's Return, Castro Tries to Keep Momentum," *New York Times,* 30 June 2000.
46. "Elián's Father Gets Medal From Castro," *Los Angeles Times,* 6 July 2000; "Castro Leads Rally Against US Embargo," *Los Angeles Times,* 27 July 2000; Bardach, *Cuba Confidential,* 336.
47. D. González, "On Free Trade, Castro Sees US Guile and Latin Dupes," *New York Times,* 2 May 2001.
48. Castro cited on 26 July 1968 in Fagen, *Transformation,* 139.
49. C. Báez cited in "Cada día que pase se alarga el sufrimiento de un niño que tenemos que rescatar," *Juventud Rebelde,* 2 February 2000, 2.
50. Bardach, *Cuba Confidential,* xvii. Castro cited on 45.
51. The main difference between Cubans arrested in the United States and those tried in Havana is that the former had indeed spied: their defense team conceded that the five men had attempted to penetrate Cuban-American groups, and the prosecution added that they had attempted to gather intelligence on the US military. They were generally underfunded and unsuccessful. See "Cuba Rallies for Release of 5 Held 'in Belly of Beast,'" *Los Angeles Times,* 18 July 2001.
52. G. Marx, "Activists Get Federal Aid to Subvert Cuba Regime," *Knight Ridder Tribune News Service,* 21 February 2005, 1.
53. W. Smith, "Bush and Cuba: Still the Full Moon," *NACLA Report on the Americas* 38: 2 (September/October 2004); M. Doyle, "Rules Impair Farm Exports to Cuba," *Fresno Bee,* 25 February 2005.
54. D. Alin, "Havana States Its Case," *Bohemia,* 18 April 2003, reproduced in *World Press Review,* July 2003, 23–25; LeoGrande, "US Policy Is Consistent—but Wrong," *Los Angeles Times,* 22 April 2001.
55. Castro cited in Bardach, *Cuba Confidential,* 357.
56. "Castro Calls Bush 'Deranged Person,'" *Deseret News* (Salt Lake City), 3 February 2005.
57. D. Farah, "Politics, Posturing Trip Up US-Panama Negotiations," *The Oregonian* 5 July 1998; P. M. Sanchez, "The End of Hegemony? Panama and the United

States," *International Journal on World Peace* 19 (September 2002): 57. O. Pérez says that the opposition to a counternarcotics center was from a "vocal minority," "Public Opinion": 2. For nationalist writings, see R. Soler, *La invasión de Estados Unidos a Panamá: neocolonialismo en la posguerra fría* (Panama City, 1992); and D. Acosta, *Patria y CMA* (David, Panama, 1999).

58. D. González, "The Big Ditch: Panama's Big Opportunity," *New York Times,* 13 December 1999.

59. Ibid.; "Historic Point in US-Latin Ties," *Los Angeles Times,* 13 December 1999.

60. "Panama Canal Sees the Last of the Stars and Stripes," *New York Times,* 31 December 1999.

61. O. Ortega Durán interview by author, tape recording, 13 October 1999, Panama City, Panama.

62. J. Lindsay-Poland, *Emperors in the Jungle: The Hidden History of the US in Panama* (Durham, 2003), 126.

63. Falcoff, *Panama's Canal: What Happens When the United States Gives a Small Country What It Wants* (Washington, 1998), 32–35; more polls are available from Pérez, "Public Opinion": 1–33. Pérez relies partly on his own polls, conducted with the help of the University of Pittsburgh, but also on others conducted for Panamanian newspapers. See also S. Dudley Gold, *The Panama Canal Transfer: Controversy at the Crossroads* (Austin, 1999), 21.

64. A. Rosenthal, "16 Americans Dead," *New York Times,* 21 December 1989; M. R. Kagay, "Panamanians Strongly Back US Move," *New York Times,* 6 January 1990; Gold, *The Panama Canal Transfer,* 104–5.

65. A. Clymer, "Panama Trouble: Who Hands Canal Over?" *New York Times,* 12 December 1999; "China's Control of Panama Canal Feared" *Los Angeles Times,* 6 October 1999; J. Darling, "'The Canal Is Ours' Is Jubilant Cry in Panama," *Los Angeles Times,* 1 January 2000.

66. J. Giannareas, "Panamá no está capacitada para defender el Canal," *La Prensa,* 29 December 1999; H. Sucre Serrano, "Neutralidad, única defensa del Canal," *La Prensa,* 30 December 1999.

67. T. Robberson, "Panama Turnabout: Yankee, Don't Go Home," *Washington Post,* 16 October 1995. Lindsay-Poland, *Emperors,* 176.

68. Wiarda, *Soul,* 317.

69. González, "The Big Ditch."

70. Pérez, "Public Opinion," 11–20.

71. Robberson, "Panama Turnabout." The responsibility of the former Zone was indeed heavy. It contained 3,600 buildings and 71,000 acres of land, much of which was decaying because of neglect. The Trans-Isthmiam Railroad had already been shut down after five years under Panamanian responsibility because of the frequency of derailments.

72. Lindsay-Poland, *Emperors,* 138–71.

73. Ibid. 138, 141, 160.

74. C. Sánchez, "Clean Up of Firing Ranges Creates Friction with United States," *La Prensa* Website trans. by BBC, 14 November 2004.

75. D. González, "As Panamanians See It, Clinton Is a Party Pooper," *New York Times,* 14 December 1999. The *New York Times* agreed, editorializing that the Clinton administration lacked courage enough to attend the ceremony, in "A Century Ends in Panama," 18 December 1999.

76. D. González, "Panama Feels Slighted When Albright Cancels Date at Canal," *New York Times,* 11 December 1999.

77. E. Schrader, "US Drags Heels as Panama Canal Transfer Party," *Los Angeles Times,* 11 November 1999; J. Peterson, "Latin Gains Displayed During Albright Tour," *Los Angeles Times,* 16 January 2000.

78. M. Archer cited in S. Wilson, "Yankee Come Back," *Washington Post,* 28 September 2002.

79. R. E. Berrocal, "Panama's Hour of Truth Has Come," *La Prensa* Website trans. by BBC, 10 January 2005; "Panama's Lobbying for FTA with US Said to Cost Millions," *La Prensa* Website trans. by BBC, 8 December 2004.

80. The board had been commissioning studies quietly since 2000 because it was wary of the cultural sensitivities this might arouse. For this reason, any proposal would go through the Congress and a nationwide referendum (planned for November 2005). C. Kraul, "$5-Billion Expansion of Panama Canal Is Considered," *Los Angeles Times,* 22 January 2005; J. Zamorano and K. Martinez, "Panama Touts Successes after 5 Years of Canal Control," *Chicago Sun-Times,* 31 December 2004.

81. H. Reich, "Panama Trying to Jazz Up Image and Lure Tourists," *Knight Ridder Tribune News Service,* 24 January 2005.

82. M. Miranda and M. Shulman, "Central America, the Forgotten Frontier War on Terrorism," *International Herald Tribune,* 23 November 2004.

83. Minister of Government and Justice Hector Alemán cited in J. Otero and R. Luna Noguera, "Alemán: 'We Do Not Need an Army'," *La Prensa,* trans. by BBC, 13 November 2004.

Chapter 8

OPTION FOR THE POOR
Liberation Theology and Anti-Americanization

David Ryan

It is an irony that, as the so-called *refolutions*[1] of Eastern Europe un-folded over the autumn of 1989, and during the "final offensive" of the Farabundo Martí Front for National Liberation (FMLN) in El Salva-dor, an elite US-backed battalion entered the Central American Uni-versity and shot six Jesuits, their housekeeper Elba Ramos, and her daughter Celina Ramos. As the democratic options were opening up in Eastern Europe, the repression by US-sponsored "national secu-rity states" was still intense. The Jesuits were perhaps the most vis-ible symbols of a liberation theology that had grown in Latin America since the late 1960s. Crucially, liberation theologians argued that "the man who is not a man" had to be humanized and made conscious of the economic and political structures that kept him in poverty. For liberation theologians, salvation was something to be sought in *this* world, not just in the afterworld. For one of the key theorists and ac-tive theologians, Gustavo Gutierrez, who published the seminal *A Theology of Liberation* in the early 1970s, the word "poor" did not sig-nify a description of an individual condition. Instead, talk of the poor involved an "element of social conflict," he wrote. "The word 'poor' is not a tranquilizing one." Instead it situates the poor as "the prod-uct, or by-product, of an economic and social system fashioned by a few for their own benefit. So a structural conflict is embedded in the reality of the poor." An awareness of their situation therefore ne-cessitated and involved the poor in a fight against those conditions.[2]

This fight meant that advocates of liberation theology and those who supported the poor were pitted against the elite, their security forces, and the imperial US economic and political systems. For the Salvadoran right and the security forces, there was little to distinguish between the Jesuits murdered that night of 16 November 1989 and the various "communist" movements within El Salvador, Nicaragua, and beyond. Their political discourse on "communism" still represented a monolithic force in a Manichaean framework, often the case in such polarized contexts. Thus, for many, and certainly for the security forces that carried out the murders, these Jesuits were seen as legitimate targets.

The end of the Cold War, the broken Esquipulas peace process, the end of the Sandinista revolution in Nicaragua, and the return to neoliberal economic structures also created two parallel phenomena. The first was the protracted settlement of the conflicts, often subverted by Washington, which prevailed in Nicaragua, El Salvador, and Guatemala.[3] In the latter part of the 1980s, these countries not only moved toward some settlement but also increasingly applied orthodox policies of economic stabilization to reduce inflation. Even Sandinista Nicaragua introduced such economic strictures from 1988. By the early 1990s most regional governments pursued similar economic objectives to stem the decade-long decline in gross domestic product per capita. Over a decade of war, increasing poverty, and exhaustion led to a "pacification" of Central America that failed to address the fundamental underlying causes of poverty and the liberation theologians' critique of the US-centered system.[4] The ensuing "regulative peace," which focuses on increased economic integration and the attendant institutions and ideologies to sustain that peace, increasingly coalesced in the process of globalization. The stability of peace was accompanied by the instability of globalization.[5]

A second consequence of the 1980s was that the Catholic church suffered the loss of substantial numbers of followers. By the early 1990s, between 9,000 and 10,000 people a day converted from Catholicism to more fundamentalist forms of Protestantism.[6] The socially conservative but consciously apolitical Protestant churches strategically situated themselves against the politicized Catholic church. The politicization of liberation theology also caused deep divisions in the Catholic church, some of which involved Vatican intervention. Pope John Paul II himself silenced the Brazilian Franciscan Leonardo Boff,[7] and he berated Sandinista Minister of Culture Father Ernesto Cardenal during the papal visit to Nicaragua in 1983.[8] The Catholic hierarchy ultimately became alarmed at the growth of Pentecostal churches in areas of US strategic concern. On occasion, they blamed the United States for the so-called invasion of the sects. In Central America there were suggestions that the Central Intelligence Agency

(CIA) was behind such Protestant advances, in an attempt to block social change and maintain US hegemony.[9] Presumably, if the "poor" were led to believe that their salvation would occur in the afterlife, they would accept their poverty as "natural," mitigating the need to attribute blame or direct their anger at the authorities in their country or at the United States. The new Protestant churches and the traditional Catholics held such views. Liberation theologians argued that the church's long-standing silence on political matters sustained an unequal and unjust status quo. Their pastoral role should include an active engagement with issues of poverty and human rights.

So, was liberation theology anti-American? It was anti-American in a subtle but fundamental way: as a critique of the domestic and international order that was closely associated with the United States. Its antecedents can be traced back to Catholic social teaching[10] and some specific conclusions of the Second Vatican Council (or Vatican II, 1962–1965). One can also find its roots in dependency theory in the economic realm and in critiques of repressive regimes that justified their legitimacy through reference to discourses on national security. Although the political elements of the critique were often more intense during periods of heightened tension and intervention, the basic outlook on the global order was a more fundamental criticism of the prevailing economic system and its impact on the poor. As Latin American societies increasingly underwent modernization, urbanization, and Americanization, the traditional Catholic church came under increased pressure because it could no longer address the pastoral needs of people stuck in deepening poverty. For liberation theologians, dependency theory explained Latin American poverty and its relationship to US wealth. Beyond the theoretical explanation, liberation theology added a moral element emphasizing the need for change. As these theologians articulated the political connections between Washington and repressive regimes in Latin America, the Catholic church experienced a division between these clergy and those who limited themselves to purely spiritual concerns.[11]

Liberation theology speaks to the concerns of the poor in the face of the US-led international economy. This paper will outline the development of liberation theology from 1968 within the context of Latin American politics. It will then address two central tenets of liberation theology: the inhumanity of the local and international economy, and the immorality of the national security state, its ideology, and its impact on human rights. While the United States and its foreign policy were often the object of direct criticism, the theology of liberation more generally set up arguments that implicated Wall Street as a key part of the problem. In this regard, it is essential to distinguish between anti-Americanism and what concerns liberation theologians, anti-Americanization. Finally, this paper will assess the attempt by liberation theologists to represent the "voice of the voiceless" in El Salvador.

The Developing Critique: Medellín to Puebla

Liberation theology emerged from particular developments within Catholic social teachings but also fit within a long-term discourse of Latin American criticism of US power. From the outset, the United States encountered resistance of various sorts, as its exceptional ideologies and economic penetration were interpreted quite differently in the global south. In the 1890s José Martí warned in Cuba that "our America," as opposed to that of the United States, was threatened by northern power. It was time for "Spanish America to declare its second independence" from US economic integration. Martí was not that concerned about political occupation, but more about the dangers of an unequal economic relationship. He argued that "the nation that buys, commands. The nation that sells, serves. It is necessary to balance trade in order to guarantee liberty. The nation eager to die sells to a single nation, and the one eager to save itself sells to more than one. A country's excessive influence over the commerce of another becomes political influence."[12] Martí's call for resistance to excessive influence resonated throughout the twentieth century. One also thinks of the nationalist resistance of Augusto Sandino in Nicaragua, or that of Farabundo Martí in nearby El Salvador prior to World War II.

After World War II, Washington became increasingly aware of the opposition and its local indigenous roots: an internal opposition generated by and for the poor against forms of economic control. During the Cold War, policy documents frequently invoked international communism; but no less an important theme was the frequent reference to Latin American nationalism. For instance, the Eisenhower National Security Council's NSC 144/1 considered that

> there is a trend in Latin America toward nationalist regimes maintained in large part by appeals to the masses of the population. Concurrently, there is an increasing popular demand for immediate improvement in the low living standards of the masses, with the result that most Latin American governments are under intense domestic political pressures to increase production and to diversify their economies. . . . A realistic and constructive approach to this need which recognizes the importance of bettering conditions for the general population, is essential to arrest the drift in the area toward radical and nationalistic regimes. The growth of nationalism is facilitated by historic anti-US prejudices and exploited by Communists.

Thus, US policy sought "orderly political and economic development in Latin America so that the states in the area will be more effective members of the hemisphere system and increasingly important participants in the economic and political affairs of the free world."[13]

Concurrently, since 1948, the Economic Commission for Latin America (CEPAL), led by economist Raúl Prebisch, developed theories of underdevelopment that sought to move the explanations for Latin American poverty from indigenous causes to exogenous factors, especially international trade and obviously the United States. Prebisch argued that the economies of the center and periphery were fundamentally different. The underdevelopment of the former was directly related to the latter. The "center obtained some of its wealth from the periphery through 'unequal exchange.'"[14] The argument was highly influential throughout Latin America and formed the basis of dependency theory. Dependency challenged the consensus on modernization.[15] Highly contested within academia, the essential ideas remained influential and were often used to form a fundamental critique of US economic policy.

Soon after its creation, CEPAL suggested that, in general, Latin American countries would face declining terms of trade with the north. There was an acute shortage of hard currency in many Latin economies, which limited trade with the north. To mitigate the effects of the international economy, inward-focused models of development became more attractive in the south.[16] Pitted against such options were the liberal capitalist models preferred in Washington. The Latin response was mixed. While some adopted policies of import substitution, others maintained liberal trade regimes. Industrialization accelerated during the 1950s, bringing with it increased urbanization, relative poverty, and the adoption of US models of economic development and national security. By the 1960s, President John F. Kennedy's Alliance for Progress was in part conceived to overcome the tensions between the two options on development. Dependency theory gained more influence and pertinence in explaining the international context of development in the wake of Washington's 1954 overthrow of the Jacobo Arbenz government in Guatemala, the work of CEPAL, and the 1959 revolution in Cuba.[17]

Dependency and revolution informed the ideas of liberation theologians. During the 1960s the political and economic context coincided with important developments in the Catholic church. First, the Second Vatican Council (Vatican II), which updated the practices and theology of the Catholic church, fundamentally altered the church's outlook; it gradually introduced a more liberal agenda focused on peace and the pursuit of social justice, including the obligation to help the

poor. The impact of Vatican II forced the church to reconsider its understanding of itself as a church based on tradition, hierarchy, and
theological stasis to one based on an understanding of the impact of
temporal change on its teachings and pastoral work. The debate
was not confined to theological issues. The Catholic church injected
various elements of contemporary social science into its thinking
and became increasingly concerned with development. Especially in
Latin America, where these changes had the greatest initial impact,
the church engaged with issues of violence, "structural change," and
economic dependency.[18]

The second major factor was the publication in 1967 of Pope Paul's
encyclical letter, *Populorum Progressio*. The document's publication
coincided with the development of liberation theology and provided
further succor. On the Christian vision of development, it asserted
that "development cannot be limited to mere economic growth. In
order to be authentic, it must be complete, integral"; it had to promote the good of people. On liberal capitalism, the letter stated that
"it is unfortunate that on these new conditions of society a system
has been constructed which considers profit as the key motive for
economic progress." It went on to say that "if it is true that a type of
capitalism has been the source of excessive suffering, injustices and
fratricidal conflicts whose effects still persist, it would also be wrong
to attribute to industrialization itself evils that belong to the woeful
system which accompanied it."[19] Part two of the document went further in explicitly injecting elements of dependency theory into a section on "equity in trade relations." Through an argument on unequal
trade, the encyclical identified the inadequacy of international assistance and argued that nations too reliant on exports were vulnerable
to price fluctuations. As a result, "the poor nations remain poorer
while the rich ones become still richer."[20] Such observations were
quite critical within the context of highly polarized societies. As the
theologian Jon Sobrino later pointed out, "remember that in [El Sal-
vador] even Paul VI was accused of being a 'communist' when he published *Populorum Progressio*."[21] Thus, while the critique of US-style
capitalism was implied, it was nevertheless very clear.

Among several authors who contributed to the development of
liberation theology, Peruvian theologian Gustavo Gutierrez was notably influential.[22] His writings were especially important because
they coincided with the 1968 meeting of Latin American bishops in
Medellín, Colombia. Shortly before the meeting, Gutierrez presented
the paper "Toward a Theology of Liberation," though his writings received far more attention after the gathering. Gutierrez had an obvious influence on the proceedings in Medellín; the legitimacy and

strength of liberation theology grew out of that encounter.[23] The Medellín gathering initiated the consolidation of liberation theology. Bishops were forced to think of the temporal dimensions of their work and affirm their commitment to fight for justice.[24] Gutierrez was one of the principal advisors to the committee responsible for writing the central document, titled *Peace*. Much of the content of *Peace* is a straightforward statement about the relationship between Latin American poverty and US wealth. According to the authors, North American development relied on the exploitation of Latin America and other "underdeveloped" regions."[25] Again, this form of implicit anti-Americanism is evident in the statement that "the principal guilt for the economic dependence of our countries rests with powers inspired by uncontrolled desire for gain."[26]

In a section dealing with neocolonialism, the document addressed what it called the "growing distortion of international commerce" as a result of "countries which produce raw materials—especially if they are dependent upon one major export—always remain poor, while the industrialized countries enrich themselves."[27] Gutierrez was more explicit. In *A Theology of Liberation*, he argued that the "domination exercised by the great capitalist countries, and especially by the most powerful, the United States of America," caused the current conditions.[28]

Perhaps the most influential passage from the document *Peace* concerned violence; it provided the basis for liberation theology's focus on addressing structural violence. The final document stated:

> As the Christian believes in the productiveness of peace in order to achieve justice, he also believes that justice is a prerequisite for peace. He recognizes that in many instances Latin America finds itself faced with a situation of injustice that can be called institutionalized violence, when, because of a structural deficiency of industry and agriculture, of national and international economy, of cultural and political life, "whole towns lack necessities, live in such dependence as hinders all initiative and responsibility as well as every possibility for cultural promotion and participation in social and political life," thus violating fundamental rights. This situation demands all-embracing, courageous, urgent and profoundly renovating transformations. We should not be surprised therefore, that the "temptation to violence" is surfacing in Latin America. One should not abuse the patience of a people that for years has borne a situation that would not be acceptable to anyone with any degree of awareness of human rights.[29]

The Medellín conference injected a sense of activism into the Catholic church. Liberation theologians no longer considered a passive pastoral role as adequate given the structural violence they had identified. At the heart of liberation theology was the notion of "conscientization"—that one had to become aware of one's own situation. It was therefore necessary to treat poverty within the context of the structural violence that exacerbated it. To many clergy members, this resulted in an active commitment to serving the poor. Within the polarized context of Latin and particularly Central America, such involvement and activism was read by the elite and security forces as subversion. For liberation theologians, the order that kept people mired in poverty was fundamentally that of the US-centered international order, which was maintained in Latin American countries through a "national security" state, which was often the recipient of military aid from Washington.[30]

El Salvador: "The Option for the Poor" and US National Security

Between the time of the 1968 bishops' meeting in Medellín and the next meeting in Puebla, Mexico, in 1979, the church divided along fault lines that were directly related to the "option for the poor." The decade between these meetings witnessed increasing polarization. Just as Castro's revolution had spurred on the left in the late 1950s and early 1960s, the electoral victory of Salvador Allende in Chile in 1970 gave the post-Medellín agenda new hope. At the Medellín meeting, capitalism had been roundly criticized in both its international and local dimensions. The US government reacted to these changes along the lines that Nelson Rockefeller, the New York Republican governor, identified in his report following his tour of the region in 1969, which provided the basis for US policy during the early 1970s. Rockefeller identified the increase in nationalism and the desire for social change throughout the region, both of which could threaten US "national security" interests and its investments. Further, he suggested that the church and the military would become the key protagonists in the evolving situation. The report welcomed the power of the military, though it was ambivalent about the direction of the church.[31] While the Rockefeller report accepted the premise of liberation theology, it did not approve of the remedy.

Given the radical criticism of liberation theologians, several Latin American leaders concluded that those who preached liberation theology had to be silenced. Clergy members and bishops were increasingly targeted for arrest, torture, expulsion from various countries, and assassination. El Salvador witnessed some of the most extreme repression of the church during the late 1970s and throughout the 1980s. The radicalization of Archbishop Oscar Romero, for example, is largely attributed to the murder of Father Rutilio Grande in 1977.[32]

Grande was amongst the first victims following the electoral seizure of power by General Carlos Humberto Romero in February 1977. At Grande's funeral in San Salvador, which over one hundred thousand people attended, ignoring the government's state of siege, Bishop Rivera Damas opined that Grande was killed in order to stop the process of evangelization and conscientization that he had worked to bring about.[33]

The 1979 bishops' conference in Puebla took place in this atmosphere of increasing polarization and violence. Despite the best efforts of conservative forces within the church to significantly shape the agenda, Puebla attendees reiterated a strong message on the "option for the poor" (which is explained in more detail below). The church was openly divided in its preparations for the conference, and indeed the Puebla document is not as uniform or coherent as that of Medellín. Increasing compromise was reached on matters of high theology, but the most noteworthy outcome was that the social content of the Puebla document reaffirmed the conclusions drawn in Medellín. That the document should do this after a decade of repression and reaction to the popular church was an extraordinary achievement. After all, it was one thing to propose a radical program, but quite another to continue endorsing it a decade later.[34] This was the true significance of the Puebla meeting, rather than the relatively minor doctrinal issues discussed.

The "option for the poor" represented a small but vital part of the document. Central to its message were the affirmation of the vast poverty throughout the continent and the recognition that the poor could become "true protagonists of their own development." The document's authors recognized the importance of the grassroots communities in these terms and ultimately, while not identifying the United States and the elite throughout Latin America specifically, stated that they would make "every effort to understand and denounce the mechanisms that generate this poverty."[35] If the language seemed weak, it represented a compromise between the liberation theologians and the conservative clergy.

The direction of the radical wing of the church, and even the rhetoric of more moderate liberation theologians, preoccupied Washington considerably. Reports indicated that the US Senate, the CIA, and the Pentagon increased their interests in the developments at Puebla "wondering whether there were any mitred ayatollahs."[36] The Carter administration's search for a path between the extremes of military repression and left-wing insurgency proved elusive. In the context of having "lost" Nicaragua to the Sandinistas and South Vietnam to the communist North, it became increasingly important to seek human rights reforms but also to help the Salvadoran regime hold power and survive. US credibility was at stake. Yet the National Security Council (NSC) reported in October 1979 that, despite some announcements toward reform, "undiminished police repression and anti-opposition violence have undermined the credibility of [General] Romero's proffered reforms." The NSC observed that the Salvadoran establishment was "demoralized" and the "economic elite is divided between advocates of harsh repression and moderate reform." But neither group had faith in General Romero to deliver either. The elite's flight from the country with their capital further widened the political divisions and inflamed "deep social antagonisms." The NSC considered both "intensified repression" and "a bloody and radical revolution . . . a distinct possibility." Though US interests in El Salvador were deemed limited, "the coincidence of turmoil there with the Nicaraguan revolution and renewed Cuban activism gives El Salvador disproportionate psychological and political importance." Moreover, unless a reforming military coup succeeded, "in a context of Soviet troops in Cuba, the general debate over the apparent decline of US global power, and the forthcoming US elections, the turmoil in El Salvador could have wider repercussions. Either a bloody revolution or direct US military involvement would become an issue in US domestic politics."[37] Within this context, Washington feared the influence of liberation theology and moved to undermine its impact, co-opt key protagonists, and support the "moderate" center.

Archbishop Romero became increasingly critical of both the regime and ultimately of the United States' supporting role. Since the murder of Rutilio Grande, Archbishop Romero grew increasingly radical and critical, starting with the refusal to attend General Romero's inauguration in 1977 until Grande's murder had been solved. His pastoral letters constantly pushed forward the central lines of liberation theology: the support for a church that situated the poor at the center of its mission, the concomitant denunciation of the political and economic systems that sustained this poverty, and the denunciation of the human rights' abuse that followed the doctrines of national security.[38] These criticisms were aimed not just at local injustices, but at two of the most fundamental aspects of US foreign policy: the aim to enhance a US-centered economic system in the region, and the military and political support for repressive regimes, which rested on ideologies of national security and "anti-Communism."[39]

Romero took pains to identify the central conclusions of Puebla and apply them to his analysis of the situation in El Ṣalvador and then to broadcast and publish his pastoral letters. "That 'muted cry' of wretchedness that Medellín heard ten years ago," he wrote, "Puebla now describes as 'loud and clear.'" He constantly denounced the increasing political violence, government attitudes, and extrajudicial killings. In his fourth pastoral letter, he wrote that

[a]bsolutizing wealth and private property brings about the absolutizing of political, social, and economic power, without which it is impossible for the rich to preserve their privileges, even at the cost of their own human dignity. In this country this idolatry is at the root of structural and repressive violence. In the final analysis, it is the cause of a great part of our economic, social, and political underdevelopment. This is the capitalism condemned by the church at Puebla.[40]

In this pastoral letter Romero addressed the issue of structural violence and intimated that violence in opposition to these conditions would be legitimate. He cited Pope Paul's *Populorum Progressio,* "according to which insurrection is legitimate" in certain circumstances. This point became explicit in his address at the University of Louvain, which conferred on him an honorary doctorate. Romero accepted the award as a gesture of solidarity with the people of El Salvador and explained that in "this situation of conflict and antagonism, in which just a few persons control economic and political power, the church has placed itself at the side of the poor and has undertaken their defense." The church could not remain removed from the realities of the daily atrocities that he enumerated. For Romero, the causes both internal and external were obvious, therefore "neutrality is impossible. Either we serve the life of Salvadorans, or we are accomplices in their death." Thus, he concluded, "we encourage all liberation movements that really lead to justice and peace for the majority of the people."[41]

The issue of violence divided liberation theologians. Following the radical Colombian priest, Camilo Torres (who joined in armed struggle against the government and was killed in 1966) and the message of *Populorum Progressio,* a number of liberation theologians accepted that violence was a legitimate response to the extreme situation they faced. The theological position on violence was relatively clear: it was justified under extreme conditions. Who could doubt that El Salvador experienced such conditions?

Ignacio Ellacuría, one of the six Jesuits executed at the Central American University in 1989, was an outspoken critic of the regime, of US backing, and of the structural violence that caused the poverty of Central America. He was the rector of the Central American University, often referred to by the Salvadoran government and the US embassy as the "intellectual leadership of the FMLN." Ellacuría had written extensively on violence and *Populorum Progressio* and described it as legitimate in certain circumstances, and even the moderate Romero hinted that it might be legitimate. Elsewhere, many liberation theologians were closely associated with revolutionary movements. Ellacuría's early position on violence was that, though it was legitimate under these circumstances, it always ran the risk of acting against certain Christian values; therefore, he argued, such questions must always be asked about the context within which violence was legitimate. Moreover, the use of violence should be ceased as soon as possible. Whether all liberation theologians understood all the nuances as to when, where, and under which circumstances violence was legitimate is doubtful. However, by the 1980s Ellacuría had come to believe that violence would ultimately not advance the situation in El Salvador and that other options had potential.[42]

Within several weeks of the Louvain address, Romero squarely identified the United States as part of the problems facing much of Latin America. Calling on President Carter to cease military aid and training to the repressive regime, he wrote, "Your government's contribution will undoubtedly sharpen the injustice and the repression inflicted on the organized people, whose struggle has often been for respect for their most basic human rights."[43]

Washington grew increasingly alarmed at Romero's public pronouncements. US officials maintained contact with him, but failed to moderate his position. Ultimately, Carter's adviser on national security, Zbigniew Brzezinski, wrote to Pope John Paul II. His letter outlined the socioeconomic origins of the crisis in Central America and argued that rapid modernization was leading to "profound economic, social and political reforms" and that most governments were responding with violence and repression. In these circumstances the extreme left was seeking opportunities to "destroy the existing order and replace it with a Marxist one," which would be equally repressive. Brzezinski ultimately argued that the Catholic church could "make a decisive contribution to furthering a process of peaceful change." While Washington recognized the constructive role played by Romero, Brzezinski noted that Romero had shifted positions. In the course of several weeks, "the Archbishop has strongly criticized the Junta and leaned toward support for the extreme left" despite Washington's "frequent and frank dialogue with Archbishop Romero and his Jesuit advisors." Brzezinski asked for the Pope's intervention.[44]

According to NSC documents, the Pope apparently followed Brzezinski's request and cautioned Romero. Romero in turn was reported to see "the hand of the US in his being called to the Vatican." However, they reported, "the Pope's message apparently has had little initial impact. . . . Romero has continued his criticism of the Junta and was also quoted in the press as justifying the use of political violence if there were no other means to achieve needed changes."[45] Still, the NSC director of Latin American affairs, Robert Pastor, wrote Brzezinski that they were looking for effective ways to "divide the left and try to get leading groups and individuals (like Archbishop Romero, MNR, Jesuits) to leave the left and support the Junta."[46]

Just over a month later, on 24 March 1980, Archbishop Romero was assassinated while giving Mass. The day before, he had pleaded with soldiers not to obey orders if they were not lawful. Two days after his death, an NSC coordinating committee opined, "Radical Jesuit priests are working with leaders of the extremist groups to plan a spectacular procession, perhaps involving 200,000 people, for the funeral of the Archbishop this weekend. The extremists will probably try to use the demonstration to spark violence and perhaps an insurrection, along the lines of what the Sandinistas did after the assassination of Pedro Joaquín Chamorro."[47] Thousands did gather at his funeral. A banner was hung on the entrance to the cathedral indicating that the conservative bishops, the papal nuncio, and the US ambassador were not welcome. Gunmen ultimately opened fire at those gathered on the steps of the cathedral, killing and wounding scores of people.[48]

Romero's death was unique only in its symbolism. Hundreds of church workers were executed over the course of the decade by US-backed government forces, especially in El Salvador and Guatemala. The year 1980 ended with the murder of four American nuns and church workers: Ita Ford, Maura Clarke, Dorothy Kazel, and Jean Donovan. Despite a brief cessation of US assistance to the Salvadoran government, military aid resumed within weeks.[49] US interviews at the time with Salvadoran officials indicated, "There is evidence of hostility between the military and the church in El Salvador and, in particular, between the military and church workers in Chalatenango. Our interviews with Salvadoran officers reinforced this conclusion; their animosity toward the church was obvious. Colonel Monterrosa was perhaps most blunt. He openly speculated that the churchwomen were probably subversives, and that the military might well have wished them dead."[50]

The approach taken by the administration of Ronald Reagan to liberation theology was set by the tone of an advisory group to the president, the Committee of Santa Fe, which argued that "US foreign policy must begin to counter liberation theology as it is utilized in Latin America. Liberation theology has played an increasing role in overthrowing authoritarian, but pro-US governments and replacing them with anti-US, Communist . . . dictatorships of the totalitarian kind."[51] Given the participation of liberation theologians in various revolutionary movements, conservatives in Washington placed them squarely on the opposite side of a Manichaean construct. The tendency was to place their thinking within the same framework of all revolutionaries and therefore, at least from Washington's perspective, as a problem relating to communism. Though they were explicitly aware of the anti-US sentiment, it was far more convenient to approach it through the bipolar paradigm rather than examine the central criticisms of liberation theologians relating to economic and political oppression.

The end of the Cold War, or the civil wars in Central America, eventually alleviated the political and overt use of violence throughout the region, but liberation theologians were concerned that the less visible "structural violence" imposed as they saw it, through the international economy would not end. Indeed, much of the structural violence would intensify with the triumph of western ideology and the increasing integration of the global economy. The International Commission on Central America concluded that "a decade of civil conflict and economic decline has devastated Central America. More than 160,000 people have died in wars or unrest. By 1990, ten million people—40% of the population—will be living in extreme poverty. The problems have deep roots in the endemic poverty and injustices that have long plagued the region."[52] Indeed, neoliberal economic orders would enhance the economic integration of the region after the low intensity conflicts.

The decade ended with the murder, by the US-backed Salvadoran armed forces, of six Jesuits, their housekeeper, and her daughter in the Central American University. The subsequent US congressional task force contended that the "murders of the Jesuits reflect problems within the Salvadoran armed forces that go far beyond the actions of a particular unit on a particular night." Similarly, Jon Sobrino, normally resident at the university could have been amongst those killed on that night of 16 November 1989, but happened to be in Thailand, later concluded that it was not so much a question of who actually did the killings as much as what he referred to as the "whole world of sin which has once more inflicted death on innocent people, people who worked for the poor." In this sense, according to Archbishop Rivera, the killers were those who had killed Romero. More broadly, at the funeral of the Jesuits, Fr. José María Tojeira explained that the murdered priests "sought the truth about the world and about the situation of this small part of it called El Salvador. They tried to move this situation forward toward justice, fellowship, dialogue, to create a space in which the poor could have their say and maintain their dignity." For Sobrino it was their work on conscientization and their words about structural injustice that explained their deaths.[53]

The Jesuits and the Futility of Violence

During the 1980s many liberation theologians realized that they could not advance the "option for the poor" through violent resistance and that they needed to develop a more sophisticated, peaceful approach while still maintaining their principles. Ellacuría was active in the intellectual development of liberation theology and also acted as a go-between for Archbishop Rivera to the FMLN. He was regarded as one of the most outspoken theologians since the death of Archbishop Romero. Despite his public and constant criticism of the regime, he had disagreed with the FMLN offensive of November 1989. In the late 1970s he had argued that violence was a justified response to the prevailing conditions, but by the early 1980s, he considered that a negotiated solution was a possibility.[54]

Nevertheless, his preference for a "third way" had no place in Salvadoran society. His colleague Ignacio Martín-Baró's work on the social polarization that results from living in conditions of perpetual violence suggests that, in such circumstances, it is common for people to undergo cognitive and behavioral changes that bring about a certain dehumanization. A part of that process is a tendency to think in terms of absolutes, ideals, and ideological rigidity. The middle ground is often displaced with "opposite extremes, with a resultant rigidification of their respective ideological positions and pressure exerted upon everyone to align himself or herself with 'us' or 'them.'"[55] Under such circumstances, it is not surprising that anti-Americanism became acute. Washington was clearly a part of the problem. It had financed the Salvadoran government, provided it with arms, munitions, and diplomatic and political legitimacy despite the fraudulent elections of the 1980s. Moreover, the colossus of the north was also perceived as central to the economic system and the poverty it generated in the south. With these perspectives and the cognitive impact of extreme repression, the brutality of the Salvadoran forces also contributed to anti-American feelings.

Ellacuría sought a different path. His preference was for a significantly modified version of socialism that would serve the poor more effectively. The moderate reforms in capitalism had not brought significant development to the peoples of the Third World or ended the repressive regimes under which they lived. A better international order was a fundamental prerequisite for the improvement in the lives of the poor. Ellacuría firmly criticized the form of development that was centered on economic issues at the expense of humanity. The United States was implicitly at the center of the system he criticized, as the economic engine and as backers of the praetorian guards that maintained the system. Ellacuría's writings frequently criticized Americanization. Shortly before he was executed in 1989 he wrote that

> truth demonstrates the impossibility of reproducing and, especially, of enlarging the present historical order significantly. It demonstrates, even more radically, its undesirability, since this present order cannot be universalized. It brings with it the perpetuation of an unjust and predatory distribution of the world's resources, and even of each nation's resources, for the benefit of a few nations. The result is that prophetic and utopian Latin America does not seek to imitate those who today are in the forefront and position themselves on top. Rather, it seeks a different order in the objective and in the subjective, an order that will allow a humane life not only for a few but for the greater part of humanity. The developed world is not at all the desired utopia, even as a way to overcome poverty, much less to overcome injustice. Instead, it is a sign of what should not be.[56]

It is somewhat ironic that such an argument should be produced at roughly the same time as Francis Fukuyama, of the State Department's Policy Planning Staff, argued in his article, "The End of History," that "the triumph of the west, of the Western *idea,* is evident first of all in the total exhaustion of viable systematic alternatives to Western liberalism."[57] Such triumphalism masked the horrendous daily realities that informed the liberation theologians' critique.

There was another irony in the timing of the Jesuits' execution. The Berlin Wall was coming down in Europe and soon the peoples and states that existed under Soviet domination pursued their paths to a certain type of freedom. There was a triumphal sense that the transitions toward democracy that had already begun in Latin America were simultaneously occurring in the Eastern Europe. Martín-Baró was skeptical about such triumphalism. He believed that one of the most difficult problems facing Latin American states was the "sequelae of the political repression carried out by earlier governments of 'national security.'" When such transitions were not mediated by a war that brought democratic forces to victory, the states found tremendous difficulties dealing with issues of justice and with the past. Martín-Baró argued that a thorough investigation needed to take place into the costs of the counterinsurgency program, and only then "can we appreciate the deception involved in wanting to wipe out history and start over." His analysis suggested that the past could not be swept under the carpet in the celebrations of the transition to democracy. A full inventory had to be taken. Implicit in this criticism of the ameliorative atmosphere was that the "truth and reconciliation" process would focus more on local agents and issues rather than on the US contribution to the systematic oppression and structural violence of the international economy. Under such conditions, anti-Americanization would similarly be forgotten. Yet the "emptiness" left by the absence of the thousands murdered or "disappeared" would still sadden and oppress countless families, and "all this damage is of such magnitude that it becomes almost ingenious or cynical to act as if it can be forgotten overnight, because fundamentally the problem is not one of isolated individuals. . . . The damage that has been produced is not simply in the destruction of personal lives. Harm has been done to the social structures themselves—to the norms that order the common life, to the institutions that govern the life of citizens, to the values and principles by which people are educated and through which the repression has tried to justify itself."[58]

Martín-Baró considered that the two common solutions to dealing with the past were inadequate. The first was the practice of limiting culpability through "owned obedience" to a few high ranking officers, who are suddenly treated as individuals rather than as part of the institutions that perpetuated the violence on a regular basis. It was not enough to merely focus on resolution of the high-profile murders that garnered the most attention in the United States. While US-trained and US-financed forces were behind the murders of the archbishop, the churchwomen, and the Jesuits, they were also the forces that perpetuated the daily atrocities. For Sobrino, it was not only important to solve the "notorious murders but more important to clear up the mass murder of peasants who die anonymously."[59] The second major response to overcoming such violence and division was to promote the idea of moving beyond the period toward forgiveness and reconciliation. The Truth Commission on El Salvador adopted this strategy, though of course the structural violence and international systemic dimensions were not formally a part of the proceedings.[60]

As mentioned previously, Martín-Baró's work examined the psychological impact of long-term and structural violence on a society in the Third World, with particular attention to the case of El Salvador. He argued that a high level of violent coercion was necessary to maintain the structural injustice that characterized the situation in Central America. The United Nations' Truth Commission on El Salvador indeed found that Salvadoran government forces were responsible for some 75 percent of the atrocities and extra-judicial killing during the 1980s.[61] According to Martí-Baró, this violence rested on more than the circumstantial image of a particular enemy. It needed a much broader justification to explain why violence was a norm for the society in question. His work advanced that of the earlier liberation theologians by arguing that the ideology of national security that had provided thin legitimacy in the 1970s had given way to a strategy and ideological assumptions centered on low intensity conflict during the 1980s. Both doctrines viewed the structural conflict in terms of a perpetual and constant state of war. The key difference was that the latter added a psychological element that aimed to "win people's 'hearts and minds' so that they accept the requirements of the dominant order and, consequently, accept as good and even 'natural' whatever violence may be necessary to maintain it."[62] However, the psychological elements of low-intensity conflict failed in these objectives. Instead, given the violence, the polarization of the decade, and the US support for the armed forces, the psychological impact of war produced a Manichaean outlook that closely identified Washington as a central element of the problem. It is therefore not surprising under these conditions that anti-Americanism and anti-Americanization were rife.

Liberation theology thus provided a basic critique of the causes of poverty and the political repression necessary to maintain that situation. In doing so its message was not directly anti-American, so much as opposed to the process of Americanization. The "solutions" of the 1990s and the treaties signed in 1992 in El Salvador, the electoral defeat of the Sandinistas in Nicaragua in 1990, and the end of the global Cold War removed, for the time being, the repressive characteristics of the 1980s. The original and central concern regarding the structural violence that created the poverty of the region, however, did not disappear. One of the central reasons for the recent growth in the evangelical churches throughout the region has been precisely because of their apolitical stance compared to that of the liberation theologians, for whom a pastoral role necessitated addressing the causes of such poverty and violence.

Though the contexts and histories are very different, a few observations from the experience in Central America can be drawn to further understand anti-Americanism in the Middle East. The deeper the United States becomes integrated in a given region, the more vociferous anti-Americanism becomes. It is particularly acute at times of polarization and US intervention. Thus, the polarization produced by the Palestinian situation and US support for Israel echoes the themes developed above. Perhaps for that reason, Martín-Baró's work has been applied to some children's clinics in Palestine. The cognitive and behavioral impact that he identified in El Salvador under conditions of war contributed to the Manichaean outlook, and "America" will often be regarded in the same framework as Israel. His work suggests that, as children grow during violent periods in their country's history, their outlook tends to grow increasingly polarized; the children therefore end up holding a more stark view of their perceived opponents. Hence, the tendency of violence was to exacerbate further anti-Americanism. Furthermore, when the nationalist opposition to the US presence in the Middle East became a spent force, anti-Americanism expressed itself through the radical theological arguments of Ayatollah Khomeini and others.[63] Finally, much of the debate about anti-Americanism's relation to the "failed states" of the Middle East needs to be situated in a broader context and to examine the international dimensions of why these particular states are not performing in certain regards.

Notes

1. The term is from Timothy Garton Ash and denotes a combination of reform from above and revolution from below. See Garton Ash's *We The People: The Revolution of '89 Witnessed in Warsaw, Budapest, Berlin and Prague* (London, 1990).
2. G. Gutierrez, *The Poor and the Church in Latin America* (London, 1984), 9.
3. D. Ryan, *US-Sandinista Diplomatic Relations: Voice of Intolerance* (London, 1995).
4. J. Dunkerley, *The Pacification of Central America: Political Change in the Isthmus, 1987–1993* (London, 1994), 3, 12–14.
5. I. Clark, *The Post-Cold War Order: The Spoils of Peace* (Oxford, 2001), 187.
6. J. Haynes, *Religion in Third World Politics* (Buckingham, 1993), 95.
7. H. Cox, *The Silencing of Leonardo Boff: The Vatican and the Future of World Christianity* (London, 1988).
8. C. Cruise O'Brien, "God and Man in Nicaragua," in *Church and Politics in Latin America,* ed. D. Keogh (London, 1990), 149; R.N. Ostling, "Berating Marxism's 'False Hopes,'" *Time,* 10 September 1984, 48.
9. J. Haynes, *Religion in Third World Politics* (Buckingham, 1993), 95–96.
10. D. Dorr, *Option for the Poor: A Hundred Years of Vatican Social Teaching* (Dublin, 1983).
11. Haynes, *Religion,* 96.
12. José Martí cited by L. Johnston, "The Road to Our America: The United States in Latin America and the Caribbean," in *The United States and Decolonization: Power and Freedom,* ed. D. Ryan and V. Pungong (London, 2000), 41.
13. NSC 144/1, "United States Objectives and Courses of Action with respect to Latin America," 18 March 1953, *FRUS* 1952–1954, IV: 6–7; D. Ryan, "US Foreign Policy and the Guatemalan Revolution in World History," Washington, D.C.: US Department of State, forthcoming.
14. J. W. Park, *Latin American Underdevelopment: A History of Perspectives in the United States, 1870–1965* (Baton Rouge, 1995), 231, 237.
15. Park, *Latin American Underdevelopment,* 230; N. Cullather, "Development? It's History," *Diplomatic History* 24 (fall 2000): 641–53. See for instance, A. G. Frank,

Capitalism and Underdevelopment in Latin America (Harmondsworth, 1969), 309–46.

16. V. Bulmer-Thomas, *The Economic History of Latin America since Independence* (Cambridge, 1994), 246; D. Ryan "US 'Colonialism' in Post-War Latin America," *The International History Review* 21 (June 1999): 285–96.

17. I. Roxborough, *Theories of Underdevelopment* (London, 1979); P. F. Klarén and T. J. Bossert, eds., *Promise of Development: Theories of Change in Latin America* (Boulder, 1986); G. Kolko, *Confronting the Third World: United States Foreign Policy 1945–1980* (New York, 1988).

18. D. H. Levine, ed., *Churches and Politics in Latin America* (Beverly Hills, 1980), 21–23.

19. Pope Paul VI, *Populorum Progressio* (London, 1967), 10, 15.

20. Paul VI, *Populorum Progressio,* 29.

21. J. Sobrino, *Companions of Jesus: The Murder and Martyrdom of the Salvadorean Jesuits* (London, 1990), 22.

22. An elaborate study is provided in P. E. Sigmund, *Liberation Theology at the Crossroads: Democracy or Revolution?* (New York, 1990), 28–78.

23. Sigmund, *Liberation Theology,* 29.

24. R. Poblette, "From Medellín to Puebla," in *Churches and Politics,* Levine, 45.

25. D. H. Levine, "Religion and Politics, Politics and Religion," in *Churches and Politics,* 29.

26. Latin American Bishops, "Peace," Medellín, Colombia, 6 September 1968. Available at http://www.shc.edu/theolibrary/resources/medpeace.htm.

27. Ibid.

28. Guitierrez cited in Sigmund, *Liberation Theology,* 36.

29. Latin American Bishops, "Peace."

30. See for instance R. H. Holden, "The Real Diplomacy of Violence: United States Military Power in Central America, 1950–1990," *The International History Review* 15 (May 1993): 283; Democratic Policy Committee, Foreign Aid to Central America, FY 1981–1987, special report, Washington, D.C.: US Congress, 12 February 1987.

31. P. Lernoux, "The Long Path to Puebla," in *Puebla and Beyond: Documentation and Commentary,* ed. J. Eagleson and P. Scharper (Maryknoll, N.Y., 1980), 12.

32. I. Martín-Baró, "Oscar Romero: Voice of the Downtrodden," in *Voice of the Voiceless: The Four Pastoral Letters and Other Statements* (Maryknoll, N.Y., 1985), 6.

33. P. Lernoux, *Cry of the People: The Struggle for Human Rights in Latin America— The Catholic Church in Conflict with US Policy* (Harmondsworth, 1980), 74–75.

34. Dorr, *Option for the Poor,* 208–9.

35. Final Document of the Third General Conference of the Latin American Episcopate, "Evangelization in Latin America's Present and Future," 27 January to 13 February 1979, Puebla, Mexico in Eagleson and Scharper, *Puebla and Beyond,* 263–67.

36. P. Berryman, "What Happened at Puebla," in *Churches and Politics,* ed. Levine, 55; Lernoux, *Cry of the People,* 444–46.

37. NSC, US Policy toward El Salvador, 12 October 1979, partially declassified, RG 273, miscellaneous documents on El Salvador, NA.

38. Martín-Baró, "Oscar Romero," in *Voice of the Voiceless,* Romero, 1–21.

39. R. Calvo, "The Church and the Doctrine of National Security," in *Churches and Politics,* Levine, 135.

40. O. Romero, Fourth Pastoral Letter, 6 August 1979, in *Voice of the Voiceless,* Romero, 119.

41. Ibid., 144; Archbishop Oscar Romero, address on the occasion of the conferral of a doctorate, Louvain, Belgium, 2 February 1980, cited in Romero, *Voice of the Voiceless,* 177–87.

42. Sigmund, *Liberation Theology*, 111.
43. Archbishop Romero letter to President Carter, 17 February 1980, cited in *Voice of the Voiceless*, Romero, 189.
44. Zbigniew Brzezinski, draft letter to the Pope, attached to Peter Tarnoff, Memorandum to Brzezinski, 31 January 1980, RG 273, miscellaneous documents on El Salvador, NA.
45. NSC, "Status report on the State Department's efforts to encourage Vatican officials to try to influence Salvador's Archbishop Romero to support moderate change through the new Junta," undated [circa 15 February 1980], partially declassified, RG 273, miscellaneous documents on El Salvador, NA.
46. Robert Pastor, memorandum for Zbigniew Brzezinski, David Aaron, and Henry Owen, SCC Meeting on El Salvador, 14 February 1980, RG 273, miscellaneous documents on El Salvador, NA.
47. Report, Mini-Special Co-ordination Committee Meeting, Bushnell, Carlucci, Aaron, Pastor, 26 March 1980, RG 273, miscellaneous documents on El Salvador, NA.
48. D. Keogh, *Romero: El Salvador's Martyr* (Dublin, 1981), 99–122.
49. Author unknown, El Salvador, Intelligence Information Cable, 20 December 1980, National Security Archives, Washington, D.C.; Peter Tarnoff, memorandum to Zbigniew Brzezinski transmitting the Report to the President of his Special Mission to El Salvador, 13 December 1980, National Security Archives, Washington, D.C.
50. H. R. Tyler, "The Churchwomen Murders: A Report to the Secretary of State," 2 December 1983, National Security Archives, Washington, D.C., 55.
51. The Committee of Santa Fe, *A New Inter-American Policy for the Eighties* (Washington, D.C., 1980).
52. International Commission for Central America Recovery and Development, *Poverty, Conflict and Hope: A Turning Point in Central America,* a report for the Committee on Foreign Relations, United States Senate, 101st Cong., 1st sess., March 1989, xix.
53. J. J. Moakley, Interim Report of the Speaker's Task Force on El Salvador, United States Congress, 30 April 1990, 6; Sobrino, *Companions of Jesus,* 26, 29–30; homily by Fr. José María Tojeira, Provincial of the Society of Jesus in Central America, 19 November 1989, in *Martyrdom in El Salvador, Church in the World* (27) (London, 1990).
54. J. Sobrino, et al. *In Memoriam: the Jesuit Martyrs of El Salvador* (London, 1990), xiv, 5, 62.
55. I. Martí-Baró, "Political Violence and War as Causes of Psychological Trauma in El Salvador," *International Journal of Mental Health* 18 (1988), reprinted in *In Memoriam,* ed. Sobrino et al., 84, 91.
56. I. Ellacuría, "Utopia and Prophecy in Latin America," in *Towards a Society that Serves its People,* ed. Hassett and Lacey, 51.
57. F. Fukuyama, "The End of History," *The National Interest* 16 (summer 1989): 3–18.
58. I. Martín-Baró, "Reparations and Democracy," in *Towards a Society,* Hassett and Lacey, 138–39.
59. Sobrino, *Companions of Jesus,* 36.
60. Report of the Commission on the Truth for El Salvador, "From Madness to Hope: The 12-year war in El Salvador," Belisario Betancur, chairman, 15 March 1993. Available at http://www.usip.org/library/tc/doc/reports/el_salvador/tc_es_03151993_toc.html.
61. M. Reid, "Truth Commission Points Finger at Salvadoran Military," *Guardian* (London), 16 March 1993.

62. I. Martín-Baró, "Violence in Central America: A Social Psychological Perspective," in *Towards a Society,* Hassett and Lacey, 341.

63. U. Makdisi, "'Anti-Americanism' in the Arab World," in *History and September 11ᵗʰ,* ed. Joanne Meyerowitz (Philadelphia, 2003), 146.

Part III

EXPLAINING THE ABSENCE OF ANTI-AMERICANISM

Chapter 9

THE UNITED STATES, COLOMBIA, AND DRUG POLICY, 1984–2004

A Study of Quiet Anti-Americanism

William O. Walker III

This chapter asks why anti-Americanism did not emerge in Colombia beginning in the mid-1980s as violence engulfed that country. The United States was all but insisting that Colombia serve as a tripwire in the growing war on drugs in the Americas. Authorities in Bogotá managed for some time to fend off demands that they treat drugs as a security issue of the first order, choosing instead to try to keep the internal conflict from completely tearing their country apart. By the time of the 2002 presidential election in Colombia, Washington had apparently gotten its way. The war on drugs and the quest for state stability had coalesced into a broad campaign against terror, in which a growing cadre of military and civilian advisers, along with US funds flowed into Colombia. To the extent that anti-American sentiments existed then, they are best characterized as a quiet, perhaps latent anti-Americanism.*

Colombia was arguably less sovereign by late 2004 than it had been two decades earlier, and its governability depended partly upon the largesse of the United States. That such a situation did not provoke displays of vocal anti-Americanism illustrates the convergence of security interests between Washington and Bogotá and the development of a common political culture. Conversely, it also reflects an exclusionary characteristic prevalent in Colombian politics and society. That is, other than among the political class and its business friends, too many Colombians appeared not to have a personal stake in the future of their country. In such a climate, it is hard to imagine anything other than a muted form of anti-Americanism taking hold. Colombia's most serious problems were fundamentally domestic in origin; the US contribution to them, however intrusive, was and remains one of secondary importance. Anti-Americanism therefore never had the capacity to be a unifying force for the nation.

Overview

Pablo Escobar confined himself to a sumptuous jail in June 1991. As was his custom, Don Pablo, Colombia's most notorious criminal, greeted visitors with no interference from authorities. Like many *colombianos* Escobar loved *fútbol;* unlike others who also found great joy in soccer, Escobar had inexhaustible resources for funding the development of national talent. Among the grateful was star goalkeeper René Higuita of Medellín, whose visits presumably brought comfort to Escobar in his cell.[1]

Drug czar Bob Martinez, director of the Office of National Drug Control Policy and former governor of Florida, threw down the verbal gauntlet in the month of Escobar's arrest by declaring, "Colombia will be on trial with Pablo Escobar." The strident Martinez was neither the first nor the last US official to berate Colombia for its presumed lack of rigor in antinarcotics activity.[2] Commencing in the late 1970s, and continuing into the presidency of Belisario Betancourt Cuartas in the mid-1980s, the United States sought to compel Colombian officials to combat drugs with measures that were demonstrably tougher than those used by the US government itself.

These efforts succeeded to a degree unanticipated in Washington. By the time Álvaro Uribe Vélez, the former governor of the department of Antioquia who was educated at Oxford and Harvard, took office as president in August 2002, Colombia was waging a multifront war on drugs: coca plantings were the object of a sustained aerial defoliation campaign; extradition of drug traffickers to the United States was a distinct possibility within the bounds of the nation's legal processes; and Colombia's security activities increasingly linked drug control and the terror brought on by the nation's civil strife.[3] These very successes, applauded by the administration of President George W. Bush, had the potential to make effective governance in Colombia more difficult.

Illicit drugs were not, of course, the primary reason for the weakness of the Colombian state, a weakness that largely explains the relatively mild nature of anti-Americanism in Colombia. For at least forty years a domestic insurgency, which in the 1980s became a bloody civil war, had plagued Colombia. The major participants in the conflict were (and still are) several: leftist rebels, principally belonging since about 1990 to the powerful Revolutionary Armed Forces of Colombia (FARC) and the Army of National Liberation (ELN); the armed forces, including the Colombian National Police; right-wing paramilitaries personified by the United Self-Defense Forces of Colombia (AUC), following its formation in 1997; and the state itself. In this mix must be included not only the thousands of wealthy, educated expatriates who fled their country but also the nearly two million internal displaced who abandoned their homes for a combination of political and economic reasons. As late as 2003, at least ten Colombians per day were dying in the conflict.

In this context, the differences between Bogotá and Washington over drug policy might have given rise to a robust form of anti-Americanism. That did not happen. Criticism of the United States was typically veiled, as in the words of Rafael Pardo Rueda, who was in charge of talks with rebel groups during the presidency of Virgilio Barco Vargas and who served as minister of defense in the early 1990s under Barco's successor, César Gaviria Trujillo: "President [George H. W.] Bush . . . established the theme of a struggle against drugs with the rhetoric of a war, in which the front line was our country."[4] Even ex-President Ernesto Samper Pizano, controversial at home and reviled abroad, carefully chose his words of criticism: "If the demand for drugs did not exist in the United States and Europe, Colombia would neither have to confront the problems nor pay the human and economic costs that it is still paying."[5]

The lack of intense anti-Americanism stems from several factors. Significantly, Colombia and the United States have not had historically contentious relations, despite strong differences over the fate of the department of Panama around 1900. US officials, first in the 1920s, as they sought to build a hemispheric relationship apart from the economic and political uncertainties of postwar Europe, and again with the Alliance for Progress in the 1960s, looked to Colombia with its relatively healthy economy as one model for growth and development in the Americas. US leaders long assumed an affinity with the Colombian populace. In that sense, Colombia's urbane, educated middle class acted as a reference point for authorities in Washington when they imagined how modernization might proceed throughout the hemisphere.[6]

Second, this image of well-being and the ties that resulted from it, while not without foundation, did not accurately reflect Colombian reality—particularly since the establishment of the National Front in

1958. The National Front amounted to a power-sharing arrangement by Liberals and Conservatives who sought to end the decade-long chaos known as *La Violencia.* In this uneasy peace, rapid urbanization, increased literacy, and a rise in longevity did not cure but rather may have exacerbated historic economic and social inequities.[7] Political elites regularly promised to implement sweeping reforms but rarely delivered on their lofty promises. The role of the state, writes Jenny Pearce of the London-based Latin America Bureau (an organization promoting social justice), "has been primarily to provide the conditions for private sector-led growth. The relationship of the state to the people is therefore one of neglect and, in many areas, abandonment."[8] This illiberal state of affairs could hardly be blamed on the United States and the diplomacy of modernization. It did, however, limit the bases for anti-Americanism while helping to create conditions in which a drug-dependent economy would flourish.

Third, those who took advantage of the state's inattention to the commonweal were a new class of entrepreneurs, latter-day oligarchs based in the environs of Medellín and Cali. They lived by their own rules, employed private security forces to safeguard their interests, and determined to coexist with the state on their own terms. If this claim to quasi-autonomy was not new, its form surely was. The incredible power of the new class derived from its willingness to intimidate or employ violence against its opponents and from its capacity to satisfy the appetites of cocaine consumers, principally in the United States. The foes of these *narcotraficantes,* as they were called, were not only state authorities—except for corrupt elements within the judiciary, armed forces, and national police—but also the left-wing groups who had been in revolt against the state since the mid-1960s.

In the years under consideration here, from 1984 through 2004, US-Colombian diplomacy operated in an environment in which strident anti-Americanism might well have emerged. As the United States failed to control drugs at home, the burden on Colombia to act forcefully weakened that nation's security. Bogotá's drug war prolonged the civil conflict in two ways. It emboldened fierce paramilitary forces to view themselves as autonomous regional actors even as their benefactors, the two major drug cartels, were broken up in the early 1990s. Also, the amorphous boundaries of the drug war arguably played a contributory role in turning the FARC and the ELN toward drugs as a source of revenue. The grisly violence of the electoral campaign of 1990, in which numerous candidates of the leftist Patriotic Union (UP) were slaughtered by right-wing forces, suggested that the government was incapable of ensuring a safe political environment even if it wanted to—something that rebel leaders had reason to doubt.[9]

Anti-Americanism, had it materialized, would have resulted from the debate in Colombia over how best to fight Washington's war. For present purposes that debate occurred in four stages: (1) from 1984 through 1990, a time of watchful waiting by the United States and of concern about Colombia's antidrug efforts; (2) from 1990 through 1994, during which time US concerns triggered disagreement over the direction of drug control; (3) from 1994 through 2000, a period marked at first by US frustration with Colombia's drug policy and palpable animosity toward President Samper and later by an increase of US influence in Bogotá; and (4) from 2000 through 2004, when convergence on security policy in the two capitols took shape and gave rise to high expectations about future success in the matter of drug control.

Colombia's Wars in the 1980s

During the 1980s, Colombian leaders underestimated Washington's determination to define bilateral relations in terms of drug control. Presidents Belisario Betancourt and Virgilio Barco, committed to reversing the near unraveling of their nation even as they guided it toward a more prominent role in regional and global affairs, downplayed signals from Washington about the primacy of drug control.[10] It is noteworthy that Barco, a former ambassador to the United States, seemed not fully to realize US priorities. He did, however, insist upon a relationship of equality with Washington, a position that limited anti-Americanism during his presidency. How? His government's discontent with North American pressure on drug policy did not spill over to the public at large. Such was one of the odd benefits of Colombia's exclusionary politics.

Coca, the natural source of cocaine, played a crucial economic role in parts of Colombia in the years following World War II.[11] US officials took greater notice in the mid-1970s when domestic consumption of cocaine surged. A House of Representatives report declared, "Colombia is a major concern to the US narcotic enforcement effort."[12] The Carter administration pressed Colombia to reduce drug production and trafficking, persuading the Liberal government of Julio César Turbay Ayala to adopt extradition as a policy priority.[13] Betancourt, Turbay's Conservative successor, initially ignored pressure from Washington to follow Turbay's lead, but by March 1984 he had adopted a more forceful stance.[14] The successful raid on the "Tranquilandia" cocaine processing complex was the first public indication of this change. On 30 April 1984, the Medellín cartel had

Justice Minister Rodrigo Lara Bonilla assassinated, unleashing an orgy of violence not experienced since *La Violencia*. Colombia, notes Pearce, "fell headlong into undeclared war."[15]

Washington's focus on Colombia's role in drug trafficking from South America to the United States helped to obscure the extent of state weakness.[16] To be sure, Betancourt did face an array of drug-related problems that threatened his ability to govern. These included the accumulation of private fortunes that altered the structure of political and economic power in parts of the country, increases in drug smuggling, and a rise in political corruption, to name only three problems.[17] More importantly, he had to contend with a growing guerrilla presence and the accusation that Colombia's democracy was largely "a sham concealing an authoritarian regime," as one observer recounted.[18] Horrific evidence of Betancourt's troubles came in November 1985 with the assault on the Palace of Justice by the urban-based leftist group, M-19—an attack that left eleven Supreme Court judges dead. Compounding these difficulties, wrote Rafael Pardo, was the "progressive deterioration of relations between the Executive and the Armed Forces."[19]

Virgilio Barco viewed US drug policy as a challenge to his nation's sovereignty, as evidenced by his strong reaction to efforts in January 1988 to punish Colombia with sanctions after a judge released Medellín *narco* Jorge Luis Ochoa from jail, an action that Barco quickly denounced.[20] Barco, who prevented the January crisis from becoming an excuse for a show of anti-Americanism,[21] used the violence of the Medellín and Cali drug cartels to counter US pressure to place greater emphasis on antidrug activity. Some thirty thousand Colombians died in violence related to drugs and the national crisis between 1984 and 1989, a fact that led Barco to demand a more equal role in relations with Washington. Indeed, Barco was not reluctant to combat drugs as part of his overall efforts to restore and protect state legitimacy. Colombia was then providing 80 percent of the cocaine and 25 percent of the marijuana consumed in the United States.[22] With limited, carefully calibrated actions—to the apparent dismay of US officials, who wanted a more comprehensive effort—Barco employed limited aerial fumigation and manual eradication to reduce the cultivation of coca and marijuana, and used the armed forces as a weapon against guerrillas and the drug trade. This latter tactic raised the dual specter of corruption and human rights abuses.[23]

Barco's primary goal was to put an end to Colombia's internal strife, especially following the murder of his likely successor, Luis Carlos Galán, by the Medellín cartel in August 1989. Galán had fought the *narcos* since 1981 when Pablo Escobar became an alternate member of Congress from Antioquia.[24] Barco declared war on the cartel, a courageous act that pleased officials in Washington. Taking on the *narcos* was merely a means to an end. In Barco's view, Colombia's problems were political and social in nature. Rafael Pardo has commented that the drug trade became pervasive "because of the indifference of many and the complacency of others," a statement doubtless directed at the arrogance of the political class. Narcoterrorism, thus, "was the violent expression of the determination of a new social class to be recognized and to find a place within Colombian society." Fear of extradition to the United States united the *narcos*, or "extraditables" as they termed themselves, making the success of Barco's efforts to achieve national reconciliation even more problematic.[25] Ironically, Barco and a segment of the public supported the controversial practice of extradition, which was then prohibited under Colombian law.[26]

US perceptions of the situation differed from those held in Bogotá. In its annual narcotics report in 1989, the Department of State flatly asserted: "Cocaine traffickers are *the* major threat to democracy in Colombia." In other words, the *narcos* were the cause, not a symptom, of the decline of state authority.[27] This conclusion set the tone for US-Colombian relations over the ensuing decade. In its simplest formulation, US policy was the creation of domestic political battles among congressional committees, government agencies involved in drug control, and the White House.[28] Moreover, drug policy reflected the multifaceted efforts to reestablish US international hegemony throughout the 1980s and into the 1990s. In that sense, there could be a Colombian road to drug control so long as that path hewed to US priorities. When it did not, a diplomatic clash was certain to ensue.[29] That the Department of State's challenge—in a published report—to Barco's priorities did not lead to an outbreak of anti-Americanism reflects Barco's skill at damage control as well as the limited importance of public opinion in Colombian politics.

Barco saw himself as defending state sovereignty on many fronts. In the months before Galán's assassination, the Department of State had endeavored, through a mix of diplomacy, intelligence sharing, and economic and military assistance, to "make the sovereignty of other nations, threatened by rampant drug trafficking, . . . our ally in mobilizing action and cooperation."[30] For its part, Congress, "increasingly frustrated with the inability to see any progress in the fight against narcotics," was putting pressure on the administration of George H. W. Bush to militarize the drug war—contrary to the traditional position of the Department of Defense.[31] Galán's murder moved the United States to consider sending one hundred advisers to train Colombian forces for counterdrug activities.[32] Thus it was that the $2.2 billion Andean Strategy, which was then in the planning stages in the White House, contained a strong military component and brought into question Washington's respect for the sovereignty of Bolivia, Colombia, and Peru when their policies did not serve US interests.[33]

Importantly, a new reality briefly set in, one that ultimately showed how difficult it would be either to alter the historic basis of US policy, namely, control at the source, or to challenge Washington's hegemonic intentions. In February 1990, at a meeting with Barco and other Andean leaders in Cartagena, Colombia, President George H. W. Bush and Secretary of State James W. Baker III suggested that a rethinking of US policy was in order. They acknowledged that consumption was as serious a problem as production and trafficking. Followed to its logical conclusion, this admission might have opened the door to a multilateral approach to drug control and greater control by Colombia over its own drug policy. Those possibilities proved illusory, though, because of domestic political considerations, bureaucratic differences, and the drug control-security nexus in Washington.[34] Accordingly, the Barco presidency ended in August 1990 amid growing disquiet in Washington over Bogotá's loyalty to US priorities in the drug war.

"A War That Is Not Ours"

In the second period of this study, 1990–1994, Barco's successor, César Gaviria Trujillo, similarly faced US insistence that he take on the cartels. US officials did not know Gaviria well, and from the outset of his presidency they doubted his commitment to strict drug control. The jailing of the Medellín cartel's Ochoa brothers, Fabio and Jorge Luis, in December 1990 and January 1991, moved Drug Enforcement Administration (DEA) Chief Robert Bonner to comment, "We will watch closely [their] prosecution by Colombian authorities."[35] The surrender on 19 June 1991 of Pablo Escobar did not alter scepticism about Colombia's antidrug commitment. Escobar was housed in the ostentatious Envigado prison, dubbed *La Catedral* (the cathedral), from which he seemed to conduct business as usual.[36]

Gaviria had assumed office in August 1990 determined to gain respect for Colombia as a combatant in the war against drugs. His primary objective, however, was to accelerate the process of democratization and national reconciliation initiated by his predecessors. To do so he agreed to rewrite the constitution to reflect a partial transfer of power from the capital to the rest of the country. He also sought to expand foreign trade on a regional and hemispheric basis.

In fact, as president-elect, he told President Bush that economic aid would be more welcome than antinarcotics assistance. With these measures Gaviria and his top advisers, including Minister of Defense Rafael Pardo, reasoned that traditional clientalism might lose its tight grip on national politics, local government would improve, and social reform could become a reality—thereby undercutting the program of the FARC and other rebels.[37]

Pardo has written, "The political system was in imminent danger of collapse." In early 1991 as elections for a new Constitutional Assembly were occurring, the FARC and other members of the guerrilla alliance, the Simón Bolívar Guerrilla Coordinating Group (CGSB), increased their attacks against the Colombian state.[38] The army responded in kind, thereby raising the price of failure for the government.[39] Gaviria also entered into an extended series of negotiations with the CGSB, but early results were disappointing—a result of the lack of trust on each side.[40] The persistence of violence and the frequent disruption of essential services like electricity cost him dearly at home. By 1992, which Gaviria pointedly termed "a very difficult year for the nation and my government," the president's once elevated public approval rating had dipped to well below 50 percent.[41]

Gaviria's policies invited controversy at home and abroad, as happened when he refused to turn over to the United States those extraditables who had agreed to submit to Colombian justice.[42] Distinguishing between drug trafficking and narcoterrorism, which Gaviria deemed an internal matter to be addressed in the process of state reconstruction, elicited Washington's wrath.[43] Some senior US officials seemed unable to comprehend the delicacy of the situation. Melvyn Levitsky, head of the Bureau of International Narcotics Matters in the Department of State, minimized the harm that the drug war could do to democracy in the Andes. He termed US-sponsored militarization there "a sign of greater overall national commitment in dealing with the [drug] problem."[44]

Gaviria thought that fighting drugs on Washington's terms compromised Colombian sovereignty. US Ambassador Thomas E. McNamara declared, and—in a break with the government—the crusading liberal newspaper *El Espectador* agreed, that it was "an error to prohibit extradition,"[45] a step that the Constitutional Assembly took on the day that Escobar surrendered, 19 June. Two weeks later the extraditables announced their determination to demobilize.[46] In opposing the emotional practice of extradition, Gaviria—who like Pardo believed that Colombia was the real victim of the traffic in cocaine and heroin—hoped to curb the violence of the Medellín and Cali cartels even as he pursued them by using Colombia's own judicial processes.[47] Unlike Barco, Gaviria was willing to call upon nationalist sentiments to boost support for his policies. In the short term, the doubts of *El Espectador* notwithstanding, rejecting extradition was a popular political move.[48] Through appeals to Colombian nationalism, with its implicit defense of state sovereignty, Gaviria was engaging in and encouraging a kind of quiet anti-Americanism. He would soon learn, however, that anger against the state ran deeper among Colombians than did antipathy toward the United States.

Ultimately, Gaviria lost the battle of public opinion.[49] Escobar's dramatic escape from Envigado in July 1992 led critics to conclude that Gaviria's road to drug control had been a dead-end street. Escobar's violent death in December 1993 at the hands of security forces with the help of US intelligence and the DEA did not silence growing criticism.[50] Many Colombians, who expressed considerable pessimism about their country,[51] worried that leniency toward Escobar and other extraditables would undermine the fragile process of democratization. Deals with the cartel leaders might result in human rights abuses from both the right and left, give indirect support to the growth of the Cali cartel, or lead the CGSB to conclude that it could continue with impunity its campaign of terror.[52]

Why the lenient treatment of Escobar did not destroy relations between Gaviria and the United States has a straightforward explanation. Without resorting to decertification and implementing the sanctions that went with it, there was little US officials could do in the short run.[53] Instead, they began to look for ways to exert greater influence upon Colombia. Gaviria, like Barco, wanted to use counternarcotics aid to attack the guerrillas as well as the cartels, pointing to the growing involvement of the FARC with drugs.[54] Authorities in Washington consistently turned down requests to use assistance against both traffickers and guerrillas, partly in response to concerns raised in Congress and by groups like Americas Watch about human rights violations associated with the Colombian military, and partly because they believed that counterguerrilla activity would harm the vital cause of drug control.[55]

In the interval between Pablo Escobar's escape and violent death, the Bush and succeeding Clinton administrations followed a two-track policy. Publicly, Gaviria received unstinting praise.[56] Whatever disappointment officials felt concerning the escape, they consoled themselves in the belief that the war on drugs in Colombia had a solid foundation. DEA and Department of Defense training missions were assisting the Colombian National Police and the armed forces; information sharing was at an all-time high; and the dollar value of military and other counternarcotics aid probably surpassed a total of

$500 million between late 1989 and 1993.[57] Also, a program funded by the Agency for International Development to restore judicial integrity began to show results.[58] At a summit held in February 1992 in San Antonio, Texas, Bush acknowledged that he had "learned" much about drugs and the Colombian economy.[59]

When relations over drug policy cooled in 1993 and 1994, and guerrilla violence rose markedly,[60] what might be termed the "Gaviria shock" brought additional troubles. Upon learning that Prosecutor General Gustavo de Grieff had secretly met with three leaders of the Cali cartel in January 1994 in an attempt to negotiate a truce between Cali's *narcos* and the government, the Clinton White House suspended a 1991 evidence-sharing accord.[61] Assistant Secretary of State for International Narcotics Matters Robert S. Gelbard, who previously served as ambassador to Bolivia where he gained notoriety for insisting that officials vigorously prosecute a war on drugs, asserted that de Grieff, and by implication Gaviria, was disrupting the existing bilateral counterdrug operations.[62]

At home, Gaviria was being criticized as well for failing to alleviate his nation's drug-related woes despite the attacks on major trafficking organizations; to curb ongoing violence against the state by paramilitaries and leftists; to negotiate an end to the conflict; and to address Colombia's most pressing economic and social needs. Some observers feared that the state was bordering on collapse.[63] The strong nature of criticism, including doubts about his drug policy, helps explain why anti-American sentiments were not more forcefully expressed in the latter stages of the Gaviria presidency. Anti-Americanism seemed a luxury that Colombians of the political class believed they could not afford.

Dismay with conditions in their homeland extended to Colombians in all classes. In a remarkable document, *The Heart of the War* in Colombia, guerrilla sympathizers—most of whom had been displaced from their homes—spoke with pain, anger, and disillusionment about the chasm between Bogotá's promises and their personal reality. The guerrillas, said Laura, the wife of a suspected guerrilla, "fight to change Colombia from this unfair system in which we are living." Marcos, a former communist, asserted, "Nothing is more widespread than betrayal." He concluded, "Power everywhere is most effective when it learns to hide its methods."[64] Perhaps the 1991 constitution would someday mean a better life and political integration for poor and rural Colombians; in the mid-1990s it was not clear if that would ever happen.[65]

Gaviria defended his record in the face of opposition from multiple sources as he prepared to leave office. He lamented differences with Washington over drug policy, saying, "Colombians do much more than what is sufficient. We are practically alone in a war that is not ours."[66] Gaviria's subtle brand of anti-Americanism, which had earlier garnered numerous adherents, found little resonance then among his countrymen and women.

The Crisis Years of Samper and Pastrana

The third section of this study, 1994–2000, began during the 1994 presidential campaign. Disquiet over the situation in Colombia increased as a result of charges, leveled by forces supporting Conservative Andrés Pastrana Arango, that the Liberal party candidate and victor, Ernesto Samper Pizano, had accepted $6 million from the Cali cartel.[67] This scandal and the reactions to it contributed to both the emergence of anti-Americanism and its limited nature. As the United States began to intrude more in Colombian affairs, the president's supporters vociferously denounced US actions, while Samper's opponents in the political class countered with their own heated denunciations of his perceived misdeeds.

By March 1996, when the Department of State refused to certify Colombia as cooperating fully in the war on drugs, revelations coming out of Proceso 8000—the special investigation into the scandal—suggested complicity by Samper in the successful effort by former campaign manager and Minister of Defense Fernando Botero to obtain "donations" from the cartel. The Department of State asserted that Samper's government had demonstrated a "lack of political will" and "lacked commitment to support the efforts of Colombian law enforcement entities and to strengthen the nation's institutions" in their fight against the corrosive impact of the cartel's activities. Although most of the seven high-level Cali drug traffickers were in jail, they continued "to manage [their] criminal empire from prison."[68] Frustration turned to rage in January 1996 when Cali leader José Santacruz Lodoño escaped from prison. DEA Chief Thomas A. Constantine thundered, "This is the Envigado scenario revisited"—a reference to the jail where Medellín's Pablo Escobar had been housed before his escape.[69] In subsequent testimony before Congress, Constantine declared: "The fate of Colombia hangs in the balance."[70]

Elected in 1994, Ernesto Samper came to office under a cloud of suspicion for his support in the early 1980s of marijuana legalization and his alleged ties to the Cali cartel. DEA agent Joe Toft derided Colombia as a "narco-democracy," an allegation that stuck to Samper's government during his four years in office.[71] Thus, it was not surprising in July 1996 when the Clinton administration forbade his entry into the United States by refusing to grant him a visa. The White House acted not because of the volume of drugs flowing out of Colombia, which had declined in recent years. Rather, President Bill Clinton—who had not made drug control a priority until 1996, when he named Gen. Barry R. McCaffrey, a Vietnam and Gulf War veteran, as head of the Office of National Drug Control Policy—had ceded control of policy to an activist, primarily Republican faction in Congress. In 1966, Clinton sought to reassert executive control over drug policy.[72]

A barrage of abusive, undiplomatic language emanated from many quarters in the United States. Said Myles Frechette, US Ambassador to Colombia from 1994 to 1997, "Washington hated the idea of Samper [as president]."[73] One Senate staff member, following Colombia's 1996 decertification, further castigated the president: "This is a decertification not of Colombia, but of President Samper. This is a vote of no confidence for him, not the country."[74] Under pressure from those in Congress who were dissatisfied with his policy toward Colombia, Clinton sounded like former drug czar Martinez and others, when he observed, "[The] United States judges its relationship between the two countries by one standard: whether they are cooperating with us in the fight against narcotics."[75] From Bogotá, Frechette urged his government to "isolate and debilitate" Samper.[76] Assistant Secretary Gelbard was equally blunt, saying that US goals have "been undercut at every turn by a government and a legislature not only plagued by corruption but which are fostering corruption in order to protect themselves."[77] In announcing the subsequent decertification of Colombia in 1997, Secretary of State Madeleine Albright said, "Senior officials [there] are failing to cooperate with us in the fight against drugs."[78]

It is remarkable that such heated rhetoric, vividly reminiscent of the days of US regional hegemony early in the century, did not utterly destroy existing patterns of US-Colombian cooperation on drugs. Decertification of Colombia led authorities to bypass Samper and create a special relationship with the Colombian National Police and its charismatic leader, Rosso José Serrano. Frechette, upon leaving his post in November 1997, would boast about the success of his efforts: "My job was to change Colombia. I have done that, and Colombia is better off for it."[79] Such bluster revealed the ultimate objective of US policy: the diminution of Colombian sovereignty in order to bring that nation more into compliance with US interests, especially in terms of drug control. Morris Busby, US ambassador to Colombia from 1991 to 1994, minced no words. "Sovereignty," he said, "was interfering with the possibility of extraditing drug traffickers and international criminals."[80] Richard Feinberg, the top Latin American expert in the

National Security Council, was similarly blunt: "Sovereignty . . . has become a refuge for scoundrels."[81]

Samper had become a scapegoat for the limitations of US drug control policy.[82] Colombian scholar Diana M. Pardo contends that Washington's disaffection with Samper "contributed to the erosion of Colombian democracy."[83] She may be right. The six months following the March 1996 decertification were the most critical time of Samper's presidency and a wrenching time for Colombia as a nation. Decertification complicated the task of answering domestic critics and implementing a counterguerrilla strategy. The celebrated Colombian writer Gabriel García Márquez defined the issue symbolized by Proceso 8000: "The real national drama . . . is the moral catastrophe of the political class."[84] Some 44 percent of Colombians blamed Samper for the decertification, while 46 percent dissented from that position.[85] Anti-Americanism was increasing among the political class, and it was not subtle. One anonymous writer asserted, "The United States decertified Samper and unjustly castigated a people." Calling the decision "arrogant," the writer acidly concluded, "The majority of Colombians have paid a high price in the drug war. Much more than that paid by the gringos."[86] An overwhelming percentage of Colombians, nearly 80 percent, believed that the United States did not possess the moral authority to censure others when it could not restrict drug consumption at home.[87]

This wave of anti-Americanism did not spill into the streets of Bogotá. Some in the political class feared that the controversy over decertification would impair Proceso 8000, whose outcome they reasonably assumed would not be favorable to Samper.[88] Leading intellectuals feared that confrontation with the United States could only hurt Colombia. Prominent among them was the scholar Horacio Godoy, who argued that reflexive anti-Americanism was "very dangerous, however appealing." He concluded that Colombians had more important things to do, given their many internal problems, than worry about perceived challenges to "national dignity."[89]

Polarization and pessimism ran deep in Colombia. Samper's exoneration could have further imperiled relations with Washington and the governing capacity of the state. More than 80 percent of those interviewed in July believed that the United States wanted Samper out of office, and nearly 70 percent were opposed to extradition because it would result in more violence at home. It is not surprising that 49 percent had a negative image of Ambassador Myles Frechette. Barely 6 percent of those interviewed by Yankelovich Acevedo and Associates, a polling firm operating in Colombia, believed that US policy toward Colombia was justified.[90]

A crisis in Colombian-US relations did not materialize, however, because of both the actions of Samper and his closest advisers and the advent of protests against the government in coca-growing regions throughout the country. In the first instance, the government considered expelling Frechette, but ultimately chose not to. Moreover, Rodrigo Pardo extended an olive branch in a column he wrote for *El Tiempo,* a liberal newspaper in Bogotá. Pardo began, "Colombia and the United States are not what they seem: enemies in the midst of a cold war." Despite using some tough language, he observed that the two countries were fighting a common enemy in drugs. And, the longer the impasse between the two governments continued, the more drug trafficking would threaten US security.[91] Evidence of Bogotá's evident desire to improve relations came in the visit to Washington in late July of María Emma Mejía, the new foreign minister.[92]

At the same time, tens of thousands of coca growers in the Putumayo, Guaviare, and Caquetá departments protested not only the chemical spraying of their crops but also the resorting to violence against the protesting campesinos by local police. One police colonel, Edgar Herrera, claimed that "guerrillas are behind" the protests.[93] However true the allegations about FARC involvement might have been, the government was in no position to respond to its critics with force. Proceso 8000 and the divisions in the political class had foreclosed that option. As observed in *Semana,* a major weekly magazine, "While government programs come to naught, guerrillas are consolidating in [Guaviare]."[94] Quick, ameliorative action by the state was therefore essential if the situation was not going to get completely out of hand. Between 60 and 80 percent of the campesinos in the three departments made their living in the illicit drug business; alternative crop development had failed.[95] One problem was determining how to persuade coca growers to grow other crops; more basic, though, was identifying with whom the state could negotiate an accord. As one official said of the coca growers of Putumayo, "They are the authority here." What was underway was a powerful social movement whose participants believed that their identity as Colombian citizens was at stake.[96]

The campesinos who resisted the government's eradication program were engaging in what I term the "anti-Americanism of the poor" (see Fig. 9.1). They carried signs reading, *"Votamos Samper, no por la DEA"* ("We vote for Samper, not for the DEA"). If their protests against US drug policy were less orderly than those of the political class, it was because they had more to lose. By mid-September, the demonstrations—an indication of the state's inability to meet pressing social needs—were over, and the government was negotiating.

Figure 9.1
Farmer in Puerto Asis, Putumayo, protests U.S.-backed defoliation programs.
Used with permission of Winifred Tate.

One legacy of this chaotic time was the formation of a women's peace movement—*La Ruta Pacífica de las Mujeres*—which opposed not only guerrilla and paramilitary violence, but also US-funded eradication programs because of their negative consequences for the poor. Samper's government had pledged to continue fumigating coca crops and to reinvigorate the national plan of alternative development, known by the acronym Plante, which had begun the previous year.[97] Had the "moral catastrophe" of the political class become a catalyst for change? It was too soon to tell, yet the message of the events of 1996 was clear: "Colombia requires new directions, not only political but also social."[98]

Driven by an overwhelming desire to compel Samper to do its bidding, the US government refused to acknowledge that punishing Samper by decertifying Colombia had harmed drug policy and allowed new groups, known as "boutique cartels," to take the place of the Medellín and Cali operations. While Samper's judgment may have been faulty, as Proceso 8000 showed, his antinarcotics record was laudable, particularly given the intensification of civil strife that occurred during his presidency. It is ironic that, prior to Uribe, it was Samper who did the most to combat drugs while trying to keep Colombia intact.[99] In that regard, it is worth noting that by the final months of his presidency, Samper's efforts were failing, according to a Department of State intelligence assessment. FARC forces had inflicted upon the army "its most disastrous defeat in 35 years of civil war." Army-paramilitary collusion was reportedly on the rise, and concern about human rights abuses threatened further to curtail US aid programs.[100]

In evaluating Samper, it is essential to recall that he kept Rosso José Serrano in office; Serrano could arguably have been seen as a US operative had Samper wished to portray him as such. Samper also took a series of actions that the United States surely would have welcomed under other circumstances. He continued aerial fumigation despite protests by coca farmers, prosecuted prominent drug traffickers, named as foreign minister María Emma Mejía, who was sympathetic to US objectives, and endeavored to restart the process of extradition—an action prohibited by the 1991 constitution.[101]

In short, Samper received far less credit than was warranted. His exoneration by the Liberal-dominated Congress from formal charges of involvement in illegal activities explains why. The US Department of State was furious about the decision not to pursue criminal charges against him, claiming that the evidence was conclusive. Spokesperson Nicholas Burns indicated that, unless Samper intensified antinarcotics efforts along desired lines, the United States might be forced to designate Colombia "a pariah state."[102]

In February 1998, the General Accounting Office (GAO) detailed the ongoing narcotics threat from Colombia and wondered about the "political will" of Samper's government to meet the challenge.[103] Yet Samper's efforts to shape his own drug policy were partly successful. In March, Colombia received a national interest certification. A less confrontational policy was in the making, and the United States was seeking ways to improve relations. Why? US officials had begun to understand the imminent threat civil unrest posed to Colombian and regional stability. Also, Samper's accomplishments against drugs could not be denied, as the GAO report noted. Additionally, Colombia would hold elections in 1998, with a new president taking office in August. Imperceptibly, Bogotá and Washington were forging a common political culture whose gestation period would last two years.

If US authorities expected Samper's successor to be a more tractable executive, someone who would essentially accept limits on state sovereignty in the name of cordial relations, they badly miscalculated. Andrés Pastrana spent his first eighteen months in office following the Barco model, whereby he assumed equality in Colombia's relations with the United States. It was Pastrana's misfortune not to possess Barco's political or diplomatic skills. A consultant to Pastrana aptly called a nascent US proposal to help Colombia's coca growers switch to alternative crops "the first admission that American eradication policy is not working."[104] The GAO did admit that "[o]ur work over the past ten years indicates that there is no panacea for resolving all of the problems associated with illegal drug trafficking."[105] Yet not all was harmonious between Bogotá and Washington.

Pastrana contended that aerial eradication of coca "has not worked," even as the House of Representatives voted to send an additional forty helicopters in order to bolster the military's presence in Colombia's coca eradication campaign (see Fig. 9.2).[106] In a visit to the United States at the end of October, Pastrana emphasized that his first priority was to negotiate with the FARC before trying to implement strict drug controls. "The root problem of Colombia's crisis is not violence, or even drugs," he said. "It is the poverty that fuels both guerrilla recruitment and the drug trade."[107] In an apparent contradiction barely two months later, Pastrana declared, "The first enemy of peace is narco-trafficking."[108]

For the Clinton administration, the question became how best to craft a position of influence with Pastrana, given his inconsistencies. Colombia's unstable environment helped US officials achieve that objective. As the identity gap between drug traffickers and guerrillas narrowed, the United States became a more active participant in Colombia's internal conflict, which some Republicans in Congress enthusiastically welcomed.[109] Sympathetic congressmen had established direct ties with Serrano's office in order to expedite the flow of military aid. Others, led by Senator Patrick Leahy (D-VT), argued that military aid in the battle against guerrillas should be closely tied to

Figure 9.2

U.S.-supplied helicopter raises fears of violence among the poor in Putumayo. Used by permission of Witness for Peace.

progress on human rights.[110] The possibility that equipment designated for the drug war might be committed to fighting the FARC or other guerrillas did not bother Serrano's friends. Pastrana himself initially neither discouraged nor actively promoted this linkage.

There existed within the Department of State a conviction that counternarcotics "assistance may be used to confront anyone, including the guerrillas, who is directly involved in narcotics trafficking."[111] Pastrana tried to give life to his assertion about the linkage between drugs and peace. He believed that coca eradication in FARC-controlled territory, a zone of distension in south-central Colombia about the size of Switzerland (created in May 1999 and dubbed *"Farclandia"*), would serve as an important symbol of rebel willingness to enter into negotiations. Pastrana reasoned that, so long as the peace process showed signs of progress, an aspiration that had little basis in reality during his first three years in office,[112] he had the freedom to subordinate drug control to other policy objectives.

What Pastrana could not have anticipated was how a growing concern about the activities of paramilitary groups by the US Congress and independent advocacy groups like Human Rights Watch and the Washington Office on Latin America would affect the bilateral relationship. The paramilitaries had strong links to Colombia's armed forces and frequently attacked suspected leftists without fear of reprisal. Reports of human rights abuses cut short Pastrana's post-election honeymoon. Whether he chose to fight guerrillas or drugs or paramilitaries, he faced scrutiny from Washington as intense as any experienced by his predecessors. Indeed, drug czar McCaffrey saw in Colombia the onset of a regional crisis.[113] Moreover, some members of the out-of-power Liberal party, including political commentator and ex-diplomat Fernando Cepeda Ulloa, aligned themselves with conservatives in the United States by advocating a greater US military role in Colombia.[114] Like Barco, Pastrana had limited expressions of anti-Americanism by the political class; unlike Barco, he could not contain his domestic critics.

Doubts were growing at home about Pastrana's capacity to govern, as were fears of deeper US involvement in Colombian affairs, which *El Tiempo* termed "a quiet intervention."[115] *Semana* captured the essence of unfolding developments in an article entitled, *"El Tío Sam al rescate"* ("Uncle Sam to the rescue"). The Pastrana presidency appeared to be gravely wounded.[116] A rescue operation became Plan Colombia, a $7.5 billion plan, ostensibly initiated at Pastrana's behest, to preserve the integrity of Colombia through a revival of "nation-building"—an ambitious program of economic development and social reconstruction, similar to that undertaken by the United States in the late 1950s and early 1960s for locales as diverse as Indochina and Latin America.[117] The US share of the cost would be approximately $1.6 billion over three years, making Colombia the third largest recipient of US foreign aid. Plan Colombia, which came into effect in the summer of 2000, returned drug control "to a status of vital importance in Colombian politics and diplomacy."[118] For the Pastrana government, this development occurred not a moment too soon, even though Plan Colombia showed the limits of Colombian autonomy vis-à-vis the United States, thus opening the door to a resurgence of anti-Americanism.

The Making of an Entente Cordiale

Pastrana began the year 2000 (and the final period of this study) by declaring, *"Aqui no hay guerra civil"* ("There is no civil war here"), which few Colombians believed.[119] By mid-year, his administration was stumbling from crisis to crisis. The interior minister resigned, peace talks showed no signs of progress, and Rosso José Serrano announced that he would soon leave office.[120] The situation was so volatile that Defense Minister Luis Fernández Ramírez welcomed additional US military aid, terming it "a new beginning."[121] Implicit in the statement was an admission that talks with the FARC and the ELN had been unproductive and that Pastrana's effort to bring peace through negotiation was failing, as much a result of government weakness as it was evidence of guerrilla strength.[122]

Clinton sought to bolster Pastrana's waning fortunes with a brief visit to Bogotá in late August. An advance team, composed of Department of State, Department of Defense, and DEA officials, revealed how desperate the United States then believed the Colombian situation to be. Department of State official Thomas Pickering tellingly observed, "I hope that in twenty-five years Colombia can reach its goal of being a peaceful nation."[123] Twenty-five years to overcome drugs, rebels, and paramilitaries: in Pickering's estimation peace was not a task to be left to Colombians alone. Without exaggeration, the political editor of *El Espectador,* Javier Hendez, observed, "The public's view of Pastrana is worse than [that] of Samper on his worst day."[124] The Clinton administration felt much the same. Assistant Secretary of State Rand Beers commented that the government's "historic neglect of the nation's outlying areas has allowed the problem[s] to fester."[125] Clinton's visit brought little relief to the beleaguered Colombian president. A series of protests against crop fumigation and a spate of guerrilla attacks across the country, which left twenty people dead, showed that opposition to US-induced drug policy was not as dormant among Colombians as the relative quiescence of the political class suggested.[126]

On its own terms, US policy had not failed. Crop eradication was effective in the Andes, seizures of cocaine and heroin shipped from Colombia were increasing, and drug consumption at home was declining. Just the same, Washington had not managed to cultivate an entirely reliable partnership with Bogotá. The quest for a steadfast ally would go on; Washington did not have long to wait for one to appear.

Álvaro Uribe, a Liberal party member who ran as an independent, was elected president in 2002 soon after the peace process broke down; Uribe sought and comfortably wore the mantle of Washington's man in Bogotá. Robin Kirk of Human Rights Watch called him "the war president to end all war presidents."[127] Welcomed rapturously by the administration of President George W. Bush, and assisted by the events of 11 September 2001 and after, Uribe persuaded the White House and Congress to ignore the fiction that funds appropriated to fight drugs would not be used for counterguerrilla operations. In the post-September 11 world, security became as indivisible in the Andes as elsewhere. Playing to his North American audience, Uribe reportedly called drug trafficking "a greater threat than Iraq."[128] Whether he believed his own words was beside the point. Unlike his predecessors, Uribe was not disposed to stray far from US preferences on so vital a matter as drug trafficking, which he knew was the acid test of his government's political will. Terrorism, real or imagined, had created a common political culture for Bogotá and Washington. It was Uribe's political genius to use the convergence for his own ends. In the process, anti-Americanism all but vanished as an important factor in Colombian-US relations.

Uribe deemed untied aid essential if his army was going to defeat the guerrillas. He cast the four-decade-old conflict as an antiterrorist operation and applauded US designation of guerrillas and the AUC as terrorist organizations.[129] Just as Uribe took office in August 2002, the United States allowed lethal assistance to be used against terrorists. US Southern Command Director of Operations Brig. Gen. Galen Jackman observed, "Our main objective is to help transform the Colombian military to a force that is capable of defeating the terrorist organizations."[130]

Uribe was getting the weapons he needed for the war he wanted. The defeat of narcoterrorism, which both countries now defined as a security priority, enabled him to depart from the antiguerrilla strategies and drug control policies of his predecessors. He freely employed extradition as a weapon in the fight, the ban on which had been lifted in December 1997 while Samper was still president.[131] For the Bush administration, Colombia was important on its own terms, and military aid was a means to a larger end. Department of State official Paul E. Simons told the Senate Drug Caucus in June 2003 that "[t]he Andean Counterdrug Initiative (ACI) is a regional effort" throughout northern South America.[132] Simons's statement anticipated what Assistant Secretary of State for International Narcotics and Law Enforcement Affairs Robert Charles told the Senate Foreign Relations Committee in October 2003: "For the record, we shall never give up the primacy of the counternarcotics mission in Colombia." He could have added, "and elsewhere."[133] This depiction of a multilateral struggle resembled what Barco and Gaviria had wanted US policy to emphasize years earlier: an arrangement that "stresses shared goals, increased cooperation, and sensible compromises."[134]

Notwithstanding Charles's reiteration of the traditional objective of control at the source, Uribe's government and the Bush administration had overcome differences that long plagued US-Colombian relations. Uribe's uncompromising approach toward the FARC and the ELN, as well as the AUC to a lesser extent, created common ground on which the mutual goal of combating terror—with its links to drugs— satisfied policymakers in Washington. By no later than early 2004 an entente cordiale existed; the United States was treating Colombia as a nominally equal partner in a joint struggle. Within such an environment anti-Americanism had no place to take root, at least not within the political class or at the government-to-government level.

How Anti-Americanism Might Reemerge in Colombia

By late 2004, the greatest bar to a resurgence of anti-Americanism was Uribe's incredible popularity—a 70 percent approval rating.[135] No recent president maintained such high ratings so long into his presidency. Indeed, many Colombians—quietly supported by the White House—wanted Uribe to serve a second term; in December, the Colombian congress voted heavily in favor of the right to run for reelection.[136] The Constitutional Court would ultimately decide whether so momentous a change was legal, which it did in October 2005.

Uribe's popularity stemmed from several notable successes in the struggle against the guerrillas and paramilitaries. A high-level FARC leader was seized in Ecuador in January 2004 with the help of US intelligence, and a military campaign, Operation New Year, was launched to recover "the credibility of the state," according to one soldier.[137] As a result of ongoing talks, some paramilitaries put down their arms, while leaders promised further demobilization and announced their intention to reinsert themselves peacefully into public life.[138] Also, coca production in Putumayo, a FARC stronghold, appreciably decreased during Uribe's first two years in office.[139] These developments appeared to justify Washington's absolute faith in Uribe and his policies, which Secretary of State Colin Powell underscored in October 2003 by applauding Colombia's human rights policy and which the US Senate affirmed by appropriating $600 million in military assistance.[140] The leading Senate Democrat, Tom Daschle of South Dakota, indicated in March 2004 that he would consider supporting an administration plan to double the number of US military personnel in Colombia to eight hundred and raise the limit on civilian contractors from three hundred to six hundred. The 2005 United States Defense Department authorization act approved these changes.[141]

The situation in Colombia was not altogether positive, however. War against rebel forces continued to force thousands of poor Colombians from their homes,[142] even as paramilitaries turned the cease-fire into a controversial, forcible grab for land.[143] Another serious, if less visible, problem was the incessant price instability in the international coffee market—a result in part of Bush administration support for free trade as seen in the entry of Vietnam into the International Coffee Organization in 2002. Some Colombian coffee farmers, who numbered eight hundred thousand throughout the country, could no longer earn a living and were turning to opium production—which Uribe deemed a crisis of grave proportions.[144]

The major challenge facing the political class was to turn historically unsuccessful alternative development projects into an economic improvement for poor, rural farmers. Bogotá's "ability to effectively coordinate eradication and alternative development activities remains uncertain," the GAO concluded. Plante, the national program for alternative development, "is weak and its funding for alternative development projects is not ensured."[145]

The vexing problems that Colombia faces as of this writing could redound unfavorably for the United States were Uribe to fall from public grace. Should the United States not adopt a multilateral approach to mutual problems in the Andes and northern South America, then the troubled history of Colombian-US relations since the mid-1980s might repeat itself. The result would likely be displays of anti-Americanism extending beyond the political class, along with widespread ridicule of Uribe's hard-won entente cordiale. A hint of what might transpire appeared in *Going to Extremes: The US-Funded Aerial Eradication Program in Colombia,* a report of the Latin American Working Group, a nongovernmental organization that promotes human rights and justice in the Americas. The report linked the chemical eradication of illicit crops with damage to food and livestock, a rise in health problems, and ongoing displacement for people inhabiting sprayed areas.[146] With alternative development aid not arriving in a timely fashion for more than a minority of farmers, antigovernment protests—as personified by the march in November 2003 of three thousand women in Putumayo in opposition to fumigation—posed a challenge (the anti-Americanism of the poor) that neither Uribe and the political class nor their friends in Washington could afford to ignore.[147]

In a January 2004 report, "*Andes 2020:* A New Strategy for the Challenges of Colombia and the Region," the Center for Preventive Action of the Council on Foreign Relations called upon the Bush administration to adopt "a shared strategy" to avert "regional collapse." Continued emphasis on narcoterrorism and drug trafficking would reduce the prospects of sustainable development and a lasting peace. The report faulted Uribe for lacking "the political leverage to reverse Colombia's historically weak state institutions," his popularity notwithstanding.[148] Jan Egeland, humanitarian coordinator at the United Nations catalogued the numerous human problems confronting Bogotá and concluded: "Colombia is therefore by far the biggest humanitarian catastrophe of the Western Hemisphere."[149] It would ultimately take much more than convergence with the United States on anti-terror measures and drug control policies to change that reality.

Two decades of drug control as a central issue in Colombian-US relations brought to the fore three strains of anti-Americanism that differed in degree of severity from earlier variants.[150] Colombian-style anti-Americanism was rarely mass-based, though it did not lack popular appeal; it was more subtle than not, though never inchoate; and it was often self-contained within the political class and its factions. As such, it never threatened to disrupt the bilateral relationship, only to strain it as disputes over the contours and pace of Colombian drug policy were negotiated. The merger of the drug war with the war on terror and the creation of Uribe's entente cordiale removed anti-Americanism from the agenda of state-to-state relations. Whether popular protests in rural Colombia would grow into hostile expressions of anti-Americanism depended upon how the political class responded to the dilemma contained in the unrealized promise of economic development and the illusion of democratic inclusion. Like it or not, the United States—through its drug control aid and anti-terror assistance—had become intimately associated with the success or failure of the Colombian state.

Notes

* I thank Alan McPherson for suggesting this formulation of "quiet" anti-Americanism.
1. A Guillermoprieto, *The Heart That Bleeds: Latin America Now* (New York, 1994), 331–36.
2. *Washington Post*, 24 June 1991.
3. United States Department of State, *International Narcotics Strategy Report for 2002*. Available at http://www.state.gov/documents/organization/18169.pdf, section IV, 18–28.
4. R. Pardo Rueda, *De primera mano: Colombia, 1986–1994: entre conflictos y esperanzas* (Bogotá, 1996), 196.
5. E. Samper Pizano, *Aquí estoy y aquí me quedo: Testimonio de un gobierno* (Bogotá, 2000), 272.
6. This argument about US-Colombian affinity in the 1920s and 1960s draws upon several sources: S. J. Randall, *The Diplomacy of Modernization: Colombian-American Relations, 1920–1940* (Toronto, 1977), 11, 55–57; P. W. Drake, *The Money Doctor in the Andes: The Kemmerer Missions, 1923–1933* (Durham, 1989), 30–31; E. S. Rosenberg, *Financial Missionaries to the World: The Politics and Culture of Dollar Diplomacy* (Cambridge, 1999), 158–60. On the 1960s, see W. O. Walker III, "Mixing the Sweet with the Sour: Kennedy, Johnson, and Latin America," in *The Diplomacy*

of the Crucial Decade: American Foreign Relations During the 1960s, ed. D. B. Kunz (New York, 1994), 53, 60.

7. Though hopeful about the prospects for modernization in the Alliance decade, US officials were not unaware of the troubles that Colombia was experiencing in the 1960s. See "Colombia: Short-term Contingency Plans," 18 June 1963, DDRS, Document number CK3100468178 (Farmingham Hills, 2004). S. G. Rabe, *The Most Dangerous Area in the World: John F. Kennedy Confronts Communist Revolution in Latin America* (Chapel Hill, 1999), 158–60.

8. J. Pearce, *Colombia: Inside the Labyrinth* (London, 1990), 115.

9. H. F. Kline, *State Building and Conflict Resolution in Colombia, 1986–1994* (Tuscaloosa, 1999), 40–43, 56, 85–86; S. Dudley, *Walking Ghosts: Murder and Guerrilla Politics in Colombia* (New York, 2004), 153–66.

10. R. Pardo and J. G. Tokatlian, *Política exterior colombiana: ¿De la subordinación a la autonomía?* (Bogotá, 1988), 181–237.

11. *United Nations Annual Reports of Governments: Colombia,* E/NR, 1948, 10 July 1949 (Lake Success, 1949), 8–10.

12. US Congress, House of Representatives, *Report of a Study Mission to Mexico, Costa Rica, Panama, and Colombia,* 6–8 January 1976, "The Shifting Patterns of Narcotics Trafficking: Latin America," 94 Cong., 2 sess., May 1976, Washington, D.C., 1976, 23.

13. M. Reina, *La Relaciones entre Colombia y Estados Unidos (1978–1986),* Documentales Ocasionales, no. 15, Bogotá, May–June 1990, 10.

14. Ibid., 42–46; F. E. Thoumi, *Political Economy and Illegal Drugs in Colombia* (Boulder, 1995), 212–13; M. J. Duzán, *Crónicas que matan* (Bogotá, 1992), 35, 36, 73–78.

15. Pearce, *Colombia: Inside the Labyrinth,* 180; Thoumi, *Political Economy,* 213–14. Pardo calls the assassination "the point of no return for drug trafficking on the path to terrorism." Pardo, *De primera mano,* 186.

16. One respected observer of Colombian affairs contends that US demands on Colombia constituted "a threat to both the regional and national security of Colombia." J. G. Tokatlian, "National Security and Drugs: Their Impact on Colombian-US Relations," *Journal of Interamerican Studies and World Affairs* 30 (1988): 133–60; quotation 133. Tokatlian points out that Colombian officials took notice of the allegations of links between the Nicaraguan *contras* and the cocaine trade even as Washington was asking Bogotá to take a harder line on drugs.

17. Generally, see F. E. Thoumi, *El imperio de la droga: Narcotráfico, economía, y sociedad en los Andes* (Bogotá, 2002), 223.

18. D. Pecaut, "Guerrillas and Violence," in *Violence in Colombia: The Contemporary Crisis in Historical Perspective,* ed. C. Bergquist, R. Peñaranda, and G. Sánchez (Wilmington, 1992), 231–32.

19. Pardo, *De primera mano,* 21.

20. J. G. Tokatlian, "Seguridad y drogas: Su significado en las relaciones entre Colombia y Estados Unidos," in *Economía y política del narcotráfico,* ed. J. G. Tokatlian and B. M. Bagley (Bogotá, 1990), 228 n. 30. See also memorandum, *Ambassador Gillespie's January 15 Meeting with President Barco, 16 January 1988,* Document number CK 3100471652, DDRS; and the memorandum by Elliott Abrams, 8 June 1988, Document number CK 3100471667, DDRS.

21. Tokatlian, "Seguridad y drogas," 229.

22. J. G. Tokatlian, *Globalización, narcotráfico y violencia: Siete ensayos sobre Colombia* (Buenos Aires, 2000), 106–11.

23. Ibid. On the human costs of the government's war on guerrillas and drugs, see generally, Americas Watch, *Political Murder and Reform in Colombia: The Violence Continues* (New York, April 1992).

24. Kline, *State Building,* 47–50.

25. Pardo, *De primera mano*, 189–94; quotations, 190, 193.

26. Memorandum, *Ambassador Gillespie's January 15 Meeting with President Barco, 16 January 1988*, Document number CK 3100471652, DDRS.

27. US Department of State, Bureau of International Narcotics Matters, *International Narcotics Control Strategy Report, March 1990* (Washington, D.C., 1990), 123; emphasis added.

28. The dispute over the control of drug policy makes explicable President Ronald Reagan's designation of drugs as a threat to US national security in National Security Decision Directive No. 221 of April 1986. Available at http://fas.org/irp/offdocs/nsdd/nsdd-221.htm.

29. This analysis derives from several sources: Tokatlian, "National Security and Drugs"; W. O. Walker III, "The Bush Administration's Andean Drug Strategy in Historical Perspective," in *Drug Trafficking in the Americas,* ed. B. M. Bagley and W. O. Walker III (New Brunswick, 1994), 1–22; idem, "Drug Control and US Hegemony," in *United States Policy in Latin America: A Decade of Crisis and Challenge,* ed. J. D. Martz (Lincoln, 1995), 299–319; H. Tovar Pinzón, *Colombia: droga, economía, guerra y paz* (Bogotá, 1999), 91–108, which is a chapter entitled: "El fin de la guerra fría y la guerra contra las drogas."

30. US Department of State, "Cocaine: A Supply Side Strategy," 15 June 1989, in "War in Colombia: Guerrillas, Drugs and Human Rights, 1988–2002," NSAEBB no. 69. Available at http://www.gwu.edu/~nsarchiv/NSAEBB/NSAEBB69/part1.html.

31. Secretary of Defense Dick Cheney increasingly supported an active drug control mission for the US military, a development that did not escape notice in Colombia. C. G. Arrieta et al., *Narcotráfico en Colombia: Dimensiones pilíticas, económicas, jurídicas e internacionales* (Bogotá, 1991), 344.

32. US Embassy Colombia cable, "Murtha and Marsh Visit Concentrates on Narco Power and Insurgency," 24 May 1988, in "War in Colombia," NSAEBB no. 69. Available at http://www.gwu.edu/~nsarchiv/NSAEBB/NSAEBB69/part1.html; *Washington Post,* 1 September 1989.

33. National Security Council, National Security Directive 18, "International Counternarcotics Strategy," 21 August 1989, in "War in Colombia," NSAEBB no. 69. Available at http://www.gwu.edu/~nsarchiv/NSAEBB/NSAEBB69/part1.html. On the Andean Strategy, see Walker, "The Bush Administration's Andean Drug Strategy in Historical Perspective."

34. See W. O. Walker III, "The Limits of Coercive Diplomacy: US Drug Policy and Colombian State Stability, 1978–1997," in *The Illicit Global Economy and State Power,* ed. H. R. Friman and P. Andreas (Lanham, 1999), 153–59.

35. *New York Times,* 21 January 1991.

36. The Escobar story is powerfully rendered in M. Bowden, *Killing Pablo: The Hunt for the World's Greatest Outlaw* (New York, 2001).

37. Thoumi, *Political Economy and Illegal Drugs,* 7; *Miami Herald,* 8 August 1990.

38. Pardo, *De primera mano*, quotation on 211, 289–91.

39. Americas Watch, *Political Murder,* 60–61, 68–73.

40. L. Boudon, "Guerrillas and the State: The Role of the State in the Colombian Peace Process," *Journal of Latin American Studies* 28 (1996): 283–84; Kline, *State Building,* 85–100.

41. *Washington Post,* 30 May 1992; the characterization of 1992 as a terrible year for Colombia is found in Pardo, *De primera mano,* 371.

42. *El Tiempo,* 3 and 8 August 1990 and 6 September 1990. Bringing *narcotraficantes* to justice meant acceptance of talks between the governments and its sworn enemies; many influential Colombians accepted the distasteful procedure as necessary, if only to try to decrease the level of violence against the state. Among those who supported negotiations was Bogotá's Conservative Mayor, Andrés

Pastrana Arango, who would lose the 1994 election in a close race with Ernesto Samper. *Washington Post*, 24 April 1990.

43. D. M. Pardo, "The US Foreign Policy Making Process Towards Colombia During the Administration of Ernesto Samper Pizano (1994–1998): The Certification Decisions" (Ph.D. diss., University of Miami, 2003), 53.

44. US Congress, House of Representatives, *Hearings Before the Subcommittee of Western Hemisphere Affairs of the Committee on Foreign Affairs*, "The Andean Initiative," 101 Cong., 2 sess., 6 and 20 June 1990, Washington, D.C., 1990, 13, 94.

45. *New York Times*, 4 June 1991; *El Espectador* (Bogotá), 20 June 1991. DEA, CIA, and the Department of State opposed Gaviria on extradition, although Ambassador Thomas McNamara in Bogotá had initially shown some respect for Colombian sensibilities; D. Farah, "The Crackup," *Washington Post*, 21 July 1996.

46. *El Espectador*, 4 July 1991.

47. Pardo, *De primera mano*, 299–309, 403.

48. Farah, "The Crackup."

49. Pardo, *De primera mano*, 302.

50. *El Tiempo*, 23 July 1992 and 3 December 1993.

51. "Pesimismo," *Semana*, 757, 5–12 November 1996.

52. The general thrust of this argument about the effects of leniency on state legitimacy and the prospects for institution building builds on Thoumi, *Political Economy and Illegal Drugs*. On Colombia's guerrillas and state stability, see Boudon, "Guerrillas and the State," passim.

53. Beginning in the mid-1980s, the Department of State certified annually the extent of cooperation by foreign governments with US drug policy. Those who failed to meet current standards faced possible decertification, which could entail a variety of sanctions. See R. F. Perl, "International Drug Policy and the US Congress," in *Drugs and Foreign Policy: A Critical Review*, ed. R. F. Perl (Boulder, 1994), 66–67.

54. Not all US agencies involved in the drug war in Colombia accepted this conclusion. See, for example, DEA, Drug Intelligence Report, "Insurgent Involvement in the Colombian Drug Trade," June 1994, in "War in Colombia," NSAEBB no. 69. Available at http://www.gwu.edu/~nsarchiv/NSAEBB/NSAEBB69/col33.pdf.

55. CIA, "Narco-Insurgent Links in the Andes," 29 July 1992, in ibid. Available at http://www.gwu.edu/~nsarchiv/NSAEBB/NSAEBB69/col24.pdf, especially 5–6.

56. US Department of State, INM, *INCSR, March 1992*, 105–9. Even after Escobar fled Envigado, John P. Walters of the Office of National Drug Control Policy averred: "Colombia remains one of our staunchest partners in the hemispheric struggle against cocaine." See US Congress, House of Representatives, *Joint Hearing before the Subcommittee on Western Hemisphere Affairs and Task Force on International Narcotics Control of the Committee on Foreign Affairs*, "The Future of the Andean War on Drugs after the Escape of Pablo Escobar," 102 Cong., 2 sess., 29 July, 1992, Washington, D.C., 1993, 41.

57. US GAO, Report to the Chairman and Ranking Minority Member, Committee on Government Operations, House of Representatives, *The Drug War: Colombia Is Undertaking Antidrug Programs, but Impact Is Uncertain*, GAO/NSIAD-93-158 (Washington, D.C., August 1993), 46–53.

58. US GAO, Report to Congressional Requestors, *Foreign Assistance: Promising Approach to Judicial Reform in Colombia*, GAO, NSAID-92-269 (Washington, D.C., September 1992), 2.

59. Bush is quoted in *New York Times*, 29 February 1992.

60. Pardo, *De primera mano*, 376.

61. *Washington Post*, 8 March 1994; *El Espectador*, 8 March 1994.

62. *Washington Post*, 21 April 1994; and see ibid., 12 June 1994.

63. Pardo, *De primera mano*, 360–83; Kline, *State Building*, 109–18; Tokatlian, *Globalización, narcotráfico y violencia*, 225.
64. C. Ardila Galvis, *The Heart of the War in Colombia* (London, 2000), 53, 59, 203.
65. A. M. Bejarano, "The Constitution of 1991: An Institutional Evaluation Seven Years Later," in *Violence in Colombia*, ed. Bergquist, Peñaranda, and Sánchez, 53–74.
66. *El Tiempo*, 12 July 1994 (quotation); ibid., 24 July 1994.
67. Ibid., 21 June 1994; *New York Times*, 23 June 1994.
68. US Department of State, INM, *INCSR, March 1996*, xxv. José Santacruz Lodoño, who together with the Rodríguez Orejuela brothers, Gilberto and Miguel, dominated the Cali cartel, died in a clash with police on 5 March 1996; *El Tiempo*, 6 March 1996. A useful introduction to the charges of corruption in Samper's administration is P. L. Clawson and R. W. Lee III, *The Andean Cocaine Industry* (New York, 1996), 119–22, 170–75.
69. DEA Press Release, 12 January 1996. Available at http://www.usdoj.gov/dea/pressrel/pr690112.htm. Constantine was less forthcoming about the DEA's view of Samper several months later in an interview with *Semana;* there did remain a critical tone. See "No investigamos corrupción ni nos metemos en política," *Semana*, 730, 30 April–7 May 1996.
70. DEA Congressional Testimony, 6 June 1996. Available at http://www.usdoj.gov/de/cngrtest/ct960606.htm.
71. R. Crandall, *Driven by Drugs: US Policy toward Colombia* (Boulder, 2002), 103, 134 n. 16; see also Farah, "The Crackup," for an extensive account of Toft's allegations and their repercussions in Colombia.
72. Walker, "The Limits of Coercive Diplomacy," passim.
73. Quoted in Crandall, *Driven by Drugs*, 101.
74. *Washington Post*, 3 March 1996.
75. *Houston Chronicle*, 14 June 1996.
76. *Washington Post*, 30 June 1996.
77. US Department of State, Daily Press Briefing, 1 March 1996.
78. *Los Angeles Times*, 1 March 1997.
79. *The Economist*, 15 November 1997.
80. *Proceso* (Mexico), 22 January 1996.
81. *El Tiempo*, 20 July 1996.
82. This conclusion is based in part upon the documents in "War in Colombia," NSAEBB no. 69, vol. III: Conditioning Security Assistance: Human rights, end-use monitoring and "the government's inability to curb the paramilitary threat." Available at http://www.gwu.edu/~nsarchiv/NSAEBB/NSAEBB69/part3.html.
83. Pardo, "The US Foreign Policy Making Process Towards Colombia," 2. Pardo's brother, Rodrigo Pardo, served as Colombian foreign minister under Samper. Other observers of the Colombian scene argue that Samper's dubious actions and poor judgement left Colombian democracy in a "deplorable state." Tokatlian, *Globalización, narcotráfico y violencia*, 232 n. 69.
84. *La Jornada* (Mexico City), 29 February 1996.
85. *El Tiempo*, 3 March 1996.
86. Ibid.
87. Ibid., 10 March 1996.
88. Ibid.
89. *El Espectador*, 12 July 1996.
90. *El Tiempo*, 26 May 1996 and 7 July 1996.
91. *Washington Post*, 13 July 1996; *El Tiempo*, 14 July 1996.
92. *El Tiempo*, 24 and 25 and 26 July 1996.
93. Ibid., 30 July 1996.
94. "El polvorín del Guaviare," *Semana*, 743, 30 July–6 August 1996.

95. *El Tiempo,* 11 August 1996.

96. Ibid., 16 August 1996; M. C. Ramírez, *Entre el estado y la guerrilla: identidad y ciudadanía en el movimiento de los campesinos del Putumayo* (Bogotá, 2001).

97. Activities of *La Ruta Pacífica de las Mujeres,* roughly translated as "women of the peaceful path," can be followed on its web site: http://www.rutapacifica.org.co/index.htm. See also *El Tiempo,* 13 August 1996. On Plante, see G. Palacio Castañeda, *Globalizaciones, estado y narcotráfico* (Bogotá, 1998), 132–38; Ramírez, *Entre el estado y la guerrilla,* 113 ff.

98. F. Cepeda Ulloa, "El desmantelamiento de la clase política," *El Tiempo,* 2 September 1996.

99. Crandall, *Driven by Drugs,* 101–41.

100. US Department of State, Bureau of Intelligence and Research, Intelligence assessment, "Colombia: Momentum Against Paramilitaries Lost," 7 April 1998, in "War in Colombia," NSAEBB no. 69. Available at http://www.gwu.edu/~nsarchiv/NSAEBB/NSAEBB69/col61.pdf.

101. Crandall, *Driven by Drugs,* 120–33.

102. *Washington Post,* 16 June 1996.

103. US GAO, *Drug Control: US Counternarcotics Efforts in Colombia Face Continuing Challenges,* GAO/NSIAD-98-60 (Washington, D.C., February 1998), 5, 6.

104. *New York Times,* 14 August 1998.

105. US GAO, *Drug Control: Observations on Counternarcotics Activities,* GAO/T-NSIAD-98-249 (Washington, D.C., September 1998), 1.

106. *Miami Herald,* 16 October 1998.

107. Ibid., 31 October 1998.

108. *New York Times,* 6 January 1999.

109. US Embassy Colombia cable, "CODEL [Congressional Delegation] Hastert's May 24–27 Visit to Colombia," 28 May 1997 in "War in Colombia," NSAEBB no. 69. Available at http://www.gwu.edu/~nsarchiv/NSAEBB/NSAEBB69/col52.pdf.

110. Crandall, *Driven by Drugs,* 106–8.

111. As the Department of State also carefully pointed out, "We do not provide assistance to Colombia for counterinsurgency." State Department cable, "Clarification of US Counternarcotics Assistance," 25 October 1997, in "War in Colombia," NSAEBB no. 69. Available at http://www.gwu.edu/~nsarchiv/NSAEBB/NSAEBB69/col57.pdf.

112. *New York Times,* 7 December 2000.

113. Ibid., 27 July 1999. McCaffrey was not alone in his concern about the regional nature of the crisis in Colombia; see Tokatlian, *Globalización, narcotráfico y violencia,* 239–40.

114. On the occasion of a conference held at Florida International University in Miami, Florida, on 15–16 March 2000, which this writer attended, Cepeda responded to a question by stating that he supported US military involvement in Colombia. Prepared remarks delivered at the conference can be found in Summit of the Americas Center, *Colombia: Conflicto armado, perspectivas de paz y democracia* (Miami, 2001).

115. *El Tiempo,* 10 August 1999.

116. *Semana,* 908, 20–27 September 1999.

117. W. O. Walker III, "A Reprise for 'Nation Building': Low Intensity Conflict Spreads in the Andes," *NACLA Report on the Americas* 35, 1 (2001): 23–28, 50.

118. Ibid., 24.

119. *El Tiempo,* 9 February 2000.

120. *El Nuevo Herald* (Miami), 14 June 2000; *El Tiempo,* 14 June 2000; *New York Times,* 12 July 2000.

121. *New York Times,* 25 June 2000.

122. An early assessment of negotiations during the Pastrana presidency is Tokat-lian, *Globalización, narcotráfico y violencia*, 232–45. For analysis of Pastrana's peace process see A. Isacson, "Was Failure Avoidable?: Learning from Colom-bia's 1998–2002 Peace Process," Dante B. Fascell North-South Center Working Paper Series, Paper No. 14, University of Miami, March 2003.

123. *El Tiempo*, 11 August 2000.

124. *Washington Post*, 18 August 2000. One opinion survey found that 60 percent looked upon his presidency in unfavorable terms, a percentage that rivaled Samper at his worst; J. Lodoño de la Cuesta, "La opinión pública colombiana frente la crisis: Una breve descripción," in *Colombia: Conflicto armado*, 12.

125. *New York Times*, 15 October 2000.

126. Ibid., 31 August 2000.

127. R. Kirk, *More Terrible Than Death: Massacres, Drugs, and America's War in Co-lombia* (New York, 2003), 279.

128. Uribe is cited in G. Marcella, *The United States and Colombia: The Journey from Ambiguity to Strategic Clarity* (Carlisle, May 2003). Available at http://www.carlisle.army.mil/ssi/pubs/2003/journey/journey.pdf, 6.

129. *Washington Post*, 6 February 2003; *El Tiempo*, 14 February 2003; *Washington Post*, 22 February 2003.

130. Jackman cited in I. Vaicius and A. Isacson, "The 'War on Drugs' meets the 'War on Terror,'" International Policy Report, Center for International Policy, Febru-ary 2003, 15.

131. Extradition remained a matter of serious, though not overly controversial, de-bate as Uribe entered the final two years of his presidential term; *Semana*, 1132, 19–26 January 2004.

132. See Simons's statement at http://usembassy.state.gov/bogota/wwwsps02.shtml. The ACI was devised to revise Plan Colombia as a regional response to drugs and terror. It recalls Operation Snowcap and the Andean Drug Strategy of the late 1980s and the early 1990s.

133. Charles's declaration is available at http://usembassy.state.gov/posts/col/wwwspc49.shtml.

134. R. Pardo, "Colombia's Two-Front War," *Foreign Affairs* 79 (2000): 64–73 (quota-tion 73).

135. *El Tiempo*, 17 January 2004; *New York Times*, 2 December 2004.

136. *New York Times*, 12 and 13 November 2003. On US support for another term for Uribe, see C. Hallinan, "Colombia: Old Domino's New Clothes," 16 March 2004. Available at http://www.americaspolicy.org. See also *El Espectador*, 1 December 2004.

137. *El Tiempo*, 4 January 2004; *New York Times*, 4 January 2004; *Washington Post*, 25 January 2004 (quotation).

138. *Miami Herald*, 3 December 2003.

139. *Washington Post*, 21 December 2003; *New York Times*, 23 March 2004. For a less optimistic view of developments in the Putumayo coca-growing regions see Memorandum by A. Isacson, Center for International Policy, 22 March 2004. Available at http://www.ciponline.org/colombia/040322coca.pdf. Isacson con-tends that coca growing spread into areas untouched by Colombia's aerial eradication program.

140. *Miami Herald*, 1 October 2003; *El Tiempo*, 31 October 2003.

141. See http://www.colombiaemb.org/extra/news_item.html (accessed 28 March 2004); *New York Times*, 11 October 2004.

142. V. Bouvier, "Colombia Quagmire: Time for US Policy Overhaul," Interhemi-spheric Resource Center Americas Program Policy Brief, September 2003, 1.

143. *Washington Post,* 20 and 25 September 2003; *New York Times,* 21 January 2004 in which one supporter of the newly displaced commented, "The land problem is at the center of the armed conflict in Colombia."
144. Statement of Sen. Patrick Leahy on the International Coffee Crisis, 23 October 2003, Oxfam America. Available at http://www.oxfamamerica.org/advocacy/art6419.html. *Washington Post,* 26 June 2003.
145. US GAO, *Drug Control: Efforts to Develop Alternatives to Cultivating Illicit Crops in Colombia Have Made Little Progress and Face Serious Obstacles,* GAO-02-291 (Washington, D.C., February 2002), 3, 12.
146. B. Marsh, *Going to Extremes: The US-Funded Aerial Eradication Program in Colombia* (Washington, D.C., 2004), 2–3, 14–15.
147. Ibid., 25–26, 37.
148. Report of an Independent Commission Sponsored by the Council on Foreign Relations Center for Preventive Action, "*Andes 2020:* A New Strategy for the Challenges of Colombia and the Region," January 2004. Available at http://www.cfr.org/pdf/Andes2020.pdf, passim (quotations iii, 2, 29).
149. *New York Times,* 11 May 2004.
150. For other expressions of anti-Americanism in the Western Hemisphere, see the essays in this book and A. McPherson, *Yankee No! Anti-Americanism in US-Latin American Relations* (Cambridge, 2003).

CONCLUSION
Common Findings and New Directions

Alan McPherson

> Surely, Latin America is in itself a distinct, significant, and interesting field of study, but its problems and its fantasies are common to other continents as well. Its resentments and fear of the United States are an exacerbated version of passions that Europe shares.
>
> J.-F. Revel, "Foreword," *The Latin Americans: Their Love-Hate Relationship with the United States*

Jean-François Revel's observation[1] makes a point worth exploring—namely, that Latin America and the Caribbean may have much to teach the rest of the world about anti-Americanism. It is beyond the expertise of this volume's contributors to debate whether anti-US sentiment in the Western Hemisphere may be an "exaggerated version" of anti-Americanism in Europe or anywhere else. Yet this conclusion proposes general lessons to be drawn from the volume's findings and suggests future research paths to explore how students of international history can draw upon this volume to inform scholarship on anti-Americanism.

To be sure, the contributors of this volume did not arrive to any of the following conclusions as a group. But it is useful to suggest seven broad findings that return in more than one chapter.[2] The first of these findings is that anti-Americanism has almost always been, and often primarily was, not an a priori ideology but a response to US policy. The more US policy offended, the more widespread, deep, and visceral anti-US sentiment became. As far as the contributors have uncovered, there was no consistent, steady rise in anti-Americanism from the nineteenth to the twenty-first centuries, but rather several spurts corresponding to changes in actual US practices. This is not to say that Latin Americans were perfectly rational and measured in their responses. Common to most of them was an exacerbation of tensions rooted in the perception that US practices increasingly betrayed common goals for the hemisphere. In other words, anti-Americanism was so reactive against abusive policies because those policies were so contrary to US ideals. From Darlene Rivas's Venezuelans to Jeffrey Taffet's Chileans, Latin Americans rich and poor turned most anti-US when policies supporting dictatorship and repression contradicted Washington's promises of democracy and freedom. The additional perception that the United States was indifferent to these criticisms caused further disenchantment.

A second common finding is that the most compelling anti-Americanism, past and present, has had economic causes. In the eyes of Latin Americans, economic power has always been more obvious— and more obviously malignant—than any other US power. Few knew what happened in the US embassy or what CIA agents were really up to. But thousands in almost every country of the hemisphere were in contact with US plantation overseers or mine managers, or they read about them in novels. The exploitation they witnessed only reinforced the belief that US economic self-interest was the primary reason for any US presence in Latin America. The growing gap in wealth between north and south in the Americas only reinforced that belief. As David Ryan, John Britton, and Glenn Dorn, among others, showed, the arguments that most compelled masses to mobilize were arguments against the excesses of US-led global capitalism.

Third, anti-Americanism was most potent when it overlapped with other ideological constructs. In other words, just as anti-Americanism was not a priori, neither was it sui generis. Most prominent among the ideologies with which anti-Americanism overlapped was nationalism. Almost every contributor to this volume located anti-US politics within a greater effort by patriots—self-described or otherwise—to erect a more robust national identity to resist US power. Running close behind nationalism were Arielism, Hispanism, indigenism, socialism, communism, populism, and so on. My own chapter illustrated the different anti-Americanisms that can manifest in Cuba and Panama.

Fourth among our findings was the prominence of ambivalence. Inhabitants of Latin America and the Caribbean learned to compartmentalize their criticisms and to appreciate the benefits and drawbacks of the United States. Ambivalence generally meant appreciating US people as "good" while berating their government's actions as "bad"—*norteamericanos* fooled by *yanqui* imperialism. Darlene Rivas showed the difficulties in maintaining such a dichotomy: even though the culturally sensitive Nelson Rockefeller charmed Venezuelans, was he not the epitome of capitalist exploitation? Was it fair to attempt to take Richard Nixon's life because of the actions of his government? And Jason Parker argued that West Indians, too, had "mixed feelings": they regretted the Jim Crow racism of the United States but appreciated the jobs created by World War II.

Fifth, anti-Americanism often did bring out the darker side of Latin American and Caribbean politics: the faulty arguments, the manipulation, the opportunism. By its very nature, anti-Americanism was a negative ideology that could be used negatively: to place the United States in a damned-if-you-do, damned-if-you-don't dilemma, to confuse voters, to distract from domestic worries, to tap into stereotypes, to dominate other countries. Kirk Bowman showed, for instance, how Brazilian public opinion came to be in a state of near-frenzy against "a nation of idiots" as it elected Lula.

Though anti-Americanism manipulates—sometimes *because* it manipulates—it does not always work. This sixth finding observes that what often seemed to unite Latin Americans during an election rarely sustained them through a serious challenge against US power. Dorn's study of Perón, for instance, charts a largely losing foreign policy as the United States, soon after Perón's successful defeat of Spruille Braden in 1946, outspent and outpersuaded the Peronists in the rest of South America and that much of Perón's own rhetoric remained on the surface.

A final insight of these studies of anti-Americanism, shared by almost all of them and discussed also in the introduction, is that anti-Americanism is strongest when the nation-state is behind it. It is fitting that John Britton's chapter focuses on national Mexican leaders because in the end it was they—and not union bosses or peasant leaders—who curtailed the power of US banks and oil corporations. William Walker's essay is the exception that proves the same rule: anti-Americanism was "quiet" in Colombia because the nation-state was ravaged by the drug trade.

Given these findings, in which direction should anti-Americanism studies head now? To be more accurate, we should speak of directions in the plural, recognizing the many questions still unanswered, avenues of inquiry to pursue further, and methodological challenges that may not even have arisen yet. Not only must scholars question the specific topics of this volume with additional sources and perspectives, but they should open up new and more creative avenues with bolder theoretical underpinnings and more diverse documents. The following are six possible directions—in no order of importance—that scholars would find fruitful in researching *antiyanquismo* whether in Latin America and the Caribbean or anywhere else in the world.

First is the intellectual construction of anti-Americanism. While scholars have focused on this topic since the 1920s, few have done it justice. Still missing are studies of the contexts, shifts, and political implications of intellectual anti-Americanism. What political, cultural, or material conditions created communities of journalists, novelists, and poets to turn their art into criticisms of the United States? How did these intellectuals interact with those in power? Who changed their minds, and why? The literature could use histories of specific anti-US ideas, "life and times" biographies, and prosopographies.

A second possible new direction is related to the first: the history of institutions. Since the nation-state was so important, how have ministries, central banks, planning directorates, propaganda organizations, juntas, universities, philanthropic organizations, and other bureaucracies constructed challenges to US power? If intellectuals are so central, what institutions organized their opposition? Were these institutions European universities or homegrown ones, and how did their structure and curricula evolve to incorporate the continent's growing resistance to US power? The Catholic church's role in spreading anti-Protestant propaganda and countering Protestant missionaries must also be further examined. What about media managers such as magazine and newspaper editors, publishing houses, and television producers? And finally, what about political parties? Very few were principally anti-US. Why not?

Third, what about generational studies? How did Fidel Castro's generation, so young when Castro took power in 1959, come to define itself so early on and so clearly against US power? Why did the generation of Simón Bolívar *not* do so, leaving Bolívar practically alone in opposing the Monroe Doctrine?

Fourth, how do we blend the histories of social movements and of anti-Americanism? Recent scholarship on civil society in Latin America and elsewhere should lead historians to ask if anti-Americanism was an early arena for the development of social movements. After all, criticizing the United States was often one of the only forms of political speech allowed in public, especially under dictatorships, since leaders had little to lose by letting it heat up. How did student movements, guerrillas, economic nationalists, women's groups, and indigenous movements emerge from (or into) anti-US moments?

A fifth area is the psychological component of anti-Americanism. Many have commented on the emotion inherent in an anti-US stance—as Revel's quotation suggests, its "fantasies" and "passions." Many of these comments aim to dismiss the phenomenon by inferring that, since emotions are irrational, ephemeral, and effeminate, therefore anti-Americanism is unworthy of serious consideration. In response, George Yúdice has written that "it is important . . . to acknowledge the intensity of Latin American emotion on the topic of anti-Americanism." What if we not only acknowledge emotion but take the analysis several steps further? Several historians have made great strides in exploring moments or institutions in history that promoted joy, anger, fear, or other emotions.[3] Anti-Americanism, if it has been as emotional as its detractors pretend, should therefore be fertile ground for a psychological dig. Shame, humiliation, envy, hatred, pessimism, resentment—all might reemerge as a consistent cluster of anti-US emotions with common cultural roots and identifiable political consequences.[4]

The sixth and perhaps boldest new direction for anti-Americanism is to uncover the anti-Americanism of the poor. This direction challenges scholars to ask a series of questions about groups for whose political opinions we have barely any evidence. Yet the implications are fascinating. When a US plantation manager in Honduras made racist remarks to his mixed-race workers, how did locals react? If a US corporation offered to buy a small farmer's land, what recourse did a family have? When local thugs fought US sailors in a bar, what motivated them? Paul Foos suggested the rich vein that historians could tap into by noting that Mexican historiography had done little on popular resistance to the US invasion of 1846 despite their being evidence of such resistance.[5] The history that this direction suggests would benefit most from research in memoirs, interviews, local archives, court records, and the letters and records that Latin Americans have kept in their homes.

Scholars have yet to develop fully the study of anti-Americanism in Latin America and the Caribbean—perhaps in any part of the world. Anti-Yankee sentiment is still largely taken for granted by scholars, as an intuitive, I-know-it-when-I-see-it phenomenon that requires little study. This volume has attempted to delve deeper into anti-Americanism in one area of the globe, whether it be cultural or more material in nature. May it inspire other scholars to nurture a scholarship still in its infancy.

Notes

1. J.-F. Revel, "Foreword," in C. Rangel, *The Latin Americans: Their Love-Hate Relationship with the United States* (New Brunswick, [1977] 1987), xiii–xiv.
2. This conclusion elaborates on the three basic themes I expressed in *Yankee No! Anti-Americanism in US-Latin American Relations* (Cambridge, 2003), 6–8.

3. G. Yúdice, "US *Prepotencia:* Latin Americans Respond," 69–84, in *Anti-Americanism,* ed. A. Ross and K. Ross (New York, 2004): 80. On emotions, see P. N. Stearns with C. Z. Stearns, "Emotionology," *American Historical Review* 90 (October 1985): 813–36; J. Pfister and N. Schnog, eds., *Inventing the Psychological* (New Haven, 1997); P. N. Stearns and J. Lewis, eds., *An Emotional History of the United States* (New York, 1998); and B. H. Rosenwein, "Worrying about Emotions in History," *American Historical Review* 107 (June 2002): 821–45.
4. R. Ardila, "Political Psychology: The Latin American Perspective," *Political Psychology* 17 (1996): 339–51; M. Montero, *Psicología política latinoamericana* (Caracas, 1987).
5. P. Foos, *A Short, Offhand, Killing Affair: Soldiers and Social Conflict during the Mexican-American War* (Chapel Hill, 2002), chapter 6.

Contributors

Kirk Bowman is associate professor in the Sam Nunn School of International Affairs at the Georgia Institute of Technology. He is the author of *Militarization, Democracy, and Development: The Perils of Praetorianism in Latin America* (University Park: Pennsylvania State University Press, 2002) and some two dozen articles and book chapters. His forthcoming book focuses on the political economy of tourism promotion in Latin America and the Caribbean. Prof. Bowman has conducted extensive fieldwork in Argentina, Brazil, Costa Rica, Cuba, Fiji, Honduras, and Uruguay. He received his Ph.D. at the University of North Carolina, Chapel Hill in 1998.

John A. Britton is Gasque Professor of History at Francis Marion University and was recently named a Francis Marion University Board of Trustees Research Scholar. His publications include *Carleton Beals: A Radical Journalist in Latin America* (Albuquerque: University of New Mexico Press, 1987) and *Revolution and Ideology: Images of the Mexican Revolution in the United States* (Lexington: University Press of Kentucky, 1995). His articles have appeared in the *Hispanic American Historical Review*, *The Americas*, *The Journal of Latin American Studies*, *Journalism History,* the *SECOLAS Annals,* and *Business History Review.* He also serves as a contributing editor to the *Handbook of Latin American Studies.*

Glenn J. Dorn is associate professor at Embry-Riddle Aeronautical University. He has published a number of articles on US-Latin American relations in the 1940s, and a monograph, *Peronistas and New Dealers: US-Argentine Rivalry and the Western Hemisphere, 1946–1950* (New Orleans: University Press of the South, 2005). At present, he is working on a study of the Truman administration's response to nationalism and communism in South America during the early years of the Cold War.

ALAN MCPHERSON is associate professor of history at Howard University. He is the author of *Yankee No! Anti-Americanism in US-Latin American Relations* (Cambridge, Mass.: Harvard University Press, 2003), a *Choice* Outstanding Academic Title in 2005 and the winner of the A. B. Thomas Award for best book of the year by the Southeastern Council on Latin American Studies. In 2006, he will also publish *Intimate Ties, Bitter Struggles: The United States and Latin America since 1945* (Washington: Potomac Books). He is also working on a book about resistance movements in Central America and the Caribbean from 1912 to 1934.

JASON PARKER is assistant professor of history at West Virginia University, where he is currently revising his manuscript on Anglo-American-Caribbean relations during the decolonization of the British West Indies. His articles on US foreign relations, transnational race-based activism, and decolonization and the Cold War have appeared or are under consideration in *International History Review,* the *Journal of African American History, Diplomatic History,* and the *American Historical Review.* His next project, for which he has received a fellowship from the Smith Richardson Foundation, will examine American Cold War public diplomacy in the Third World.

DARLENE RIVAS is associate professor of history at Pepperdine University and the author of *Missionary Capitalist: Nelson Rockefeller in Venezuela* (Chapel Hill: The University of North Carolina Press, 2002). Her current project explores U.S. efforts to promote economic development through technical assistance programs in Central America in the post-World War II era.

DAVID RYAN is currently a member of the Department of History, University College Cork, Ireland. He is the author of a number of books and articles on US foreign relations including *US-Sandinista Diplomatic Relations* (New York: St. Martin's Press, 1995), *US Foreign Policy in World History* (New York: Routledge, 2000), and *The United States and Decolonization* (New York: St. Martin's Press, 2000). He is currently working on a history of U.S. intervention in regional conflict and collective memory since Vietnam.

JEFFREY F. TAFFET is an assistant professor of history at the United States Merchant Marine Academy at Kings Point, New York. He earned his Ph.D. in 2001 from Georgetown University in the history of US foreign relations. His research focuses on foreign aid programs and US-Chilean relations in the 1960s. He has published articles on Chilean folk music, Chilean editorial cartoons, and the approach to gender issues among Chilean leftist parties. He is currently working on a book about the Alliance for Progress.

WILLIAM O. WALKER III is professor of history at the University of Toronto. He is the author of two books on drugs and US foreign policy, *Drug Control in the Americas* (Albuquerque: University of New Mexico Press, 1981, 1989) and *Opium and Foreign Policy: The Anglo-American Search for Order in Asia, 1912–1954* (Chapel Hill: The University of North Carolina Press, 1991). He is also the editor of *Drugs in the Western Hemisphere: An Odyssey of Cultures in Conflict* (Wilmington, Del.: Scholarly Resources, 1996). He is working on a book about US-Andean relations since 1960.

INDEX

A

Ackley, Gardner, 127
activism, 222; church, 221; Cuban, 224;
    West Indian, 166, 168, 169, 181;
    youth, 99
activist networks, transnational, 141,
    145, 146, 147, 148–149, 155, 159, 166
activists, 40; West Indian, 169, 170,
    172–173, 175, 178, 181–182
Afghanistan, 22, 23; war in, 22
Africa, 176
African Americans, 27, 169, 175, 177,
    181; and cartoons, 68, *69, 70*
Agency for International
    Development, 124, 249
aid, 105, 260, 263; anti-drug, 248, 257;
    alternative development, 262;
    economic, 155, 159, 247; foreign,
    26, 75–76, 107, 114, 115, 128–129,
    133, 258, 202; international, 220;
    military, 159, 222, 226, 227, 256,
    259, 260, 261; as political tool,
    125–126, 134–135; reliance on, 131;
    renunciation of, 132
aid programs, 20, 113, 115, 119, 123,
    124, 126, 132–133, 134–135, 152,
    255. *See also* Alliance for Progress;
    Loans
Al Qaeda, 207
Albright, Madeline, 206, 251
Alemán, Hector, 206
Alemán, José Miguel, 206
Alessandri, Jorge, 120, *122*
Allende, Salvador, 21, 113, 114, 116,
    222; overthrow of, 148; victory of,
    133–134
Alliance for Progress, 20, 113, 119,
    123–126, 133–134, 152, 219, 241

alliances, 24, 181; Andean, 85;
    guerrilla, 247; labor, 72, 73;
    military, 10, 12; political, 145;
    transnational, 149; wartime, 151
Allies, 150–151
Altimirano, Carlos, 131
Amazon, 157
ambivalence, 7, 85, 86, 191, 192, 272;
    Panamanian, 204; West Indian, 166,
    168, 169, 170, 175, 176, 182
American Colonization Society, 175
American colony, 90–91, 92, 99
American Federation of Labor, 64,
    73–74, 75
American International Association, 93
American Popular Revolutionary
    Alliance, 17, 71, 75
American Revolution, 10, 11
Americanization, 98, 217, 230, 232
Americas Watch, 248
Amorín, Celso, 144
Anaconda copper company, 120, *121,*
    127, 128, 129
Anarcho-Syndicalism, 20
Andean Counterdrug Initiative, 260
Andean Pact, 107
Andean Strategy, 246
Anglo-American Caribbean
    Commission, 173, 174, 178
annexation, 175–176, 181, 192, 200
anti-Americanism, 1, 22, 43, 65, 72, 77,
    189, 209, 217–218, 228, 231–233,
    271–273; ambivalent, 98, 101;
    Argentine, 25–26, 61–62, 64, 66, 68,
    74, 77; from below, 13; Brazilian, 26,
    140–141, 142, 145, 147, 149, 152,
    153, 155, 156–158, 159; changes in,
    7, 13, 18, 22; Chilean, 113–114,
    116–117, 118, 121, 133, 134;

images, 8, 42, 151; animal, 12; media, 26; of United States, 6–7, 23, 119, 158, 160, 196
immigrants, 192
imperialism, 14, 15, 24, 50, 89, 93; Argentine, 75, 76; cultural, 21; European, 165, 190; models of, 141; political, 147; resistance to, 2; theory of, 145–147; US, 16–17, 20–21, 58n22, 64, 90, 97, 156, 184n29, 198; Wall Street, 64, 68; Yankee (*yanquis*), 18, 63, 64, 67, 71, 73, 95, 97, 105, 272
import substitution industrialization, 21, 150, 152
imports, 103, 142; barriers to, 91, 104, 150; cost of, 47; petroleum, 88, 98, 99
income distribution, 204
income gap, 272
independence, 41, 50, 71, 75; Argentine, 63; Chilean, 113, 116, 132, 133, 134; Cuban, 192, 193, 208; declarations of, 11, 13; economic, 54; Mexican, 40; movements for, 11, 19, 75, 132; Panamanian, 188, 195, 203, 206, 208; political, 191; West Indian, 170, 173, 174, 176–177, 182; Spanish American, 218
Independent Foreign Affairs, 152
India 14, 159; aid to, 114
indigenism, 17–18, 21, 272
indigenous groups, 23–24
Indochina, 258
Indonesia, 114
industrialists, Venezuelan, 103
industrialization, 47, 63, 66, 151, 152, 219, 220
industry, 150; tourist, 142
inequalities, social, 4, 21, 23
inflation, 127, 128, 130, 216
influences: Argentine, 71; foreign, 27, 102, 104, 190, 194; global, 190; political, 218; Protestant, 192; Soviet, 148; US, 20, 44, 87, 108, 114, 120, 123, 169, 172, 181, 195
injustice, 2–3, 224, 226, 228, 230; structural, 229, 231
Institutional Act Number 5, 153
insurgency, 103, 223, 227, 241; efforts to combat, 27, 230
intellectuals, 5, 7, 15
Inter-American Association for Democracy and Freedom, 98

Inter-American Conference, 12, 151
interdependence, 206
interest, 141, 192–193; harmonies of, 145–148, 149, 150–151, 154, 155, 159–160; shared, 178, 189; US, 86, 87, 90, 92, 96, 148, 150, 152, 246, 251; Venezuelan, 86, 94, 95, 109; West Indian, 171
Interests Section, US, 198, 200, 202
interference, 102–103, 154
International Coffee Organization, 262
International Commission on Central America, 228
International Criminal Court, 143, 155
International Monetary Fund, 22, 24, 61, 78, 79, 145
internationalism, 108
Internet, 158
interventions, 25, 41, 63, 64, 66, 152, 232, 275; attitudes toward, 14; in Cuba, 196; economic, 40; fear of, 44; justifications for, 41, 55; in Mexico, 39, 42, 50; military, 18, 22, 43, 45, 48, 49, 55; opposition to, 38; quiet, 258; resistance to, 54; tendency toward, 51; threats of, 38, 76, 77, 101; Vatican, 216, 226
investments: foreign, 26, 88, 89, 109, 150, 152, 154; private, 85; US, 4, 14, 66, 94, 95, 103, 190, 204, 222
Iran, 143, 158
Iranian Revolution, 6
Iraq, 38, 85, 143, 158, 260; war in, 22, 23, 140, 143, 156
Irisarri, Antonio José de, 11
Islamist movements, 6
Israel, 114, 232–233
Italy, 52

J

Jackman, Galen, 260
Jagan, Cheddi, overthrow of, 148
Jamaica, 165, 167, 168, 180
Jamaican Progressive League, 170
Japan, 115, 144, 148
Jefferson, Thomas, 195
Jesuits, 215–216, 225, 227, 228, 230, 231
Jim Crow, 13, *69*, 166, 170, 174, 175, 177, 179, 180, 181, 182, 273
jobs, 273
Johnson, Lyndon, 26, 124, 125, 126, 127–128, 129, 133, 134, 135, 153